FIERY DRAGONS

NIAS – NORDIC INSTITUTE OF ASIAN STUDIES
Monograph Series

73. Vibeke Børdahl: *The Oral Tradition of Yangzhou Storytelling*
74. Cecilia Nathansen Milwertz: *Accepting Population Control*
75. Sharifah Zaleha Syed Hassan & Sven Cederroth: *Managing Marital Disputes in Malaysia*
76. Antoon Geels: *Subud and the Javanese Mystical Tradition*
77. Kristina Lindell, Jan-Öjvind Swahn & Damrong Tayanin: *Folk Tales from Kammu – VI*
78. Alain Lefebvre: *Kinship, Honour and Money in Rural Pakistan*
79. Christopher E. Goscha: *Thailand and the Southeast Asian Networks of the Vietnamese Revolution, 1885–1954*
80. Helle Bundgaard: *Indian Art Worlds in Contention*
81. Niels Brimnes: *Constructing the Colonial Encounter*
82. Ian Reader: *Religious Violence in Contemporary Japan*
83. Bat-Ochir Bold: *Mongolian Nomadic Society*
84. Shaheen Sardar Ali & Javaid Rehman: *Indigenous Peoples and Ethnic Minorities of Pakistan*
85. Michael D. Barr: *Lee Kuan Yew: The Beliefs Behind the Man*
86. Tessa Carroll: *Language Planning and Language Change in Japan*
87. Minna Säävälä: *Fertility and Familial Power*
88. Mario Rutten: *Rural Capitalists in Asia*
89. Jörgen Hellman: *Performing the Nation*
90. Olof G. Lidin: *Tanegashima – The Arrival of Europe in Japan*
91. Lian H. Sakhong: *In Search of Chin Identity*
92. Margaret Mehl: *Private Academies of Chinese Learning in Meiji Japan*
93. Andrew Hardy: *Red Hills*
94. Susan M. Martin: *The UP Saga*
95. Anna Lindberg: *Modernization and Effeminization in India*
96. Heidi Fjeld: *Commoners and Nobles*
97. Hatla Thelle: *Better to Rely on Ourselves*
98. Alexandra Kent: *Divinity and Diversity*
99. Somchai Phatharathananunth: *Civil Society and Democratization*
100. Nordin Hussin: *Trade and Society in the Straits of Melaka*
101. Anna-Greta Nilsson Hoadley: *Indonesian Literature vs New Order Orthodoxy*
102. Wil O. Dijk: *17th-Century Burma and the Dutch East India Company 1634–1680*
103. Judith Richell: *Disease and Demography in Colonial Burma*
104. Dagfinn Gatu: *Village China at War*
105. Marie Højlund Roesgaard: *Japanese Education and the Cram School Business*
106. Donald M. Seekins: *Burma and Japan Since 1940*
107. Vineeta Sinha: *A New God in the Diaspora?*
108. Mona Lilja: *Power, Resistance and Women Politicians in Cambodia*
109. Anders Poulsen: *Childbirth and Tradition in Northeast Thailand*
110. R.A. Cramb: *Land and Longhouse*
111. Deborah Sutton: *Other Landscapes*
112. Søren Ivarsson: *Creating Laos*
113. Johan Fischer: *Proper Islamic Consumption*
114. Sean Turnell: *Fiery Dragons*
115. Are Knudsen: *Violence and Belonging*

Fiery Dragons

Banks, Moneylenders and Microfinance in Burma

Sean Turnell

NIAS – Nordic Institute of Asian Studies
Monograph series, No. 114

First published in 2009
Reprinted in 2013 by NIAS Press
Øster Farimagsgade 5, 1353 Copenhagen K, Denmark
tel (+45) 3532 9501 • fax (+45) 3532 9549
email: books@nias.ku.dk • website: www.niaspress.dk

British Library Cataloguing in Publication Data

Turnell, Sean, 1964-
  Fiery dragons : banks, moneylenders and microfinance in
  Burma. - (NIAS monographs ; 114)
  1. Financial institutions - Burma - History 2. Burma -
  Economic conditions 3. Burma - Economic policy
  I. Title II. Nordic Institute of Asian Studies
  332.1'09591

ISBN: 978-87-7694-041-6 (hbk)
ISBN: 978-87-7694-040-9 (pbk)

Typeset by NIAS Press
Printed in Great Britain by Marston Book Services Limited, Oxfordshire

For Peter and Diana Turnell, Lisa Brandt –
and for U San Lin, U Po Sa, Lawrence Dawson, and all
who struggle for freedom and prosperity in Burma

Contents

Preface • *xi*

Acknowledgements • *xiii*

Note on Names and Places • *xvii*

Commonly Used Abbreviations • *xix*

Timeline of Events in Modern Burma • *xxi*

1. Introduction • 1

2. The Chettiars • 13

3. Cooperative Credit to the Rescue? • 53

4. One Bank, Two Countries: Imaginings of a Central Bank in Colonial Burma • 74

5. Aristocratic Eagles: The Commercial and Exchange Banks • 104

6. Reconstruction, a Currency Board and the Union 'Banks' of Burma • 137

7. Agricultural and Commercial Banking in the Parliamentary Democracy Era • 172

8. The Road to Ruin: Credit and Banking under Military Rule • 223

9. 'Reform' under the SLORC/SPDC • 256

10. The Crash • 297

11. Microfinance in Burma • 319

Afterword • *353*

Bibliography • *359*

Index • *381*

TABLES

2.1   Paddy Prices and Land under Cultivation, 1845–1900 • 15

2.2   Paddy Prices, 1926–1939 • 36

2.3   Classification of Land Holdings in the 13 Principal Rice-Growing Districts of Burma • 37

2.4   Chettiar Lending Rates, 1929 • 40

2.5   Indian Bank Rate, 1931–1941 • 42

2.6   Chettiar Borrowing and Lending Rates, 1935–1942 • 42

3.1   The Rise and Fall of Cooperative Credit, 1905–1935 • 64

5.1   Scheduled Banks Operating in Burma in 1941 • 106

6.1   Selected Monetary Indicators, 1948–1952 • 147

6.2   Selected Monetary Indicators, 1950–1962   166

7.1   Agricultural Loans and Repayment Rates, 1949–1962 • 195

7.2   GA Loans to Agriculture, 1945–1962 • 200

7.3   Moneylender Credit and Interest Rates, 1953/54 • 203

7.4   State Commercial Bank: Selected Assets and Liabilities, 1955–1962 • 207

7.5   Private Commercial Banks in Burma in March 1963 • 210

7.6   Measures of Commercial Bank Development, 1950–1962 • 214

7.7   Size Classification and Source of Outside Financing to Burmese Industrial Enterprise, 1953/54 • 215

7.8   Credit Programme, Four-Year Plan for the SAB • 218

8.1   The Nationalised Banks • 226

8.2   Allowable Bank Interest Rates, 1964 • 229

8.3   Private Lending and Quasi-Money Creation, 1962–1968 • 230

8.4   UBB Lending to Government/Money Supply, 1962–1966 • 236

8.5   Currency in Circulation, 1963–1964 • 240

8.6   SAB and Village Bank Loans and Repayments, 1958–1967 • 242

8.7 Advance Purchase, Procurement Price/Market Price, 1972–1989 • 245

8.8 MEB Lending to State Enterprises and the Private Sector, 1975–1986 • 251

8.9 Money Supply and Inflation, 1984–1989 • 253

9.1 Burma's Private and Semi-Private Banks • 260

9.2 Private Bank Loans and Deposits, 1992–2002 • 270

9.3 MADB Seasonal Loans, 2003/04 • 283

9.4 MADB Seasonal Lending, 1999–2004 • 284

9.5 MADB Term Lending, 1998–2003 • 284

9.6 MADB Source of Funds, 1998–2004 • 286

9.7 MADB Profits, Capital and Reserves, 1997–2003 • 287

9.8 CBM Lending to Government, Banks and Inflation, 1989–2002 • 291

9.9 Burma's Exchange Rates, 1988–2002 • 292

10.1 Private Bank Loans, Deposits and CBM Assistance, 2001–2006 • 310

10.2 CBM Lending to Government, 2001–2006 • 315

11.1 Selected Indicators (DRMO) • 328

11.2 Selected Indicators (DZMO) • 331

11.3 Selected Indicators (CRDI) • 333

11.4 UNDP Microfinance Institutions, Operational and Financial Sustainability, 2005 • 335

Preface

In 2002 Burma's new private banks were on a roll. From a standing start just a decade earlier they were rapidly growing in number and size, and seemed to be sweeping all before them. At the vanguard of the 'market reforms' instigated by Burma's military regime, the success of the banks seemed to suggest that, after decades of mismanagement, Burma's economy was at last on track.

It was in 2002 that I first took a serious interest in Burma's banks. Long an observer of Burma and its economy, a previous incarnation as a central banker led me to write a series of papers in an effort to discover what was going on in Burma's rapidly expanding banking sector. What I found, however, whilst not exactly surprising, was most troubling. The 'numbers' surrounding Burma's banks were indeed spectacular but, to put it mildly, they did not 'add up'. A country's financial sector is driven by all manner of things at any particular point in time, but in the end its health depends upon certain 'fundamentals'. Such fundamentals did not justify the narrative of astonishing success that Burma's banks seemed to present. And, as economists are wont to say, what cannot last, will not last. A reckoning did not seem far away.

As it turned out, my timing and assessment were serendipitously prescient since at the end of 2002 Burma suffered a spectacular banking crisis. The crisis was an important and terrible story which was picked up by a number of Burma watchers and commentators. Much of their assessment, however, missed a deeper story within: that this episode was less a discrete 'event' than a continuum of crises that reached back to the earliest days of modern Burma – a parallel narrative of the country that shed much light upon the broader picture. It was in order to tell this 'parallel narrative' that this book was conceived.

Acknowledgements

In undertaking a project of this scale one necessarily incurs a veritable mountain of debts. Most of these, like the sums owed to the creditors of Burma's collapsed banks, cannot possibly be repaid. Nevertheless, it is hoped a 'thank you' here might offer some modest return.

I must begin, however, by acknowledging my sources within Burma who, for their safety, cannot be thanked by name. That individual public thanks are not possible in the normal way for such people grieves me, for without their help (and in granting this, their courage, commitment and patriotism), an undertaking like this would not be possible. Of course, to those familiar with Burma this incongruity is a familiar one, and is a sad little vignette of the greater tragedy that is Burma today.

But there are many people outside Burma who I can and must thank for the myriad ways in which they have assisted the telling of the story in these pages. In alphabetical order these kind creditors include David Arnott, Bernard Attard, Aung Din, Debbie Aung Din, Maureen Aung-Thwin, Christian Baron, Swapna Bhattacharya, Anne Booth, Ian Brown, Michael Charnley, Priscilla Clapp, Stefan Collignon, John Conroy, Liz Curach, David Dapice, Freda Dawson, Rajeev Deshpande, Michael Dobbie, Jon Fernquest, Marianne Gizycki, Tyrell Haberkorn, Geoff Harcourt, David Henley, Jonathan Hulland, Andrew Huxley, Nimali Jayasinghe, Carrie Keju, Kyi May Kaung, Curtis Lambrecht, Lin Lin Aung, Tze May Loo, Craig Macmillan, Maung Maung Myint, Mya Than, Myint Cho, Dietmar Rothermund, Sai Oo, San San Hnin Tun, Monique Skidmore, David Steinberg, Andrew Selth, Magdalena Sokalska, Alison Tate, Tin Maung Maung Than, Tinzar Lwyn, Jeremy Woodrum, Glenn Worley, and Zaw Oo. Of course, almost certainly I have forgotten someone central, and for this I can only beg forgiveness.

I must especially thank my publishers at NIAS Press in Copenhagen over and above that which is simply 'pro-forma'. The very idea for this book was initially theirs, the product of an opportune meeting at the 2002 Burma

Studies Conference in Gothenberg, Sweden, with the then Commissioning Editor, Janice Leon. Janice has since moved to the other side of the world altogether to live in New Zealand – but my gratitude to her is boundless. Since Janice's departure this project has been in the very capable hands of Gerald Jackson, Karen Mikkelsen, and Leena Höskuldsson. Many, many thanks to them for their patience, and much else besides.

In undertaking the research for this book I have necessarily made use of a score of archives and libraries around the world. The restrictions on access imposed by Burma's current government to its own records, and the somewhat haphazard way it collects and preserves them, necessitates for studies such as this the use of collections from all corners of the globe. From these I was able to access a vast array of documents – not just personal papers and specific bank records and the like, but Burmese government reports whose existence is sometimes confined to one or two crumbling physical copies. We can hope that one day a more stable and prosperous Burma can bring them all together under one roof. In the meantime, however, in researching this book I had the privilege of consulting the following archives, libraries and collections: the Oriental and India Office Collections, the British Library; the Archives of the Bank of England; the National Archives of the United Kingdom, Kew; the Centre of South Asian Studies, University of Cambridge; the National Archives of Australia, Canberra; the National Archives of India, New Delhi; the Institute of Southeast Asian Studies, Singapore; the Library of Congress, Washington DC; the Kroch Library, Cornell University; the Bodleian Library, University of Oxford; the University Library, University of Cambridge; the Central Library, University of Calcutta; the archives of the Reserve Bank of Australia, Sydney; Macquarie University Library; the Matheson Library, Monash University; the collections of the School of Oriental and African Studies, University of London; the New York Public Library.

Much of this book was written whilst I was a visiting fellow at the Southeast Asia Program (SEAP), Cornell University. The people at SEAP, and especially its Associate Director, Nancy Loncto, could not have been more generous or helpful. The warm friendship of this genuine community of scholars is something I shall treasure always. Lengthy sojourns were also spent at the Department of Economics, Queens College, City University of New York, whose hospitality was similarly munificent. Otherwise, the rest of this book was written at my home base at the Economics Department at

Macquarie University in Sydney. My deepest thanks to all of my colleagues there.

Perhaps the single greatest pleasure of my work on Burma has been the close collaboration I have enjoyed with my fellow founders of *Burma Economic Watch*, and two of my dearest friends, Alison Vicary and Wylie Bradford. Their intellectual acuity is matched only by their moral courage, and they inspire me daily.

Leanne Ussher has had a most profound impact on this book, and upon its author. Her manifest kindnesses, intellectual insights and general *joie de vie* has sustained me in more ways than she knows.

Finally, I would like to thank my family. To my sister Lisa, my brother-in-law Michael, and nephews Timothy and Mitchell, thank you for your love and for making me laugh. My debts to my parents, Peter and Diana Turnell, are of such a magnitude that the IMF should be called in. It is to them that this book is humbly dedicated.

A Note on Names and Places

Place names in Burma are subject to substantial volatility, the most obvious source for which has been Burma's contemporary military government and its efforts to expunge any vestiges of colonialism. This expedient, which joins the inconsistencies and inaccuracies to begin with in the rendering of many Burmese place names into English, can present long-period narratives such as this book with considerable terminological difficulties. In the face of these difficulties, however, we deal with the question of changing names in a straightforward and relatively uncontroversial way. Simply, places are named in the book according to how they were popularly known and accepted at the time of the episodes examined. Thus, for instance, 'Moulmein' is employed through the colonial and early post-independence years, but 'Mawlamyaing' for more recent times. The same goes for such places as Akyab (Sittwe), Magwe (Magway), Pagan (Bagan), and so on. Where a change of name has not become generally accepted, within or outside Burma (such as 'Yangon' for 'Rangoon' for instance), we stick with the earlier standard. Either way, clarity and a desire to avoid unnecessary distraction is the principle followed.

Consistent with this assumption too (but more controversially), we have chosen to refer to the country itself throughout as 'Burma' rather than 'Myanmar'. The latter is the name chosen by Burma's current military regime, and it is the name accepted by the United Nations. However, for many people (in and outside Burma), it is a name tainted by its regime associations and by an alleged privileging of Burma's dominant ethnic group.[3] This last consideration is an important one with respect to the choice made here, but it is equally matched by the fact too that, for the vast majority of the time period covered here, 'Burma' was the (largely) uncontested label. These are deep waters, of course, but in making this choice we believe we have chosen the least-worst, and least diverting, alternative.

Burmese personal names are likewise often a source of confusion to those unfamiliar with the country and its people. This is especially the case with the Burmese custom of preceding personal names with traditional honorifics. In this volume the most prevalent of these is the title 'U' (essentially 'uncle' or 'mister', a designation of esteem to an older man, or a man of standing), and its female equivalent 'Daw'. In order to avoid any confusion on this score the practice adopted here is to normally only use such honorifics at the first reference to a person, and to omit them thereafter. There are, however, exceptions to this 'rule' when, as is not uncommon, an honorific is integral to the popular name of the individual concerned. Famously this includes (of particular relevance here), Burma's venerable post-independence premier, 'U Nu'.

Commonly Used Abbreviations

AFPFL	Anti-Fascist People's Freedom League
AWB	Asia Wealth Bank
BCB	Burma Currency Board
BoE	Bank of England
BPBE	Burma Provincial Banking Enquiry
BSPP	Burma Socialist Programme Party
CBM	Central Bank of Myanmar
CRDI	Credit for Rural Development Institution
FAO	Food and Agriculture Organisation of the United Nations
DRMO	Delta Region Microfinance Organisation
DZMO	Dry Zone Microfinance Organisation
FATF	Financial Action Taskforce
IMF	International Monetary Fund
KTA	Knappen, Tippetts, and Abbott Engineering Company
MADB	Myanma Agricultural Development Bank
MEB	Myanma Economic Bank
MFTB	Myanma Foreign Trade Bank
MICB	Myanma Industrial and Commercial Bank
OECD	Organisation for Economic Cooperation and Development
PBUB	People's Bank of the Union of Burma
Rs	Burmese Rupees
SAB	State Agricultural Bank
SAMB	State Agricultural Marketing Board

SCB	State Commercial Bank
SLORC	State Law and Order Restoration Council
SPDC	State Peace and Development Council
UBB	Union Bank of Burma
UNDP	United Nations Development Programme

Timeline of Events in Modern Burma

The story of Burma's financial system is understandably closely interlinked with the country's history more broadly. In order to better orientate the reader, in the timeline below we link the various events in Burma's financial history within this (highly truncated) broader narrative.

1826   First Anglo-Burmese war brings Arakan and Tenassarim into the British Empire. The first Chettiars move into Burma.

1852   Second Anglo-Burmese war brings about the British appropriation of Lower Burma. In its wake King Mindon, Burma's penultimate king, initiates a series of economic, monetary and institutional reforms.

1869   Opening of Suez Canal stimulates the commercialisation of Burmese agriculture. The Irrawaddy Delta is transformed into the 'rice bowl' of the British Empire.

1885   Third and final Anglo-Burmese war. Burma becomes a province of British India.

1905   Cooperative credit is introduced into Burma as a counter to the influence of moneylenders such as the Chettiars.

1920s   Renewed nationalist sentiment and unrest in Burma. Imperial authorities initiate limited political reforms, but real power remains in the hands of the British.

1930s   Paddy prices collapse in the wake of the Great Depression. Immense hardship amongst Burmese cultivators leads to substantial land alienation to Chettiars and other lenders. Increased unrest culminates in 'Saya San' rebellion. A new generation of nationalist leaders (including Aung San and U Nu) emerges in the 'Thakin' movement. Towards the end of the decade Burma is beset by strikes and Indo-Burmese and Sino-Burmese race riots. Plans for a central bank for Burma are drawn up.

1937   Burma is given cabinet self-government under a new constitution, but the British Governor retains critical powers. Ba Maw becomes the first Prime Minister of Burma under the new constitution.

1942   Japanese invasion of Burma. Exodus of Europeans and Indians – and the banks. Ba Maw, Aung San and many other nationalists align with the Japanese. A 'government in exile' settles in Simla.

1943   Burma is declared 'independent' by the Japanese and Ba Maw becomes head of state. Various financial institutions are proposed, but none are successfully established before war's end. During the war Japan's occupation currency is printed in vast quantities, delivering hyperinflation and undermining trust in fiduciary money.

1945   The Anti-Fascist People's Freedom League (AFPFL) emerges as principal domestic opposition to Japanese rule. Aung San and others turn against the Japanese. Allied forces accept the surrender of the Japanese in Burma.

1947   The Attlee–Aung San Agreement determines that Burma will achieve full independence in 1948. The Panglong Agreement between most of Burma's ethnic groups is concluded. Elections are won by the AFPFL, and Aung San becomes Burma's presumptive head of government. On 19 July Aung San and other ministers are assassinated. The Burma Currency Board is established.

1948   Burma achieves independence, with U Nu as Prime Minister. Within weeks ethnic and communist insurgencies commence, and Burma is engulfed in civil war.

1952   The Union Bank of Burma is established as Burma's first 'true' central bank. U Nu launches the 'Pyidawtha Plan', centrepiece of Burma's mildly socialist economy. An economic boom commences on the back of rising paddy prices.

1958   The AFPFL splits into opposing factions. General Ne Win heads a military 'caretaker' government until democracy is briefly restored in 1960. Burma's monetary and fiscal conditions deteriorate.

1962   On 2 March Burma's parliamentary democracy comes to an end following a coup by Ne Win. A 'Revolutionary Council' government is established. The 'Burmese Way to Socialism' becomes the ruling 'ideology'. Burma turns inwards and four decades of economic stagnation begins.

1963   Mass nationalisation of economic enterprises in Burma takes place, including the banks. They lose their individual identity, and are ultimately merged into the monolithic 'People's Bank of the Union of Burma'.

1964   The first 'demonetisation' episode takes place in Burma.

1974   Burma formally becomes the 'Socialist Republic of the Union of Burma' and the Revolutionary Council regime is replaced by the rule of the 'Burma Socialist Programme Party' (BSPP). Ne Win, however, remains in charge.

1975   The People's Bank monolith is broken up.

1980   Ne Win resigns as head of state, but remains chairman of the BSPP.

1985   Burma's second demonetisation episode takes place.

1987   Burma's third demonetisation episode sparks riots and unrest. Burma applies for, and is later granted, 'least developed country' status by the United Nations.

1988   A year of turmoil and tragedy. Demonstrations and strikes throughout the year and across the country are crushed by government troops. Ne Win 'resigns'. Aung San Suu Kyi emerges as a spokesperson for democracy in Burma. On 8 August hundreds of democracy activists are killed, thousands are arrested and many more seek sanctuary beyond Burma's borders. An internal military coup brings to power the 'State Law and Order Restoration Council' (SLORC).

1989   The SLORC announces that Burma would now be known as 'Myanmar'.

1990   Elections take place which are overwhelmingly won by the National League for Democracy. The results are not recognised by the SLORC. The National Coalition Government of the Union of Burma (NCGUB) is formed in exile. The SLORC introduces a series of economic reforms, including new laws that allow the formation of private banks.

1990s   Fitful economic reforms continue, which are largely overshadowed by Burma's political turmoil.

1992   The first private banks are established.

1997   The UNDP microfinance schemes are implanted.

2001   Burma is first named by the Financial Action Task Force of the OECD as a 'non-cooperative' jurisdiction with respect to money-laundering. Such a designation is assigned annually until 2006.

2002   A banking crisis commences that brings about catastrophic damage to Burma's nascent private banking sector.

2003   The United States applies sanctions against Burma's financial system as a jurisdiction, and against particular banks labelled 'primary money-laundering concerns'.

2004   Some of Burma's private banks recommence operations, some are closed because of money-laundering, and many more remain moribund.

2007   Popular unrest erupts throughout Burma. As has so often been the case, economic hardship and arbitrary regime decision-making provide the trigger. Nearly six decades after it achieved independence, Burma remains without a properly functioning financial system.

2008   Cyclone Nargis sweeps through Burma, damaging much of the best rice-growing land in the Irrawaddy Delta.

CHAPTER 1

Introduction

*A country's currency and credit is no less important for economic develop-
ment than other spheres of economic activity. In its own sphere it has problems
which affect other areas of the economy, in the same way as other economic
problems affect it. Therefore a study of the working of Burma's Currency and
Credit system in both pre-war and post-war years is necessary.*

U Tun Wai, 1953

*The decrepitude of the buildings in Rangoon is almost grand. The surfaces
are shabby, but the shapes are extravagant, and the workmanship is obvious ... names are given in medallions at the top of each building ... Dawson's
Bank and the Chartered Bank (both painted out but legible).*

Paul Theroux, 1971

At the dawn of the twentieth century Burma was the richest country in
Southeast Asia. At the dawn of the twenty-first century it was the poorest.

The journey between these poles is the political and economic history
of modern Burma. It is a history of repression and release, and repression
again. It is a history of economic construction, reconstruction and decay.
It is a history of plans, and of chaos. It is a history of hope, and hopes
dashed. Common through all the travails, however, is that at no time did
Burma's leaders manage to fashion the institutions necessary for sustained
economic growth. One of these institutions is a proper, functioning
financial system.

This book tells the story of Burma's financial system – of its banks,
moneylenders and 'microfinanciers' – from colonial times to the present
day. It argues that Burma's financial system matters, and that the careful
study of this system can tell us something about Burma – about its descent,
its current circumstances and, perhaps, about finding a way forward.

Burma's financial system matters because financial institutions play a critical role in a country's economic development. Such an idea has been around since the times of Adam Smith, but it is only in relatively recent times that a coherent narrative has emerged as to why this might be so.[1] We now recognize numerous ways in which financial institutions promote development. Financial institutions mobilise a country's savings (its surplus above subsistence), and channel those savings into their most productive uses. Financial institutions create the media of exchange through which we conduct economic activity beyond simple barter. This allows specialisation – the very source of the 'wealth of nations' identified by Smith in 1776. Financial institutions also create credit. Credit permits economic expansion in response to developments in the 'real' economy (technical progress) which might otherwise be stymied by a barter or a purely commodity monetary system. Financial institutions aggregate funds for investment in amounts larger than that which would be allowed by the savings of single individuals. This allows greater economies of scale, but it also reduces the risk of investment to particular individuals, and thereby encourages innovation. Financial institutions, by providing a safe vehicle for savings and by advancing personal credit, allow individuals to 'smooth' consumption and better insure themselves against unexpected events. Finally (though this list is far from exhaustive), and so long as they are not distorted through inappropriate government intervention, the 'prices' determined by financial institutions (such as interest rates) act as critical 'signals' conveying information – to policy makers, to investors, to everyone.

But a theme of this book is that financial institutions *especially* matter in Burma. Events in the financial and monetary sphere have been unusually, spectacularly, prominent in Burma's turbulent modern history. From the Chettiars and the alienation of the land, to the backlash against the foreign moneylender. From the great state banks of the democracy years, to the Orwellian 'people's banks' of the Burma way to socialism. From the bizarre demonetisation experiences, to the rise and crash of the entrepreneurial bankers. And from the money-launderers, to the practitioners of microfinance. The story of Burma's financial system and its players is one that has shaped the country. It is a dramatic story, and it is an important story.

THE BOOK'S STRUCTURE AND OUTLINE

The story of Burma's financial system outlined in this book is organised in a roughly chronological order and, within this overall organising principle, into thematic chapters that take up the narrative of various sectors and institutions. Thus, the first chapter begins more or less at the time of the arrival of the British in Burma, and the final chapter concludes with developments in early 2008. The ten chapters of the book (not including this introduction) are more or less evenly divided between the colonial and post-colonial eras – a division consistent with the chronology. Within this partition the recognisable political eras of modern Burma are apparent: the colonial era proper (1826–1942); the wartime and 'interregnum' years of British flight and return (1942–1948); the years of independent Burma's parliamentary democracy (1948–1962); military-rule socialism (1962–1988); 'market-reform' military rule (1988 to the present). This combination of chronological and thematic sequencing allows us to identify critical continuities and disjunctures, whilst avoiding simply telling a general narrative history.

The book begins (Chapter 2), as both chronology and significance demands, with the story of the Chettiars – the financiers whose impact on Burma, for good or ill, arguably far surpasses that of any other players. A community of moneylenders indigenous to Chettinad, Tamil Nadu, the Chettiars operated throughout the Southeast Asian territories of the British Empire. But they played a particularly prominent role in Burma, where their provision of capital to Burmese cultivators gave the impetus for the dramatic emergence of the Irrawaddy Delta as a major force in the global rice trade in the latter half of the nineteenth century. The chapter details the Chettiars' role in the rise of Burma as it became the world's largest rice exporter, but it also explores the way that British land title law aided and abetted the Chettiars in significant ways. All of this was to rebound severely later when, with the arrival of the Great Depression of the 1930s, the confluence of cultivator indebtedness to the Chettiars and British land title law led to the catastrophic alienation of Burmese farmers from their land. This in turn led to a popular backlash against the Chettiars, and they became demonised figures, perfect scapegoats for all the vices concomitant with a colonial economy. That said, the Chettiars concerns were ultimately for their financial security back in their Tamil homelands, and they felt little responsibility for Burma as an entity independent of Britain's Indian Empire.

Yet, whilst not shying away from outlining the problems associated with the Chettiars in Burma, the chapter reappraises their contribution and finds generally in their favour. Employing modern economic theory to the issue, the chapter finds that the success of the Chettiars in Burma lay less in the high interest rates they charged, than it did to patterns of internal organisation that provided solutions to the inherent problems faced by financial intermediaries. In so doing, we dispute the charge that the Chettiars were stereotypic and usurious moneylenders, but argue instead that they are best regarded as proto-financial intermediaries from whom much could have been built. A proper functioning, *formal* financial system could have provided better solutions for Burma's long-term development, but Burma did not have such a system, then or latter.

In Chapter 3 we take up the story of cooperative credit – the device employed by the British throughout their Empire in an effort to solve the universal problems of agricultural indebtedness and to lessen the influence of groups such as the Chettiars. Originating in schemes from rural Germany, cooperative credit was transplanted into Burma in 1905 with something of an evangelical zeal to solve all manner of perceived economic and social ills. By 1920 several thousand cooperative credit societies had mushroomed across the country with the vague hope they would be a suitable replacement for the Chettiars, and become the base upon which a formal rural credit system could be established in Burma.

As the chapter reveals, however, the hopes and ideals that propelled the cooperative credit system were cruelly dashed in the late 1920s. The problems were essentially internal to the system. Cooperative credit was, in the modern lexicon, a 'top down' solution to a problem that required the inculcation of the 'spirit of cooperation' on the ground. Soon the Depression would arrive in any case, and the same destruction that would be so damaging elsewhere put paid to cooperative credit. Exemplary of that reformist component of British imperialism, the importation of cooperative credit was also a fine example of official myopia as to the cultural, historical and economic differences between the people of Burma and their imperial rulers. The chapter concludes with the findings of the various official enquiries commissioned into the failure of the cooperative credit system – within which a number of Burmese nationals destined for greater things first made their impact.

Chapter 4 takes up the beginnings of the 'macroeconomics' of banking and finance in Burma by bringing to light the efforts to fashion a *central bank* for the country during the colonial era. Of course, as formally a province of 'British India' in the imperial scheme, policy questions of money and finance in Burma were mostly the preserve of the *Raj* in Calcutta and New Delhi. And, yet, against this backdrop a small cadre of imperial officials planned and plotted for a Burmese central bank that would return monetary policy-making to Burma itself. These plans were never realised in the colonial era. They were, however, indicative of a political economy discourse in colonial Burma that was much more vigorous, and more theoretically sophisticated, than is commonly supposed.

In Chapter 5 we take up the development of *commercial* banking in Burma by following the entry into the country of the great 'exchange banks'. These banks were drawn to Burma by the opportunities for trade finance opened up by Burma's emergence as the world's great paddy exporter. The exchange banks, which included institutions that dominate global finance to the present day, touched the ground lightly in Burma. Few ventured beyond Rangoon, and few sought to promote banking in Burma beyond that of the provision of trade finance. Nevertheless, by providing funds to rice millers as well as the Chettiars, the funds outlaid by the exchange banks played their own crucial role in the 'industrialisation' of Burmese agriculture. As with all other financial institutions in Burma, the exchange banks suffered severe losses in the Great Depression. The nadir for them, however, would take place the next decade when, upon the Japanese invasion of Burma in 1942, the banks were forced to flee the country. In this chapter we bear witness to some of the extraordinary scenes of this flight, and also briefly examine some of the institutions the Japanese military and their allies in Burma attempted to put in their place. Amongst the latter were some tantalizing 'might have beens'. The chapter concludes with the return of the exchange banks after the war – to a very different Burma.

In Chapter 6 we examine the efforts to reconstruct Burma's financial system after the war through its central banking arrangements. We start with the 'Burma Currency Board' which lasted from 1947 to 1952. Created by the British to serve their own interests, it nonetheless delivered monetary stability to the first governments of newly independent Burma. We then move on to examine the 'Union Bank of Burma', Burma's first central bank. In fact, as we shall see, there were two Union Banks. The first incarnation, which accompanied the currency board, was not really a central bank, but simply a government-owned bank that undertook a limited array of banking activities for the state. The second Union Bank, which was commissioned in 1952, became Burma's first true central bank, and returned to the country the monetary sovereignty long desired. We explore the performance of the Union Bank during Burma's parliamentary democracy years. A sound and impressive institution in its early years, towards the end of Burma's democratic era the pressing financial demands of the state had begun to overwhelm its erstwhile prudence. A harbinger, alas, of the chaos ahead.

Chapter 7 takes as its subject the development of agricultural and commercial financial institutions during Burma's years of parliamentary democracy. It begins with both the high hopes and the civil war chaos of the early independence years, and the efforts to finally provide the Burmese cultivators with the credit they needed via a new state agricultural bank. The governments of Burma's parliamentary democracy years were committed to a form of mild socialism and, reinforced in this conviction by foreign advisers, drew up an extraordinary array of 'plans' for the future of Burma's economy. Apart from the state agricultural bank, these plans conjured up the creation of a state commercial bank and a network of state organs designed to bring about the 'Burmanisation' of the country's financial sector, as well as its development. Alas, state-ownership and national planning would prove to be disappointing as elixirs of growth, and increasing financial demands of the state would 'crowd out' many of the new institutions. Meanwhile, as the 1950s progressed, Burma became increasingly under the sway of its military and their allies. In this context the chapter examines the hand-over of power in Burma to a military 'caretaker' government in 1958. This government remained in charge long enough to enact a number of policies that would prove inimical to the proper functioning of financial institutions.

In 1962 parliamentary democracy in Burma came to an end via an explicit military coup. Titled 'the road to ruin', Chapter 8 explores the policies of what, for the next 26 years, would be a military regime of extreme socialism and an even more extreme nationalism. For Burma's financial system the effects of these years were catastrophic. Within a year of its coming to power, this 'Revolutionary Council' government would nationalize the banks, within two years it would conduct the first of Burma's serial 'demonetisation' episodes, and by the end of the decade Burma's financial system would consist of a single institution – the 'People's Bank of the Union of Burma'. This monolith would not last, but the uninformed and disastrous presumptions upon which it was created would persist until well into the 1980s. The chapter explores the continuing failure to provide Burma's agriculturalists with adequate credit, a failure made more so in this era by the dismantling of many of the existing institutions of rural credit in favour of 'advance purchase' by the state. The chapter concludes with the latest and most bizarre of Burma's demonetisation rounds, whose effects would trigger the tragic events of 1988, and bring about the dénouement of this version of military rule in Burma.

In Chapter 9 our story takes up the 'reforms' announced by the self-styled State Law and Order Restoration Council (SLORC) in response to the chaos of the military-socialist years. These reforms, ostensibly designed to steer Burma onto the path of a market economy, included a number of significant new laws that transformed the country's financial system and its institutions. The most important of these laws allowed the formation once more of privately-owned banks in Burma, recreated the country's central bank and established a number of new state-owned institutions. In this chapter we critically evaluate the rise of Burma's private banks, and find that what appeared for a while as a considerable success story was a mask for a much less impressive reality. We also explore the changes made to agricultural finance, but we conclude that these did little to alleviate the chronic difficulties facing Burma's farmers. Finally, we explore the establishment of Burma's new central bank, and its comprehensive failure as both an arm of monetary policy, and as a financial system regulator.

Chapter 10 paints a quasi-morality tale of 'chickens coming home to roost', as the private banks that seemed of such promise just a few years earlier crashed in spectacular fashion in a banking crisis that engulfed Burma in 2002–2003. We detail the story of the crisis, its causes and effects, and the failure of Burma's monetary authorities to do anything much about it. The chapter pays particular attention to the question of money-laundering in Burma, and takes the developments on this front up to the present day. Money-laundering was one of the triggers of the 2002–2003 crisis, but its ill-effects last well beyond it. The crisis described in these pages dramatically re-fashioned Burma's financial system, and we conclude the chapter with a survey of what remains.

Chapter 11 concludes our chronological story with a narrative that could, in more encouraging political environments than Burma's, be one of hope and renewal. The subject is microfinance in Burma. Currently riding a wave of acclaim as it garners Nobel prizes and other honours, microfinance is sometimes painted as a 'silver bullet' for poverty alleviation and economic development. Of course it is not this, but microfinance is the sort of vehicle that could bring a significant chunk of what is needed to a financial system such as Burma's. The chapter takes up the promise of microfinance, and explores the methodologies and instruments that differentiate it from conventional approaches and institutions. One of the most notable methodologies of microfinance is the preference given to lending to women – a preference we argue is well suited to Burma, where women arguably play a dominant role in both indigenous moneylending and the management of household finances. Significantly, we also detail microfinance as it currently exists in Burma. Although they are little known, there are already substantial microfinance schemes operating in Burma. Some of these are large, even by global standards, and a few stand at the cusp of becoming the sort of institutions that could make a difference. Whether they ultimately do this will depend upon the Burmese government, which at present seems unwilling to provide the legal and other infrastructure microfinance needs. We also report, more ominously, on the ways Burma's oppressive political system may render ineffective the mechanisms of trust and accountability upon which microfinance relies. The chapter concludes somewhat pessimistically, opining that without significant political reform in Burma, microfinance will more than likely continue the dismal tradition of financial institutions in the country – of a good and well intentioned idea, gone wrong in application.

As will be apparent from the above outline, the timeframe examined by this book is limited. Commencing the narrative shortly after the initial British annexation of Burma following the first Anglo-Burmese war in 1826, it does not examine in any systematic way financial arrangements in pre-colonial Burma. There are a number of reasons for this. Firstly, in the wake of the final subjugation of Burma following the third Anglo-Burmese war in 1885, most of the institutions of pre-colonial Burma were eliminated and replaced by ones imported from British India. As such, very few arrangements and practices, especially those concerned with finance, continued through from the pre-colonial era. The nature of the very different 'state' and economy following Burma's colonisation likewise created an altogether new set of financial needs and institutions designed to meet them. In the years following Burma's independence the façade of older practices was sometimes revived, but they bore little trace of the substance of the pre-colonial order. Of course, where there does exist the traces of earlier practices and traits (especially relevant in the context of moneylenders, and various norms regarding interest rates), these are examined as they arise.

Secondly, and notwithstanding the recent and sterling efforts of such scholars as Toe Hla (1987), Saito (1997) and Thant Myint-U (2001 and 2006), we still know relatively little about Burma's pre-colonial moneylenders and financiers, and certainly not enough to apply meaningful economic analysis to their practices. This is an area in which further research is likely to yield rich dividends, and the identification and exploration by the authors above of the *thutays*, middlemen between early-modern Burma's royal courts, tributary nobles and local authorities, raises all sorts of interesting questions. Upon all of this as yet, however, the author of this book can have little to say.

SOURCES AND DATA

Accessing reliable and accurate data on almost anything to do with contemporary Burma is extraordinarily difficult – except when it is utterly impossible. Burma no longer publishes national accounts for instance, and many other data categories that might be taken for granted elsewhere are unavailable, and often not even collected. This book proceeds fully cognisant of Burma's 'data pathology', and employs a number of devices designed to at least partially surmount it.[2] These are mostly common-sense measures – for instance, checking for internal inconsistencies in data, cross-checking data between different issuing agencies, comparing Burmese data to that of peer countries, evaluating published data against the author's own sources and interviews, correlating official data with 'proxy' indicators to verify plausibility, and so on. With respect to non-official sources of information (of particular relevance to Chapters 9, 10 and 11), the 'two source' confirmation test is employed. With regard to confidential sources, a necessity (ethically and otherwise) if one is really to understand what is going on in contemporary Burma, we eschew that which is not subsequently confirmed by events in the public arena. This book also uses data from the IMF and similar multilateral agencies. Such data, even though ultimately sourced from Burmese authorities, is usually subject to at least a degree of 'filtering' by the international agency concerned. Of course, to such data the verifying measures outlined above are nonetheless likewise still deployed. Despite all of this, as well as requisite care and discretion, it is

9

not possible to be certain with respect to any data emanating from Burma today. We are, however, confident with regard to the broad direction and orders of magnitude of most of the data in these pages, given the efforts taken. Nevertheless, Dapice's caution (2003: 14) that economic analysis in Burma is 'a series of more-or-less informed speculations rather than a standard exercise in processing data' is valid for these pages too.

With respect to the data from the colonial era in Burma the problem is almost the opposite. The vastness of the data collected by the British imperial authorities, and its survival for the use of modern scholars, lends it a certain 'false precision'. This is particularly the case with respect to the relative importance attached to what we might call 'formal' and 'informal' activity. The latter will almost of necessity be granted less weight because simply much of it went unobserved and unrecorded, but the resultant picture will be one rather more 'ordered' in ways directed by the imperial authorities than might actually have been the case on the ground. The colonial government in Burma largely understood this and, as shall be outlined in these pages, it went to considerable lengths in commissioning all manner of reports and surveys to gain a better understanding. Of course, whether such surveys themselves only added to the confusion by asking questions 'culturally loaded' to elicit certain responses must always be borne in mind.

PREVIOUS HISTORIES

The financial institutions of *India* have long held a special fascination for economists. John Maynard Keynes's study of India's banking system on the eve of the First World War was that renowned economist's first step on a path of discovery that would revolutionise economics, but countless others before and since have used India as a backcloth for some of the most profound insights into monetary affairs. So it is a curious fact then, since for most of its colonial history it was a province of British India, that such a fascination never did extend to Burma.

The number of works devoted to the study of Burma and its monetary and financial institutions are few. Of the works that have appeared, most are micro-studies of particular events, or are simply components of larger studies of general Burmese history. Although theirs is a story rich in drama and significance, Burma's banks and bankers have largely been without their chroniclers.

One book that did appear in which Burma's monetary and financial institutions were central characters was *Burma's Currency and Credit* by U Tun Wai. Published in 1953 and in a revised second edition in 1962, Tun Wai's book was a seminal work not only for Burma, but for the study of financial institutions generally in what we now call the developing world. Tun Wai would later go on to the United Nations and the International Monetary Fund, joining that band of Burmese economists (a non-exhaustive list that includes the likes of Hla Myint, Mya Maung, Khin Maung Kyi and Ronald Findlay) who would achieve world recognition within their profession. Tun Wai wrote his book to influence policy-making in Burma but times and events would move against him. The first edition appeared as Burma's monetary system was revolutionised with the elimination of the currency board, the second on the eve of the military coup that nationalised and all but destroyed Burma's financial system. The coup kept Tun Wai out of Burma, as it did so many of the country's best and brightest, their expertise wasted in the country of their birth.

This present book differs in significant ways from Tun Wai's. Firstly and obviously, it carries on the tale of Burma's 'currency and credit' beyond 1962 and all the way up to the present day. These four and a half decades have included many of the most extraordinary and significant events in Burma's monetary and financial history, few of which could have been foreseen in 1962. This book is also a more detailed *history* of Burma's financial institutions than *Burma's Currency and Credit*. As noted, Tun Wai's purpose was that his work would be something of a practical handbook for policy-makers. It was not devoid of historical analysis and, indeed, on this front it was deeply insightful, but the focus was always on the contemporary scene. This present book too has a strong focus on contemporary issues (and is also written in the hope that it will be profitably read by policy-makers), but now there is much more history to be told. Of course, economic and financial theory has also changed mightily since 1962. Tun Wai was a sharp critic of government folly, but his work was nonetheless infused with the confidence that in 'plans and planners' were the answers to many economic problems. History has shaped today's economists to be rather more modest in their claims on this front if, perhaps, more dismal in their vision.

Two other books with a narrower focus than Tun Wai's are also worthy of mention. *The Coins and Banknotes of Burma* by Michael Robinson and Lewis Shaw (1980) is an exceedingly rare, privately published account of Burma's currencies. Written for and by numismatists, its painstaking attention to detail makes it a valuable resource for broader canvasses such as this. In a similar vein, Marilyn Longmuir's *The Money Trail: Burmese Currencies in Crisis, 1937–1947* (2002), is a finely honed work that constructs an exquisite history of Burma's monetary affairs during the Second World War and the Japanese occupation. The comprehensiveness of Longmuir's work on this period has meant that this present book has been able to pare down its own focus on the war years, more or less exclusively to the fate of particular institutions.

NOTES

1 Especially since the seminal work of authors such as Gurley and Shaw (1955), Gershenkron (1962), Goldsmith (1969), McKinnon (1973), Shaw (1973) and King and Levine (1993a, 1993b). For Adam Smith's anecdotal aside as to the importance of banks, see Smith (1910 [1776]: 262). Up until the last few decades some economists maintained that the causal link between financial institutions and economic development was in the opposite direction to that posited here. In the inimitable words of Joan Robinson (1952: 86), 'where enterprise leads, finance follows'. The now wide consensus against this view was as a consequence of works such as the above – but for a most recent empirical study into the matter, and in the context of Asia, see Fase and Abma (2003).

2 To use the expression evocatively employed by Bradford (2004a).

3 On the idea that 'Myanmar' proclaims the 'political suzerainty' of the majority 'Burmans' (Myanmahs) over Burma's ethnic minorities, see Mya Muang (1991: 258)

CHAPTER 2

The Chettiars

Tersely and pointedly speaking, Chettiar banks are fiery dragons that parch every land that has the misfortune of coming under their wicked creeping. They are a hard-hearted lot that will ring out every drop of blood from the victims without compunction for the sake of their own interest ... [T]he swindling, cheating, deception and oppression of the Chettiars in the country, particularly among the ignorant folks, are well known and these are, to a large extent, responsible for the present impoverishment in the land.

Testimony of a Karen witness to
the Burma Provincial Banking Enquiry, 1929[1]

You represent a very important factor indeed in the life of this province ... Without the assistance of the Chettiar banking system Burma would never have achieved the wonderful advance of the last 25 to 30 years ... The Burman today is a much wealthier man than he was 25 years ago; and for this state of affairs the Chettiar deserves his thanks.

Sir Harcourt Butler, Governor of Burma,
to Chettiar representatives, 1927

The economic history of Burma contains many controversial themes, but few have been as divisive as the role of the Chettiars.[2] Renowned as the crucial link between Burma and international finance, and as the providers of the capital that turned the country into the 'rice-bowl' of the British Empire, they were simultaneously vilified as predatory moneylenders whose purpose was to expropriate the land of the Burmese cultivator. The truth was more nuanced. The Chettiars *were* the chief providers of capital to Burmese cultivators throughout the colonial era, and the combination of the collapse of paddy prices in the Great Depression, the Chettiar insistence on land as collateral, and the imposition of British land-title laws, *did* bring about a substantial transfer of Burma's cultivable land into their hands. But the Chettiars did not charge particularly high interest rates – indeed, their rates were much lower than indigenous moneylenders. Nor did the Chettiars set out to become landlords, fearing that this would only provoke the local population and lead to reprisals against them. Their fears were prescient, for in the end the Chettiars were expelled from Burma, in the process losing the land they had acquired and much of their capital.

In this chapter we reappraise the role of the Chettiars in Burma. We begin by examining the role played by the Chettiars in the reclamation of the Irrawaddy Delta for rice growing, and the extent of their operations subsequently throughout the country. We trace the origins of the Chettiars, their arrival in Burma, and their activities in other territories of the British Empire. Following this, the source of Chettiar capital is examined, emphasising the extent to which Chettiars functioned as quasi-financial institutions rather than as stereotypic moneylenders. The chapter then details Chettiar banking business – highlighting their lending, deposit and other products. The chapter uses modern economic theory to attempt to account for the Chettiars' success in Burma, a success that was owed more to strengths in their internal organisation than it did to high interest rates. In the wake of this theoretical discussion the narrative shifts in tone to examine the period in which all went wrong for the Chettiars – the arrival of the Great Depression, and the land alienation that followed in its wake. High Chettiar interest rates have often been put forward as a cause of land alienation in Burma. The chapter examines the truth or otherwise of this claim, and largely exonerates the Chettiars. Modern economic theory is likewise employed here, to find that Chettiar interest rates were determined by the usual forces shaping the conduct of 'informal finance'. The chapter briefly concludes with a verdict on the Chettiars in Burma.

FINANCING THE 'RICE-BOWL'

Burma's emergence as the 'rice-bowl' of the British Empire came as a result of what Furnivall (1956: 116) lauded as the 'epic bravery and endurance' of the country's cultivators in reclaiming the swamps and jungles of the Irrawaddy Delta. An enterprise motivated by Burma's entry into the commercial imperatives of the British Empire following the second Anglo-Burmese war of 1852, the conversion of the Delta into rich paddy-producing land initially required little capital. Britain's great 'exchange banks' took care of shipping, milling and other export-finance needs (see Chapter 5), and up until the middle of the nineteenth century the amount of capital required 'on the ground' in land preparation was slight. In the early years of British rule in 'Lower Burma' the growth in rice exports was founded on cheap and surplus labour within cultivator families, and on abundant land that required little more than clearing. What capital needs there were outside family networks could be met by 'successful agriculturalists, local shopkeepers and rice merchants' (Adas 1974b: 388).

The opening of the Suez Canal in 1869 transformed Burma's prospects as a centre for commercial agriculture. Cutting shipping times to and from Europe by half, the Canal not only directly opened up European markets to rice exports from Burma, it also stimulated demand for the commodity more generally in a region suddenly exposed to greatly expanded commercial opportunities.[3] The price of rice accordingly soared, as did the acreages of land under cultivation in Lower Burma, as Table 2.1 below indicates:

Table 2.1 Paddy Prices and Land under Cultivation 1845–1900

Year	Wholesale Paddy Price (Rs per 100 Baskets)	Paddy Land Annual Average* Acreage Lower Burma (000s of acres)
1845	8	354
1850	24	679
1855	45	993
1860	45	1,333
1865	50	1,627
1870	70	1,965
1875	65	2,704
1880	85	3,402
1885	95	4,011
1890	95	4,865
1895	95	5,765
1900	95	6,832

*For five-year interval beginning in year indicated.
Source: Table derived from data in Cheng Siok-Hwa (1968: 25)

Rising paddy and land prices, as symptomatic of Burma's expanding 'rice frontier', were critical factors in motivating Chettiar entry into Burma.[4] Equally important, however, was the introduction into Burma of British land-title law. In this context the seminal event was the implementation of the *Burma Land and Revenue Act* of 1876, introduced into Lower Burma (and subsequently the whole of the country following the third Anglo-Burmese war in 1885) to consolidate and accelerate agricultural expansion through the creation of 'peasant proprietors' and, it has to be said, to provide the basis for a system of land revenue via which to finance the colonial apparatus. Under the *Burma Land Act,* occupiers of land acquired ownership of land via their occupation and payment of twelve successive years of land revenue.[5] Importantly, such ownership under the *Burma Land Act* was in the 'full sense' that had developed over countless generations in Britain itself – with land title bringing with it permanency of tenure, transfer and inheritance rights and, importantly, the ability to pledge land as collateral. It was this last 'property right' that distinguished the imported British land title forms from the categories of land tenure that had existed before the British annexation.[6] Prior to the British there had been a number of land tenure regimes in different parts of Burma *and* under successive kingdoms – but the British authorities understood that 'non-state' land existed under customary laws that assigned 'use rights' to those who cleared and then cultivated the land (*dama-ugya*). In settled areas such land mostly stayed within families for generations (thus becoming land known as *boba-baing-myay*) who, even if they 'mortgaged' the land in some form, retained a right of return. Such land was allodial in that it was not beholden to anyone apart from the occupier, but equally it was not 'private' since 'the holder did not have full rights to dispose of the land as he or she saw fit' (Thant Myint-U 2001: 41).

In Lower Burma, the sparseness of population and the fact that much of the land was only cultivated in the sunset of Burma's Konbaung dynasty (if at all) made for a variety of landholding forms – most of which involved simply squatting for a time before moving on as diminishing returns from the soil set in. Writing in *The Economic Journal* in 1909 the famed Burma scholar and official, J.S. Furnivall, observed that in Lower Burma 'there was for the most part no ownership in land' as understood by the 'Western mind, saturated with the idea of private property'. In the same article he cited (1909: 555) a 'Colonel Ardagh', Duty Commissioner for Rangoon District, who described land tenure arrangements in the Delta in 1862 as follows:

> In the majority of instances, the villagers regard land, especially paddy land, to be common land, which, if unoccupied, any villagers have a right to take up, and which when they have done with it they have an equal right to throw aside. If not taken up, it remains the common fallowland of the villagers for a few years, until it finally, on being overgrown with jungle and long grass and the bunds partially obliterated, takes its place in the wasteland of the village tract.[7]

In fact, as Thant Myint-U (2001: 228) noted, the understanding of British colonial authorities of Burmese land tenure arrangements (which, in any case, had been rapidly evolving under Burma's last Konbaung dynasty) were 'extremely rudimentary'. Nevertheless, for the purposes here this scarcely matters, for what the British did *correctly* understand was that the alienation of land, as a consequence of its surrender as collateral, was neither final nor complete until their own arrival.

THE SCOPE AND SIGNIFICANCE OF CHETTIAR OPERATIONS

The first Chettiars seem to have arrived in Burma at the outset of British rule – in 1826 accompanying Indian ('Madrassi') troops and labourers in the train of the British campaign in Tenasserim. Their activities, however, were petty and remained so even after the first formal Chettiar 'office' was established in Moulmein in 1850 (Cooper 1959: 30). It was, however, the opening of the Suez Canal in 1869 and the passing of the *Burma Land Act* noted above that brought about the first substantial movement of Chettiars into Burma. By 1880 the Chettiars had fanned out throughout Burma and by the end of the century they had become by far the 'the most important factor in the agricultural credit structure of Lower Burma' (Cooper 1959: 30). According to the *Burma Provincial Banking Enquiry Report* (BPBE), the most dependable source on the extent of Chettiar operations, in 1905 there were 30 Chettiar offices in Burma, but this had increased to 1,650 by 1930 (BPBE 1930a: 203). The distribution of Chettiars in Burma was, however, highly uneven, with the vast preponderance of Chettiar offices being (not unexpectedly) located in Lower Burma. According to the BPBE's reckoning (1930a: 203), 1,443 (87 per cent) of Chettiar offices were in Lower Burma, with 343 of these in Rangoon alone. Conveying more graphically the ubiquity of Chettiar offices, the BPBE concluded (1930a: 203) that in 'nearly every well-populated part of Lower Burma there is a Chettiar within a day's journey of every cultivator'.

The ubiquity of Chettiar offices in Burma created and supported the vast capital they employed in the country. Here the 'numbers' are necessarily less precise, but once more the BPBE provides an estimate around which most commentators on the Chettiars have reached a broad consensus.[8] According to the BPBE (1930a: 210–211), Rs 650 million was the 'unassailable minimum' of Chettiar capital employed as loans in 1930, Rs 800 million being its own estimate, but it conceded that 'Rs 750 million cannot be seriously wrong'. Cooper (1959), Siegelman (1962), Ray (1995) and Rudner (1989 and 1995) more or less accept the Rs 750 million figure. Furnivall (1956: 190) estimated that total Chettiar loans outstanding as at 1939 at £50 million, a figure, he noted, which was 'the equivalent of all British investments in Burma combined'. At the then rigidly fixed exchange rate of £1:Rs 13.33 (or Rs 1:1s, 6d), Furnivall's estimate translated to approximately Rs 670 million – a figure not inconsistent with the BPBE's given that Furnivall's estimate was for a time *after* the Depression had done its work.[9]

The uneven distribution of Chettiar offices across Burma was replicated in an uneven distribution of capital employed. According to the BPBE (1930a: 210) little more than Rs 40 million (5 per cent) of Chettiar capital was in the form of loans granted in Upper Burma. Based on the Rs 750 million consensus total, this left Rs 710 million for Lower Burma, of which an extraordinary Rs 330 million (46 per cent of lending in Lower Burma, 44 per cent of the country total) was written in Rangoon. As the BPBE (1930a: 210) acknowledged, however, the Rangoon numbers were somewhat misleading since a substantial portion of lending written in the capital was by large Chettiar firms but 're-lent' by associate offices in outlying areas.

Of course the above are 'stock' figures (overall loans outstanding) rather than the 'flow' (new lending) each year. Regarding the latter, the scarcity of data once more precludes absolute precision, but the BPBE (1930a: 68) reported that for 1929–1930 Chettiar firms lent something between Rs 100 and Rs 120 million in Lower Burma, an amount it estimated to be around '70 per cent' of all borrowings from all sources. Cooper (1959: 83) estimated that annual Chettiar lending represented about 80 per cent of total lending, but once more precision, in this case on Chettiar 'market share', remains elusive. The survey that accompanied the BPBE, for example, found that in the (agriculturally important) Hanthawaddy and Tharrawaddy Districts, the Chettiars essentially accounted for *all* lending (BPBE 1930a: 68).[10] In other regions the economic significance of Chettiar lending was disguised by their relatively common practice of financing *other* lenders who in turn lent to agriculturalists.

What were Chettiar loans used for? In terms of functional distribution, Chettiar loans were overwhelmingly employed in agriculture. Two-thirds of all Chettiar loans outstanding in 1930 were held by agriculturalists, the remainder roughly categorised as 'trade'. Of the loans given to agriculturalists, one component was 'crop-loans' – 'given and repaid every year and corresponding immediately to the annual expenses of the cultivators' (BPBE 1930a: 211). Others were less narrowly concerned with the sowing of crops, but with meeting the needs of agriculturalists more generally in covering the timing mismatch between their expenditure and income from the harvest. Chettiar loans were also advanced to agriculturalists for land improvement, housing and other 'longer-term' purposes. Interestingly, the functional distribution of Chettiar lending was very different in Upper Burma – where 'three-quarters' went to trade (BPBE 1930a: 211).

Chettiar lending was secured against collateral, and mostly against title to land. According to the Chettiar representative on the BPBE, the Diwan Bahadur A.M.M. Murugappa Chettiar [*sic*], two-thirds of loans to agriculture in Lower Burma were secured by mortgage. For trade loans the proportion was somewhat less, with between one half and two-thirds of such loans secured by mortgage on land. For the *crop* component of agricultural lending the proportion was lower again, with mortgage security backing only around one-third of all loans. Once more there was something of a geographical divide, however – with only around half of all agricultural loans in Upper Burma being secured against mortgage over property (BPBE 1930a: 212).

A deeply significant role played by the Chettiars was the way in which they functioned as a 'bridge' between what had formerly been the subsistence agricultural economy of Burma, and the European financial institutions that had newly become interested in the country. The precise magnitude of exchange bank lending to the Chettiars will be examined later, but of concern here is the broader issue – of the way the Chettiars undertook the task of taking banking and finance into those areas of Burma that the exchange banks deigned not to notice. This role was celebrated by the Diwan Bahadur A.M.M. Murugappa Chettiar, for example, who described their role thus:

> The banking concerns carrying on business on European lines did not and do not care to run the risk of advancing money to indigenous cultivators and traders; and it is left to the Chettiars to undertake the financing of such classes, dealings with whom are naturally a source of heavy risks. So far as banking business is concerned the Chettiar banker is the financial backbone of the people (BPBE 1930b: 760).

Subsequent scholars of Burma, notably Adas (1974a, 1974b) and Ray (1995), have likewise noted this cultural 'bridging' role performed by the

Chettiars in Burma, the latter noting the symbiotic relationship between the 'commanding heights' of Burmese finance (the exchange banks) and what he referred to as the 'expanding intermediate sphere of Asian commercial credit' (such as the Chettiars) whose:

> (...) function within the new colonial trade order was to maintain the supply lines and marketing channels in the interior which enabled the European banks and corporations to sustain the export of produce to Europe and the distribution of foreign goods among the native population (...) Without the internal monetary regulation of the seasonal flows, the machinery of imports and exports would have ground to a halt (Ray 1995: 485).

Origins

The Chettiars, or more properly the *Nattukottai* Chettiars, came from the Chettinad tract of what is now Tamil Nadu.[11] Chettinad, literally 'Chetti land' in the Chettiars' native Tamil, was a collection of 76 villages which, at the time of their activity in Burma, stretched from Ramnad District and into Pudukottai State of (southern) 'British' India (BPBE 1930a: 190, Siegelman 1962: 122). A distinct sect of the *Vaisya* caste, the Chettiars numbered little more than 40,000 people in 1920 (Rudner 1994: 2).[12] Originally involved in salt trading, sometime in the eighteenth century they became more widely known as financiers and facilitators for the trade in a range of commodities. By the early nineteenth century *finance* had become the primary specialisation of the Chettiars, and they became famed lenders to great land-owning families (*zaminders*) and in underwriting their trade in grain through the provision of *hundis* (more on which below). Of course, they became known to the British imperial authorities in this context, for whom the narrative of the Chettiars as bankers who had been 'for centuries developing and perfecting to a remarkable degree a system of indigenous banking' quickly became the accepted wisdom (BPBE 1930b: 759).[13]

The first, substantial, expansion of Chettiar financial activities beyond Chettinad and the Madras Presidency was to (what was then) Ceylon, sometime in the second decade of the eighteenth century. The motivation seems to have been simply the offer of higher returns there – 10 to 12 per cent on capital employed in Ceylon, compared to 8 to 9 per cent at home (Ray 1995: 524). Establishing links with European financial institutions, they followed the British Empire into Malaya and the Straights Settlements (Malaysia and Singapore), Burma, and even into 'Netherlands India' (Indonesia), Siam (Thailand) and French Cochin China (Vietnam, Laos and Cambodia) (Rudner 1994: 67–88). As with Ceylon, the returns to their overseas operations (especially in Burma) easily exceeded those at home, with the result that during their period of colonial expansion the Chettiars increasingly retreated from business in their homelands.

Of all their overseas spheres of operations, however, it was Burma that dominated. The tin, rubber, tea and opium trades of maritime Asia created a ready demand for Chettiar capital, but this was significantly overshadowed by the volume of credit demand, and the quality of the collateral, that could be yielded from the expanding 'rice frontier' of Burma. The BPBE estimated a total of Rs 1,200 million in Chettiar lending in *all* of their operations in 1929–1930 of which, as has been noted, Rs 750–800 million (roughly two-thirds) was employed in Burma.

Sources of Chettiar Capital

Conventional financial intermediaries 'finance' their lending and other activities primarily by taking in deposits. Recycling these deposits – transforming them into loans and advances – is the primary role played by financial intermediaries. Of course, financial intermediaries do not lend out the whole of the deposits they take in. For prudential and other reasons (not least that some depositors will want their deposits back), a certain proportion of deposits are held apart by the intermediary in the form of cash or reserves. Reserves aside, a process of 'money creation' is set in motion since, just as deposits create loans, so loans create deposits (lodged by the ultimate recipients of the spending created by the loans). Such deposits, in turn, are *re-lent* by the intermediary minus (once more) a portion held back as reserves. So the process goes on – and along the way financial intermediaries 'create' (deposit) money. This money creation story, which continues to fascinate even the modern student of economics (for whom the process is known as the 'money multiplier'), is the closest approximate in the discipline to the fabled 'free lunch'. Money is created allowing greater production, greater consumption, more trade – the creation of real goods and services – and a growing economy. The role of the funds of the proprietor of the financial intermediary in this story is crucial – to 'kick off' the lending/deposits cycle and to act as an assurance of their commitment to the intermediary's solvency.[14] Importantly, however, as the money creation process outlined above proceeds, this proportion of 'proprietors funds' to the loans and deposits created becomes relatively small.

The behaviour and economic contribution of a financial intermediary described above is not traditionally applied to the operations of money-lenders who, it is mostly assumed, simply lend out of their own funds and do not take deposits. As such, they are not perceived as performing an 'intermediation' function. They do not recycle deposits into loans. They do not 'create' money.

Most accounts of the Chettiars in Burma (for instance, the BPBE, Brown [1993], Cooper [1959], Tun Wai [1953, 1962] Siegelman [1962], Chakravarti [1971]) explain Chettiar funding arrangements in terms of the traditional moneylender narrative – that is, of a relatively unsophisticated financial structure in which the funds employed by each moneylender come out of his own pocket. Representative of this line was Cooper (1959: 36), who asserted that 'the Chettyar banks operated on the basis of their owners' capital; deposits were the exception rather than the rule'. Likewise the BPBE (1930a: 211), working on their figure of Rs 750 million of Chettiar loans outstanding in 1930, places on the liabilities (funding) side of this equation a figure of Rs 535 million that it describes as being provided by the 'proprietors' of Chettiar firms. This estimate, it notes, was 'in accordance with (...) the general acceptance amongst Chettiars that "on average about two-thirds" of the working capital in Burma is supplied by the proprietors'. The BPBE acknowledged that Chettiars sourced some of their funding from deposits but, whilst these were considered as being important at the margins and in signaling confidence in their operations, were seen as constituting a small place in Chettiar financing. Putting some numbers to its belief, the BPBE (1930a: 213) estimated that around one-seventh of Chettiar liabilities (around Rs 100 million) were deposits of non-Chettiars. These constituted: loans from chartered banks in Burma, Rs 30 million; general (non-bank) deposits in Rangoon, Rs 50 million; general (non-bank) deposits in the rest of the country, 7 million; loans from Madras-based chartered banks, Rs 13 million; non-bank deposits from Madras, Rs 2 million. In addition to these, however, the BPBE and other sources also noted that Chettiar firms placed any idle capital with other Chettiar firms. Inter-firm deposits of this kind, the BPBE estimated, would come to about Rs 150 million, assuming once more that total advances amounted to about Rs 750 million (BPBE 1930a: 213).

Accepting the BPBE's dissection of the liabilities side of Chettiar banking in Burma would indeed suggest that their operations were consistent with traditional moneylender narratives. According to the BPBE's analysis, only about Rs 250 million (or one-third of Chettiar lending) was financed by the taking in of deposits and less than half of this was from non-Chettiars. In this sense, Chettiars did little in the way of financial intermediation, and little in the way of credit creation by recycling deposits into new loans. Few other authors have ventured into the complex territory of Chettiar funding but, of those who have at least attempted some understanding, most differ little from the BPBE's verdict. Tun Wai (1953: 42), for example, uses the BPBE's numbers and his own 'back of the envelope' calculations to arrive at a ratio of proprietors' capital to total Chettiar lending at 60 per cent. Once more this is consistent with a traditional moneylender tag for the Chettiars, rather than anything more complex.

In the late-1980s, however, this picture of the Chettiars as stereotypic moneylenders came under question – and an alternative image emerged of the Chettiars as proto-financial intermediaries who, amongst other things, 'created money'. This new picture was primarily the creation of David Rudner (1989, 1994), an anthropologist who, apart from spending time in Chettinad and interviewing surviving Burma-based Chettiars, examined a cross-section of (hitherto believed lost) account books and other documents of Chettiar operations. Rudner's vital contribution was to make the distinction between what was truly proprietors' own capital (*mudal panam* in Tamil) and what were, in his analysis, 'deposits' of other Chettiars. In other works, but especially the BPBE, Chettiar deposits were classified as 'deposits by close relatives' (*sontha thavanai panam*) and, as such, regarded as part of the capital contribution of the proprietors. In the BPBE's own words (1930a: 214) 'both (*mudal panam* and *sontha thavanai panam*) are in fact the proprietor's capital'. According to Rudner, however, these were better understood simply as 'deposits' (*mempanam*), with no ownership connotations attaching to them. The deposits belonged, for the most part, to 'kinsmen' – original inhabitants perhaps of the same village in Chettinad, distant relatives, fellow 'clan' members – but *not* to close family members.

In Rudner's analysis, then, the BPBE *et al.* failed to understand how 'loose' the relationships usually were between Chettiars placing deposits with each other – failed, in short, to properly distinguish between Chettiar inter-lending and what was truly the 'owners' capital' of each firm. In the case of the BPBE specifically, this failure was curious – since in places in its report the BPBE referred to the deposits of other Chettiars as 'borrowed capital', and acknowledged that the returns to it were in the form of a 'fixed interest rate' (BPBE 1930a: 215). This latter piece of evidence should have been conclusive – since it would be an unusual form of 'owners' equity' that generated fixed interest payments rather than an entitlement to a share in profits.[15]

Rudner's findings were not trivial, nor an arcane issue of interest perhaps only to an archaeological accountant. Using, for example, the BPBE's own numbers for capital/deposit categories, *but* re-classifying them in terms Rudner's scheme, yields a story for Chettiar operations in Burma that is very different from the moneylender stereotype. Proprietors' capital shrinks from providing 65–85 per cent of Chettiar lending to 10–20 per cent. Deposits (and their recycling into new loans), by contrast, rise – from 10–20 per cent to as high as 90 per cent (Rudner 1989: 446–447). At this latter proportion the extent to which Chettiars 'multiplied' the available money-base in Burma through the deposit/lending creation process would have been as high as many modern banks. Unfortunately, however, we cannot be too precise in this matter since we have little real idea of the proportion of reserves the Chettiars held against deposits taken. Nevertheless, the overall picture is unambiguously one in which the Chettiars behaved more like conventional financial intermediaries than previously realised, including by 'creating' financial (and subsequently real) resources.

Funds Supplied by the Exchange and Other Banks

A celebrated source of Chettiar funding was the 'exchange' and other banks 'organised along Western lines'.[16] The Chettiar member of the BPBE, the aforementioned Diwan Bahadur A.M.M. Murugappa Chettiar, put loans from banks to Chettiars in 1929 at Rs 40 million (comprised of a mix of direct loans and overdraft advances). The largest lender to Chettiars – by far – was the Imperial Bank of India, which accounted for about half of all bank lending to them. Two other major lenders to Chettiars were Lloyds Bank (an estimated Rs 7 million in advances) and the National City Bank of New York (Rs 5 million). A few of the other major exchange banks in Burma, including the Hong Kong and Shanghai Banking Corporation and the Yokohama Specie Bank, did not lend to Chettiars at all (BPBE 1930a: 216).

Christian (1942: 118) claimed that the Chettiars 'borrowed much of their capital from European banks'. The validity or otherwise of this statement would clearly depend upon what was meant by 'much'. Certainly, however, the BPBE's figure of Rs 40 million was not insubstantial – especially, just as in the case of deposits, this amount would be 'multiplied' as it was on-lent by the Chettiars, generating in turn more deposits, more loans, and so on. On the other hand, if Christian's implication was that a majority of Chettiar funding was sourced from the European banks – then this book would argue, based on the analyses above, that he was clearly wrong.

Exchange and other bank lending to Chettiars was, not surprisingly, heavily concentrated in Rangoon, and fully Rs 17 million of the Imperial Bank's Rs 20 million of loans to Chettiars in 1929 were written there. Bank lending to Chettiars was also highly concentrated on a few, large, Chettiar firms who 'on-lent' to smaller firms and agents across the country. Loans and overdrafts from banks to Chettiars were secured against immovable property (house title-deeds worth no less than twice the value of the maximum advance), and government securities (BPBE 1930a: 216).

CHETTIAR BANKING BUSINESS

The Chettiars carried on an extraordinarily wide range of banking business in Burma. They made loans, took in deposits, remitted funds, discounted *hundis*, honoured cheques, exchanged money, dealt in gold, and kept valuables for safe-keeping. They were, in essence, a 'one-stop-shop' that covered pretty much the gamut of financial needs, especially those of agriculturalists and cultivators. In the following we consider in more detail some of these products and services, highlighting the more important and/ or particular functions of the Chettiars in Burma.

Loans and Advances

Above all, the Chettiars were known for *lending* money. According to the BPBE (1930a: 196), Chettiars were anxious to avoid 'speculative loans', but were otherwise 'ready to lend their money for *any* enterprise which offers ready security and profit' (emphasis added). As such, their loans were 'not determined by the purpose of the loan or the kind of borrower' – a *commercial* virtue that brought with it the considerable *social* virtue that they 'dealt with all races and classes on equal terms' (BPBE 1930a: 233). As noted earlier, Chettiar lending overwhelmingly went to agriculturalists, but this was because it was precisely this sector that most fulfilled their profitability and security prerequisites, rather than any philosophical predisposition to rural pursuits.

Crop-loans and loans for land purchase, redemption and improvement, were the most common forms of Chettiar lending to agriculturalists.

Cultivators typically drew multiple loans from their Chettiar lender throughout the year according to season – for the purchase of seed, transplanting and broadcasting, for payments to labourers, for the purchase of cattle, to repair dykes and borders, and to meet general expenses.[17] These multiple loans constituted a type of 'revolving credit' facility, upon which repayment was due only once a year, after the sale of the cultivator's crop. Recognising the essential fungibility of money (a fact often overlooked by other lenders in Burma), Chettiars also lent for a range of other cultivator needs – for marriage expenses, funerals, religious and other social festivities, and for household contingencies generally. One aspect of Chettiar loans highlighted by the BPBE (1930a: 233) was the speed at which they could be arranged: 'the time elapsing from the first application for a mortgage-loan (...) until the document is executed and the loan paid over is often not more than an hour'.

Beyond agriculturalists strictly defined, the Chettiars lent money for a range of economic activities – to wholesalers, rice millers, shopkeepers, petty industrialists and artisans of various types. A 'considerable amount' of Chettiar lending was also made to other moneylenders (BPBE 1930a: 232–233). These were mostly Burmese, and were a mix of professional moneylenders and land-owning agriculturalists who on-lent Chettiar loans to their employees. Burmese moneylenders enjoyed certain 'informational' advantages over their Chettiar funders that enabled them to reach a (poorer) clientele that the Chettiars rejected because of their lack of collateral. The BPBE (1930a: 200) painted the issue thus:

> The Chettiars are generally at a disadvantage in comparison with a Burman lending to persons of his own race living in his own village; they cannot have quite the same intimate knowledge of the borrowers (...) Thus most clients of Chettiars are landowners or tenants of good standing or shopkeepers. Borrowers who cannot give security to the satisfaction of a Chettiar must find a local lender who can accept the additional risk because he is in closer contact, and they must generally pay a higher rate of interest accordingly; labourers of all kinds fall into this class and rarely borrow from Chettiars.

With collateral security critical to Chettiar lending it is not surprising to find that Chettiars extended credit to cultivators mostly on the basis of the mortgage of land. Gold was especially well-regarded as collateral too but, as the BPBE noted (1930a: 234), it was 'usually not available'. There was, however, a degree of flexibility with regard to Chettiar collateral requirements and the pledging of jewellery, houses, paddy and other crops was not uncommon. In cases where crop was pledged it was often the case that 'the Chettiar alone has the key of one lock of the godown in which it is stored and he keeps a watchman there at the expense of the borrower' (BPBE 1930a: 233). Some of the 'less common' forms of collateral accepted by Chettiars included motor vehicles and boats, shares, stocks, and government securities (BPBE 1930a: 233).

Deposit Types

Chettiars provided a number of different deposit products in Burma. But unlike loans these products were not so universally available. Large Chettiar firms typically offered the full range of deposit types outlined here, but many small and outlying firms did not actively seek deposits of any form beyond those from other Chettiars. The most important deposit devices offered by Chettiars in Burma included:

(1) 'At call' or demand deposits placed by Chettiar firms with each other. Such deposits, called *kadai kanakku* in Tamil (literally 'shop' deposits) were a subset of the inter-Chettiar deposit system outlined above. Though callable at any time, they could remain for a day or indefinitely. Substantial quantities of such Chettiar funds were 'floating' in this form in normal times, the necessary result of the different seasonal needs for funds in the regions and countries the Chettiars operated in. On such deposits was paid the *nadappu vatti* (essentially 'current rate', but literally 'walking rate') – the 'basic rate' of interest upon which most other Chettiar interest rates were calculated and which functioned like the 'prime lending rate set by the central bank of a modern nation state' (Rudner 1989: 433). The comparison was apt, as can be readily seen from this description of the setting of the *nadappu vatti* in Burma by the BPBE (1930a: 225):

> [The *nadappu vatti*] is fixed in the evening of the 16th of every Tamil month at a meeting held at 9.00pm in the Chettiar temple at Rangoon, and it holds good for all the current Chettiar month including the sixteen days already passed. At this meeting the local heads of all Chettiar firms may attend if they wish; those who lend to Chettiar firms outside Rangoon are the mostly deeply interested and always try to attend (...) The meeting discusses the general financial situation, and fixes the current [*nadappu*] rate for the current month with this, taking into account the current pitch and tendency of the thavanai rate [see (2) below], the rates current amongst the Marwaris, Multanis, and Gujaratis [other Indian banking communities in Burma, operating on

a much smaller scale than the Chettiars] and the rates for advances by the joint-stock banks to Chettiars. As every firm has both income and expenses determined largely by this rate, great care is taken to fix the rate according to the needs of the situation.

Not surprisingly, the *nadappu vatti* varied with the season – peaking when the demand for funds rose in January–February, and falling when funds were plentiful in August–September. The rate was typically expressed in its per-month equivalent, in terms of annas per 100 rupees (BPBE 1930a: 225–226).

(2) Fixed or term deposits were likewise a subset of the inter-Chettiar deposit system outlined earlier. Known as *thavanai kanakkus* (literally 'period' deposits in Tamil), these were 'fixed' deposits of a minimum term of two months.[18] Most *thavanai* deposits were 'rolled over' beyond their initial term, with compound interest being paid every two months. The interest rate on *thavanai* deposits (*thavanai vatti*) was fixed across each two-month term.

Thavanai deposits provided Chettiar firms with a relatively stable channel of funds. Establishing the *thavanai vatti* at an appropriate rate for the prevailing conditions was accordingly critical – arguably more important than getting the 'call rate' (*nadappu vatti*) right since, not surprisingly, it was the longer-term *thavanai* deposits that any particular Chettiar firm was most desirous of attracting. Indeed, as the BPBE (1930a: 227) noted, the calculation of the *thavanai vatti* was not dependent on the prevailing *nadappu vatti* – rather, and in contrast to interest rate determination in modern financial markets, the relationship seems to have been the reverse – the course of the *thavanai* rate being a consideration when fixing the current rate.

Of course, given that both rates reflected underlying monetary conditions, they tended to move together, though the *thavanai* rate was typically 'at least half-an-anna below the current rate'.[19] As with the establishment of the *nadappu vatti*, setting the *thavanai vatti* was a formal process strongly reminiscent of modern (central bank) policy-making. Unlike the *nadappu vatti*, however, the *thavanai vatti* was set weekly:

...a systematic way every Sunday evening at 9 o'clock by a meeting in the Rangoon temple (...) generally the decision is a foregone conclusion, and, unless the rate is standing particularly high or low or an abrupt change is expected, few attend (BPBE 1930a: 227).

(3) 'At-call' or 'demand' deposits available to non-Chettiars. Known as *katha kanakku*, these were heavily patronised by Burmese and Chinese moneylenders and traders, as well as non-Chettiar Indian business interests and individuals. According to Chakravarti (1971: 60), these demand deposits 'worked on the principle of savings accounts; no cheques could be drawn but withdrawals were permitted on presentation of a pass-book by the depositor where the deposits and withdrawals, and the credit balance would be entered by the Chettyar'. Interestingly, the efficiency of inter-firm Chettiar deposit/lending meant that few Chettiars seem to have kept cash reserves against demand deposits, trusting rather in 'temporary borrowings' to meet unexpected cash withdrawals.[20]

(4) Fixed or term deposits available to non-Chettiars. Called *veyan vatti* in Tamil, these were fixed for periods of three months to a year, and also paid an interest rate typically 1 to 2 per cent above the *thavanai* rate. Like the former, these were often rolled over indefinitely and tended to be confined to larger merchant interests (Chakravarti 1970: 60).

HUNDIS

One of the most important financial products provided by the Chettiars in Burma were 'hundis'.[21] Hundis were (and are) bills of exchange that could be used both to remit funds and to advance credit. An ancient financial device used in India and surrounding countries well before the dominance of Europeans in regional commerce, they were integral to the operation of indigenous bankers such as the Chettiars.

In Burma the Chettiars offered two main varieties of hundis – 'demand' hundis and 'usance' hundis. Each are examined in turn:

Demand Hundis

A demand hundi was simply a remittance instrument, a device for sending money from one part of Burma to another through a network of Chettiars. The logic of a hundi was simple: Suppose that person 'A' in Rangoon wanted to send a sum of money to person 'B' in a village in the Burmese countryside. Banks were unapproachable for most people, and sending money through the post or in person was risky and/or expensive. So person A approached their local Chettiar with whom, more than likely, they had done business before. We will call this Chettiar, 'Chettiar A'. Chettiar A, like nearly all

Chettiars, had contacts with other Chettiars throughout Burma, including in the village where person A wanted their money sent. We will call Chettiar A's contact in the village, 'Chettiar B'. The links are now in place.

Person A pays Chettiar A the sum of money they want to send person B. Chettiar A, in return, issues a hundi which orders Chettiar B to pay the bearer, upon presentation of the hundi, the sum of money written upon it. The bearer of the hundi is person B, to whom the hundi has been sent through the post or delivered by some other means. At this point various security measures made for varying practices – some hundis were payable on sight, but most were payable only when presentation was followed by advice from the 'ordering' Chettiar (Chettiar A in this example) conveyed via post or telegraph. This last practice carried the benefit that the final recipient of the money (person B) was protected against the theft of the hundi.

Of course, in the example outlined above there remains the issue of settlement between the two Chettiars (A and B). This was accomplished in a number of ways in practice, all of which relied upon the 'trust' between the counterparties which (as shall be examined below) was a virtue of the entire inter-Chettiar system. One way was to deal with sums owed as inter-firm deposits/lending in the manner described above, upon which the interest rates likewise outlined above were levied. Other methods included making payments through branches of the Imperial Bank, authorised via telegraphic transfers. Finally, some settlements were completed in cash. The BPBE (1930a: 49) evocatively described a regional snapshot of this mechanism thus:

> Chettiars send a considerable amount of money to and from Rangoon in the form of currency. It is said that the money brought in by Chettiar clerks from stations along the Prome railway-line to four Rangoon firms alone amounts to half a million rupees a day (...) and large sums are sent in also from Wakema, Moulmeingyun and other delta towns.

Chettiars generally did not charge for hundis issued to people who were otherwise their customers as borrowers or depositors. For people for whom they had no existing relationship, charges were not much more than a couple of 'annas' per 100 rupees (BPBE 1930a: 166).[22] Such charges were very competitive with other remittance forms, but perhaps the greatest competitive advantage enjoyed by the Chettiars was the ubiquity of their presence – enabling hundis to be sent to Rangoon, and to cities throughout South and South-East Asia, from all but the humblest of villages.

Usance Hundis

Usance or 'discount' hundis differed from demand hundis in that, in addition to performing a remittance function, they provided credit too. This credit was arrived at in a remarkably straightforward way – a function simply of allowing a period of time to elapse before payment had to be made to the remitting Chettiar by the customer. Usance hundis were, in this way, little different to the exchange or trade bills employed by European banks, and provided similar stimulus to trade in Burma as such bills had delivered to international commerce.

Usance hundis were the most common form of hundi offered and used by the Chettiars in Burma, who generally only applied the label 'usance' (a label favoured by the exchange and other European banks) when they needed to distinguish them from the less numerous demand hundis. An important difference between usance hundis and European bills of exchange was that usance hundis were not written against a specific transaction, but did provide a specific *quantity* of credit. The period of 'delayed payment' which gave usance hundis their credit function could vary – from 30 to 120 days. The latter, the longest period of a usance hundi allowed, was also the most common (BPBE 1930a: 153).

Chettiars themselves re-discounted *usance* hundis with other financiers, especially the Imperial Bank and certain of the exchange banks. This mechanism provided yet another financial link between the Chettiars and the exchange banks, but it was one that was only really available to the larger Chettiar firms based in Rangoon. These, however, could discount usance hundis from smaller firms and then present them for re-discount at the banks – giving the latter the 'two signatures' on such instruments sometimes required before they would advance funds (BPBE 1930a: 154–155). Usance hundis were written on special 'hundi-paper' that was sold by the colonial government of Burma for a price that represented the 'stamp duty' on each instrument. The BPBE recommended the promotion of usance hundis to the extent that they became 'the ordinary mode of financing trade' and – together with the possibility for discounting at the banks – would provide the essential 'elastic margin' to the provision of credit in Burma (BPBE 1930a: 156). To this end the BPBE urged (1930a:156) the reduction of stamp-duty on hundis, as well as the bringing of hundis *written in Burmese* under the *Negotiable Instruments Act* (BPBE 1930a: 155–156).[23]

THE BASIS FOR CHETTIAR SUCCESS

How to account for the extraordinary dominance of the Chettiars in rural finance in colonial Burma? The standard answer, which retains great explanatory power, emphasises the links between the Chettiars and 'Western' banks. In part this explanation is a sub-set of a broader assertion as to the reasons for the Indian dominance of many of the institutions of colonial Burma. Typical of such accounts is Harvey (1946: 70), who wrote of Indians in Burma as having the advantage over the Burmese of 'a couple of centuries start' in their contacts with the European commercial world. They had, he continued (1946: 71), 'the good will of our trade, they handled the new business we introduced (...) for long they monopolised the professions, legal, medical, accountancy, engineering, as no Burman was qualified'.

The extent to which the 'Western' banks were a source of Chettiar capital has, as this book has noted, been exaggerated, yet their funding certainly had an impact 'on the ground' in many parts of Burma. It was also the cause of no little resentment, as a Burmese moneylender from Pyapôn Town made clear, complaining to the BPBE (1930b: 99), that 'the Imperial Bank and other joint-stock banks give too much support to the Chettiars and little or none to the Burmese moneylenders'. Certainly too, the Bank of Chettinad, a 'bank' formed in 1929 from two prominent Chettiar firms in Rangoon, enjoyed strong support from a number of foreign banks, especially the Chartered Bank, the Imperial Bank, the National City Bank of New York and Lloyds Bank.[24] This support crucially involved advancing funds during the periods of seasonal shortage.

Chettiar Organisation

Another answer as to the reason for the success of the Chettiars in Burma, which to a large extent has only come to light in relatively recent times via the work (already cited) of the anthropologist David Rudner (1989, 1994), and the historian R.K. Ray (1995), emphasised the nature of Chettiar organisation in Burma. And, of particular importance in this context, their identification of 'trust' as the keystone of Chettiar finance. Of course, trust is the foundation of finance of all kind. Financial intermediaries of any stripe depend upon trust, without which their assets (merely promises to pay when all is said and done) are worthless, and without the trust of depositors and investors there would be nothing to 'mediate' in any case. In modern banking systems such trust is established by norms of behaviour that have been centuries in evolution, shaped by the state, the law, and other institutions easy to identify but hard to replicate.

In the case of the Chettiars, 'trust' was a function of caste and kin rather than more impersonal institutions. This trust was manifested in a number of ways, but not least the way in which Chettiar firms were formed by partnerships of individuals connected through marriage, home village ties and other loose forms of kinship. Interestingly, because of Hindu inheritance laws based on primogeniture, partnerships were generally not formed between close 'blood' relatives' (Ray 1995: 525). This trust was also the engine behind the inter-firm lending/deposit system between Chettiars. The worth of this system as a principal source of individual firm capital has already been noted, but it also constituted a most intriguing framework of 'prudential' arrangements that acted to dampen systemic risk. Alleviating systemic risk in a modern financial system is the responsibility of a central bank, but in the Chettiar arrangements this role was subsumed by collective 'caste' responsibility. According to Rudner (1989: 451), the identifiably caste system of 'inter-depositing banks' employed by the Chettiars (implicitly) ensured 'the regulation of reserve levels', and with it 'confidence in individual Chettiars as representatives of the caste as a whole'.

Perhaps the most important way through which trust was manifested in the *spread* of Chettiar operations in Burma was as it was embodied in their 'agency arrangements'. The device 'that enabled the Chettiar bankers to extend their far-flung banking network into Southeast Asia', the use of 'agents', allowed Chettiars without financial means to establish their own firms to act as agencies for their more financially secure kinsmen (Ray 1995: 525). Ray (1995: 526) described the Chettiar 'banker–agent' relationship as 'a particular form of creditor–borrower relationship in which the agent did business with the capital advanced by his patron', an arrangement that usually lasted until the agent 'had enough savings to set up on his own'. According to the BPBE (1930a: 209), the sums advanced by the patron to the agent were often large, and the only security 'an unstamped receipt on a piece of palmrya leaf'.

Chettiar agents had almost complete discretion on the lending out of their patron's money and they usually enjoyed 'power of attorney' generally over what might be regarded as the activities of the 'joint' firm.

The arrangement seems to have been enormously successful in creating appropriate incentives for the agent, the BPBE (1930a: 526) reporting that 'some Chettiars believe that their agents are more earnest in trying to make their business a success than are employees of banks, and even advance this as a reason against attempting to establish in Burma banking on "western lines".[25] The BPBE was certainly impressed with another aspect of 'trust' in the Chettiars agency system, declaring in its report (1930a: 207) that it had found 'practically no cases of dishonesty' between firms and agents.

Chettiar agents typically served in Burma for three years, the last six months of which were spent training their replacement. At the completion of the three years they invariably returned to Chettinad for three years of leave, before returning to Burma to begin the cycle again. Particularly successful agents could be offered partnerships in the firm they represented after their three year stint, a few may even have assembled enough capital with which to create their own firm (BPBE 1930a: 209). This triennium service pattern seems to have proved efficient in producing and training Chettiar bankers, but it was the cause of resentment amongst their clients. The issue emerges time and again in the BPBE surveys, typical of which was the testimony of a cohort of paddy-millers in Kyaiklat. They complained (BPBE 1930b: 104) that the agency-handover often involved the recalling of loans that the incoming agent was not comfortable with, the unilateral variation of interest rates, and the costly re-issue of mortgage deeds.

The Chettiars sent into the Burmese countryside as agents were exclusively male, and were almost never accompanied by spouses or other family members. Most seemed to have lived an extraordinarily frugal existence. Typically between half and two-thirds of their entire triennium salary was paid a month after taking up their station, whereupon it was mixed in with the proprietor's capital advance and employed in making loans (BPBE 1930a: 209).

Bankers Born and Bred?

In giving weight to the argument that various 'internal' factors might have accounted for the success of the Chettiars in Burma, the issue of education within the community – especially of young males – is worthy of note. This aspect of Chettiar culture fascinated contemporary observers of the Chettiar phenomenon, even though their observations read somewhat archaically today, rich as they are in moneylender stereotypes and other prejudices. Nevertheless, it would be less than complete *not* to record such observations. Representative of these is this from the renowned Edgar Thurston, whose work on 'castes and tribes' of the 'East' commissioned by the colonial government of India remained a seminal work for many decades:

A *Nattukottai Chetti* is a born banker. From his earliest childhood he is brought up on the family traditions of thrift and economy. When a male child is born in a *Nattukottai Chetti's* family, a certain sum is usually set aside to accumulate at compound interest and form a fund for the boy's education. As soon as he is ten or twelve, he begins to equip himself for the ancestral profession. He not only learns accounting and the theory of banking, but he has to apply his knowledge practically as an apprentice in his father's office. Thus in a *Chetti's* training, the theory and practice of banking are not divorced from each other, but go hand in hand, from the very start. When a boy is married he attains a responsible position in the family. Though, being a member of the joint Hindu family system, he may not make a separate home, yet he must bear his own financial burden. He is allotted a share in the paternal, or ancestral, estate and he must live on it. He alone enjoys all that he may earn and suffers for all that he may lose. So he naturally grows self-reliant and ambitious, with a keen desire to build a fortune for himself (...) Strict economy is scrupulously practised, and every little sum saved is invested at the highest rate of interest possible (...) So particular are the *Chettis* where money is concerned that, according to the stories current about them, if they have a visitor – even a relative – staying with them longer than a day he is quietly presented with a bill for his board at the end of the visit (Thurston 1909: Vol. V, 252).

LAND ALIENATION AND THE 'HOSTILE SYMBIOSIS'

Chettiar success in Burma came to a shuddering halt with the onset of the global Depression of the 1930s. An event with severe economic repercussions in most countries, in Burma these were manifest primarily in the near total collapse of paddy prices. Paddy prices had been trending downwards across the latter half of the 1920s, as can be seen in Table 2.2 (overleaf) but they went into a precipitous decline in 1930 and remained at unremunerative levels until after the Second World War.

The impact of the collapse in paddy prices was soon felt amongst the cultivators of Burma's lower delta, whose general situation was neatly summarised by the Commissioner of Settlement and Land Records in his annual report to the Government for 1930–31:

Table 2.2 Paddy Prices 1926–1939 Rs/100 baskets[26]

Year	Price	Year	Price
1926	202	1933	64
1927	190	1934	70
1928	169	1935	93
1929	169	1936	89
1930	133	1937	97
1931	80	1938	90
1932	92	1939	97

Source: Author's calculations from data in Wickizer and Bennett (1941: 332–333)

The year was one of extreme depression for agriculture in Burma. The (...) agricultural economy had for many years been based on the assumption that the price of paddy would be Rs.150 or more per 100 baskets. The result was that contracts for wages were made and loans were taken on the same scale as in previous years at the beginning of this cultivating season. Consequently when the crop was harvested, after the labour had been paid for at the rates agreed upon, and the rents paid in kind at the old rates, the tenant, though left with the same share of produce, found its value reduced by half, and was unable to repay his loan and often not even able to pay the interest. The landlord found himself receiving produce worth only half as much as in the previous year with large irrecoverable loans outstanding and the land revenue to pay at the same rates (Government of Burma [GoB] 1932: 10).

Of course, at the end of this cycle of distress were the Chettiars. Unable to collect even interest payments on their loans, increasingly Chettiars came to foreclose on defaulting borrowers and to seize the pledged collateral. For the most part this was land. Table 2.3 (opposite) eloquently conveys what followed:

The alienation of much of the cultivatable land of Lower Burma, a tragic and seminal event in the political economy of Burma, would also prove to be the equally tragic climax to the story of the Chettiars in the country. Exposed to the understandable anger of indigenous cultivators and the demagoguery of Burmese nationalists, they became easy scapegoats not just for the current economic distress, but the foreign domination of Burma's economy:

Alien in appearance and habits, the Chettyar was the butt of the Burmese cartoonist, he was depicted as Public Enemy No.1, and the violence of the mob was directed against him, a canalization, a projection of the people's own faults and failings on to a convenient victim (Harvey 1946: 56).

Table 2.3 Classification of Land Holdings in the 13 Principal Rice-Growing Districts of Burma (000s/acres)*

Year	Total land under cultivation	Land occupied by non-agriculturalists	Land occupied by Chettiars	Proportion of non-agriculturalist land occupied by Chettiars	Proportion of total land occupied by Chettiars
1930	9,249	2,943	570	19	6
1931	9,305	3,212	806	25	9
1932	9,246	3,770	1,367	36	15
1933	9,266	4,139	1,782	43	19
1934	9,335	4,460	2,100	47	22
1935	9,408	4,687	2,293	49	24
1936	9,499	4,873	2,393	49	25
1937	9,650	4,929	2,446	50	25
1938	9,732	4,971	2,468	50	25

* The thirteen districts were then Pegu, Tharrawaddy, Hanthawaddy, Insein, Prome, Bassein, Henzada, Myaungmya, Maubin, Pyapon, Thaton, Amherst and Taungoo. Table derived from GoB (1938: 39).

In the vernacular press the demonisation of the Chettiars soared to extreme heights, and they were accused of all manner of barbarities well beyond a mere rapacity for land. Nevertheless, it was the latter alleged sin that was the most difficult to rebut. In February 1930, for example, the Maubin District-based newspaper *Thuriya* reported that the Chettiars had 'aimed at obtaining possession of agricultural land' through the artifice of loan arrears, a strategy which in the past three years alone had secured them '30,000 acres' of the District's best land.[27] Like much of the vernacular press it called for the outlawing of foreign ownership of land and called upon Burmese everywhere to 'raise an outcry'.[28] In this particular instance the *Nattokottai* Chettiars Association attempted to answer the charges laid against their members, asserting that the Chettiars in Maubin were doing their best to help local cultivators avoid foreclosure.[29] Unusually, in the same rebuttal against the *Thuriya's* accusations there contained something of a threat too, with the Association emphasising that Chettiars 'already had business in various countries, that men with capital could make a living anywhere, and that if newspapers in Burma tried to spoil the good terms now existing between the agriculturalists and the Chettiars they would close down their Burma business and invest their capital elsewhere'.[30]

In the immediate post-independence period most observers of Burma, but especially ex-colonial officers, tended to side with the nationalist press in condemning the role of the Chettiars in the land alienation of the 1930s.

J.S. Furnivall (1956: 116), whose comments ascribing the reclamation of the Delta to the 'epic bravery and endurance' of the Burmese cultivator has been cited already, wrote that this same epic concluded 'with a picture of imposing government offices and business houses in Rangoon, and gilded Chettyar temples in Tanjore, while in the rice districts, the source of almost all of this wealth, nearly half the land is owned by foreigners and a landless people can show little for their labour, but debt'. Sir Bernard Ottwell ('B. O.') Binns (who was to play a critical role in the creation of rural credit institutions in Burma post-independence) was even more scathing, calling the Chettiars 'a useless class of parasitic middlemen' (Binns 1946: 10). One contemporary observer who stood aside from the general condemnation of the Chettiars was J.R. Andrus. He wrote later (1947: 68) that Chettiars often 'nursed' their debtors, reduced interest rates to allow at least some measure of payment and were anxious as far as possible to keep the original owners on the land. He also noted a compromise device often employed by the Chettiars 'whereby part of the land was left in the hands of the former owner, free of mortgage, while the remainder was deeded to the Chettyar without lawsuit' (Andrus 1947: 68).

Although the Depression and the collapse in paddy prices had provided the trigger, the conditions for the land alienation of Burma's indigenous cultivators had been underway for some time. As noted earlier in this chapter, almost from the moment it came under 'industrial' cultivation, Burma's lower delta became a vast arena in which the fluctuating fortunes of cultivators, moneylenders, millers, traders and others in the paddy production chain were contested. Most often it was the cultivators who lost out, the vagaries of agriculture forcing them to surrender title to the land they enjoyed (or were in the process of establishing through continuous occupation). This on-going struggle between what was, in essence, 'three economic systems in Burma' (the European, the Indian and the Burmese) created a situation in which, as a Financial Commissioner in the country famously observed as early as 1895, 'land in Lower Burma was transferred as readily as shares on the London Stock Exchange'.[31] In the 1930s, however, this situation of 'musical chairs' came to an end. The 'closing' of the rice frontier as the best land in the Delta was taken up, and the resultant increase in land prices and rents – coupled with the declining prices of its principal output – meant that the hitherto boundless supply of cultivators willing to buy land forfeited to moneylenders dried up. In this sense, what happened in the wake of the Depression then was simply that what had been a '*sub rosa'* alienation of the land was replaced by *explicit* alienation: revealing the extent to which Burma's lands had passed into the hands of absentee (and foreign) landlords (Siegelman 1962: 249).

The demonisation of the Chettiars in the vernacular press and at the hands of the demagogues, as well as the question of *sub rosa* land alienation before the Depression, found voice in the BPBE and its surveys. Regarding the latter, the evidence of J.M. Clark, Deputy Commissioner of Tharrawaddy District, was representative of a large body of Indian Civil Service (ICS) officers:

> Before the annexation (...) there were few sales of land and mortgages. Money was tight and ostentatious display rarely resorted to for the fear of the 'Myosa'. But with the advent of the British the Myosa disappeared, the Chetty arrived, money became easier, land increased in value, mortgage became common, the number of Chetties increased and more as each year passes, the land is passing into or through their hands, and little by little each year disappears the possibility of a peasant proprietary. We could not do without the Chetties but in my view they should no longer be allowed to enjoy their present monopoly (BPBE 1930b: 734).

Within the BPBE there was disagreement regarding the Chettiars' desire to control land. The four Burmese members of the Enquiry, as well as H.S. Jevons, the then Professor of Economics at Rangoon University, agreed that in recent years there had 'been a tendency for Chettiars in general to become land owners and for this *purpose* to seize land more readily when loans are in arrears' (BPBE 1930a: 199, emphasis added).[32] Strong exception to this assessment, however, was taken by the BPBE Chairman, S.G. Grantham of the ICS, and Lawrence Dawson, Managing Director of Dawson's Bank (the one 'Western' bank whose main business was lending to Burmese cultivators). Grantham and Dawson took issue with both the *Thuriya's* accusations regarding Maubin in particular, as well as the broader point of a change in Chettiar desires regarding land. Their statement asserted that (1930a: 200):

> The Chettiar's predilection is to be a financier, and he would rather have for his assets loans which he can transfer to another Chettiar when he wants to go back to Madras than land which cannot be transferred in the same wholesale way (...) the present increase of land in Chettiar hands is a reflection of the depression in business of paddy cultivation, and will disappear when that depression disappears, and is not an indication that the Chettiar's heart has changed and made him greedy to get possession of land.

CHETTIAR INTEREST RATES

One component of the hostility to the Chettiars was the accusation that the interest rates they charged were usurious and, as such, were the means by which loan default and the seizure of land was activated. Accusations to this end were especially prevalent in the wake of the events outlined above – the principal *plausible* variant of which had it that Chettiar interest rates failed to follow other interest rates down during the Depression.

The question of Chettiar interest rates is not easily settled, and Goldsmith's (1983: 75) caution on this issue regarding India, that 'quoted interest rates must be taken with several grains of salt in a country in which the money and capital markets were little developed [and] in which many interest rates have conventional features and do not often change', is at least equally applicable to colonial Burma. Of course, critics were in little doubt that Chettiar rates were exorbitant. Especially loud in making such accusations were borrowers without collateral such as small stall-holders. One such group from Myingyan Town in Upper Burma claimed in the BPBE commissioned surveys (BPBE 1930b: 146) that Chettiars charged 'from 4 to 5 per cent per month' (around 70 per cent per annum). Peam (1946: 16) asserted that Chettiar rates ranged as high as 45 per cent per annum, while Kyaw Min (1945: 38) alleged rates of 25 per cent were applied even to loans secured against land.[33] Throughout the BPBE surveys (the Myingyan Town testimony was unusual), Chettiar rates were seldom reported beyond 25 per cent per annum, and even these rates *only* applied to loans unsecured by collateral. The last illustrated a universal truth of Chettiar lending: the applicable interest rate depended nothing on the purpose of a loan, but everything upon demand and supply in the lending market, the creditworthiness of the borrower, the security they offered, and the size of the loan.

Chakravarti (1971: 65) constructed the following table of Chettiar lending rates based upon the BPBE Report and surveys:

Table 2.4 Chettiar Lending Rates, 1929

Type of Collateral	% p.a.
Land and Immovable Property	9–15
Precious Metals and Jewellery	12–15
Promissory Notes backed by Collateral	12–15
Unsecured Promissory Notes	15–24

Source: Chakravarti (1971: 65)

Chakravarti was not an unbiased source perhaps, and certainly his 1971 article was a spirited defence of the role of the Chettiars generally. Nevertheless, his quoted lending rates were not in dispute with other reputable sources. Tun Wai (1953: 53) came up with some very similar numbers (Table 2.6 below, though for almost a decade later), and nor are these rates inconsistent with the BPBE (from which Chakravarti drew freely) or the other major studies of the Chettiars (Brown [1993], Cooper [1959], Siegelman [1962], Rudner [1989 and 1994]).

Of course this does not yet imply that Chettiar rates were reasonable, since for that we would need to know the rates that they in turn had to pay on deposits and on other funding. Once more the most reliable source on this was the BPBE, which put the cost of Chettiar working capital (which it took to be represented by the *nadappu vatti*, the Chettiar 'current rate') at 'between 2 and 3 per cent above bank rate' (BPBE 1930a: 226). Bank rate in this context was the rate at which the Imperial Bank made advances against securities of the colonial government of India. Across the 1920s the BPBE estimated that Bank rate ranged from a low of around 6 per cent (in 1925) to a high of 11.5 per cent in 1926. In 1929, the latest relevant year for its report, the BPBE had Bank rate ranging from 7 to 10 per cent. Given that the Chettiars had to pay 2 to 3 per cent above bank rate, we can estimate from this a *nadappu vatti* at about 10 per cent for 1929. In evidence given to the BPBE by a group of the largest Chettiar firms in Rangoon the figure of 10 per cent was likewise cited as the 'average cost of their working capital' (BPBE 1930a: 214).

With a funding base that 'cost' around 10 per cent the lending rates in Table 2.4 do not look usurious. This is especially so when we remember that at this stage no other 'costs' to Chettiar firms have as yet been factored in. Such costs will be considered more fully below, but suffice to say at this stage that even in 'normal' (that is, pre-Depression) times, these could not have been less than about 5 per cent of each individual loan. So far then, the Chettiars seem to be exonerated from the usury charge.

And yet, not so fast. The chief complaint of Tun Wai (1953: 53–55) was that Chettiar lending rates *did* suddenly look exploitative in the 1930s when, as he pointed out, interest rates throughout the world steeply declined. Goldsmith (1983: 69) traced the Indian bank rate thus:

Table 2.5 Indian Bank Rate, 1931–1941

Year	% p.a.	Year	% p.a.
1931	7.0	1937	3.0
1932	5.5	1938	3.0
1933	3.6	1939	3.0
1934	3.5	1940	3.5
1935	3.5	1941	3.5
1936	3.0		

Source: Goldsmith (1983: 69)

According to Tun Wai, the collapse in interest rates in the 1930s dramatically decreased the cost of Chettiar funding, allowing them to bring down 'the current rate of interest [*nadappu vatti*] by 60 per cent during the depression'. This reduction in the cost of their liabilities was not matched, he alleged, by a similar reduction in Chettiar lending rates. Table 2.6 recreates Tun Wai's (1953: 53) 'depression-revised' table of Chettiar borrowing and lending rates.

On the face of it, Tun Wai's revisions look damning. Chettiar funding rates unquestionably fell over the course of the 1930s, but their lending rates are scarcely different than the BPBE/Chakravarti numbers for 1929. Surely now the usury charge could be applied to the Chettiars?

Table 2.6 Chettiar Borrowing and Lending Rates, 1935–1942

Borrowing rates	% p.a.	Lending rates	% p.a.
Nadappu vatti (Current) Rate	3.00–3.25	Land and immovable property	9–15
Thavanai (Fixed) Rate	2.80–3.25	Precious metals and jewellery	12–15
Advances from Banks	4.0–5.0	Promissory notes backed by collateral	12–15
Veyan Vatti (Fixed) Rate	4.25–5.75	Unsecured promissory notes	18–24

Source: Tun Wai (1953: 53)

Once more, however, a reasonable appraisal of the situation would still have to deliver an answer of 'not guilty' with regard to the Chettiars. The reason for this is simple. However much low deposit rates had fallen in theory, in practice there were scarcely any new deposits available to most Chettiar firms. As Tun Wai himself acknowledged (1953: 44–50), fresh Chettiar deposits more or less dried up from the mid-1930s and few banks were willing to lend to them. It was true that Chettiar firms could pay lower interest rates on existing deposits, but since the bulk of these belonged to other Chettiars, the net effect on the Chettiar 'system' was not one to alleviate their funding squeeze.

On the *asset* (lending) side of Chettiar balance sheets there were even firmer grounds on which to dismiss this variant of the usury charge. Once more the reason is simple, and once more Tun Wai himself alluded to the answer: the Chettiars had, in large measure, ceased to become lenders in the 1930s. Reluctant though the shift may have been, by 1934 the Chettiars were as much landlords in receipt of rent (to the extent that this too was paid) as they were money lenders. In short, whatever interest rates may have nominally been charged by Chettiars at this time, there were few loans that they applied to. Tun Wai (1953: 44–45) calculated that across 1935–42 Chettiar assets (which as late as 1929 had consisted entirely of cash, hundis and loans) had transformed 'from a liquid to a solid form' as these categories were largely replaced (87 per cent of the total) by 'land and houses'.

In examining and, where necessary, defending, the interest rates charged by the Chettiars, one must also consider the rates offered by their peer competitors – the credit provided by Burmese moneylenders, shopkeepers (indigenous and non-indigenous), landlords, employers and so on. And, likewise on this score, the Chettiars compared favourably. Interest rates charged by non-Chettiar moneylenders in Burma varied enormously, but it is amongst this cohort that 'true usury' was perhaps apparent. This was especially the case with regard to so-called *sabape* loans, advances made 'in kind' (usually in rice) to cultivators to be repaid after harvest. Such loans, most often made by Burmese landlords to their cultivator tenants and farm labourers, were subject to all manner of social norms, but the interest rates applicable on them usually ranged from 8 to 10 per cent per month, in *per annum* terms between around 150 and 220 per cent. In one case reported in the BPBE survey for the Tharrawaddy District, *sabape* rates of between 600 and 1,500 per cent per annum were claimed.[34] Of course, given that such loans were generally for periods considerably shorter than a year, such astronomical implicit *annual* charges are somewhat misleading.

A Modern Appraisal of Chettiar Interest Rates

The interest rates charged by moneylenders such as the Chettiars have, until recently, attracted little in the way of intellectual attention. This is understandable. For centuries the actions of moneylenders have been simply dismissed as the manifestation of malice and greed. As such, very little in the way of nuance or sophistication was required to explain the charges of 'usurers', 'parasites', 'loan sharks', 'shylocks', 'leeches', 'vampires', 'dragons' – and all the other derogatory labels that have been created for the moneylender down the ages.

Of course there were, and no doubt still are, many examples of rapacious moneylenders bent on expropriating land and bonding labour through debt. Economists, however, are (arguably) rarely satisfied with simple answers that ascribe generalised economic behaviour to moral predilections. As such, especially over the last three decades, a large literature has grown up that has attempted to explain the behaviour of moneylenders and the markets they operate in. Central to this have been the theories that attempt to explain interest rate determination by moneylenders, usually in terms of (1) transaction and opportunity costs; (2) risk premiums; (3) monopolistic competition.

(1) Transaction and Opportunity Costs

In the context of moneylending, 'transactions costs' is the umbrella term used by economists to refer to the expenses that creditors confront when making a loan. These include the costs of identifying and screening borrowers, processing and dispersing loans, collecting and monitoring repayments, assessing collateral, 'policing' and salvaging loan delinquencies, and so on. Such costs are essentially invariant to the size of the loan – meaning that they loom larger, *in percentage terms*, the smaller the size of the loan. Of course, it is precisely such 'small' loans that are usually the stock and trade of moneylenders.

Very little data has survived regarding transactions costs for the Chettiars in Burma, nor were such issues given much attention in the BPBE and its surveys. Timberg and Aiyer (1984: 56), however, found that for Chettiar bankers *in the 1980s*, total administrative costs came to around 5 per cent of their loan book. Given advances in information technology in the intervening decades, it is difficult to imagine that the administrative costs of the Burma Chettiars could have been any less. More broadly, the World Bank (1974: 40) found that 'just the administrative costs of an *efficient* agricultural credit institution lending to small farmers equal 7–10 per cent of its total portfolio' (emphasis in original). There remains much controversy over the extent to which transaction costs can reasonably explain high moneylender interest rates, but if the numbers above are only proximately accurate for the Chettiars in Burma, their interest rate charges (given their own cost of capital) hardly seem usurious.

A 'flipside' to the transaction costs burden on moneylenders such as the Chettiars is that their services imposed relatively *lower* transaction costs on their customers. Borrowers, like lenders, face a raft of transaction costs when seeking a loan, costs which are, for the most part, simply the mirror image of the transaction costs noted above on lenders. Borrower costs, especially for rural clients, rise according to the degree of 'formality' of the arrangements imposed by the lender. The more 'formal' the arrangements, the less 'access' poor, and/or geographically marginalised people have to credit. This is important since, as Helms and Reilla (2004: 3) remind us, the 'poor generally consider ongoing access to credit more important than the actual cost of the credit'. The low transaction cost attributes of moneylenders were acknowledged by Robinson (2001: 210) thus:

> Moneylenders are conveniently located for people who need microcredit; they live in the same or a nearby village, or in the nearest market town. Loan procedures are minimal, and cash is available quickly. Loan amounts, maturities, and payment chedules are flexible. There is little transportation cost or opportunity cost of time spent travelling or waiting.

Robinson's summary of the 'virtues' of moneylenders was readily apparent in the operations of the Chettiars in Burma. Their readiness to approve loans in 'not more than hour' has been noted already, but this was but one of many similar testimonies given to the BPBE and noted in other narratives.[35] Representative was this summary of Chettiar 'office arrangements' by the BPBE (1930a: 239):

> Chettiars have no fixed hours and do not observe public or official holidays. Except for their own festivals of *Pangani Uthram* (in March or April) and *Thaipusam* (in January), when business may be stopped for about four days in all, they are ready to transact business on any day and at any time. This is often a great convenience to depositors who wish to withdraw money, and also to some borrowers whose circumstances make it desirable for them to conceal from others the fact that they are borrowing.

Chettiar accessibility was also manifested in their willingness to lend for almost any purpose – so long as the security and 'price' was right. Unlike more 'formal' lenders, Chettiars did not lend merely for 'productive' purposes. Instead, recognising the essential 'fungibility' of money, Chettiars lent for purposes that their clients themselves deemed necessary, purposes that Tun Wai (1977: 311) noted were sufficiently and subjectively 'urgent' that 'the farmer was willing to pay high rates of interest'. The issue of fungibility was lost on contemporary and later critics of the Chettiars, typical of which was Siegelman's (1962: 247) reproach that Chettiars were willing to lend to the cultivator for anything, 'foolishly for gambling, or willy-nilly on the bare necessities of existence'.[36] In a similar admonishing vein, Christian (1942: 118–119) noted that 'less than ten per cent of the money loaned on Burma rice lands was used actually to improve the land or to purchase additional holdings'. Such criticism over the purposes of Chettiar loans was misplaced. As noted above, it missed the fungibility of credit: advances earmarked for productive purposes clearly 'free up' an equal amount of money to be spent elsewhere, on anything. Fisher and Sriram (2002: 39) succinctly put the modern understanding of the issue, which was implicitly recognised by the Chettiars, that 'credit needs start with consumption purposes'.

(2) Risk Premiums

The losses associated with loan default must also be covered by the interest rates moneylenders charge across their loan portfolio. The greater the likelihood of default, the greater the need for an interest rate margin sufficient to cushion the lender against loss. Arguably, moneylenders have always lent to borrowers, and into economic environments, of greater risk than considered acceptable to more formal lenders. Indeed, one of the hitherto assumed advantages moneylenders possess over their more formal competitors – their proximity to their clients – is an example of the heightened risk they face from being less geographically diversified and more exposed to covariant shocks.

The Chettiars in Burma lent into what would become an increasingly risky economic environment. Ultimately even their fallback security, the title over land, would fail as political events swept away the laws and institutions that once must have seemed unimpeachable. We have some idea of the day-to-day riskiness of Chettiar lending, however, from the BPBE and its surveys, and other reasonable sources. In its 1923 Annual Report, for instance, Dawson's Bank (as previously noted, the only formal bank that lent to Burmese cultivators in a major way) reported that:

> ...the difficulties in the way of financing produce are considerable. It is not easy to obtain good security. Even with land as security there are sometimes risks. The absence of record-of-rights makes it difficult to be sure

about title and the investigation of title is sometimes a long and laborious proceeding.[37]

Dawson's Bank itself charged 14.5 per cent per annum on its loans – somewhat lower than the Chettiar average, but not dramatically so and only (as the Bank itself acknowledged) by taking 'the cream of the security'.[38]

Testimonies presented to the BPBE told of loan default rates rather greater than that which would be presumed by a formal bank. In Pyapôn Town a Chettiar reported that he lost 'one-sixteenth' of his loans' (BPBE 1930b: 93). Another in Kyaiklat Town said that 'one eighth' of their loan book was in default. Such Chettiars also experienced the problems in realising property security noted by Dawson's Bank, the Chettiar in Pyapôn complaining of the expense of litigation and his Kyaiklat counterpart that the 'interval between the final decree and the sale of the property' was too long (BPBE 1930b: 101). Both complainants pointed to the erosion of collateral coverage from such problems, and the concomitant increase in the inherent risks the Chettiars faced.

In his concluding thoughts on Chettiar interest rates and their relation to risk, Cooper (1959: 41) captured the essence of the matter, well before economic theory had turned its gaze towards the moneylender;

> ... in coming to any conclusion with respect to the fairness of Chettyar interest charges and the efficiency of his business operations, the standards of western banking practices should not be used as criteria (...) in the west the banker operates on the theory that his principal will be returned and in part to assure this is willing to accept a low rate of interest. On the other hand, Chettyar operations, like those of moneylenders throughout Asia, operated on the theory that the return of their principal was doubtful and charged high interest to compensate for this.

(3) Monopolistic Competition

The one aspect of modern economic research into moneylending (and moneylenders) that is somewhat sympathetic to the traditional 'exploitation' narrative is that which explains high moneylender interest rates as a consequence of 'monopolistic competition'. A phenomenon theoretically first identified by the great English economist Joan Robinson (1933), monopolistic competition describes a situation in which, notwithstanding the possible existence of competitors, firms are able to exploit varying degrees of 'monopoly' pricing power. That they are able to do this is because of obstacles that inhibit direct competition and segment the market. In the case of moneylenders, such obstacles typically include their geographical dispersion and the information they accumulate on their clients, information not available to potential competitors but essential for profitable lending in specific markets.

Practices that reflected degrees of monopolistic competition were in evidence amongst some Chettiars in Burma. In Dedaye Town, for example, Burmese moneylenders and millers complained to the BPBE that local Chettiars had agreed 'not to lend' at less than 1.4 per cent per month, or 'pay a fine to the local temple' (BPBE 1930b: 106–107). Meanwhile two BPBE committee members, U Ba Maung and U Mya, alleged similar practices amongst Chettiar firms in Myingyan Town, albeit in this case the minimum interest rate was 1.75 per cent per month and was allegedly accompanied by an agreement that they would not compete for each others' customers. Of course, these are examples of explicit collusion; more powerful probably was simply the pricing power a local Chettiar might enjoy from the fact that their isolation precluded their customers from going anywhere else.

But whilst there was some evidence of monopolistic competition amongst some Chettiars in Burma, there was also much to suggest the phenomenon was not dominant – indeed, that a high degree of *competition* amongst Chettiars was more typical. The BPBE documented fierce competition between the 22 Chettiar firms in Kyaiklat Town for instance, in which all components of Chettiar charges were up for grabs (BPBE 1930b: 100). It reported a similar situation in Myingyan Town, challenging the account of its two committee members above (BPBE 1930b: 141). Meanwhile a 1916 Settlement Report (for Tharrawaddy District) made what would become a familiar refrain from Government officials, that competition amongst Chettiars was too vigorous, prompting each 'in making reckless loans' (GoB 1916: 14). Finally, perhaps the most remarkable demonstration of competition amongst moneylenders in colonial Burma was that which took place in the Taungtha and Natogyi Townships of Myingyan District where, according to a deposition to the BPBE, 'local *Burmese* moneylenders lowered their rates sufficiently to bring about the closure of the limited Chettiar operations in both towns' (BPBE 1930b: 146).

GUILTY OR INNOCENT?

The Japanese invasion of Burma in 1942 brought with it many harrowing scenes, but few would match that of the flight of the diaspora of Indian merchants, workers, administrators and financiers who had done much to transform Burma in the colonial era. Prominent amongst those fleeing the onslaught of the Japanese, just as they had been prominent in the transformational role played by Indians in Burma beforehand, were the Chettiars of Tamil Nadu. Scapegoats then and now for the misfortunes that heralded the breakdown of Burma's colonial economy, the Chettiars were not allowed to return to their lives and livelihoods following the granting of Burma's independence in 1948. Portrayed by British colonial officials and Burmese nationalist politicians alike as almost pantomime villains in Burma's twentieth-century dramas, they left the stage as unambiguous victims.

The purpose of this chapter has been to demonstrate the central role played by the Chettiars in the development of Burma's colonial economy. Forming a critical bridge between 'Western' finance and the Burmese cultivator, the Chettiars were crucial players in the advancement of Burma's 'rice frontier'. In contrast to the received wisdom, however, this chapter paints a picture of Chettiar operations that escapes the moneylender stereotype to present them instead as proto-financial institutions that created monetary, and ultimately real, resources in Burma. The chapter has also attempted to rebut, using conventional economic theory, the notion that the Chettiars charged 'usurious' rates of interest with the objective of acquiring land. The chapter does not conclude, however, that all aspects of the Chettiars role in Burma were positive or even benign. Forever outsiders, they had little commitment for instance, to Burma independently of its identity as a component of Britain's Indian Empire. Also, although the Chettiars were financial institutions of a 'proto' form, Burma needed fully-fledged financial and other institutions that history tells us are conducive to economic growth and development. These were imperfectly created in colonial Burma and, as we shall see, they would remain so.

NOTES

1   Proof that such demonisation lives on in Burma is provided by efforts by the country's ruling military regime to label (opposition leader and Nobel Laureate) Aung San Suu Kyi as a Chettiar. For more on this, see Skidmore (2004: 136).

2   'Chettiar' (often spelt 'Chettyar') is the honorific plural for the members of the caste that is the focus of this chapter. Numerous variants of their name – Chetti, Chetty, Chety, Shetty, Setti – abound, but Chettiar was both used by members of the caste themselves when rendering their collective name into English, and it is this spelling that also most often appears in official and other contemporary reports of their activities. Brief details of the caste background of the Chettiar are given below, but a comprehensive account is provided in Rudner (1994).

3   The opening of the Suez Canal also allowed for the introduction of steamships on the Europe-Asia routes, which had previously been excluded from the Asia trade because of the lack of coal stations along the vast coasts of Africa. Accordingly, the dramatic reduction in sailing times occasioned by the opening of the Suez Canal was a function of the combination of technological advances with changes in 'geography'. For a discussion of sailing times and related matters, see Ray (1995: 476).

4   'Rice frontier' was the evocative phrase employed by Adas (1974a) and Furnivall (1956) to sum up the advancing production in the Delta.

5   Other types of land-title, such as the so-called *patta* (grant) system and various lease and colonisation schemes were also introduced during the colonial years, mostly in response to the problems of land alienation that will be outlined further here. For more, see Furnivall (1956: 51–55), Cheng Siok-Hwa (1968: 137–170) and Thant Myint-U (2001: 227–235).

6   The issue of land-title in Burma *before* the British annexation is a topic of immense complexity and depth, and it is considered here only in the briefest of outlines as necessary for an understanding of subsequent events involving the Chettiars. The numerous *Settlement Report* series and *Land Revenue Manuals* are a most comprehensive source, though they suffer from the colonial mindset familiar in such documents. Furnivall (1956), Cheng Siok-Hwa (1968), Adas (1974a) and Government of Burma (1938) offer more approachable, but intellectually similar, readings. Two recent, Burmese, accounts that deal with the topic in hitherto novel ways are Toe Hla (1987) and Thant Myint-U (2001).

7   Furnivall's citation was from an unpublished memorandum by Ardagh entitled 'The Mode of Tenure by Which the Greater Portion of the Land in Burma is Held'.

8   For the debate on some of the relevant issues, see Rudner (1989: 424–428).

9   Prior to decimalisation in 1971, £1 sterling was made up of twenty shillings (*s.*) which, in turn, were equal to twelve pennies (*d.*).

10   The survey appeared as the second volume to the BPBE Report, and is denoted in the list of references in this book as BPBE (1930b).

11   Though uniformly simply labeled 'Chettiars', the peoples who were to become the renowned money-lenders throughout South and South-East Asia were in fact a sub-set of the Chettiar community who were referred to by other Chettiars as the Nattukottai ('people with palatial houses in the countryside' in Tamil). (Rudner 1994: 1). They referred to *themselves* as the Nakarattar (roughly translating as 'city dwellers' in Tamil) (Rudner 1994: 2).

12   *Vaiśya* is one of the four major status or 'caste' divisions of Hindu society in India. It is generally held to consist of merchants, farmers, traders and 'professions' of various sorts. Based on interviews with the community, Rudner (1994: 2) estimated the number of Chettiars in 1980 at 100,000. This number has subsequently been

confirmed by the author in correspondence with members of the international Chettiar community.

13 A narrative that was fortified intellectually by L.C. Jain's influential 1929 book, *Indigenous Banking in India.*

14 An assurance formalised in modern banking systems via the 'universal' minimum capital requirements stipulated under the Basel capital accords. This issue is re-examined in Chapter 9.

15 There are genuine *equity* instruments that, in present-day financial systems, generate 'interest' as well as dividends – but they were unknown in the context of the systems described here.

16 To borrow the phrase employed by the BPBE and by Tun Wai (1953 and 1962) to categorise the European banks and their practices and instruments in Burma.

17 This list of typical purposes to which Chettiar loans were put by cultivators is yielded from the BPBE surveys of cultivators contained in BPBE (1930b).

18 Ray (1995: 527) wrongly implies that *thavanai* deposits were primarily provided to outsiders to the Chettiar community. In fact, *thavanai* deposits of non-Chettiars were both rare and insignificant.

19 In modern financial markets, rates on 'at call' deposits tend to be lower than their fixed equivalents – reflecting the benefits to those placing them from greater liquidity.

20 An example of such reliance was given in evidence to the BPBE by a Chettiar in Pyapôn Town, see BPBE (1930b: 93).

21 The word 'hundi' is derived from Sanskrit and means simply to 'collect'. Though renowned as a financial instrument as described here, its origins can be readily identified by the fact that 'hundi' is also the word employed to describe the collection box in a Hindu temple. Today 'hundis' are more known for their use in alternative remittance systems than anything else, and in this context the word 'hundi' has an identical meaning to 'hawala', 'hui kwan', 'chiao hui', 'poey kwan' – and various similar but differently *named* instruments. There are many works devoted to the study of such 'indigenous' banking instruments, but a good introduction is Jost and Sandhu (2000).

22 A rupee was worth 16 annas, implying a typical hundi charge in percentage terms of around one-eighth of one per cent.

23 The latter would also have the effect of making them more attractive to the banks for rediscounting. At the time, hundis written in a language other than English were limited in status under the *Negotiable Instruments Act* to the practices of *local usage* only – and thus lowering their reliability relative to European bills of exchange in the eyes of Western-style banks (BPBE 1930a: 150).

24 The Bank of Chettinad was capitalised at Rs.30 million and was run by a prominent Chettiar family from Kanasakatham in Chettinad. Based in Rangoon, in 1932 it expanded offshore to open an office in Colombo, Ceylon. The Bank survived, albeit at a fairly low level after the late 1930s, up until 1965 (after being 'nationalised' with all the other 'foreign' banks in 1963). Very little information is available on the Bank, but Weerasooria (1973) has as much as seems to be known.

25 In their agency arrangements the Chettiars solved what is known within the discipline of economics as the 'principal and agent' problem. In the modern world, solving the problem – which simply refers to the dilemma of how to ensure that the agent acts in the best interests of the principal – has generated all manner of methods, including franchising, incentive contracts, commission-based payments, and so on.

26 Prices as at Rangoon docks. The 'basket' was the standard unit of account for paddy, and was the equivalent of around 21 kilograms.

27 The newspaper's claim, made in its edition of 19 February 1930, is cited and discussed in BPBE (1930a: 198–199).

28 *Ibid.*

29 The *Nattukottai* Chettiars' *Association* had been formed in 1923 to represent the interests of Chettiars in Burma. The response of the Association to the *Thuriya* accusations is cited from BPBE (1930a: 199).

30 *Ibid.*

31 The Commissioner's comments are cited in Furnivall (1956: 86). On the idea that the economic struggle in Burma's lower delta was the clash of three distinct economic systems, see the contemporary account of Andrus (1936).

32 The Burmese members of the BPBE were: U Aye, a member of Burma's Legislative Assembly and representing the Chinese and Burma-Indian Chambers of Commerce; U Ba Maung, Manager of the Pegu Central Co-operative Bank and the representative of the co-operative movement; U Mya, Manager of the Myingyan Electric Company who was listed as representing 'urban interests', and: U Shwe Tha, a retired Deputy Commissioner listed as the representative of 'agricultural interests in Upper Burma' (BPBE 1930a: 4–5).

33 Kyaw Min's claim sits oddly with other sources, and in the view of this author should not be regarded as a particularly reliable source.

34 This claim was made by Saw Pah Dwai, the Karen MLC whose comments are employed at the top of this chapter. His evidence appeared in the BPBE survey volume (BPBE 1930b: 758).

35 This particular example of Chettiar lending efficiency is noted in BPBE (1930a: 233).

36 But similar moral pronouncements are endemic across the literature dealing with the 'credit culture' in Burma, and all are similarly wrong-headed.

37 The Annual Report is here cited from Government of India (1928: 255).

38 *Ibid.*

CHAPTER 3

Cooperative Credit
to the Rescue?

It was natural of course that the Government of India should take over the administration of Burma when it was added to the British Crown and it was also natural that the Government of India should make the mistake of supposing that Burma was just another of the Indian Provinces. And in this, I submit with the greatest respect lies the cause of the failure of the Burmese to make any real progress, particularly in the direction of acquiring a 'money sense'.

Captain J.M. Clark, Deputy Commissioner,
Tharrawaddy District, 1930

Cooperative credit was the British Empire's favoured device for the marginalisation of moneylenders such as the Chettiars. Its establishment a key recommendation of the Indian Famine Commission of 1901, it was given official and legal sanction under the *Cooperative Credit Societies Act* promulgated by the government of British India in 1904. Thereafter, the cooperative credit movement spread rapidly. Driven by the 'enthusiasm and driving power of a select body of officers' within the Indian Civil Service, by 1930 there were over 100,000 cooperative credit societies with 4 million members across the provinces of British India (Kumar 1983: 800–802). [1]

One of the 'provinces' of British India into which cooperative credit was imported was Burma but, as a Burmese government enquiry noted many years later, '[i]t may fairly be surmised that Burma had no place in the thoughts of the Government of India when the new policy was formulated (...) nor is there any evidence that defects in Burma's credit structure were in mind' (GoB 1938: 85). Yet, despite this lack of consideration, it must have seemed the ideal device for addressing what the colonial government already recognised as the growing indebtedness of the Burmese cultivator

53

to the Chettiars, and the increasing alienation of their land. The cooperative credit movement in Burma grew as rapidly as it did in the Indian Empire as a whole and by 1929 there were over 4,000 cooperative credit societies across the country embracing almost 100,000 individual members (GoB 1929: 5). As events were soon to prove, however, this extraordinary growth masked a less successful reality. Poorly implemented, culturally out of place and historically before its time, Burma's cooperative credit movement would collapse even before the effects of the Great Depression laid waste to the country's economy.

The story of cooperative credit in colonial Burma, as outlined here, begins with an examination of its historical and intellectual foundations. Its genealogy ultimately traceable to the 'Rochdale Pioneers' and their like, the actual form taken by cooperative credit in the British Empire owed more to German models than to anything from the metropolitan centre of the Empire. The chapter then outlines the organisational structure of the cooperative credit system of colonial Burma. A structure designed in three tiers to meet expected difficulties in monitoring and in raising funds, it would prove to contain critical flaws that would bring the movement down. The chapter tells a chronological story of the rise and fall of cooperative credit in Burma, from its optimistic beginnings to its despairing implosion in the midst of the Great Depression. Logically following this, the chapter examines the findings of the so-called 'Calvert Committee', the official enquiry commissioned by the colonial government in Burma to discover what had gone wrong, and concludes with the findings of other official diagnoses.

THEORETICAL AND HISTORICAL FOUNDATIONS

Cooperative credit arrived in Burma at the behest of its colonial government to provide an alternative to moneylenders such as the Chettiars, and to offer a solution to the malaise it saw more generally in the country that arose from its 'somewhat violent transition from a self-sufficing domestic economy to a commercial money economy' (GoB 1920: 1). Principal amongst the problems of this 'violent transition' was the indebtedness of the cultivator, the causes and facts of which the government openly admitted:

> There can be no doubt that debt per head has increased in the last forty years and the causes, generally speaking, of this increase are the rapid transition to a money economy; the absence of any machinery for saving; temporary loss

54

of ballast and extravagance; improvidence; the heavy expense of breaking new land and pioneering without a proper system of financing the pioneer; an unduly expensive credit system; the fact that much of the country is under one crop only, which prevents frequent mobilization of capital; that kind of speculation which always accompanies any land or produce boom; and latterly *habit* (GoB 1920: 5, emphasis in original).

In the government's view the underlying cause of all of the above was what it saw as the 'entire absence of organization of the weak, that is, of the cultivators, who form the mass of the population, and of the poorer inhabitants of the rural market towns' (GoB 1920: 1). Notwithstanding the seriousness of the issues, the government was nevertheless at first reasonably sanguine about the situation. It had, after all, a remedy at hand – cooperative credit.

An idea that was imported from India and imposed by the imperial government upon Burma, in its origins cooperative credit belonged to Europe. Ultimately an application of 'cooperation' as inspired by the 'Rochdale Equitable Pioneers' and their famous 'weavers' cooperative', and as adhered to by social reformers generally, cooperative *credit* was essentially a German invention. The pioneers (and bitter rivals) of Germany's cooperative credit system were Hermann Schulze-Delitzsch (1809–1883) and Friedrich Raiffeisen (1818–1888).[2] Both provincial politicians, their two movements shared a philosophy of member ownership and control, 'self-help' and (mostly) independence from the state. *Schulze-Delitzch's* movement, however, was essentially an *urban* phenomenon dominated by small craftsman and small business – groups with growing credit needs as a consequence of increasing mechanisation. *Schulze-Delitzsch* societies were reminiscent of joint-stock companies and were formed with limited liability. Members' 'shares' paid a dividend and were relatively high-priced – sufficient, together with reserves from retained earnings, for the societies to be able to ultimately fund their own loan book. They also tended to be managed by paid staff, loan turnover was relatively rapid and loans were usually short-term. For all of these reasons *Schulze-Delitzsch* tended not to be suited to agriculture. The first *Schulze-Delitzsch* cooperative credit society was formed in 1850 (Guinnane 1997: 251–274).

Contrarily, given the predominantly *rural* credit needs in Burma, the earliest credit cooperatives in the country were of the *Schulze-Delitzsch* type. The first was established in Myinmu township in March 1905, and had 19 members. By 1908 16 other *Schulze-Delitzsch* cooperatives had been formed, but even by this time the sun was setting on this form of cooperative society in Burma and they were outnumbered by the 55 of the *Raiffeisen* variety (Khin San Yee 1997: 52).

By far the most prevalent type of cooperative credit society in Burma were those based on the *Raiffeisen* model.[3] The *Raiffeisen* movement began in 1864 and was mostly concerned with agriculture and the financial needs of farmers and rural peasantry. Though it shared many of the cooperative principles of *Schulze-Delitzsch*, to a much greater extent than the latter ethical and moral considerations were a primary motive in its formation and propagation. The primary purpose of the movement was to provide credit (at the lowest possible interest rate) to those who could not normally borrow except from moneylenders. This included both the poor and those without collateral. Significantly, *Raiffeisen* societies were established with *unlimited liability* for their members against the entire borrowings of each society. This was to counter the problem of the lack of collateral by substituting for it the security of strong member incentives to monitor each other's repayment performance. In order to aid such monitoring, each *Raiffeisen* society was restricted to a relatively small geographical area. To keep entry barriers to the poor as low as possible, shares in *Raiffeisen* societies were of a nominal value only and they did not pay a dividend. Retained earnings were maintained in a reserve which would only be disbursed if a society was wound up – and even then not to members, but to fund 'some useful public work' (Wolff 1893: 75). Office bearers in *Raiffeisen* societies were not meant to draw any form of remuneration, but in Germany the movement employed a body of 'roaming auditors' who travelled 'from association to association, examining books, and inspecting accounts, and overhauling the whole business of every association, at least once every two years' (Wolff 1893: 74).

The *Raiffeisen* movement excited the interest of social reformers in Britain, and officials throughout its Empire, to a degree that dwarfed its rivals. Henry Wolff was particularly taken with its possibilities. Wolff's 1893 book, *People's Banks: A Record of Social and Economic Progress*, was enormously influential and a source of inspiration to those who ultimately established Burma's cooperative credit system (BPBE 1930a: 13). In the book Wolff even feared, he wrote, 'of falling into a strain of rhapsody' in describing *Raiffeisen's* achievements and potential. Regardless, he ventured forth, describing a 'new world' in which '[t]he idle man becomes industrious, the spendthrift thrifty, the drunkard reforms his ways and becomes sober, the tavern-hunter forsakes the inn, the illiterate learns to read and write' (Wolff 1893: 11). Wolff's contemporary assessment was overblown, of course, but before the First World War there were very real grounds for optimism for the movement. By 1910, for example, an estimated 15,000 *Raiffeisen* societies had been established across Germany (with 1.4 million members), and *none* with unlimited liability had failed (Bannerjee *et al.* 1994: 503).

Raiffeisen animated nineteenth-and early-twentieth-century social reformers generally, but the movement's structure and organisational principles also exercised (and continue to exercise) the interest of economists and those concerned with industrial organisation. *Raiffeisen's* efforts to replace collateral as the basis for lending with the discipline of 'peer monitoring' was especially noteworthy – not least in that by providing a substitute for collateral it held out the promise of a new paradigm for lending to the poor. A label made prominent by the Nobel Prize-winning economist, Joseph Stiglitz in the 1970s, peer monitoring was based on the idea that the members of a cooperative credit society not only possessed great knowledge of each other, but via unlimited liability (and the hope for future loans) had an incentive to maintain and extend that knowledge (Stiglitz 1990: 315–366). Members of a cooperative credit society, moreover, who had long-term interactions with each other (economic *and* non-economic) were in a better position to sanction opportunistic behaviour than people in institutions organised purely on commercial lines. Seen from the vantage point of economics, unlimited liability could also be regarded as a powerful 'signalling device': convincing others that a cooperative society *must* be soundly run since its members (transparently) had much to lose if it were not.

Such issues were (and are) not just of theoretical interest however. In recent decades, for example, great hope has been entertained for what has become known as 'microfinance' in delivering to the world's poor both economic security and a potential route out of poverty (we examine modern microfinance in relation to Burma in Chapter 11). Microfinance has a myriad of organisational forms, but amongst the most prominent schemes (those employed, for instance, by the famed Grameen Bank), great reliance has been placed on 'peer' or 'group' lending in providing for a viable mechanism for low cost credit without collateral. In the latest parlance, peer lending provides the 'social capital' through which microfinance institutions can lower their 'transaction costs'. The hazardous flipside of such schemes, which (as shall be examined below) was of great relevance to conditions in colonial Burma, was that when this social capital was missing, the whole system was imperiled.

COOPERATIVE CREDIT IN BURMA: A STRUCTURE IN THREE TIERS

Primary Credit Societies

Colonial Burma's cooperative credit system was organised in three tiers. The first tier consisted of the 'primary credit societies'– associations of individuals who were borrowers, savers or both. Those societies organised under *Raiffeisen* principles were formally known as 'Rural Cooperative Credit Societies' (hereafter, 'Credit Societies') and were organised usually on a 'one per village' basis. Typically they remained small, however, and in 1920 the average Credit Society in Burma consisted of only 21 individuals (GoB 1920: 11). Consistent with *Raiffeisen* principles, members had unlimited liability for the debts of the cooperative. Credit Societies raised their funds through the sale of their shares to members (a nominal amount of Rs 10), deposits placed in them by members, any accumulated profits, and borrowing from 'Central Banks' (tier three below). Dividends were not paid on shares.

Credit Societies could only lend to their (shareholder) members, and (in marked contrast to the Chettiars) only for 'productive purposes' such as cultivation expenses, the purchase, improvement or redemption of land, the purchase of livestock or for the extinguishment of debts to moneylenders. Lending 'for religious purposes or for buying luxuries or for speculation' was explicitly prohibited (GoB 1920: 5). This prohibition was to be one of the factors that brought about the failure of cooperative credit in Burma. It failed to recognize the essential 'fungibility' of money and, as such, was a measure that could never have succeeded in its seeming objective of instilling a 'money sense' in any case. In Burma as elsewhere, the doctrinaire refusal to lend for 'non-productive' purposes was also one of the principal reasons why cooperative credit failed to make the inroads expected into a market hitherto dominated by Chettiars and other moneylenders.

Credit Societies paid an interest rate of 10 per cent per annum on deposits, and lent out to members at rates ranging from 12 to 15 per cent. The highest rate was reserved for lending to pay off moneylender debts. Loans were classified in three categories according to term. 'A' class loans, for cultivation expenses, were repayable in full at harvest. 'B' class loans, for the purchase of livestock, were payable in two or three annual installments. 'C' class loans, for the purchase, improvement or redemption of land, *and* the elimination of moneylender debts, were repayable in four annual installments. A one year extension on loans in all categories could be given for 'good cause' (GoB 1920: 52). Interest was levied twice annually, but *did not* compound. The Government's *Handbook on Co-operation* was confident that loan defaults would not be a serious problem in Burma's Credit Societies, since 'the bye-laws require that only honest men be admitted'.

Great emphasis was placed by the colonial government on the role cooperatives could play in mobilising savings, and not just in apportioning credit. This was a somewhat unusual objective at the time, though today it is very much at the forefront of thinking on the role played by financial institutions in economic development.[4] In its propagating literature the colonial government was at pains to point out the advantages of saving money via a cooperative society rather than 'hiding it in the ground', or using it to buy gold and jewellery. The latter methods of 'saving' were, of course, time-honoured and widely practised in Burma. They had distinct disadvantages, however, including being 'baits for dacoits and robbers'. Burying wealth in the ground also uniquely exposed a family to loss 'if the owner dies suddenly without having disclosed the hiding place' (GoB 1920: 65). Also targeted by the government in this respect were pawn-shops, which otherwise made saving in a 'physical form' attractive. Pawn-shops, however, created the circumstances whereby the owner effectively paid 'interest on his own money' and, in any case, were only able to realise 'three-quarters of the value of the articles pawned' (GoB 1920: 65). The colonial government extolled the broader national benefits of formal savings too, noting that it allowed those with idle funds to earn interest while those without funds, but with good business ideas, could use it for 'productive purposes'. All in all, 'by making such deposits the power of production is increased and Burma as a whole benefits' (GoB 1920: 66).

Ultimate authority in the internal governance of each Credit Society was vested in the 'General Meeting' of its members (one member, one vote), which was held four times a year (Khin San Yee 1997: 49). This in turn elected an Executive Committee which decided upon all the major issues: the maximum borrowing and lending of the Society, the maximum borrowing of individual members, supervision of repayments, interest rates and the other activities of the Society. The accounts were kept by the Society's Secretary, who was selected by the Executive Committee from amongst their number. The Secretary was also meant to play the key role in promoting the 'spirit of cooperation'. Consistent with *Raiffeisen*, neither the Secretary nor the members of the Executive Committee were supposed to receive any remuneration, or any favourable treatment from the Society. In *Raiffeisen* societies in Europe, the Secretary was usually the village schoolmaster. The decline and politicisation of schools in Burma (which accelerated in the 1920s) denied Burma's cooperatives a similarly credible village-based authority figure to fulfil the role.[5]

Burma's Credit Societies were regulated by the '(Burma) Provincial Registrar of Co-operative Societies'. Curiously, the Registrar was not based in Rangoon, but in the 'hill station' town of Maymyo (the colonial government's 'summer capital'). The Registrar was responsible for auditing, or arranging for the audit, of each Society annually and had the power to place a Society in liquidation if it was found to be insolvent or operating improperly. The primary objective of the Registrar's function was 'to show why money deposited with Co-operative Societies is safe' (GoB 1920: 67). No '*responsibility* or *liability* for the debts of Societies' was accepted by the Registrar, however, and there was nothing in the way of modern deposit insurance or guarantees. Nevertheless, the government was confident that its regulatory regime was working well. In 1920 it boasted:

> As the proof in the pudding is in the eating it may be added that in the 14 years since the Co-operative movement was first introduced into Burma, 225 Societies have been wound up for bad working. They were wound up because they were the worst among all those registered. *In no case has any depositor lost anything* (GoB 1920: 68, emphasis in original).

Unions

The second tier of Burma's cooperative credit system was occupied by the 'Unions', associations of geographically-proximate Credit Societies (ranging in number from five to about twelve) grouped together to achieve objectives that were thought beyond individual Societies on their own. In the words of the Government: '[j]ust as a Co-operative Society is an Association of a number of individual persons, so is a Union an association of a number of Co-operative Societies' (GoB 1920: 57).

Unions existed in other countries where *Raiffeisen* and other credit cooperatives operated, but elsewhere their function was little more than to act as an exchange for disseminating 'best practices'.[6] In Burma, however, their role was critical. Motivated by the fact that the *human capital* of individual Credit Societies was probably insufficient for the ambitions the colonial government had for the cooperative movement, the burdens placed on the Unions were wide ranging, often contradictory and very heavy:

> A Union is (...) an association formed for *the purpose of mutually guaranteeing* the borrowings of affiliated Societies from non-members, of teaching co-operative principles, of providing regular inspection of the accounts and working of affiliated Societies, of assessing the credit to be allowed to each affiliated Society and recommending loans for them, of forecasting repayments and requirements for the guidance of the Central Bank [tier three, below], of assisting the Registrar in deciding whether or not to register new Societies in its neighbourhood and, lastly, of generally furthering the spread of sound co-operation (GoB 1920: 12, emphasis added).

The Unions had paid staff – a Supervisor and at least one clerk, whose salaries were met by a 'Union fund tax' levied on its member Societies. Consistent with cooperative principles, ultimate authority for the management of the Unions rested in their 'General Meetings', held three times a year. The General Meeting in turn elected a Chairman and Union Committee. Together with the paid staff, this leadership team came to conduct the regulatory, prudential and auditing functions that increasingly were delegated from the Registrar (GoB 1920: 53). As shall be seen below, this was to have far-reaching repercussions.

The federation of Credit Societies in Burma into Unions began in 1909. Since it was the collective 'guarantee' that was the focus of much attention regarding the Unions, they were popularly known as 'guarantee unions'. The number of Unions reached its peak, of 558, in 1925 (Khin San Yee 1997: 55).

'Central' Cooperative Banks

The third tier of Burma's cooperative credit system consisted of what became known as the District 'Central Banks'. Established to raise funds for the entire movement by 'attracting deposits from well-to-do members of the public' (largely European), their creation in 1909 was essentially an admission that individual Credit Societies had been less than successful in attracting deposits sufficient to fund their lending. A distinct advantage the Central Banks had over individual Credit Societies was that they offered better deposit products – including 'current' and 'at call' deposits as well as those for fixed terms. The Central Banks played no role in the supervision or regulation of individual Credit Societies (this was left to the Registrar and the Unions). Rather, they were created simply to help finance them. The first Central Bank was formed at Pakôkku in 1909, and what was to be by far the most significant, the 'Mandalay District Co-operative Bank', was formed a year later. At their peak (in 1926), there were 23 Cooperative Central Banks across the length and breadth of Burma (GoB 1920: 10).

The Central Banks provided funds to Credit Societies via the Unions. As noted above, the Unions were required to assess the borrowing capacity of Credit Societies and, when this exceeded their actual ability to raise funds via shares and deposits, to approach the relevant Central Bank for the remainder. In this manner, and given the problems faced by the Credit Societies in raising deposits, Central Banks provided the largest portion of funds to the cooperative movement throughout its history. The Unions' credit assessments were carried out annually, from which was derived a matching 'overdraft' facility of each Society with its Central Bank. Of course, it was in this context that the 'guarantee' of the Unions was critical – since each Society in a Union guaranteed the debts of each other with their Central Bank. As such, the risk to the latter from Credit Society defaults should have been minimal. According to a government leaflet describing the role of the Central Banks, they were 'justified in relying upon the assessments made by Unions because Unions guarantee the liabilities of their Societies' (GoB 1920: 69). The obvious flaw in this arrangement would be exposed if Unions as a whole, or in substantial number, were in trouble. Each 'borrowing' Society was required to take up shares in their Central Bank, proportionate to the size of their loans. The Central Banks came to be owned therefore by the Credit Societies that borrowed from them, although shares in the Central Banks were sold to individual investors as well. The Central Banks paid an interest rate on deposits of around 6 per cent per annum, and charged borrowing Credit Societies between 10 and 15 per cent (GoB 1920: 69).

Amongst the Central Banks, the Mandalay District Co-operative Bank stood out in such a way that it really must be considered separately from all the others. Its importance can even be traced in its changing name – first to the 'Upper Burma Central Bank' and finally, in 1920, to the 'Burma Provincial Bank'. Formed in 1910 from a firm of solicitors in Mandalay that had become a prominent agency for placing funds in individual Credit Societies, the Provincial Central Bank became over time the 'central bank' for the other Cooperative Central Banks, and provided them with funds which they in turn lent on to their member Societies and Unions (GoB 1929: 4). It also stood as a ready source of liquidity to the other Central Banks, providing them with funds, for example, when there occurred (usually due to seasonal factors) temporary mismatches between their deposit and loan books. In addition to providing funds to the other Central Banks, however, the Provincial Bank continued to lend to individual Credit Societies via the Unions. At its peak in 1925, the Provincial Central Bank had a total working capital of Rs 11.2 million and had loan outstandings of Rs 8.8 million to 2,200 individual Credit Societies in 22 districts (thus supplying almost half of the latter's lending) (Tun Wai 1953: 73).

THE GROWTH AND COLLAPSE OF COOPERATIVE CREDIT IN BURMA

Burma's cooperative credit system enjoyed spectacular growth in the first two decades of its existence. After a slow start following the passing of the *Co-operative Societies Act* in 1904, growth in the movement's 'numbers' for twenty years thereafter was almost exponential. In 1910 there were 252 Credit Societies throughout Burma, with just over 6,000 individual members and a share capital of Rs 79,000. Five years later there were 1,252 Credit Societies, over 30,000 members and share capital of Rs 700,000. By now the structure of the movement was changing too, with the second and third 'tiers' of the edifice in place in the form of 4 Central Banks and 189 Unions (GoB 1950: 16). Burma was at the periphery of the First World War and the conflict did little to slow the growth of cooperative credit which, in the decade to 1925, reached its apogee. In 1925 there were 4,057 Credit Societies, over 92,000 members, 21 Central Banks, 575 Unions, share capital of Rs 3.56 million and almost Rs 18 million in advances available or lent to members (GoB 1950: 16).

Even at its peak in 1925, however, Burma's cooperative credit system – though seemingly of great promise – accounted for relatively little of the credit needs of Burma's cultivators. During 1925 total aggregate *new* loans of the 4,000 or so Credit Societies came to Rs 6.6 million (Tun Wai 1953: 71). This was a not an insignificant sum, but it was little more than 3 per cent of the Rs 200 million that the BPBE estimated cultivators required each year. The remainder, as always, was primarily sourced from private moneylenders (mostly Chettiars).[7] The seemingly triumphant year of 1925 would also prove to be a turning point in the trajectory of cooperative credit in Burma, but even before this epochal year various warning signs had begun to appear suggesting all was not as it should be. In the Registrar's Annual Report for 1924–25, the idea that the growth in cooperative credit had been 'too rapid' over the past decade found official voice. Perhaps, the Report pondered, 'societies were being registered too easily, loans were being made too easily [and] repayments have become slack'. The movement, moreover, was 'clogged with bad societies' (GoB 1950: 18). Meanwhile, rumours had begun to surface about the solvency of the Provincial Bank. For now these were rebutted by the government. The Burma Provincial Central Bank, the government announced in 1925, had maintained its reputation for 'sound finance' (GoB 1938: 93).

The retrenchment of Burma's cooperative credit system, which in truth was its near complete collapse, took place in the decade following 1925. Of course, this interval included the years we think of as comprising the Great Depression, but the collapse of cooperative credit in Burma preceded this. Breaking the decade into two five year periods illustrates the point. In 1930 the 4,157 Societies of the movement's peak (1925) had declined to 2,191, the 92,000 members to 50,000, the share capital to Rs 2.7 million and the loans advanced and available to 70 per cent of the 1925 total. The Great Depression, the wholesale collapse of paddy prices as well as the various insurrections and communal conflicts of a country in political turmoil, provided the *coup de grace*.[8] By 1935 a greatly diminished cooperative credit system in Burma comprised 1,371 Societies with just over 29,000 members, share capital of Rs 1.5 million and loans previously advanced (*nothing* was available for new loans) of Rs 8 million. Only 10 of the Central Banks survived into 1935 and the Unions had been almost completely destroyed as a category. A mere 57 of the 575 that had existed in 1925 survived through the following decade (Khin San Yee 1997: 51). Table 3.1 provides a snapshot of the rise and fall.

Table 3.1 The Rise and Fall of Cooperative Credit, 1905–1935

Year	No. of credit societies	No. of individual members	Share capital Rs 000s
1905	9	568	18
1910	252	6,116	79
1915	1,252	30, 130	700
1920	3,319	72,816	1,873
1925	4,157	92,005	3,561
1930	2,191	50,074	2,774
1935	1,371	29,712	1,471

Source: Khin San Yee 1997: 51

The collapse of Burma's cooperative credit system was also illustrated in the sad story of its 'apex' bank. As noted above, rumours regarding the Burma Provincial Bank had been around for quite a while, but they had been brushed aside by a government anxious to maintain confidence in a movement in which it invested much (idealistic as well as financial) capital. In November 1927, however, matters came to a head when the Provincial Bank approached the government to effectively guarantee it against default. In fact, the problems facing the Bank were longstanding, and had been recognised (by it at least) since 1921. From this year until the crunch in 1927, the Bank had consistently (but privately) warned the Registrar that the other Central Banks, as well as a high proportion of the Credit Societies and Unions that it had lent to, were withholding repayments. According to a later government report on the events, in 1921 a mere Rs 21,000 was repaid to the Bank out of a total of Rs 268,000 due that year. Similar delinquency rates were reported in following years but, as the same report noted, the 'gravity of the situation was clearly not grasped by the Registrar' (GoB 1938: 93).

The government of Burma refused the Provincial Bank's request in 1927, but following panicked withdrawals of deposits it was forced to finally intervene in 1928. Arranging for a cash loan for the Provincial Bank of Rs 1.4 million from the Imperial Bank of India, the government was also forced to commission a committee of enquiry into both the operations of the Provincial Bank, and the cooperative credit system as a whole. The 'Calvert Committee' as it came to be known, reported its findings in 1929. Determining that the Provincial Bank was insolvent, the Committee recommended that it 'be wound up forthwith' (GoB 1929: 85). As it turned out, the Provincial Bank was not liquidated until 1932, and only after the government stepped in to reimburse depositors to the tune of Rs 5.8 million (GoB 1950: 5). Seizing the security pledged to the Bank, and pursuing the debts owed to it by errant Credit Societies, was to consume much of the following decade.

The Calvert Committee

The Committee chosen to investigate and report on 'Co-operation in Burma' was headed by Hubert Calvert, then Registrar of Co-operative Societies in the Punjab, and a member of the 1928 Royal Commission on Agriculture in India (which featured an investigation into cooperative credit in British India as a whole). Calvert had been a leading advocate of the cooperative movement in British India, and instrumental in its introduction. He was joined on the investigative Committee by E.P. Stocker of the Imperial Bank of India and H.O. Reynolds of the ICS. The three other members of the Calvert Committee were Burmese – U E Pe, the Chairman of the Burma Urban Co-operative Federation, U Hla Bu, Chairman of the Yamèthin District Co-operative Association and U Ba Tib, Assistant Commissioner of the Co-operatives Department (GoB 1929: 3). At the time the Calvert Committee was deliberating, Burma had its own Governor and a limited elected assembly, but it was still a province of British India and was dominated commercially by European and Indian interests. Nevertheless, as can be seen in microcosm here, a small but high calibre cohort of Burmese civil servants were beginning to make their presence felt.

The Calvert Committee's Report, which was tabled in March 1929, made for grim reading for the champions of cooperative credit in Burma. The Committee found that external circumstances – bad harvests in 1919/20 and the growing agricultural recession (Calvert reported before the Great Depression fully hit) – had played a role in the extent of the difficulties facing Burma's cooperative credit system, but they were not the cause of the crisis (GoB 1929: 8). The cause of the virtual collapse of Burma's cooperative credit system, rather, was internal, structural, and thus rather more fundamental to the movement.

The primary culprit of the crisis in Burma's cooperative credit system was, according to Calvert, from the second tier of the system – the Unions. As has been noted, these played a larger role in Burma's cooperative credit system than was usual in comparable schemes. Their prominence had been presented as positive and innovative, and an extension of the principles of cooperation from individuals to the Societies themselves. The Calvert Report saw this as self-delusion. According to the Report, the enhanced role of the Unions in Burma had less to do with the extension of principle, than it had in Government 'penny-pinching' and myopia. Since the entire system had expanded 'beyond the capacity of the Registrar to control', Calvert found that more and more responsibilities (especially those of a prudential and educational nature) had been devolved to the Unions (GoB 1929: 8). This had been done, however, 'before adequate provision had been made for [these] non-official agencies to take over the work' (GoB 1929: 18).

The principal specific failure of the Unions concerned the role they were meant to play in ensuring against default – of both individual borrowers, and of Credit Societies themselves. The logic of the former role was that it was expected that the Unions 'would show less weakness and soft heartedness and more business in the dealings of village with village' (that is, Society with Society), than that likely within a Society when dealing 'man with man' (GoB 1929: 43). Practice, however, did not follow the logic and from the Unions as well as individual Credit Societies 'excessive leniency' was the order of the day. Worse, 'fictitious figures', 'paper adjustments' and the granting of new loans so that defaulters could pretend to repay old ones, were measures commonly resorted too. Worryingly for what it implied with regard to the respect with which participants regarded 'cooperative principles', Calvert concluded that such practices 'could not have persisted and reached the dimensions it did unless connived by everyone concerned' (GoB 1938: 88). This did not necessarily imply corruption as such (though Calvert found some evidence of this, as noted below), but what the Committee called (in typically patronising tones) 'an inherent weakness (...) characteristic of the Burmans of a certain delicacy in dealing with the faults and misdemeanours of their neighbour [they] prefer to put up with administration or malpractices in the hope that (...) the Government may one day come and put things right' (GoB 1929: 1). The Unions had the power to expel individual members as well as to liquidate 'bad Societies', but such measures were 'rarely resorted to' (GoB 1938: 88).

The failure of the Unions to act against defaulting borrowers, and their turning what amounted to a 'blind eye' to borrowing Societies efforts to obfuscate their true financial position, highlighted the failure of the Unions in auditing their Credit Society constituents. Auditing too had been a function originally assigned to the Registrar, but devolved to the Unions when the workload on the former proved too much. The conduct of proper audits was to prove too much for the Unions too, leading to the unhealthy practice of Credit Societies paying their own auditors under private arrangements. Calvert found a consistent failure of auditors to discharge their basic responsibilities which, in the case of a Primary Credit Society, included simply confirmation that 'loans were made fairly, for proper periods and objects and on adequate security' (GoB 1929: 20). As a consequence the malpractices noted above – 'fictitious figures', 'paper adjustments', new lending to disguise bad and doubtful debts – were 'so common that it [was] almost impossible to determine what real work the Societies have been doing' (GoB 1929: 23). Asset valuations likewise were 'negligent', a situation that greatly exacerbated the problems of liquidation when that was to prove necessary for many Societies. In its only passing comment made on possible fraud within the cooperative system, Calvert noted that auditors had largely ignored the 'too large a share' of lending in many Credit Societies made to 'co-operative chairmen and committee members' (GoB 1929: 29).

The problems of the internal operations of Credit Societies aside, Calvert found that the Union system fared no better when it came to ensuring the movement against broader default – that is, of whole Credit Societies and even of Unions themselves. Their principal weapon in checking such 'systemic' problems was, as noted above, the 'guarantee' scheme: Societies in the Union guaranteed the liabilities of each other. Alas, however, this aspect of the Unions' role was astonishingly ill-conceived. What seems never to have occurred to the designers of the arrangements was the legal identity of Credit Societies when dealing with each other. Unlimited liability was a central principle of Raiffeisen, but this only applied to the relationship of a Society to its members, and not to their relationship to other Societies. A guarantee made between two Societies was a guarantee made between two legal entities – and implied nothing for the members of either. In short:

> [A] call from the Union to shoulder a share of the debt owing by a defaulting society (...) could not be passed on to individual members which had undertaken the guarantee, and so it was only the Society which could be proceeded against (GoB 1929: 45).

Thus the famed 'guarantee' scheme of the Union system, central though it was to the security underpinning the entire cooperative credit system (the Central Banks lent on the basis of no other security) was a mirage.

The education, indeed the propagation, of 'cooperative principles' was yet another function of the Unions delegated from the Registrar. It was an important task for a system that depended for its proper functioning on what today would be called 'social capital'. But the educative task was more important in Burma since, as a later government report provocatively noted, cooperative credit 'was not a natural growth', but was 'imposed from above and was inspired by the desire of Government' (GoB 1938:87). Alas, education was not forthcoming. Calvert noted that they 'found everywhere a sad lack of knowledge of all that is meant by co-operative banking' (GoB 1929: 13). Writing of the Union staff employed to supervise member Societies and to spread the cooperative message, it declared them to be 'untrained, uneducated in co-operative banking or co-operative principles and unfit to be let loose amongst any body of co-operators' (GoB 1938: 90). Calvert's final take on the Unions was unequivocal: 'We have no hesitation in recommending that the Union guarantee should be abolished as soon as this is practicable' (GoB 1929: 46).

The problems surrounding the Unions had a contagion effect upon the institutions 'above' them – the Cooperative Central Banks. It will be recalled that these had no independent credit assessment processes when lending to Credit Societies, but were expected to rely upon the Union system and its 'guarantees'. Given that these guarantees proved to be worthless, once the cooperative credit system began to fail in Burma the position of the Central Banks likewise became precarious. At the time of the Calvert Committee's deliberations four were either in liquidation, insolvent or moribund (GoB 1929: 66). While most of the Central Banks' problems came via the troubles of the institutions below them, some were closer to home. Calvert found that internal controls within the Central Banks were lax and irregularities abounded. One such irregularity was the common practice of borrowing Credit Societies appearing also as depositors in the Central Banks' accounts, via the simple but highly deceptive expedient of deducting a portion from the loans advanced to them and booking it as a 'deposit'. Calvert also cautioned against the practice of Central Banks offering 'current' and 'at call' accounts. The Central Banks were not 'intended to do the same business as commercial banks'. Their governing legislation, the Co-operative Societies Act, was meant rather 'for simpler institutions carrying on a much simpler business' (GoB 1929: 85). With respect to the Burma Provincial Central Bank, the point has been made already that a number of the other Central Banks were in default to it from the early 1920s. In addition, however, Calvert found it suffered from many of the same problems that had afflicted the other Central Banks: the failure of the Union guarantees, the lack of machinery for assessing the credit-worthiness of Societies independent of the Unions, as well as problems in internal controls. Amongst the most egregious examples of the latter included the Provincial Bank's practice of crediting interest income to profit – whether it had actually been paid or not.

Other 'Official' Verdicts

The Calvert Committee Report was the most detailed and comprehensive investigation into the failure of cooperative credit in Colonial Burma. The episode and its implications remained alive, however, and it was to recur as a theme in the numerous enquiries commissioned by the colonial government of Burma into credit and agriculture in the decade preceding the Second World War. These enquiries tended to draw heavily on the Calvert Committee and seldom disagreed on questions of detail. In terms of the 'bigger picture', however, on support for the principle of 'cooperation' itself, and on the appropriate role of government, there were differing views, harbingers of the ideological divides ahead.

The most comprehensive report into Burma's monetary and financial system ever commissioned, the BPBE (noted throughout Chapter 2), was tabled in 1930, mere months after Calvert. The BPBE was in agreement with Calvert on most details, but its findings highlighted that 'cooperation' as an organising principle for the allocation of credit in Burma continued to enjoy strong support in official circles. The BPBE cautioned that whilst it would be 'a mistake to make a fetish of co-operation', it remained 'in Burma (...) the proper basis on which to build'. In some respects a defence of the liberal traditions of economic policy under British rule in Burma, the BPBE remained suspicious of government involvement in the cooperative sector. According to the BPBE, 'in Burma the character of the people is such that a system of official control cannot succeed.' The appropriate role of the government in the internal organisation of a Credit Society was to create 'rules setting reasonable bounds to the sphere in which *the Society exercises its independence and self-government*' (BPBE 1930a: 176, emphasis in original).

In 1937 Burma was granted what was called 'responsible parliamentary government'. The British Governor retained pre-eminent power, exclusive authority on certain issues (including foreign relations and defence), and the right to veto all laws – but much in the way of domestic policy passed to the governments formed out of the new Burmese legislature. From 1937 and until the Second World War three governments were formed – under Ba Maw, March 1937 to February 1939, U Pu, February 1939 to September 1940, and U Saw, September 1940 to (effectively) December 1941 (Maung Maung 1980). All three Governments would attempt to enact various measures designed to achieve agricultural and credit reform. However it was the first administration, under Ba Maw, that was the most energetic. On coming to power in 1937 it appointed a 'Land and Agriculture Committee' (LAC) with a wide remit for investigation and advice. The LAC was a mix of Burmese and British officials, with the former in a strong majority. It was chaired by U Pu, then Minister of Agriculture and Forests, and consisted of U Htoon Aung Gyaw, the Minister of Education, James Baxter, Financial

Adviser to the government, U Tin Tut of the ICS, U Tin Gyi, the Registrar for Cooperative Societies, B.O.Binns, Commissioner of Settlements and Land Records, J.P.Buchanan, Administrator of Government Estates, U Ba Tin, Deputy Registrar for Cooperative Societies and U Maung Gale, the retired Deputy Commissioner (GoB 1938: 1).

The LAC was charged with two main tasks: to examine and report on (i) 'all questions pertaining to the ownership of land and in particular to advise on the measures (...) facilitating and regulating the acquisition and retention of land by the agriculturalist; (ii) the problems arising from the indebtedness of the agriculturalist and (...) on measures necessary to secure the establishment of an organised system of agricultural finance' (GoB 1938: i–ii). The Committee ultimately produced four reports: Part I, Land Tenancy; Part II, Land Alienation; Part III, Agricultural Finance; Part IV, Regulation of Money Lending. Part IV was not completed until the eve of the Japanese invasion.

Cooperative credit was the primary subject of Part III of the Report. As with the BPBE, the LAC rarely took issue with the specific measures recommended by Calvert. Of all the official reports that dealt with the problems of cooperative credit, however, the LAC was by far the most critical of the broader picture, and of a movement it regarded as a 'premature creation' (GoB 1938: 96). In what can only be described as robust language, it declared that:

> ...it is hardly too much to say that the co-operative ideal was put before [the people of Burma] with the fervour of a new revelation which they were *bribed* to accept. Co-operation must at one time have seemed to the villager like money for nothing (emphasis added, GoB 1938: 100).

Yet, still the LAC declared itself in favour of the extension of cooperative credit in Burma – going so far to say that 'no other means of getting controlled credit to the small cultivator (...) has yet been devised' (GoB 1938: 109). Consistent with the caution above, however, it urged a certain modesty of aims, adopting a tone of prosaic practicality that was a self-conscious rejection of the aspirations of the past:

> We hope that co-operation will not again be preached as a faith, a religion of celestial origin but as a humdrum matter of business for the satisfaction of purely celestial needs (GoB 1938: 100).

AN IDEA THAT REFUSED TO DIE

As we have seen in this chapter, cooperative credit was zealously promoted as the solution to two of the most intractable problems in the political economy of colonial Burma – namely, the growing indebtedness of the cultivator and, as a direct consequence of this, the increasing alienation of their land to non-agriculturalist (and primarily non-resident) moneylenders. Adopted from models that originated in Europe, but as modified and apparently successfully employed in other provinces of British India, Burma's cooperative Credit Societies appeared to their advocates as ideal institutions not only to provide credit, but to instil in their members the virtues of a modern capitalist society. This was not to be. The principles behind Burma's cooperative credit system were sound, but their implementation was not. A system constructed around a spirit of 'cooperation' and 'self-help' derived from its members was, in practice, a system that was imposed from above and a system in which responsibility and accountability were notable only by their absence. A top-heavy and overly-layered structure of institutions was likewise a feature of Burma's cooperative system, and tellingly indicative of a movement without sincere grassroots support. Established with the best of intentions, the experiment of cooperative credit in colonial Burma was a failure.

Yet, as the conclusion of the LAC above indicates, the *promise* of cooperative credit, and its younger 'kin' in the form of microfinance, would never leave Burma. An idea seemingly for all seasons, cooperative credit and its like would prove a recurring theme in the discordant symphony that is the story of agricultural credit in the country. Whether lessons were learned from this first movement, however, will be seen in the chapters ahead.

NOTES

1   Sir Edward Maclagan in the Foreword to Darling (1947: viii).

2   The dispute between the two movements, which was as much philosophical as it was personal, was to continue well beyond the deaths of the founders. Indeed, the alternative viewpoints staked out by each of the movements remain highly contested terrain to this day, not only amongst practitioners of cooperative credit, but also amongst the rapidly rising microfinance movement.

3   A small number of (predominantly urban) cooperative credit societies in colonial Burma were based on the 'Luzzatti' model, an Italian derivative of the Schulze-Delitzsch approach, but which shared many Raiffeisen principles too. This model was named after Luigi Luzzatti, the founder of Italy's Banche Populari (GoB 1920: 10).

4   For more on this, see Robinson (2001: 46–100).

5   The author is grateful to Professor Dietmar Rothermund for this curious but important fact.

6   See, for example, the very minor role assigned to 'Unions' in Wolff (1893: 79).

7   The BPBE estimated that, for 1929, Rs 120 million of the Rs 200 million was supplied by the Chettiars. For an analysis of the credit needs of Burma's cultivators at this time, see Binns (1946: 28–29).

8   The 1931 communal riots were particularly harmful to agriculture in Burma, resulting in the flight of countless Indian agricultural labourers and causing much land to lie fallow. Of course, the value of land as collateral declined commensurately.

CHAPTER 4

One Bank, Two Countries:
Imaginings of a Central Bank in Colonial Burma

To a large degree the history of central banking or, shall we say, the lack of it,
in India is also the history of central banking in Burma.

Tun Wai, 1953

For most of the history of colonial Burma, the 'big' questions of money and finance were decided upon in India. Under British rule Burma's currency was the rupee, its land, property, revenue and usury laws were based on Indian templates, and for the longest period its financial institutions were scheduled by authorities in Calcutta and Delhi. Meanwhile, in India itself financial innovation and evolution proceeded steadily, and monetary affairs passed out of the hands of the antediluvian Presidency and Imperial Banks, ultimately becoming the preserve of the Reserve Bank of India (RBI). This institution, established in 1934, was the embodiment of both political compromise and cutting-edge monetary thought. The RBI acted as Burma's central bank from its inception until the penultimate years of British rule.

It is, however, a little-known fact that plans to establish a central bank for Burma *alone* were promoted well before the country achieved independence in 1948. These plans, which peaked in the maelstrom of monetary reform advocacy that followed the Great Depression, were never realised in the colonial era. They were, however, indicative of a political economy discourse in colonial Burma that was much more vigorous, and theoretically sophisticated, than has commonly been supposed.

In this chapter we bring to light the efforts to create a central bank in Burma in the years in which the country was a province of British India.

74

The chapter begins with an account of the institutions that determined monetary and financial matters in Burma during the earliest colonial years. These institutions, an amalgam of India's Presidency Banks and operations of the central government itself, were joined together in the form of the Imperial Bank in 1921. The manifest shortcomings of this institution for Burma are the subject of the next section of the chapter. In 1929, the *Burma Provincial Banking Enquiry* provided the arena in which advocacy for a stand-alone central bank for Burma first found voice. This advocacy, which became more relevant with the growing expectation of Burma's separation from British India, is the subject of the penultimate section of the chapter. Burma did not get its central bank, and the 'compromise' that saw the RBI take upon the twin roles of central bank to both India *and* Burma concludes this part of our narrative.

EARLY MONETARY ARRANGEMENTS IN COLONIAL BURMA

At the conclusion of the third Anglo-Burmese war in 1885, the whole of Burma came to be a component of the monetary and financial system of British India. In 1885 this system was, in central banking terms at least, a rudimentary and hybrid affair. British India's currency, the rupee, was at this moment a paper standard issued by the government and backed by nothing but its assurances. From 1839 to 1861 the right of paper currency issue *had* rested with the famous Presidency Banks – of Bombay, Madras and, above all, of Bengal. Under the *Paper Currency Act* of 1861, however, the Presidency Banks' exclusive rights of issue passed to the government and from this moment their remaining 'central bank' functions consisted of currency distribution, and in being the depositories of government balances and the buyers of government bonds (Keynes 1913: 143). Of the three Presidency Banks it was only that of Bengal that had any presence in Burma prior to the final annexation. This presence was in the form of three branches – Rangoon (established in 1861), Moulmein (1865) and Akyab (1866) (Robinson and Shaw 1980: 102).

The final absorption of Burma into British India coincidentally took place in the wake of the *Indian Paper Currency Act* of 1882, the belated outcome of the (many) inquiries commissioned on Indian monetary affairs throughout the nineteenth century, and designed to bring India onto the gold standard.[1] In fact what would emerge from the 1882 Act was India's celebrated 'gold-exchange' standard. This system, famously eulogised by

Keynes, was based upon the recognition that so long as there was confidence that a currency could ultimately be *converted* into gold, gold itself did not need to physically circulate *within* a country in order to realise the benefits a gold standard currency would bring. Thus, following the 1882 Act, the rupee became a token currency only, but convertible at a fixed rate into sterling and gold. This 'exchange rate' was set at one rupee per 7.53344 grams of fine gold, which implied a rupee-sterling exchange of Rs 15 to £1 (or 1*s*. 4*d*. per rupee).[2]

British India's rupee currency notes were distributed within 'circles' centred on the provincial capitals. This was not only for efficiency of distribution, but also because of the fear that confidence in the paper currency could be shaken by the emergence of localised note shortages or surpluses according to the different agricultural seasons. With the absorption of Burma these circles expanded to seven, with centres at Calcutta, Bombay, Madras, Karachi, Cawnpore, Lahore and *Rangoon* (Kumar 1983: 769). The currency notes had the status of legal tender, but only within the circles within which they were distributed. As such, British India was something less than a 'unified currency area'. The currency notes were issued in denominations of 5, 10, 20, 50, 100, 500, 1,000, and 10,000 rupees, though neither the 1,000 nor 10,000 notes were physically available in the Rangoon circle. The Burma notes were identical to the Indian notes in most respects, the principal difference being the inscription of 'Rangoon' (in green letters) as the city of issue (Robinson and Shaw 1980: 102).[3] Interestingly, throughout this period and beyond, paper currency was more popular in Burma than it was in British India as a whole (where the 'silver rupee' coin enjoyed a certain cachet for decades after it stopped being minted). According to a later government report:

> Currency reports for many years have commented upon this; there have been returns of rupees from circulation even in the busy season, and the rice crop and other principal crops are bought almost entirely with notes. Cultivators like to have some [silver] rupees and small change for convenience in their daily household transactions; but subject to this they prefer notes to coin (BPBE 1930a: 47).[4]

The exchange level of the rupee, and controversies over the monetary standard generally, were to be something of an *idée fixe* in the monetary history of British India (though curiously not in Burma itself) – a fact that some have speculated clouded the 'more basic problem' of a still undeveloped banking system that hindered the creation of an elastic money supply responsive to seasonal (and other) needs (Kumar 1983: 774). Such a system required at its centre an appropriately constituted central bank, but progress at creating such an institution (beyond the limited functions of the Presidency Banks) was glacial. This was not for a want of 'plans', the appearance of which was more or less a constant, beginning with Warren Hasting's conception for a 'General Bank of Bengal and Bihar' in 1773. Many other plans followed, before forming what Kumar (1983: 789) described as a familiar 'bureaucratic cycle of enthusiastic initiatives, prolonged discussions (...) objections, and finally, postponement to a more propitious future occasion'.

A seminal event in the history of money and finance in British India was the appointment of a 'Royal Commission on Indian Finance and Currency' in 1910. This was chaired by Austin Chamberlain, but is renowned amongst economists for marking the public policy emergence of John Maynard Keynes. Keynes's appointment to the Commission, and the publication of his first book, *Indian Currency and Finance* (1913), represented both the high point of his involvement in India and the beginnings of his long trek from economic orthodoxy. Keynes highlighted the theoretical innovation and practical efficacy of India's 'gold exchange' standard as indicated, but his evidence and subsequent book also included a proposal for a central bank – the lack of which Keynes believed was a significant missing element:

> The objections to the existing arrangements largely arise out of the absence of a state bank (...) I feel little doubt that India ought to have a state bank, associated with a greater or less degree with the government. The government is drifting year by year into doing more business of an essentially banking character; and as time goes on it will become increasingly objectionable to dissociate some of the functions of modern state banking from others (Keynes 1913: 41).

Keynes argued that British India needed a central bank to deal with this 'business of an essentially banking character', which included currency distribution, the management of the government's accounts, the administration of foreign exchange, and (at this stage the still very limited) prudential supervision and regulation of the commercial banks. In addition, Keynes also set out other reasons for the creation of a central bank for India, a number of which pre-empted developments in central banking theory to come. The most significant of these, however, was his call for 'elasticity in the system' by creating a central bank that could expand the volume of currency on issue in response to seasonal demands – in modern terminology, a degree of monetary policy 'discretion' in response to the needs of the 'real' economy. Keynes did not believe, however, that the Bank of England offered a useful model for British India;

> ... let the framers of the new bank's constitution put far from their minds all thoughts of the Bank of England. It is in the state banks of Europe, especially in that of Germany, or in Holland or Russia, that the proper model is to be found (Keynes 1913: 168).

Keynes's advocacy for an Indian central bank went the way of all those before them, though in this case 'benign neglect' was joined by the arrival of the First World War in burying the issue for a time. Ultimately, however, the war also provided an impetus for a central bank in India – demonstrating the necessity of concentrating financial resources in order to alleviate India's industrial dependence and, from yet another angle, the benefits of an 'elastic' note issue. The Indian Industrial Commission of 1918, ultimately convened to explore ways in which India could be more self-sufficient in war materiel, reported that 'the better organisation of banking', including the provision of a central bank, was 'an important preliminary step towards the advancement of Indian industries' (BPBE 1930a: 1).

THE IMPERIAL BANK AND ITS CRITICS

With the issue of the industrialisation of British India to the fore, the first substantial, practical, step towards an Indian central bank occurred in 1921 with the fusing of the three Presidency Banks to form the Imperial Bank of India. Like the Presidency Banks that now formed its component parts, however, the Imperial Bank remained a somewhat ambiguous hybrid. Its central banking functions were primarily centred on its (enhanced) roles as 'banker to the government' and 'banker' to the other banks. Regarding the former function, the Imperial Bank became the *sole* banker to the government, while retaining the Presidency Banks' tasks of currency distribution and management of the public debt. The Imperial Bank's responsibilities as the central institution around which the commercial banks were encouraged to orbit was likewise enhanced. However, commercial banks were not *compelled* to keep reserves or otherwise follow its lead. Rather, the Imperial Bank was presented simply as the institution at which other banks' bills would always be discounted, and from which they could expect assistance in a crisis (Sayers 1952: 218). Finally, there was something of a 'developmental' aspect to the Imperial Bank. Aiming to employ it as an instrument in spreading modern banking practices across the country, Section 10 of the *Imperial Bank of India Act* (1921) required that it establish 100 new branches across the length and breadth of British India 'within five years' (BPBE 1930a: 46).

Yet, in so many important ways, the Imperial Bank resembled much more a monolithic commercial entity than a central bank. Despite Keynes's injunction, the Imperial Bank was *not* given responsibility for the note issue (thus maintaining that 'want of elasticity in the system' he had inveighed against). Its 'bankers' bank' functions were not backed by compulsion and, as with its Presidency bank forebears, it was prohibited from engaging in foreign exchange activity, thus excluding it from any role in determining the value of the rupee. Equally, the expanded scale of its own commercial operations also had the effect of hampering its role as a central bank since, not unreasonably, the other commercial banks were suspicious that in a crisis their greatest competitor would put its own commercial interests ahead of that of the financial system as a whole. Of course, like its predecessors and like other commercial banks, the Imperial Bank was a privately owned joint-stock company, even while its managing governors were government appointees. Most of the Imperial Bank's shareholders were British (resident in Britain and India), as were the top and middle ranks of its management (Goldsmith 1983: 87).

The Imperial Bank was the subject of much contemporary criticism in India. This had many components, but not least the Imperial Bank's hybrid status of being a commercial banking operation but with *some* central banking functions. This 'awkward division' created a situation that, according to Kumar (1983: 791) 'continued to bedevil the conduct of monetary affairs in India' throughout the life of the Imperial Bank's responsibilities as a central bank. Other issues also rankled, including the notion that the Imperial Bank competed unfairly with other banks via its privileged position with the government, and that it did little to integrate or support indigenous financial institutions and credit cooperatives (Sayers 1952: 220). Finally, the Imperial Bank's largely British ownership and management was a sore point – the root of a more generalised complaint that the Imperial Bank was 'unsympathetic to the needs of Indian business and (...) overly partial to European interests' (Kumar 1983: 778).[5]

The Imperial Bank in Burma

In Burma, the Imperial Bank's central banking functions were more pronounced than those for British India as a whole. Its 'public good' activities included, for example, the operation of Burma's only cheque-clearing system in Rangoon, which naturally provided it with a central function vis-à-vis the commercial banks. All of the exchange banks operating in Burma were members of the system and, more broadly, treated the Imperial Bank as 'a central bank to the extent of keeping their reserve balances with it and looking to it for advances when other ordinary sources cannot supply them' (BPBE 1930a: 39). The criticism, in India proper, that the Imperial Bank failed to support the integration of indigenous moneylenders and credit cooperatives into mainstream finance likewise had less force in the context of Burma. Amongst the banks in Burma the Imperial Bank was the largest supplier of funds to such institutions, and the *Burma Provincial Banking Enquiry* concluded generally that the Imperial Bank lent 'to financiers working otherwise than on western lines as well as to other persons' (BPBE 1930a: 39).

The requirement that the Imperial Bank open 100 new branches within five years of its formation yielded three new branches in Burma, at Mandalay (1921), Bassein (1921) and Myingyan (1924). These joined the three branches in Rangoon, Moulmein and Akyab that the Imperial Bank inherited from the Presidency Bank of Bengal (BPBE 1930a: 46). Interestingly, the perception in India that the Imperial Bank discriminated against indigenous enterprises was not widely reported in Burma, the BPBE expressing its view that:

> We find it difficult to believe that the European direction and management of the Imperial Bank would sacrifice on sentimental grounds business which is sound and profitable or would neglect opportunities of that character for which it had funds (BPBE 1930a: 40).

More pointedly perhaps to critics in India, the BPBE offered 'the reminder that in Burma a bank under Indian management would not be regarded by the majority of the non-Indian population as less foreign than a bank under European management' (BPBE 1930a: 41).

A Central Bank for Burma?

If the Imperial Bank suffered less opprobrium in Burma than it did in British India broadly, it cannot be said that it nevertheless was regarded as fulfilling the functions desired of a central bank. This was readily apparent in the findings of the BPBE – so far primarily just a source of information in this study, but in actuality a most profound and revealing investigation into Burma's financial system as at the end of the 1920s and, indeed, a weighty insight into the nation's political economy more broadly.

The BPBE was not commissioned to examine the issue of a central bank for Burma. Although in essence a sub-committee of the 1929 *Central Banking Enquiry Committee* (a broader inquest into financial arrangements than its title suggested, and applying to the whole of British India), the BPBE was given the broad remit of examining Burma's credit needs, in agriculture, industry and internal trade. Central banking, and various other topics, were meant to be the exclusive domain of the all-India enquiry. In the course of its work, however, the BPBE extended its mandate, a decision it said was informed by 'the political agitation in Burma for political separation from India' (BPBE 1930a: 3). This required a 'more comprehensive view of its duties than was necessary for committees in other provinces', and the BPBE regarded conditions in Burma as being sufficiently distinct for constructing their report as one 'for a separate country' (BPBE 1930a: 4).

The composition of the BPBE Committee reflected this implicit recognition of Burma's distinctiveness within British India. Chaired by S.G. Grantham of the Indian Civil Service, it nevertheless had a distinctive local flavour that recognised both the dominance of European commercial interests in the country and, yet, also gave hitherto unprecedented representation to Burmese nationals (who comprised precisely half of the Committee's membership). The Committee included: U Aye M.L.C., representing the Burmese, Chinese and Burman-Indian Chambers of Commerce; Lawrence Dawson, Chairman of Dawson's Bank and the representative (sic) of agricultural interests in Lower Burma; the Diwan B.M.M. Chettiar M.L.C., Director of the Indian Bank and representing indigenous bankers; Professor H.S. Jevons, Professor of Economics at Rangoon University; U Ba Maung, Manager of the Pegu Central Co-operative Bank, representing the co-operative system; U Mya, Manager of the Myingyan Electric Company; and U Shwe Tha, Deputy Commissioner (retd.), representing agricultural interests in Upper Burma. U Hla Bu of Pyinmana had been appointed to the Committee but was prevented by ill-health from taking part in any of its deliberations (BPBE 1930a: 4–5).

The BPBE's advocacy of a separate central bank for Burma was contained in the final chapter of its report, and a section devoted to what it labeled 'the essential problem' of credit and finance in Burma. This 'essential problem' was a holistic one: simply an undeveloped financial system that provided Burmese agriculture, industry and trade with too little capital at too high interest rates. The BPBE put forward a number of reasons for Burma's high interest rates, including the 'strong seasonality' of the capital requirements of agriculture, and what it alleged were 'traditional expectations' of high rates in the country (BPBE 1930a: 343). It suggested that the solution to the high interest rate problem in Burma was identical to the solution to the problem of the lack of finance itself: the creation of a banking system that created credit. Such credit creation was part and parcel of economic development in 'communities which are advanced in banking', but in Burma credit creation scarcely occurred. This was especially the case outside of Rangoon where, the BPBE reported, the creation of credit was 'almost restricted to Government' (BPBE 1930a: 346).

Solving Burma's essential credit problem was the BPBE's daring proposal for a central bank. But this was no ordinary central bank of the (functionally limited) Bank of England variety. Rather, what was envisioned was a 'spearhead (...) a new banking organisation which would hold the banking reserves of the country, issue the only paper-money of the country as its own bank-notes, and provide the desired elasticity and mobility of currency and credit' (BPBE 1930a: 350). This central bank, which was given the name 'Bank of Burma' (BoB), would establish branches across the country, 'at every important commercial centre', financed from the seigniorage profits the bank would earn as the issuer of the currency (BPBE 1930a: 352). These branches would provide a range of 'commercial' banking services, including deposit and remittance facilities, and they would be able to make advances to other financiers on bills of exchange. Such services would make the branches economically viable according to the BPBE, which believed that the biggest threat to its ambitions for an extensive branch network was simply the matter of finding enough qualified staff to operate them (BPBE 1930a: 354).

Clearly then, and consistent with Keynes's injunctions for India decades earlier, the Bank of England and other central banks of the kind that typically existed in well-developed financial centres were not the models the BPBE had in mind for Burma's central bank. Such institutions were appropriate in countries where deposit-banking was well established, but they were not appropriate in countries in which 'bank-notes' (that is, paper currency) were still preferred over cheques and other deposit-based payment instruments.

The BPBE pointedly observed (1930a: 351) the typical experience of other countries historically, in which '[n]ote-issue banking [had] always preceded deposit banking because the acceptance of bank-notes makes less demand upon the public confidence than the making of deposits and the acceptance of cheques'. The confidence required for deposit-banking, the BPBE observed (1930a: 351), came only 'after years of sound banking'.

This did not mean, however, that there were no instructive role models from overseas – and in this context the Bank of France found particular favour with the BPBE. Compared with Britain and some other European countries, private banking in France had developed little in the nineteenth century and the Bank of France, as the central bank, had played a 'relatively more important role' in the country's financial system than other central banks (Davies 1994: 556). The Bank of France had been given a monopoly of note issue in 1848 and – breaching the boundaries of central banking of an orthodox (BoE) variety – had been given responsibility for spreading modern banking practices to all corners of the French economy, including the rural hinterland. By 1900, at which time the BoE had eight branches in Britain, the Bank of France had offices in 411 towns across France (Davies 1994: 556).

It was the Bank of France's rural extension facilities that most captured the attention of the BPBE. The Bank of France's branch network provided precisely the sort of deposit, remittance and credit facilities they desired to see extended by Burma's own central bank. The remittance facilities were regarded by the BPBE as especially critical since, in Burma as in France, they expected 'for some time notes will continue (...) to be used more than cheques'. Later they observed that 'good facilities for remittance are as important to a country as good communications' (BPBE 1930: 353).

In extending credit to rural areas the BPBE did not envisage that the Burma central bank itself would lend to individuals:

We do not pretend that a bank of the nature proposed would be able to provide *directly* the finance required by peasant cultivators and petty traders. Indeed the responsibility of the note-issue requires that the bank should be worked upon true central bank lines as far as possible, and should not discount one-name paper. We conceive of the banks [that is, branches of the central bank] reaching the cultivators and traders through co-operative societies and Chettiars and other private financiers and later through other banks (BPBE 1930a: 354).

Rather than lend directly then, what the BPBE was proposing was a central bank that would provide 'wholesale' funds to other financiers (including the Chettiars and the cooperative societies). This would be done largely by discounting bills of exchange, not as issued by the parties directly seeking credit, but as subsequently endorsed by Chettiars, cooperatives and other banks. Such bills were known as 'two-name paper' since they were 'endorsed' with promises to pay by both the ultimate receiver of the funds and the financier directly lending the funds. In this way the BPBE provided that the central bank would be able to expand available credit in Burma, without being exposed to the credit risk of the borrower. Once again, this was a practice employed by the Bank of France, but highly relevant to the long-standing efforts in Burma to create a viable cooperative credit sector:

> District co-operative banks would provide a second endorsement on the bills of co-operators in the same way as the Caisses Régionales (district banks) in France endorse again, for discount at the Bank of France, the bills endorsed for their members by the Caisses Locales (village societies), and so connect the villager with the credit controlling authority while still giving the latter the requisite special security for its advances (BPBE 1930a: 354).

All the while, the BPBE was sure of the broad, developmental role played by the proposed BoB in the process:

> The district branches of the Bank of Burma would be able (...) to have local knowledge of village societies as well as of the district co-operative bank. We think also we should in this way provide the best safeguard for the sound development of the co-operative system, which would be compelled to satisfy the standards of commercial credit continuously, but would obtain access to the general money-market (BPBE 1930a: 355).

High interest rates were one of the pathologies identified by the BPBE in Burma's existing financial arrangements, so it celebrated (1930a: 355) what it thought was the solution provided by their version of a credit-expanding BoB:

> By financing suitable banks, Chettiars, non-Chettiars and co-operative societies, the competition needed to keep down the rates of interest would be provided.

The BPBE's vision for a *commercially active* central bank would be sure to raise the hackles of the commercial banks already operating in Burma, just as had the operations of the Imperial and Presidency Banks before it. The BPBE was alive to such objections however, and offered the rebuttal against any suggestion that its BoB proposal would result in a state monopoly that would strangle competition. The BPBE pointedly noted that there was not much competition to begin with in Burma, and it also once more drew upon the model provided by the Bank of France, especially in the way its 'two name' bill discounting requirement fostered the intermediation of *other* banks. Given that this issue is a critical one in grasping the scale of the objective the BPBE set out to achieve with the BoB, its reasoning in this context is worth quoting at length:

> The fact [is] that under present conditions so few banks have grown up either in Burma or in India outside the ports and a few of the larger business centres. Indeed we think that so far from preventing the growth of other banks the plan offers the best chance of getting other banks established, and of building up an organised credit system. The plan offers in fact the quickest road to the establishment of deposit-banking and acceptance-credit. The Bank of France has not only the advantage of the note-issue but also freedom to enter the money-market in competition with other banks. Yet other great banks have not only grown up under its shadow, but actually have been founded (...) for the purpose of providing the additional signatures required for its discount of bills. In the same way the establishment and development of joint-stock banks in Burma would be encouraged. We think in fact that it is more practical to have such a bank as we project, and to retain power to deal with abuses as they arise, than to expect deposit-banking to be established without being preceded by note-banking as it has always been preceded in more advanced countries with better financial and educational development (BPBE 1930a: 356).

Forestalling the BPBE: The Separation Question

Burma did not get its central bank in the wake of the BPBE. The enquiry's three volumes and over 1,000 pages appeared in April 1930 – just in time for some of the worst Indo-Burmese riots the country had experienced. These were sparked (largely) by precisely the resentment against money-lenders that the BPBE elsewhere had tried to grapple with.[6] Likewise, Burmese nationalist agitation had reached levels hitherto not seen in the colonial period. This was manifested in many ways, from formal political maneuvering, to various popular uprisings, to a series of national strikes.[7] Amongst the latter was one that shut down the Government Printer and delayed the publication of the BPBE Report itself. Of course, more broadly and more damagingly for the implementation of its recommendations, the BPBE's Report also appeared just as the depression (and the collapse of paddy prices) was cutting a swathe through the economic assumptions upon which the BPBE's proposals were based. Finally, two months after the appearance of the BPBE Report, the findings of the so-called 'Simon Commission' that examined the potential for political reform in British India were released.[8] The Simon Commission recommended that Burma be formally separated from the rest of British India, understandably generating great controversy and almost completely submerging any public or political impact that the BPBE Report might have had.

Nevertheless, the imprint of the BPBE's recommendations made their mark – and not least in the considerations of what to do regarding Burma's monetary arrangements if, indeed, separation from India was to occur. Burma had been a largely self-governing 'province' within British India since 1923, when the Montagu-Chelmsford reforms created the so-called 'Dyarchy' constitution, under which the Province was subsequently headed by a Governor (previously Burma had had to make do with a *Lieutenant-Governor*) and gained a Legislative Council to which were transferred certain 'nation-building' subjects (Tinker 1957: 3).[9] Other subjects were 'reserved' for the Governor. This limited arrangement proved unsatisfactory for almost all concerned, leading the way to the Simon Commission's findings both on separation from India and in devising a workable government for Burma. In 1935 these received practical expression in the *Government of Burma Act*, which not only separated Burma from India, but gave the 'new nation' a constitution that created a parliamentary-based Cabinet government. The new legislature was a bicameral affair, with a (fully-elected) House of Representatives and a Senate that was half elected, half Governor-appointed. In the traditions of Westminster, the person commanding majority support in the House of Representatives would become Premier, and effective head of government. The Governor was obliged to accept the advice of ministers on most issues. Nevertheless, though it was a smaller list than under the Dyarchy arrangements, the Governor retained sole power over certain subjects, including defence, foreign affairs and, of importance in the context of this book, monetary policy (Tinker 1957: 5).

What was effectively responsible Cabinet Government did not find favour, however, with many elements in the indigenous Burmese community, and the question of separation from India raged as the 'most important political issue which Burma faced' from the time the Simon Commission report was handed down until the final implementation of the *Burma Act* in 1937 (Cady 1958: 322). 'Separationist' and 'anti-separationist' parties formed to contest post-Simon elections in the Dyarchy legislature and, in 1932, the anti-separationist party of Dr Ba Maw won a stunning victory. The 'rising star [of Burma's] political firmament', Ba Maw's opposition to separation from India seems, at first glance, perplexing. Not so on closer inspection, however. Like many Burmese opposed to separation, Ba Maw's opposition was tactical. He feared that if Burma was decoupled from India it would quickly fall behind that country's political reform process (driven by its powerful Indian National Congress). Staying attached to India, so such reasoning went, joined Burma with a powerful ally in the ultimate goal of securing true independence. Ba Maw and similarly-minded others later changed their position on separation (while retaining suspicions of the British) and crafted political careers within the framework established under the *Burma Act*. Ba Maw himself became Burma's first Premier (Cady 1958: 336–338).

It was into this heady mix of nationalism, geo-politics and the personal aspirations of both would-be national saviours and imperial recalcitrants that the question of a central bank for Burma was thrown in 1930. Whereupon, as noted above, it was quickly subsumed into the related question: What form should monetary relations take in a Burma that remained part of the British Empire (this was never in doubt from the perspective of the colonial government), but which was separate from British India?

Assigned to come up with an answer to this question was Thomas Lister, then the Finance Secretary to Burma's colonial government.[10] In a memorandum penned for the government in November 1930, Lister essentially took up from where the BPBE left off, but there was one substantial difference in his proposal: Lister did not believe that Burma should (yet) have a central bank *in name*.[11] Instead, Lister advocated the continuing use of the Imperial Bank, albeit, and as shall be examined below, with full central banking powers and a localised 'board' for Burma.

Lister's belief that the time was not yet ripe for a 'Bank of Burma' was centred on the uncertain political environment: the timing and nature of separation from India, the constitutional forms this might take, what resources (and debts) Burma might be apportioned, and the political controversies that would shape events and institutions. Thus for these practical reasons Lister set himself the task of making 'proposals *only* for the currency arrangements immediately after separation', a period in which there was 'not sufficient material to lay down a permanent system'.[12] Yet, Lister also clearly believed that Burma was as yet *structurally* unsuited for a central bank of its own. The economy was 'too small' and the 'general credit basis for central banking was rudimentary'.[13] More basically, Burma lacked sufficient personnel with requisite skills and experience, a lack of a 'banking tradition' and even the lack of 'a suitable building' within which to house a central bank.[14] Lister was also fearful of the implications of a 'too early' adoption of a central bank in shaking the credibility of a nascent Burmese monetary system. He wrote that there were already rumours a new Burmese currency would 'become inconvertible' with sterling. The whole situation would be exacerbated by the fact that Burma and its government would be an unknown political and economic quantity, resulting in an initial 'mistrust of the currency of that Government until confidence is established by sound management of the finances, favourable budgets, and the creation of substantial reserves'.[15]

So Lister did not think it necessary or desirable for Burma to have its own central bank at this stage. This did not mean, however, that he thought Burma's existing monetary arrangements were satisfactory. Indeed, far from it. In words that echoed the BPBE, but in more strident terms, he declared in his memorandum to the government that Burma required an 'elastic' monetary system that expanded the volume of currency according to the needs of the country. What Burma needed then, especially as a country unusually subject to seasonal fluctuations, was an institution that could provide an elastic currency issue by endorsing bills of exchange (he referred to them as trade bills) along the lines advocated by the BPBE (and Keynes and others before them). In Lister's formulation:

> The amount of currency required in a country varies with the volume of trade and the variation is particularly marked in an agricultural country. This will certainly be the case in Burma which is an agricultural and almost a one-crop country. The required elasticity of the currency to meet variations in trade is provided if a proportion of the reserve consists of trade bills. As *bona fide* trade bills are presented for rediscount currency expands. As the bills mature the currency is automatically contracted.[16]

In order to create such a system, it was necessary that at least a proportion of the security reserve 'backing' of the currency consist of trade bills. Under the existing arrangements, however, with currency issued by the government, trade bills played no part in the reserves of the 'gold-exchange standard' backing the rupee.[17] The only elasticity that was allowed was that created by allowing a proportion of the reserves to consist of (government-issued) rupee securities. Lister argued (correctly) that institutions such as the Federal Reserve System of the United States, and similar systems where a reserve formed a fixed percentage of the note issue, routinely included trade bills into such reserves. Once again, his argument is worth quoting in full:

> In the Indian system these trade bills are regarded as an abnormal item of the reserve. They are, however, on account of their automatic expansion and contraction according to the needs of the country, a more suitable backing to a paper currency than ordinary rupee securities. In the case of ordinary securities the authority which manages the currency has to arrive at a deliberate judgement regarding the desirability of expanding or contracting the currency (...) Errors of judgement are thus possible. Such errors are less liable to occur in the case of true commercial bills covering genuine commercial transactions.[18]

Of course, such 'dynamic' currency backing had to be managed by a central bank, rather than the government. Continuing the existing arrangements, with the government controlling the note issue, exposed Burma to the danger long feared by central bankers of the 'subordination of monetary principles to political considerations'.[19]

Burma needed a central bank post-separation then, but, as indicated, in Lister's view not yet a *Bank of Burma*. His chosen instrument rather was the Imperial Bank, something of an obvious choice amongst existing institutions given that it already undertook a good proportion of the functions normally assigned to a central bank. These functions would be greatly extended as a fully-fledged central bank, most obviously in that the Imperial Bank would become the issuer of the currency and in one step, removing 'currency management from government'. Of course, the Imperial Bank would remain the government's banker and Lister re-emphasised its importance as a device for extending remittance facilities across Burma (even advocating that remittance facilities be provided 'without any charge whatsoever' for amounts up to Rs 10).[20] Lister envisaged that the Imperial Bank would manage the debt of the Burmese government and, underlining the significance of its role as a central bank, would be its primary lender. To this end he recommended that the Bank should be 'required to establish a branch of the Public Debt Office in Rangoon' and to make arrangements 'for ways and means advances and for the issue of treasury bills'.[21] Not surprisingly, given his stress too on both the *interim* nature of the Imperial Bank's role and the lack of relevant expertise in Burma, Lister highlighted that the use of the Bank would 'solve the difficulty of Burma obtaining a staff versed in currency matters' and ultimately facilitating 'the final complete management of the currency by a [future] Reserve Bank'.[22]

Consistent with the 'best practice' of central banks elsewhere, Lister's conception of the Imperial Bank as a central bank had it divided into an 'Issue' and 'Banking' Department. As their titles implied, these kept at arms length the roles of the Imperial Bank as issuer of the currency and the manager of its security 'backing', and those functions – banker to the Government, manager of the public debt and so on – that pertained to its role in banking more broadly. As a way of giving credibility to this division, and establishing confidence that backing was being maintained, Lister advocated that the 'Imperial Bank should be required to publish weekly both Issue and Banking statements showing (...) deposits and the notes on issue and details of the reserves held against them'.[23] Interestingly, Lister did not include amongst the 'banking' functions of the Imperial Bank any enhanced role for its *commercial* activities. Indeed, according to Lister these should be greatly scaled back during the Imperial Bank's stint as Burma's central bank. In a blunt contradiction of the recommendations of the BPBE above, Lister sided with the general orthodoxy of not mixing central and general banking, and in this context quoted the Irish Banking Commission approvingly:

> While there are central banks which do thus compete from day to day with other banks on more or less equal terms for ordinary business, at least in certain narrowly and well defined branches of lending, it is not a wholesome state of affairs, and is one which is being gradually eliminated in practically every country of modern banking organisation.[24]

Although Lister did not believe existing political considerations allowed for a solely Burmese central bank, he was alive to the circumstances in which events and issues in India were hampering, and would hamper into the future, the conduct of monetary affairs in Burma. These events and issues were partly political and partly nationalist. The former included the latest round of Congress-inspired boycotts of British goods in India, as well as the on-going difficulties in the Indian legislature over when, and if, a

Reserve Bank of India bill would ever be passed (more on which below). Regarding the nationalist question, Lister recognised that currencies were an important symbol of national independence and, as such, Burma would not want to be seen forever as an appendage of India. But there were genuine economic concerns about an Indian-dominated central bank too. Above all, there was no reason to suppose that India's interests in monetary matters would always coincide with Burma's, and should there be a clash of interests there was little reason to suppose that it would be Burma's that would prevail.

Lister's solution to these problems was to insist that the Imperial Bank in Burma be presided over by a 'Local Board' and a 'Local Head Office'. Such a Board was necessary, according to Lister, both to ensure that Burma was 'as free as possible in the management of currency operations' and for 'close collaboration' between the (Burmese) government and the Bank. Lister favoured government nominees for the Board, which he thought should include Burma's Auditor-General and Financial Commissioner. He was also anxious to ensure that the Burma Local Board was 'in no way inferior' to any other Board of the Bank, and suggested amending legislation to bring this about.[25]

The most important matter the Local Board would control in Lister's scheme was the note issue. In his 1930 memorandum, Lister believed that while Burma should maintain the Indian rupee as its currency, it should have its own notes – designed and printed in Burma and depicting Burmese scenes and figures. Lister estimated that, based on the relative size of the economies, the volume of Burma notes should number approximately 'one-ninth of that of India'.[26] The notes should be printed and ready from 'day one' after separation, from which time India notes would remain legal tender only for 'three months after the appointed day'.[27]

As noted previously, the responsibility for the note issue would rest with a separate and distinct 'Issue Department' within the Imperial Bank (under the authority of the Burma Local Board). This would be responsible not only for the physical distribution of notes in Burma, but also for managing the reserve 'backing' for the notes – what Lister referred to as the 'Paper Currency Reserve'. This Reserve would, in the first instance, be created by simply transferring across to the Imperial Bank's 'Burma Issue Department' a sum of reserves necessary to maintain the existing backing. Thus in Lister's formulation if Imperial Bank 'Burma notes' were circulated at a volume equivalent to 'one-ninth' of the note issue for the whole of British

India, then 'one-ninth' of the Paper Currency Reserve should likewise be held by the Burma Issue Department of the Imperial Bank.

But the most complex task of the Issue Department would be to manage (post-separation) that 'elastic' part of the note issue that would be backed by trade bills. The ability of the Imperial Bank to provide an elastic currency issue in response to the needs of the economy was, of course, fundamental to Lister's schema – and to his advocacy of a *central bank* rather than government note issue. In his own words:

> The trade bills will provide an elastic element in the reserve which will permit of the expansion of the currency for financing the movement of crops. And if the expansion is carried out by the acceptance of commercial bills covering the crops and assets the expansion and contraction will take place almost automatically and will be in accordance with the needs of the country. These bills should bear two good signatures and should have a maturity of not more than 90 days.[28]

Ideally, Lister believed that around 25 per cent of Burma's currency reserves should be in the form of trade bills. But this provision required 'an active bill market' which was not, at present, in existence in Burma.[29] The Imperial Bank should do all it could to encourage the development such a market, but in the meantime Burma's relatively sparse financial markets meant that a figure of '10 per cent' was probably all that could be managed as a 'permanent' trade bill backing for the time being. Over and above this, however, Lister proposed that an extra '4 to 5 crores' of notes (40–50 million rupees, an increase of 20 to 25 per cent of the total note issue) could reasonably be issued against trade bills at certain times of the year, especially at harvest time.[30]

The Imperial Bank's (Burma) Issue Department would earn profits ('seigniorage') from its circulation of currency notes (issued at near enough to zero cost apart from printing and distribution) that were partly backed by interest-bearing securities of various forms. These seigniorage profits, which are earned by all note issuing authorities' would come in useful, in Lister's design, when Burma finally achieved a central bank of its own. How? According to Lister, it was important that seigniorage profits be used to build up a reserve of sterling securities:

> Burma should neglect no means of acquiring a reputation for prudent finance. Later on, when Burma has its own system, the question of devoting

some of the interest of the development of banking in Burma may be considered.[31]

One aspect of Burma's monetary system that would *not* fall under the authority of the Local Board of the Imperial Bank in Lister's schema was the value of its currency in terms of other currencies – that is, the rupee exchange rate. This would remain the responsibility of the Indian Head Office and the full Board of the Imperial Bank. Lister did not see any reason why the rupee's historical value to sterling needed to change in the short term, but should 'India' seek to make a change, it should give 'sufficient notice to Burma to enable Burma to consider whether, in the altered circumstances, it should still continue to form part of the Indian monetary system'.[32]

The Fate of Lister's Plans

Lister's memorandum on using the Imperial Bank as a central bank for Burma (following separation) became a template for discussions amongst a range of Imperial and Indian Government officials throughout 1931–1932. It did not fare well, especially at the hands of finance officers at the India Office, the British government department which was the final authority and arbiter for most things to do with British India as a whole. At a meeting between Lister and various such officials in London in December 1931, for example, Lister was told that his scheme posed grave problems for the maintenance of the value of the rupee.[33] Specifically, the India Office told Lister that they had two fears. Firstly, that Burma might over-inflate the note issue. Secondly, that if Burma notes drove out the (Indian) rupee in Burma, such rupees could subsequently be presented for redemption in India for gold and/or sterling and thus exacerbate that country's existing 'excess rupee to reserves' problem.[34]

Other meetings followed, in Calcutta as well as in London, but the issue seems to have been laid to rest at a final meeting in March 1932 (in London) between Lister and a 'heavyweight' delegation of India Office officials led by Sir Louis Kershaw, the Office's Under Secretary of State.[35] Retaining their broader objection to Lister's Burma proposals as being potentially bad for *India*, the India Office advanced new concerns now as to the state of the global economy as being a reason to reject the idea of a 'Burmanised' central banking division of the Imperial Bank and, above all, a separate Burma note issue circulated from it. The 'present condition of world affairs' it said, made 'the time inappropriate for the introduction of a new currency into Burma'.[36]

A BANK FOR TWO COUNTRIES

Events have a way of overtaking even the best laid plans, and so it turned out both for Lister's Imperial Bank scheme and, indeed, for the critiques of it. In this context the 'event' was the looming establishment of the Reserve Bank of India (RBI). As noted above, this institution was long on the drawing board, but following the strong recommendations of the Royal Commission on Indian Currency and Finance in 1926, and after failures to get relevant legislation through the Indian assembly in 1927, 1928 and 1933, the RBI was finally established (for the whole of British India, including Burma) on 1 April 1935 (Kumar 1983: 791–792).[37] Contrary to the recommendations of Keynes and others down the years, it was a privately-owned (shareholder) institution modelled on the Bank of England. As with Lister's scheme, it was divided into 'issue' and 'banking' departments. The Issue Department was given sole responsibility for note issue in the whole of British India. It also managed the reserves backing these notes. The reserves were conservatively apportioned to include 'no less than' 40 per cent of the note issue as gold and/or sterling securities. Yet, there was room for an elastic note issue, with up to 25 per cent of the reserves being allowed to consist of rupee securities. As Sayers (1952: 227) noted, this allowed for quite substantial monetary 'accommodation' during the early years of the RBI when it handled the affairs of Burma.

Adding an additional 'elastic' component to the note issue arrangements were the activities of the Banking Department. The RBI, unlike the Imperial Bank, was *purely* a central bank and undertook no commercial banking operations. Nevertheless the Banking Department, like its namesake at the Bank of England, engaged in a range of activities that could considerably ease (or tighten) monetary conditions. These included directly lending to the Indian and Provincial governments (including Burma's, but only for terms of up to three months), and lending to commercial banks and credit cooperatives. The RBI also carried the full array of instruments then considered 'normal' for influencing domestic monetary conditions, including a 'bank rate' at which the RBI would be prepared to rediscount bills of exchange and other eligible securities. This could have functioned much along lines identical to Lister's proposals with respect to advances on trade bills but, as Sayers noted (1952: 224), it was unlikely that such an instrument 'would prove suitable to an economy that was still relatively underdeveloped, and where financial institutions were not fully integrated into a "system"'. Of course, such a criticism could have been as equally levelled against Lister's plans, to which it might be replied that a start had to be made sometime. As it was, the RBI did establish a bank rate (initially set at 3.5 per cent, then at 3 per cent – where it remained for 15 years), but the facility was very little used. According to Sayers (1952: 228), 'the only regular customer of the Bank [in this context] was the Government', and there was little in the way of large-scale discounting of bills with the RBI.

As noted, the RBI was a 'shareholders' bank owned, primarily, by private investors. Capitalised at Rs 50 million, the shares were initially distributed between five different registers – part of the effort to make the RBI truly inclusive of the widely varying peoples and polities of British India. One of these registers was in Rangoon, which was given Rs 3 million of shares for sale in Burma, six per cent of the RBI's total share capital.[38] This was, of course, rather less than Burma's 'one-ninth' share of the currency distribution for British India estimated by Lister – demonstrating perhaps that the RBI was even less 'Burma's' than it should have been. Such a view was certainly held by Tun Wai, who noted (1953: 99) that even this low equity share held in Burma was ephemeral, with a large proportion of Rangoon registered shares 'soon migrating to the Bombay Register'. On the day the RBI opened the Rangoon Register contained its Rs 3 million worth of shares in the names of 3,157 separate shareholders. By 1940 only Rs 1.85 million worth of these remained on its books (Tun Wai 1953: 100).

Also of relevance to the question of control of the RBI, and the related matter of whose interests it served, was the composition of its board. In fact, echoing Lister's proposals, the RBI had multiple boards. The 'central' and overarching board had twelve directors, eight appointed by shareholders via the five share registries, and four appointed by the government. The Governor of the RBI and two deputies were also government appointees – significantly leveraging the state's power over it. In addition to the Central Board, however, were Local Boards for each of the five registry centres. These had eight directors, five elected by the shareholders of each registry and three appointed by the *Central Board*. Importantly (and in contrast to Lister's proposal), the Local Boards served in an advisory capacity only. Overall the RBI then was ostensibly a very 'mixed' institution. Part private, part official, part centrally controlled, part provincially focused. The *realpolitik* was of an institution that was highly centralised, and identifiably a creature of the colonial government of British India.

An important function given to the RBI (as noted earlier, much neglected under previous arrangements) was the prudential supervision of banks in British India. To be a 'scheduled' bank under the RBI Act, a financial institution had to have paid-up capital of no less than Rs 500,000 and to maintain (in the form of deposits with the RBI) reserves of 'no less than 5 per cent of demand liabilities (deposits) and 2 per cent of time liabilities'. In addition, scheduled banks had to file weekly returns to the RBI detailing their balances and financial position (Sayers 1952: 225). The RBI was given responsibility for maintaining the rupee exchange rate vis-à-vis sterling. This meant an obligation to buy and sell sterling to maintain an average rate at (the now traditional) Rs 1:1s.6d.

Separation from India

In April 1937, the implementation of the *Government of Burma Act* (1935) brought about the long-awaited separation of Burma from British India. But the RBI continued to be Burma's central bank following partition. The RBI maintained its presence in Burma via its one branch in Rangoon, and no changes were made to its Local (Burma) Board.

The separation of Burma from British India necessitated legislation to amend the RBI Act, and this emerged in the *India and Burma (Burma Monetary Arrangements) Order* (1937). Coming into force at the same time as the *Government of Burma Act* itself, the *Order* essentially set out the legislative changes required to make the RBI the central bank for *two* countries. Mostly these changes were cosmetic – the most common amendment being simply to replace 'references to India and British India' with 'references to Burma and British Burma'.[39] The 1937 *Order* also set out the procedure that would follow a dispute between the Indian and Burmese governments, which would be decided upon by an agreed arbiter or, if an arbiter could not be agreed upon, by the 'Secretary of State for India and Burma'.[40] Ultimate power, in other words, continued to rest with Westminster.

The 1937 *Order* required the RBI to issue, as soon as possible after separation, 'bank notes of distinctive design, to be known as Burma bank notes'.[41] Under the 1937 Order, the RBI had sole right of note issue, the government of Burma being expressly forbidden from issuing its own notes. The first distinctive Burma notes were issued in May 1938. The name 'rupee' was retained as the official name of Burma's currency. In the earliest notes issued (the five and ten rupee notes, issued in May and June 1938 respectively) 'rupees' appeared unadorned, however in later issues (such as the 1,000 rupee note, issued in July 1939) the distinction '*Burma* rupees' appears. The notes bore the name of the 'Reserve Bank of India' as issuer, but also the inscription that the Bank's promise to pay applied to 'any office of issue in Burma' only. In other words, the Burma notes were not legal tender in India. The notes were inscribed in three languages, English, Burmese and Shan. By July 1939 there were five denominations of Burma notes in circulation (5, 10, 100, 1,000 and 10,000 Burma rupees). All featured King George VI on one side but, giving them the required 'distinctive design', featured on the obverse side various Burmese motifs – of peacocks, elephants, tigers, sailing vessels and ox-carts.[42]

As an interim measure before the first distinctive Burma notes were ready, certain new (RBI) India notes were circulated in Burma with the overprint (in red) 'Legal Tender in Burma Only'. The volume of these notes issued was under the control of the RBI and, in themselves, they presented little difficulty for the RBI's broad monetary objectives. However, their issue highlighted the fact that, as a central bank for *two* countries, the RBI had little control over the volume of currency in Burma. Indeed, for the entirety of the RBI's tenure in Burma five quite separate (legal tender) currencies circulated:

1. Notes issued by the government of India. These were notes circulated before the creation of the RBI took note issue away from the government. Such notes could have been distributed originally from Rangoon as part of the 'Rangoon circle', some could have come into Burma via Indian traders, workers and so on.

2. For a brief period following the decision to separate India and Burma, but *before* the RBI had started printing its own notes, an issue of government of India notes was made that bore an overprint (in red) 'Legal Tender in Burma Only'.

3. New RBI India notes that, as per (1) above, entered Burma via its symbiotic economic relationship with India.

4. RBI (India) notes over-stamped 'Legal Tender in Burma Only'.

5. The RBI's 'Burma notes' (Robinson and Shaw 1980: 106–107).

Controlling the volume of currency on issue within its jurisdiction is one of the key functions of a central bank. The RBI, overseeing what was, in essence, a common currency zone encompassing the whole of what was British India, was unable to control the supply of the currencies of the type in (1), (2) and (3) above in Burma. 'De-monetisation' of the older issues was a partial solution, but given the economic ties between India and Burma two separate central banks – with distinct powers over their respective currencies, was a far better one. Alas, this was not on the table.

The RBI did not keep separate reserve 'backing' against its Burma currency note liabilities. Rather, a consolidated reserve for the note issue of both India and Burma persisted beyond separation. Section 7 of the 1937 *Order*, however, provided for the division of the reserves should the RBI cease to function as Burma's central bank, in which case, there would 'be transferred from the Issue Department of the Bank to the government of Burma assets which (...) have together a value equal to the total liability in respect of the Burma notes outstanding'.

The 1937 *Order* provided that any RBI profits from its operations in Burma should accrue to the government of Burma. Such profits would derive from two sources. Firstly, there was the income earned from the RBI's 'banking' functions (banker to the government, banker to other banks, and so on). Secondly, and more importantly, there were the seigniorage profits that would come from the note issue. Here, however, a problem emerged that, once more, came as a consequence of Burma's 'not-quite' separate monetary system from that of India. Put simply, whilst Burma notes (and those overprinted as such) were legal tender only in Burma, India notes (of the type in Burma outlined above) were legal tender in *both* countries. Burma earned seigniorage revenue only from the RBI Burma notes; the seigniorage from the India notes widely circulating in Burma was taken up by the government of India.

The issue of profit distribution was not a trivial one, and it may be recalled that the earning of such profits, and their accumulation as future reserves for Burma, was a significant motivation for Lister's argument that the country should have a central bank of its own. Though there was an attempt to adjust the profit distribution to take into account the India notes it was, according to Tun Wai (1953: 110–111), done in an 'arbitrary manner' that was 'not fair to Burma'. Tun Wai argued that what the RBI had not taken account of, even presuming that they judged the proportion of India notes in Burma accurately, was that as Burma notes left the country (in the hands of Indian migrant workers and traders) seigniorage profits accruing to Burma were automatically reduced. This was because, as such notes were 'encashed' at Indian branches of the RBI for Indian rupees, reserves flowed from the Burma Issue Department of the RBI to its Indian equivalent. India notes, on the other hand, retained their earning value either side of the border. All in all, Burma faced a more or less constant drain of seigniorage profits while ever its monetary system remained 'open' to its larger neighbour.

Post-separation, the RBI became 'government banker' to the government of Burma as well as that of India. In this role it was tasked with the usual array of central banking duties: keeping the government's accounts, managing the public debt, providing occasional advances to the government and its agencies, promoting remittance facilities, and so on. Because of their separate political standing, a specific provision of the 1937 *Order* extended these functions to the management of the 'Federal Fund' of the Federated Shan States too. Previous arrangements with the Imperial Bank, however, which undertook many of these roles in locations in Burma and the Shan States where the RBI was not represented, were maintained.

The extent of banking operations actually undertaken in Burma by the RBI fell short of the potential suggested above. In September–October 1937 the RBI managed a government of Burma Treasury Bill issue to cover an unexpected revenue shortfall, but no direct advances by the RBI to the government were ever made. The RBI sold most of the treasury bills to Indian investors (almost 90 per cent of the Rs 9 million issue), which was illustrative of both the shallowness of the debt market in Rangoon and the RBI's propensity to court Indian investors (Tun Wai 1953: 109). Of course, one of the functions of the RBI in Burma was to encourage the development of indigenous financial markets, but it seems to have extended little effort to this end. The government of Burma (on account of Burma's consistent trade surpluses with India) built up substantial reserves of Indian rupees over 1937–1941, but (apart from a small take up of securities issued by the Port of Rangoon Trust) the entirety of these were reinvested in Government of India Treasury Bills and other Indian securities. It was not only the potential for investment in Burma that was denied by this policy but, as Tun Wai (1953: 140) also pointed out, the Burma note issue (and the seigniorage revenue accruing to it) also declined:

The implication of this short term investment policy of the Government of Burma is that there must have been a deflationary effect on the Burmese economy, because the Reserve Bank was managing the note issue. As the Government of Burma handed [over] the Burma notes, and asked for India notes to purchase Indian securities, the Reserve Bank of India withdrew those Burma notes from circulation in Burma, and increased the circulation of India notes in India.

Since its creation the RBI had been given responsibility for the supervision of scheduled banks in British India. This continued after separation, but under the 1937 *Order* a 'second schedule' of banks was created for banks whose functions were confined to Burma, and which were headquartered in the country. The Burma scheduled banks were supervised by the Rangoon branch of the RBI, with oversight from the Local (Burma) Board. The prudential requirements upon them were identical to those applying to scheduled banks in India in most important respects (capital requirements and reserve ratios for instance), but the Burma banks faced what appeared to be rather tougher reporting requirements, a function, no doubt, of the need to build trust during the difficult transition period. Every week each Burma scheduled bank had to send to the RBI:

(a) the amounts of its demand and time liabilities respectively in Burma,

(b) the total amount held in Burma in India notes and Burma notes respectively,

(c) the amounts held in Burma in India rupee coin, India subsidiary coin and Burma coin respectively,

(d) the amounts of advances made and bills discounted in Burma respectively, and

(e) the balance held at the Bank [RBI].[43]

Recognising the importance of the cooperative banking sector in Burma, the RBI Act also had provision for the RBI (Rangoon) to require cooperative (central) banks to supply the same information to it as the scheduled banks.

Even on this front, however, certain negative outcomes arose from the fact that Burma remained in most fundamental ways a part of India's monetary and financial system. Once more the issue was what was, in essence, a form of 'capital flight' – in this case represented by the *location* of the reserves the RBI required the banks to hold. These did not have to be located at any particular office of the RBI, so the almost universal practice of banks active in Burma and India was to hold the reserves in India rather than Burma, regardless of the size of the business done in the respective countries. The disparity, indeed, was of such a magnitude that whilst the banks comfortably held reserves above that required for their activities in *both* countries, for Burma in isolation the reserves held at the Rangoon office of the RBI were actually a *negative* proportion of Burma liabilities. The motivation of the banks was understandable, but something of an indictment of the failure to establish a properly functioning financial system in Burma. Simply, 'the banks did not want to keep their money lying idle in Burma (...), they preferred to invest it in India' (Tun Wai 1953: 146).

NOTES

1   Narratives of the entire 'monetary reform' process in India are legion – but some of the best include Bagchi (1989), Goldsmith (1983), Kumar (1983), Sayers (1952) and, for a contemporary account from one of the 'players', Keynes (1913).

2   Prior to decimalisation in 1971, £1 sterling was made up of twenty shillings (*s.*) which, in turn, was equal to twelve pennies (*d.*).

3   At various times, on certain denominations, the inscription of the city of issue was replaced by a single initial – 'R' for Rangoon, 'C' for Calcutta and so on.

4   The popularity of paper money did not extend to the Shan States or 'other outlying areas', however, where 'silver rupees or gold' remained preferred.

5   Tun Wai (1953: 98) and Sayers (1952: 220) likewise note the perception that, at the time, the Imperial Bank was 'anti-Indian'.

6   See BPBE (1930a), Chapters XIIIa and XIIIb.

7   Political protest had greatly increased throughout the length and breadth of Burma in the 1920s. Mostly this took what Cady (1958: 261) called a 'traditionalist pattern' of village uprisings against various injustices and which were often led by monks (*pongyis*). In the 1920s the most prominent of the latter, and the most dangerous to the British colonial authorities, were the rebellious *pongyis* who went under the names of U Ottama and U Wisara. Both were imprisoned, as were many of their supporters, and in 1929 U Wisara died in gaol after a lengthy hunger strike. U Wisara's death provoked unrest throughout Burma, but in 1930 the unrest exploded in what became known as the 'Saya San' Rebellion. A reactionary figure who drew upon Burmese royal as well as religious traditions, Saya San emerged in essence as a 'pretender' to the throne vacated by Thibaw, Burma's last king. After much bloodshed the rebellion was put down in 1932 and, after a trial in which he was represented by the nationalist politician Ba Maw (the later Premier), Saya San was executed in November 1937 (Cady 1958: 309–318). Of course, the above is but a most cursory account of these complex (and still controversial) issues. For more detailed accounts, see Cady (1958), Maung Maung (1980) and Thant Myint-U (2006).

8   Formally the 'Report of the Indian Statutory Commission'. The Simon Commission did not have any Burmese members (nor, indeed, did it have any Indian members, who boycotted it as a result). It travelled to Burma in February 1929 where it met a committee of Burmese representatives appointed by Burma's Legislative Council. Much of the evidence on Burma, however, it took from British officials in the Indian Civil Service assigned to Burma. The discussion on political reform in Burma was confined to volume XI of the Simon Commission Report.

9   These subjects included education, health, some agricultural issues and the management of cooperatives. The 79 members of the Legislative Council were elected according to a limited franchise, the remainder were nominated by the Governor (Tinker 1957: 3–5).

10   Later Lister was made Secretary to the Government in charge of the 'Reforms Office', and, in this role, was to be instrumental in drafting the *Government of Burma Act* (1935) that separated Burma from India.

11   Lister's memorandum was titled 'Currency Arrangements in Burma after Separation', and was dated 11 November 1930. It is not widely available, but a copy can be found in the C.W. Dunn Papers at the South Asian Archive, Centre of South Asian Studies, University of Cambridge, Box III. Dunn was a colleague of Lister's and Financial Commissioner for Burma, 1927–1932.

12   *Ibid.,* p. 14.

13   *Ibid.*

14   *Ibid.*

15   *Ibid.,* p. 13.

16   *Ibid.,* p. 4.

17   In fact, a proportionate reserve system along the lines advocated by Lister had been in place for India since 1920 – but in Lister's view (p.7) it was both little and ill used by the government.

18   *Ibid.,* p. 6.

19   *Ibid.,* p. 3.

20   *Ibid.,* p. 18.

21   *Ibid.*

22   *Ibid.,* p. 17.

23   *Ibid.*

24   *Ibid.,* p. 15.

25   *Ibid.,* p. 17.

26   *Ibid.,* p. 18.

27   *Ibid.,* p. 19.

28   *Ibid.,* p. 21. Of course, 'two good signatures' just implied that the Imperial Bank would provide funds on trade bills advanced to it by banks, credit cooperatives and the like, and not their (non-financial institution) customers. The 'not more than 90 days' maturity injunction was a prudential measure designed to protect the Imperial Bank from undue default risk.

29   *Ibid.,* p. 20.

30   *Ibid.*, p. 21.

31   *Ibid.*, p. 22.

32   *Ibid.*, p. 16.

33   A set of minutes of this meeting on 30 December 1931, written by Lister and titled 'Financial safeguards and currency arrangements in Burma', can be found in the C.W. Dunn Papers, Box III.

34   *Ibid.*

35   Minutes of this meeting written by Lister, which was held on 7 March 1932, can be found in the C.W. Dunn Papers, Box III. Other members of the delegation included: Sir Henry Strakosch, a leading and somewhat eccentric business figure in British India who had served on the Royal Commission on Indian Money and Finance in 1925; Sir Cecil Kisch, the Secretary of the Finance Department of the India Office and the recent author (1928) of a book on central banking; Sir George Baxter, 'Principal' of the Finance Department of the India Office; Sir David Monteath, then Assistant Secretary of State, India Office, who later became Under Secretary of State for (the separated) Burma, 1937–1941.

36   *Ibid.*

37   The *Reserve Bank of India Act* was passed by the Indian legislature and granted consent by the Governor General of India in 1934, even though the Bank was not established until 1935.

38   The other registries were Calcutta (Rs 14.5 million shares), Bombay (Rs 14 million), Delhi (Rs 11.5 million) and Madras (Rs 7 million) (Tun Wai 1953: 99).

39   *The India and Burma (Burma Monetary Arrangements) Order, 1937* (hereafter '1937 *Order*'), s.11.

40   Who, under the Government of Burma Act (1935), was the same person. 1937 *Order*, s.10.

41   *Ibid.*, s. 6.

42   Reproductions of these notes can be seen throughout Robinson and Shaw (1980).

43   1937 *Order*, s. 15.

CHAPTER 5

Aristocratic Eagles:
The Commercial and Exchange Banks

Burma had no banks before the annexation by the British.
Tun Wai, 1953

Imperial Bank, National Bank and the kindred ones are aristocratic eagles that soar on high and never come near the bushes beneath and therefore need not be touched here.
Saw Pah Dwai, evidence to the BPBE, 1930

Commercial banking, in a form that we would recognise today, arrived in Burma only in the wake of the wars that brought the country into the commercial *pax* of the British Empire. Initially the preserve of trading houses such as the famed Wallace Brothers, commercial banking in Burma soon came to be dominated by banks proper: the ubiquitous British 'exchange banks', the so-called 'Presidency Banks' of British India we have seen already, and a limited number of banks from countries outside the British imperial sphere. As shall be examined, very little in the way of what might be regarded as banks 'indigenous' to Burma were created before the country achieved independence in 1948.

The banks that established themselves in Burma during the colonial era were overwhelmingly concerned with trade, in particular the trade in Burma's great export staple, rice. They rarely established branches beyond Rangoon and, at first glance (as the testimony of Saw Pah Dwai above attests), appeared to touch the ground in Burma lightly. In fact, their role was greater than perhaps supposed, partly as a consequence of their support of Chettiar lending. One bank that did venture beyond Rangoon, and indeed attempted to become a viable alternative to the Chettiars throughout the country, was

Dawson's Bank. An institution now largely forgotten by history, Dawson's Bank was founded to alleviate the condition of the Burmese cultivator. Dawson's Bank barely survived the 1930s depression and, along with the other commercial and exchange banks, was forced to flee Burma upon the invasion of the Japanese in 1942.

In this chapter we begin by examining the exalted role of the exchange banks in Burma. We investigate the instruments and operating principals of these banks, before turning our attention to the role of specific institutions. We also examine two rare and unusual 'Burmese' banks of the colonial era. One of these is the aforementioned Dawson's Bank, the other a gold mortgage company of singular enterprise. Both, however, were outliers so we also explore why it was that more Burmese banks did not emerge. Following this we take up the story once more of the depression of the 1930s, and the damage wrought thereby in Burma, but now in the context of the formal banking sector. We outline the nadir of the experience of 'western' banks in Burma as they were put to flight by the Japanese invasion. The chapter then continues the wartime theme by examining some of the institutions created by the Japanese occupiers, before briefly touching upon the triumphant (but ephemeral) return of the 'aristocratic eagles'.

THE 'EXCHANGE BANKS'

What Tun Wai describes as 'western' banking first arrived in Burma courtesy of the great trading firms that dominated the country's commercial relations with the outside world in the nineteenth century (Tun Wai 1953 and 1962, *passim*). Such firms which, in the modern revisionist lexicon of British Empire studies, could be considered the vanguard of the 'gentlemanly capitalism' that was expanding the *pax Britannica*, were emblematic of the unequal struggle between the deconstructing kingdoms of Burma, and the economic imperatives presented by the European colonial Empires.[1] Whilst for some of these firms banking was ancillary to their trading activities broadly, for others (notably the firm of 'Wallace Brothers') it was to become an increasing focus – an example, indeed, of the well-worn transition between merchant and 'merchant banker'.[2]

By the end of the nineteenth-century, however, the merchants and traders that had hitherto been the 'bankers' of the British Empire gave way (or evolved into) institutions whose sole activity was international banking. These institutions, referred to at the time and since as the 'exchange banks' (their title thus describing their principal activity), were the financial pillars of the commercial space that was the British imperial system. By 1941, and the late evening of the colonial order, there were 24 of these banks in Burma. As Table 5.1 reveals, the majority were headquartered in London or other capitals of the Empire:

Table 5.1 Scheduled Banks Operating in Burma in 1941[3]

Bank	Branches	Bank	Branches
Britain		*Burma*	
Chartered Bank of India, Australia and China	1	A. Scott & Co.	1
		Gillander Arbuthnot & Co.	1
Lloyds Bank	2	Dawson's Bank	10
Imperial Bank of India	8	U Rai Gyaw Thoo & Co.	1
Mercantile Bank of India	1	*China and (other) Asia*	
National Bank of India	2	Overseas Chinese	2
Thomas Cook & Sons (Bankers)	1	Banking Corporation	
Hongkong and Shanghai Banking Corporation	1	Bank of China	2
		Bank of Communications	1
USA		*(British) India*	
National City Bank of New York	1	Central Bank of India	1
Japan		Reserve Bank of India	1
Yokohama Specie Bank	1	Mohaluxmi Bank	5
Netherlands		Calcutta Commercial Bank	1
Nederlande Handelsbank	1	Indian Bank	1
Netherlands Trading Society	1		

Neither the exchange banks, nor other western-style banks (with but one or two exceptions), sought to conduct much business in the Burmese countryside, or with the population at large. Confined for the most part to Rangoon, they stuck to the financing of trade (and principally just the paddy crop) and the provision of limited advances to European companies involved in government-funded projects. The banks financed most of this activity from funds raised offshore (mainly in London), but over time they increasingly took in deposits, primarily from high-income European managers and professionals in Burma, but also from a growing number of wealthy Burmese and Indian business owners. Collectively, the exchange banks held roughly a half of all bank deposits in Burma just before the Second World War (Tun Wai 1953: 27).

But some exchange bank funds did manage to percolate through into the Burmese countryside, one avenue for which was their financing of European export firms in Rangoon which, in turn, 'made cash advances to up-country mills' (Brown 2005: 32). Such advances were usually made early in the trading season (from January to about March), collateralised against the delivery of rice at harvest-time. Being 'drawn up country' in such a manner was typical of the experience of exchange banks throughout the British Empire. It was a phenomenon that increased over time, often under the pressure of exchange bank managers on the ground who, as Jones (1993: 85) relates for exchange banks generally, often 'argued that advances to producers and merchants within the country formed part of the total process of trade finance, even though they themselves did not involve exchange business'.

Lending to the Chettiars

The primary avenue, however, through which the funds of the exchange banks that *did* penetrate more deeply into Burma was via their lending (in various forms) to the Chettiars. As noted in Chapter 2 of this book, the importance of bank lending to the Chettiars should not be exaggerated (since the bulk of Chettiar lending came from their own funds, and those created through the Chettiars' deposit creation mechanisms). Yet, it is equally true that, for the banks, the Chettiars' role was critical indeed to the extension of their influence. In essence, the Chettiars in Burma fulfilled the role undertaken for the exchange banks by *compradors* elsewhere in the British Empire: giving the banks a parallel stream of activity that brought exposure to the high profits potentially available in indigenous rural credit markets (but at much lower risk), together with their more conventional business of providing financial services to expatriate firms.

The exchange banks provided funds to the Chettiars in the form of loans and overdrafts, in a roughly two-thirds/one-third ratio. The dominant bank lender to the Chettiars was the Imperial Bank which, taking as guide the seasonal lending peak in 1929, supplied Rs 20 million of the Rs 36 million provided by the banks collectively. Next, in descending order, were Lloyds Bank which lent Rs 7 million, the National City Bank of New York (Rs 5 million), the Chartered Bank and the National Bank (around Rs 1 million each), with Rs 2 million in aggregate provided between the Central Bank of India, the Netherlands Trading Society, the Mercantile Bank and the Allahabad Bank. Only the Imperial Bank and the National Bank of India lent to Chettiars from branches beyond Rangoon, albeit, in the case of the National Bank, the only other lending location was Mandalay. The Imperial Bank made loans to Chettiars from four branches beyond Rangoon which, in order of importance, were Moulmein, Mandalay, Bassein and Akyab (BPBE 1930a: 216).

The exchange banks made *loans* on the presentation of promissory notes payable on demand written by the borrowing Chettiar firm, and signed by another Chettiar firm as a guarantor. Though payable on demand, in practice the convention was that a bank would only expect the payment of principal and interest at the end of a pre-arranged period of time, which was usually three months. The interest rates charged by the European banks varied. Chettiars could borrow from the Imperial Bank at a rate that averaged from about 1.5 to 2 per cent above Bank rate (as noted in Chapter 2, the rate at which the Imperial Bank [later the Reserve Bank of India] would 'rediscount' the highest quality securities – hence, the base from which other interest rates could be calculated according to counterparty risk). The exchange banks were rather more expensive, charging the Chettiars from 2 to 3 per cent above Bank rate. The Imperial Bank and the National Bank of India charged a further 0.5 per cent interest on their Chettiar loans made outside Rangoon (BPBE 1930a: 217).

Overdrafts were typically provided against the collateral of government of India securities or promissory notes payable on demand. The latter, however, required collateral security of the 'title deeds of house-property situated in Rangoon and worth twice the maximum of the overdraft' (BPBE 1930a: 217). Interest rates charged on Chettiar overdrafts by the Imperial Bank were typically levied at between 1.5 and 2 per cent above the prevailing Bank rate. Continuing the pattern established on loans, the other exchange banks charged a further 0.5 to 1 per cent more. Also consistent with the pattern for loans, any overdraft established outside Rangoon attracted a further charge of around 0.5 per cent (BPBE 1930a: 217–218).

The Chettiars bitterly resented the margins above Bank rate that the exchange banks charged them on their loans and overdrafts. Their primary complaint was that the exchange banks did not regard the Chettiars as 'fellow bankers' but, rather, 'ordinary merchants' (BPBE 1930a: 243). In a similar vein they also complained that the exchange banks did not sufficiently accept for security on loans anything much beyond government securities. The Chettiars did not invest much in such assets, but made loans primarily against paddy godowns and land titles, as we have seen. Such items were 'equally good security' as government paper, they argued, and should be accepted as such by the exchange banks. Exacerbating this grievance was a more explicit charge of discrimination, with the Chettiars consistently alleging that loans merely 'on the security of goods in godowns *are* made to firms and companies under European management' (BPBE 1930a: 243, emphasis added).

Trade Finance and Bills of Exchange

But it was 'self-liquidating' trade finance that was the core activity of the exchange banks, and their *raison d'être*. The basic instrument for carrying this out was the ubiquitous 'bill of exchange'. A simple instrument that revolutionised global trade in the nineteenth century, the bill of exchange was essentially a device that allowed an exporter to receive the proceeds of their exports immediately upon sale, and in their own currency. The provider of these funds were the exchange banks which, via the bill of exchange, simultaneously provided credit as well as took on foreign exchange risk otherwise shouldered by exporters and importers. Tun Wai estimated (1953: 35) that before the Second World War the issuing, redeeming and trading of bills of exchange accounted for over 60 per cent of the business done by the exchange banks in Burma.

The bills of exchange provided by the exchange banks in Burma were usually very short term – mostly for 60 days, sometimes for 30, and never more than 90. Of course, such short-term 'lending' was consistent not only with the practice of exchange banks elsewhere, but with British banking generally. In contrast to their emerging rivals in continental Europe, and to a lesser extent the United States, British banks avoided long-term advances whenever they could. This is, perhaps, hardly surprising. Trade finance, and the emerging practice of providing well-qualified firms with overdrafts, was low risk, enjoyed high turnover (thus increasing the returns on a given capital stock) and was a known quantity. All this was in stark contrast to the 'dubious profits earned from interest on advances, which might never be repaid' (Jones 1993: 85). Of course, as Drake (1980: 161) points out, the short-term nature of British bank lending should not be exaggerated, since 'a significant number of nominally short-term overdrafts were repeatedly renewed to the point where they actually constituted a long-term line of credit for the borrower'. This was especially the case, moreover (of relevance to Burma), in the case of 'financing the capital works of expatriate agricultural enterprises' (Drake 1980: 161).

In colonial Burma, the long-term lending that was undertaken by the exchange banks (usually to 'European' firms) typically required collateral that was both of exceptional high quality (and liquidity), and against which the banks lent only with a considerable security 'buffer' against asset price fluctuations. Such collateral included government of India securities (10 per cent buffer required), gold bullion (also 10 per cent), primary commodities (25 per cent), share equity in local companies (25 per cent) and immoveable property (25 per cent) (Tun Wai 1953: 36). As per Drake (1980) above, these loans tended to consist of indefinitely revolving overdraft facilities, rather than fixed long-term advances.

The British exchange banks possessed considerable competitive advantages in the 'globalised' economy of the nineteenth century, many of which were the simple consequence of being at the centre of the world's largest trading empire. Then, as now, the financial institutions of the world's dominant economy were given a substantial head-start on their rivals, not least from the fact that they serviced the largest and most extensive global businesses. Critical too, however, were the benefits bestowed by the use of sterling – by far the world's most trusted and accepted currency. Sterling was used in two-thirds of international transactions by the end of the nineteenth century, and the exchange bill issued in London was the world's basic financial instrument (Jones 1993: 61). Coupled with the fact that sterling was itself credibly fixed at the centre of the gold (exchange) standard, Britain's banks were substantially free from home-generated foreign exchange risk.

SPECIFIC INSTITUTIONS

The account thus far has provided an outline of the activities and operating principles of the exchange banks *in general* – but this obscures what, in fact, were very great divergences of practice between individual institutions. Such divergences provide illuminating vignettes into the nature of commercial banking and economic life generally in colonial Burma. In the following we take a closer look at some of the individual banks that made the greatest impact on Burma, or that in other ways made important contributions.

The British Banks

In considering the operation of formal banks in Burma, one is compelled to start with the Imperial Bank. By far the most important 'western' bank in Burma, we have seen (Chapter 4) that it functioned as a quasi-central bank for much of the colonial era. But the Imperial Bank was also a strong commercial player. Excluded from the exchange trade by its Indian charter, it concentrated instead on providing funds and financial services to the colonial government and its agencies, and to a myriad of businesses *within* Burma (mostly, but not exclusively, European). As we have noted above, it was also the leading bank in providing what amounted to 'wholesale' finance to the Chettiars, and through them was an important financier of Burmese agriculture.

The number of branches of the Imperial Bank reached its maximum of eight immediately before the Second World War. These were located in the leading provincial cities and towns: Mandalay, Akyab, Bassein, Moulmein, Myinyan, besides three branches in Rangoon. The branches in Moulmein and Akyab, and one of the branches in Rangoon, had been inherited from the Presidency Bank of Bengal upon its absorption into the Imperial Bank. The others were the product of that condition of the *Imperial Bank of India Act* (1920, and noted in Chapter 4) that specified the creation of 100 new branches of the Imperial Bank across the whole of British India.

The gap left by the Imperial Bank in foreign exchange business was amply filled by what were always referred to in India and Burma as the 'exchange banks'. As this label implies, the exchange banks were concerned with foreign trade, and in this role they played 'an important role in the economic development' of Burma (Tun Wai 1962: 25). The majority of the exchange banks were British, and were either headquartered in London or in other capitals of the Empire.

Two of the most eminent names in the fraternity of British exchange banks operating in Burma were the 'Chartered Bank of India, Australia and China', and the 'Hong Kong and Shanghai Banking Corporation'. Both live on to this day as major global financial institutions (the former as 'Standard Chartered Bank', the latter as popularly known by its acronym, 'HSBC'). The Chartered Bank had arrived in Burma in 1862, just nine years after its formation in London by merchants and shipping interests with a view to financing the trade between Asia and Australia. In fact, the Chartered Bank was never to enter the Australian trade, but concentrated its efforts in Asia and other 'emerging markets'. For most of its tenure in Burma it only had one branch (Rangoon), but its influence on the finance of Burmese agriculture (through loans to millers primarily) was, as we shall see, rather greater than this suggests. In 1927, the Chartered Bank took over the P&O Banking Corporation, which in turn owned the Allahabad Bank (which also had a branch in Rangoon) (Jones 1993: 406). The two branches were soon incorporated in the Chartered Bank's opulent offices in downtown

Rangoon. The Chartered Bank was more active in Burma than most of the exchange banks, but it steered clear of long-term lending, and played a negligible role in financing (often government-sponsored) railways, river, port and other activities it regarded as 'outside the province of an exchange bank'.[4]

The Chartered Bank was the most prominent of all the exchange banks in financing agriculture in Burma *on its own account*. This prominence was achieved as a consequence of the Chartered Bank's deployment of what it called a 'produce guarantee system' in Burma, through which it financed the storage and milling of rice, as well as the storage and marketing of products such as sessamum and groundnuts. The produce guarantee system was a simple enough arrangement by which the Chartered Bank lent against the security of the stored commodities, upon the advice of an independent broker as to their quantity, quality and expected market value. The broker received a commission from the Bank of around 1 per cent of the value of the loan. As an incentive to ensure an accurate estimate of the value of the commodities, the Chartered Bank required the broker to place on deposit an amount of 2.5 per cent of the loan (upon which, however, they were paid interest) (Tun Wai 1953: 28–29). The bank typically lent up to 75 per cent of the nominated market value of the stored commodities. An interesting innovation, and a forerunner of what today is known as a 'margin call', was a requirement that, if the price of a commodity fell so that the 75 per cent collateral ceiling was breached, the borrower had to repay some of the loan immediately, and/or put up additional stocks until the 75 per cent collateral limit was re-established. Another interesting sidelight was that, in this era in which fires were common in 'godowns', and to guard against simple theft, the Bank inspected storehouses, held the only keys to the locks on their doors, and employed its own security guards to protect them (Tun Wai 1953: 30).[5] Altogether, just over a half of all of the Chartered Bank's lending in Burma was made via the produce guarantee system. It was an inventive solution to the problem of providing security against risky agricultural lending, and the Chartered Bank later extended the system to its paddy-lending in Vietnam (Jones 1993: 84).

The Hong Kong and Shanghai Banking Corporation (HSBC) was established in Hong Kong in 1865 by 'taipans of several nationalities', and by the time it entered Burma in 1891 had become something of a pillar of the British Empire in Southeast Asia. (King 1987: xxvii). As with the other British exchange banks in Burma, HSBC was chartered under

British colonial banking regulations but, uniquely, was headquartered in Asia rather than London. Successful in entrenching itself in China, even becoming 'banker and adviser' to the *Chinese* imperial government, HSBC had quickly expanded throughout Southeast Asia and by the 1880s had branches in India, the Philippines, Malaya and Singapore, (what was then) the Dutch East Indies, Ceylon and even the ports of French-ruled Cochin China. Though its principle activity was the financing of intra-regional trade, it was the 'bank of choice' for a number of colonial and sovereign governments (King 1987: 6). HSBC's branch in Rangoon was lavish even by the sumptuous standards of the exchange banks, and incorporated within it what had been a Catholic church (Collis 1965: 107).

Curiously, and notwithstanding its links to so many countries in the region and its strong position in the London capital markets, HSBC's initial operations in Burma were overwhelmingly concerned with Burma–Malaya trade, and with providing remittance products for Chinese businesses operating in Burma and the Straights Settlements (including Singapore). This trade was not particularly profitable and, as a result, the Rangoon branch was consistently one of the *least* profitable of HSBC's outposts. It made a substantial loss in 1902, and even more substantial losses in the early 1930s with the onset of depression (King 1988a: 60, King 1988b: 192). HSBC did significant business with Chettiar moneylenders in Ceylon, but surprisingly seems to have had very little involvement with them in Burma (BPBE 1930a: 216). An interesting sidelight to HSBC's Rangoon operation was that the branch served as something of a nursery for what the Bank called 'birds of passage' – young bankers being groomed for greater things, and for whom a stint in Burma was seen as a vital part of their training (King 1988b: 279).

One of the final 'Burmese' projects that HSBC was to be involved in before the Second World War was far more ambitious than the Bank's usual business in Burma: the provision of a loan in 1938 to the Chinese (Kuomintang) government (then besieged by the Japanese invasion), to construct a 'Burma–Szechuan Railway'. The Bank was part of a syndication of French banks (known as the 'Groupe Unie des Banques Francaises') and the American government-financed China Development Finance Corporation. The deteriorating situation in China brought about the abandonment of the project, however, in December 1938 (Dayer 1988: 306).

The Chartered Bank and HSBC were more or less 'pure' exchange banks, with insignificant operations in the United Kingdom itself. The one exchange bank that simultaneously was a major player in Britain as well as Burma was Lloyds Bank. The only big British 'clearing' (domestic) bank to have operations in Burma, the lack of others reflected the Bank of England's opposition to the entry of the major clearing banks into multinational banking. It was said that Montagu Norman (the legendary Governor of the Bank of England) 'had a particular dislike of Lloyds' operations in India', which he described in 1925 as 'less justifiable than any other venture' (Jones 1993: 238). Ironically, however, it was the very same Norman who promoted the entry of Lloyds into Burma by arranging for it to take over the troubled operations of 'Cox and Co.' in 1923 (Jones 1993: 240). A trading firm along the lines of Wallace Brothers, Cox had begun as a firm of agents specialising in handling financial and other matters for the British Army. It opened its first branch in India (Bombay) in 1905, and thereafter established branches throughout British India (including one in Rangoon). Cox gradually evolved into a bank, and in Burma was mostly engaged in discounting bills of exchange and in providing remittance services to British troops and other British nationals. Interestingly, in 1918 another Burma 'connection' opened for Lloyds when it took over the National Bank of Scotland, the bank that had long been the backer of Wallace Brothers (Jones 1993: 143). Lloyds did not have a happy time with Cox. Jones (1993: 145) reports that Lloyds experienced management problems with it, and 'a severe loss' at the Rangoon branch at the end of the 1920s that revealed 'poor controls over lending and inadequate senior management'. In fact Jones is referring here to the 'Beng Huat' scandal, more on which below. Lloyds had a big share of the deposits that were placed with the exchange banks in Burma and was a major lender to such leading British firms as Steel Brothers and the Burmah Oil Company. Regarding the latter deals, however (and revealing the limitations imposed on Lloyds overseas posts), arrangements were invariably made with Lloyds' head office, 'the branch in Rangoon merely acting as transfer agency' (Tun Wai 1953: 28).

The banks thus far examined were major institutions of Britain's mercantile Empire, but our Table 5.1 above also includes some others that might be best regarded as imperial 'foot soldiers'. Representative of this cohort were the 'Mercantile Bank of India', and the 'National Bank of India'. Despite their names, both of these were very much British concerns. The Mercantile Bank, for instance, was often referred to in Burma as the 'Mercantile Bank of *Scotland*' because of its preponderance of Scottish staff (Jones 1993: 50). Both banks confined their activities in Burma to the financing of international trade (mostly paddy) via the issuing of exchange bills. Both were essentially conservative institutions and would not lend against the security of either land or commodities beyond trade (Jones 1993: 406). Thomas Cook and Sons was also listed as a scheduled 'bank' in Burma but, not unexpectedly, this famous travel company confined its banking activities to the issuing and redeeming of travellers cheques and letters of credit, and small-scale (tourist-based) foreign exchange transactions. It had just the one office in Rangoon.

Non-British Exchange Banks

British banks dominated formal banking in colonial Burma as noted, but there were other banks from outside the British sphere that played significant niche roles in Burma. One of these was the 'National City Bank of New York' (now globally known as 'Citibank'). The first American bank to set up substantial operations in Asia, the National City Bank was established in New York in 1812. Unusually for an American bank, it had a global focus from early in its existence, and was keen to fashion its international operations according to the practices and structures of the British exchange banks. To this end, the Bank was an enthusiastic recruiter of the staff of the British banks (seeming to target the officers of the Chartered Bank in particular). According to the official historian of the Bank's operations in Asia, 'the general structure of the bank was similar to that of its British competitors, until significant numbers of American staff arrived in the 1930s' (Starr 2002: 30). The Bank's sole office in Burma (in Rangoon) was opened in 1919. The Bank employed local Burmese, but a high proportion of the 'local' staff were Sino-Burmese and resident Indians. Later the training of the Bank's staff greatly distinguished it from the 'on the job training' approach of its British competitors, and after the First World War the Bank 'developed a special programme with several American universities which included some practical training in international banking' (Jones 1993: 171). The National City Bank was a conservative lender in Burma, with much of its lending being in the form of letters of credit issued primarily for the trade between Burma and China (Starr 2002: 45–47).

Another significant non-British bank active in colonial Burma was the 'Yokohama Specie Bank' (YSB). The first bank in Japan permitted to establish operations abroad, the YSB had been founded in 1880, specifically to counter the challenge of the West and with one overriding objective – 'to collect specie, in coins of whatever sort with a high gold and silver content, from anywhere in the world' (Tamaki 1990: 191). The YSB engaged in exchange banking all over the world, and by 1919 it handled 44 per cent of all Japanese trade transactions. It was especially active in Southeast Asia where it competed 'head-to-head' with the British exchange banks. Effectively controlled by the Japanese government from the outset, from the 1930s the YSB came increasingly to serve the Japanese military, closely following the army into Manchuria and other places and according to Tamaki (1990: 213) facilitating 'militarism' generally. As shall be seen, the YSB performed a central role in Japan's occupation of Burma during the Second World War. Before the war the bank had just one branch (in Rangoon), which it was asked to vacate upon Japan's attack on the US base at Pearl Harbour, Hawaii, on 7 December 1941, and the immediate declaration of war on Japan by the US and Britain.

Three Chinese banks arrived in Burma on the eve of the war in order to exploit opportunities created by the completion of the famed 'Burma Road' in 1938. Two of these banks, the 'Bank of China' and the 'Bank of Communications', were under the control of the Chinese (Kuomintang) government, which had given them a mandate to accumulate as much foreign exchange as possible. The Bank of China, which entered Burma only in 1940, quickly established two branches, one in Rangoon, and one at Lashio at the terminus of the Burma road. The Bank of Communications arrived in Burma in 1939, establishing its one and only branch in Rangoon. The third bank, the 'Overseas Chinese Banking Corporation' (OCBC), had been formed in 1932 via the merger of three existing Chinese banks in the Malay peninsula. It too entered Burma (in 1939) in response to the boost to Burma–China trade occasioned by the opening of the Burma Road, but found its most lucrative customer base in Chinese rice-millers in the Irrawaddy Delta. In this business it consciously copied the approach of the Chartered Bank. In this and other activities the OCBC was a keen competitor, taking small margins and offering competitive interest rates. Like the Bank of China, the OCBC had branches in both Rangoon and Lashio. All three of these 'Chinese' banks found an additional profitable business in handling the remittances of Chinese nationals in Burma (Brown 1990: 170–180, Tun Wai 1953: 30).

Finally, two Indian (but not *British* Indian) banks operating in Burma in the late colonial era are worthy of note. The first, the 'Central Bank of India' (CBI) had been founded in 1911 – famously as the first modern 'western' commercial bank in India to be founded, owned and operated by Indians. The

CBI had one office in Rangoon, and its operations were concentrated in the trade between Burma and India. The primary instrument of this trade was the 'telegraphic transfer' (TT) and, as such, the CBI was a leading exponent of this method of transferring funds. The use of the TT dramatically shortened transaction times relative to exchange-bill-financed trade, and as such the CBI's advances were extremely short-term. Unsurprisingly, the CBI's profits in Burma were derived mostly from foreign exchange commissions and margins. The CBI also made loans in Burma against land, produce and other assets, mostly to Indian businesses (Tandon 1988: 67–68). The second bank, the 'Indian Bank', had been founded in 1907 in Madras by a number of leading Chettiar families (but it was not a 'Chettiar bank' as such). Formed to play a role in the *swadeshi* (self-sufficiency) movement directed against British rule in India, the Indian Bank had a very brief tenure in Burma. Its only branch (in Rangoon) opened in 1940, and closed in 1941 on the eve of the Japanese invasion (Seshadri 1982).

TWO 'BURMESE' BANKS

Four banks listed in Table 5.1 (p. 106) were 'scheduled' *in Burma* in 1941. In fact, two of them, A. Scott and Co. and Gillander Arbuthnot, were not really banks at all. The latter was primarily a ruby miner and trader, the former a stockbroker. The other two banks, Dawson's Bank and U Rai Gyaw Thoo and Company, were more or less 'banks' in the conventional sense. It is to these rare institutions that we now turn.

Dawson's Bank

Founded in 1905 by Lawrence Dawson, a liberal idealist of the type we have met before in the context of the cooperative credit movement (Chapter 3), Dawson's Bank was created with the express purpose of 'assisting Burmese agriculturalists to redeem their lands from Indian money-lenders' (Tun Wai 1953: 78). In Burmese, Dawson referred to his purpose as *'pakon pyoungde'* ('changing shoulders'), to illustrate the firm's objective in lifting the burden of debt from the shoulders of the Burmese cultivator. In a later deposition to the Burmese government, he was clear in nominating that his target was the Chettiars, and what he alleged were their practices:

> The business of the Bank was confined to the redemption of agricultural lands which had been mortgaged to Chettiars. This was induced by the offer of an appreciable reduction in rates of interest, but the principle sought to

be applied with respect to mortgages which the Bank took over, was that of amortization of the debt, by obtaining equated annual repayments of principal and interest over a period of years, so as to extinguish the whole debt at the end of that period. This banking principle was contrary to the practice of the Chettiar, who were not concerned with securing annual repayments of principal and who advanced to agriculturalists much more than was sufficient for their needs. The higher rates of interest which they had succeeded in maintaining, predisposed them to pay little or no regard for the ultimate security of the principal sum advanced and to accept the risk readily. The Bank, on the other hand, by discouraging agriculturalists from borrowing unnecessarily and by insisting on annual repayments, sought to   encourage savings and thrift (...) the principles followed by the Bank strengthened the economic position of the borrower, whereas the tradition of the Indian money-lender was   to keep his debtor in thrall.[6]

For most of its long life Dawson's Bank was headquartered not in Rangoon but in Pyapôn Township, in the heart of the rice-producing Irrawaddy Delta. At its peak the Bank had nine branches apart from the Pyapôn head office – in Bassein, Bogale, Dedaye, Kamakalu, Kyaiklat, Maubin, Moulmeingyun, Myingagon, and Rangoon. For most of its history Dawson's sought to expand its branch network, and it consistently complained that government regulation and obstruction, together with difficulties in finding suitable staff, stymied this. Lawrence Dawson told Tun Wai (while the latter was researching his 1953 book) that the Bank's branch 'outreach' philosophy was:

(1) To have branches as close to the cultivator as was possible so that he would not be tempted to spend the money in the city, and to enable him to come to the bank for comparatively low rates, rather than go to a loan shark and pay exorbitant rates;

(2) To have a field staff to see that money granted was used for the purpose for which it was lent, *i.e.* for productive purposes, the employee being chosen for his knowledge of people, and given courses in agriculture so that he could be guide, philosopher and friend to the agriculturalists (Tun Wai 1953: 82).

Dawson's Bank was initially founded as a private firm. In 1914 the Bank was formally incorporated as a private company under the name of Dawson's Agricultural Loan Company Limited and finally, in 1921, as a public company as Dawson's Bank (BPBE 1930b: 98). It engaged in both short-term and long-term lending to cultivators. Its short-term lending was mostly in the form of crop-lending. Long-term lending was mainly for the purposes of land redemption (from moneylenders), the purchase of new land, land improvement, farm housing and other farm building (mills, granaries and the like). Crop loans were made seasonally according to purpose (ploughing, planting and harvesting). Long-term loans were usually secured by mortgage over land, while crop loans were most often secured by a lien over the crops, although cultivators could also get overdraft facilities secured by land mortgage. Dawson's also lent to paddy traders, village stores and to local industry, provided that adequate security was pledged (BPBE 1930b: 98). Notwithstanding its professed mission of reaching the Burmese cultivator, the Bank's formality in procedure sometimes precluded this – a group of Burmese landlords telling the BPBE, for instance, that notwithstanding the Bank's lower relative rates, they 'always borrow from the Chettiars; never from Dawson's Bank'. Their reason was that 'the Chettiar lends on a simple promissory-note, whereas the bank requires *preliminaries*' (BPBE 1930b: 102, emphasis added).

Up until the Great Depression, Dawson's Bank's lending grew inexorably – Rs 1.6 million in 1921, Rs 4.3 million in 1926, Rs 7 million in 1930 (BPBE 1930b: 98). These numbers were not inconsiderable – the 1930 total, for instance, was not far short of the total lending of the *entire* cooperative credit movement at this time. Nevertheless, it was still a long way from the advances made available by the Chettiars collectively, who remained (Dawson's efforts notwithstanding) the dominant lenders in the Burmese countryside.

Dawson's Bank's lending was financed primarily via deposits, both current (18 per cent of the total) and fixed term (82 per cent). The Bank's high ratio of fixed deposits gave it a very stable funding base, and was a primary source of its strength and resilience. Fixed deposits ranged in term from six months to ten years, with an average of (a remarkably high) four years. Deposits peaked at Rs 9 million in 1930. Depositors were mostly Europeans in Burma (primarily British) but the Bank reported increasing deposits from Burmese before the crisis of the 1930s (BPBE 1930b: 99).

In addition to deposits, Dawson's Bank was able both to access and place its own funds with the exchange banks. It had a particularly strong relationship with both the Yokohama Specie Bank and Lloyds Bank, with whom Dawson's Bank would place surplus funds from January through to October, and withdraw them (and/or drawdown on its overdraft) in November/December according to harvest demand. The funds placed with

Yokohama and Lloyds formed a part of Dawson's liquid reserves. Such reserves were costly, however, the deposits with the banks yielding a mere 2 per cent per annum, as against 10 per cent and more from lending (Tun Wai 1953:81).

On the question of interest rates, Dawson's Bank was cheaper than the Chettiars (more than was apparent than when simply comparing interest rates themselves – given Dawson's stress on reducing the loan *balance* too), and comparable to those charged by the cooperative credit societies. The Bank charged 10 per cent per annum on overdraft lending, 12 to 16 per cent on land mortgage, and 18 per cent on small loans not secured on land. The Bank paid just over 6 per cent on fixed deposits, and slightly more than 4 per cent on demand deposits. As Tun Wai (1953: 79) notes, Dawson's 'built up a reputation of good management', and maintained a liquid assets to liabilities ratio of 40 per cent. Lawrence Dawson admitted that maintaining such a high ratio of liquid assets 'sacrificed much profit', but it was a prudential measure that served the Bank well in all but the most extreme of times.[7]

The Bank was also conservative in its lending on land, advancing only 60 per cent of agreed valuation (even though the collapse in land prices after 1930 would prove that even this was not conservative enough) (Government of the Union of Burma [GuB] 1950: 13). But if the Bank was prudent, it was also usually highly profitable – delivering dividend returns of not less than 10 per cent across the 1920s and peaking at 16 per cent in 1929. Dawson's Bank undertook a number of capital raisings in the 1930s, each oversubscribed, and held capital of Rs 750,000 in 1930 (Tun Wai 1953: 79). This represented a high capital commitment relative to the Bank's liabilities even by modern standards. In addition to granting loans and taking in deposits, Dawson's Bank also did a large business in providing remittance services – over Rs 150,000 per day, mostly via telegraphic transfer (BPBE 1930b: 99–100). In this it was a keen competitor with the Imperial Bank.

U Rai Gyaw Thoo Company

In the colonial era there was only one Burmese-owned and-operated scheduled bank. This was the U Rai Gyaw Thoo Company, which was based in the township of Akyab (now Sittwe) on Burma's western Arakan coast. The Bank grew out of a complex trading, shipping and moneylending entity. As a *bank*, however, its main business was to make advances on gold and land mortgage, and by 1941 it had total assets of Rs 2.3 million. The Bank took deposits, but such deposits (which in 1941 totalled only Rs 170,000) were a minor source of its liabilities (Tun Wai 1962: 56). The Bank funded its lending, rather, primarily from the capital of its owners and, at seasonal peaks (January-February), via an overdraft facility at the Imperial Bank. As with other lenders, U Rai Gyaw Thoo became a substantial landowner during the depression years of the 1930s through loan foreclosure. Tun Wai noted (1962: 57) that the bank was a generous lender to its *own* shareholders, a practice which, he acknowledged, 'by western standards, must be considered a malpractice'.

U Rai Gyaw Thoo charged interest rates on its loans of between 9 and 12 per cent per annum depending upon the security offered – enjoying a substantial margin on the rates it paid on deposits (a meagre half a per cent per annum), and on its overdraft with the Imperial Bank (three and a half per cent). Tun Wai noted that the Bank's market share had been declining in the decade before the Second World War (partly as a consequence of dynastic succession problems), losing out to less formal (but Burmese) moneylenders (Tun Wai 1962: 58). Nevertheless, the existence of the U Rai Gyaw Thoo, together with its vigorous competitors, was a prime reason that Akyab district was one of the very few in colonial Burma that was able to source most of its credit needs from indigenous lenders, and 'where Chettiars and other Indian firms have not been able to penetrate much' (Tun Wai 1962: 58).

WHY WERE THERE SO FEW BURMESE BANKS?

Of course, the existence of this 'one' Burmese-owned bank raises the broader question as to why there were no others. Tun Wai (1962: 55) put up four reasons behind the failure of indigenous Burmese to establish formal banks, even after the British had established the critical infrastructure (secure property rights, sound currency, establishment laws and so on) to do so:

(a) Their energies have been taken up in the colonization of the Delta;

(b) There are no Burmese Tatas or Birlas;[8]

(c) Burmans do not have the experience, and to gain it they would have to work long hours in banks, which they are disinclined to do;

(d) More than in other kinds of business, banking needs the form of the joint stock company with large capital to be successful, which requires confidence in the Burmese promoters, directors and managers, and this simply does not exist.

Other Burmese writers have taken a similar line to Tun Wai, but with even greater stress on 'cultural' factors. Mya Maung (1991: 62), for instance, stressed that '[c]ulturally, professions connected with finance, trade, and commerce are contrary to both traditional and Buddhist sanctions, while economically natural affluence in basic necessities and an abundance of land tend to promote a low propensity to save, invest and innovate'. Other authors, reflecting what is perhaps a consensus view, cited economic segregation in colonial Burma as being the primary reason as to why Burmese nationals did not establish banks (nor indeed, other complex capitalist institutions). Such a view is famously associated with the 'plural society' thesis of J.S. Furnivall, who criticised British 'laissez-faire' economic policies in Burma as creating a society in which various racial groups existed side-by-side, each dependent on the others for the performance of their 'own special economic functions', but 'meeting only in the market place' (Furnivall 1958: 22). Within this division of labour, moreover, most Burmese were essentially confined to agrarian pursuits, the Burmese elite to politics and the bureaucracy, but with finance the preserve of foreigners. Furnivall noted that, even at school, Burmese were deterred from taking courses (such as economics and finance), that may have broadened their horizons and that 'foreign rule brought Burma into economic contact with a larger world, [but] Burmans were halted at the threshold, and they could not learn to live in it'. Van Schendel (1991: 85), like other recent writers (Brown 2005a, Pham 2005, Mya Maung 1991), essentially agreed with Furnivall's thesis, but extended upon it by noting that, in contrast to the experience elsewhere, in Burma 'colonial annexation had not been preceded by the insinuation of European capital in local business and state institutions'. Such an 'insinuation' did not occur before or across the Anglo-Burmese wars (the economic aspects of which were exclusively related to the extractive industries) and, as such, Burma was denied the partnership between local and European capitalists that had been the foundation of indigenous banks in other colonial territories.

Of course, in the absence of formal banks, other institutions that relied on traditional practices of 'saving and borrowing' lived on in colonial Burma – the most important of which was the pawnbroker, allied with the simple and ancient habit of 'hoarding' precious stones and metals. Mostly such 'hoards' were in the form of gold ornaments and jewellery, and more often than not 'worn' by Burmese women. The BPBE estimated that, in the 1920s, the 'typical' land-owning cultivator had on average between Rs 50 to Rs 120 of such jewellery and ornaments. Other groups also engaged in the practice to varying degrees, to an extent that depended mostly on their relative wealth. Thus the BPBE also estimated that blacksmiths and artisans had about Rs 50 in gold and jewellery, small shopkeepers between Rs 50 to Rs 150, and tenant-farmers between Rs 10 to Rs 50. Rural labourers, it found, usually had nothing (BPBE 1930a: 268). The BPBE also came across a curious phenomenon in its eyes – that many people had jewellery *even while* they had debts of an equal or greater amount. Indeed, it found that many wearers of jewellery possessed it 'on pledge'. This, the gentlemen of the BPBE opined (and they *were* all men) was a 'ruinous practice' – requiring the payment of annual interest that amounted each year to around one-eighth to one-sixth of the value of the jewellery. Yet, somewhat gallantly, the BPBE concluded;

> ...it is unlikely that the Burmese women will ever give up using jewellery: and we do not think it altogether desirable that they should. The use of jewellery is not entirely a matter of vulgar ostentation and emulation. The Burmese people have artistic qualities and are bound to express themselves in the use of beautiful articles, which will often be made of gold so as to be free from tarnish (...). Universal condemnation of investment in jewellery, such as is sometimes heard, is out of place (BPBE 1930a: 268–269).

The pawnbrokers of colonial Burma were often Chinese, or of Chinese origin. This was particularly the case in Rangoon where Chinese pawnbrokers were as ubiquitous in petty urban-lending as the Chettiars were in agriculture. A European traveller's anecdote around the turn of the century observed that the Chinese-quarter of Rangoon 'bristled with pawnshops', making the entire town appear as if it 'consisted chiefly of pawnshops and pagodas' (Fraser 1899: 89). We cannot know of the relevant proportions, but (especially beyond the major towns), indigenous Burmese played a leading role as pawnbrokers. An authority on such pawnbrokers was Tun Wai, whose own background (as noted earlier) allowed him close acquaintance with gold-mortgage pawnbrokers in Akyab. Writing about the practices of such pawnbrokers between the world wars, Tun Wai (1962: 60–61) noted that they gave advances of a minimum of 80 per cent of the value of mortgaged gold. Interest rates on gold mortgage loans were invariably not compounded, were calculated monthly, and varied according to seasonal demand (but averaged around 9 per cent across the cycle). According to Tun Wai (1962: 61), there was a high degree of collusion amongst the pawnbrokers on interest rates, and he records that in Akyab in the 1930s the practice was that lenders 'agreed among themselves that if any one of them changed his rates he had to inform the others'. On this score, however, it was not all one-way traffic, a common scam amongst borrowers, for instance, being the pledging of 'false gold' – ornaments that were gold on the outside, but lead underneath.[9]

THE COMMERCIAL BANKS AND THE GREAT DEPRESSION

The commercial banks in Burma faced increasing difficulties following the First World War. The 1920s, universally and falsely remembered today as a time of boom and excess, were in reality years of decline and retrenchment. This was especially the case with respect to the international trade in commodities, the prices of which, buffeted by the surpluses built up amongst the former combatants, and by the increasing quest for food 'self-sufficiency' around the world, suffered falls across the decade. Paddy prices were not immune to this phenomenon. In 1925, for instance, the price of Rangoon export rice was down 8 per cent from the price it commanded in 1920, and by 1928 it was down a further 9 per cent again (Wickizer and Bennett 1941: 330). Of course, the exchange banks were also suffering at this time from the great disruptions to capital flows that were a consequence of the war and, increasingly, the exchange controls, tariffs and other barriers that were being erected all over the world.

The negative global outlook impacted upon the earnings of the exchange banks and, for most of them, Burma was not a highly profitable place (King 1988a: 60). Matters were made worse, moreover, by a major fraud scandal towards the end of the 1920s that brought about the collapse of the Chinese firm of Beng Huat, then Burma's most significant rice exporter. At the time of its collapse Beng Huat had loans outstanding of Rs 16 million (£1.25 million) to four of the largest banks in Burma – HSBC, Lloyds Bank, the Netherlands Trading Society and the Yokohama Specie Bank (Brown 2005a: 33). This event by itself caused a contraction in the credit these (and other) banks were willing to supply to Burmese rice millers and exporters generally and, as Brown (2005a: 33) notes, made them 'more cautious in the troubled times which were to follow'.

Such troubled times arrived in Burma with a vengeance in the early 1930s. As revealed in Chapter 2, rice prices went into catastrophic decline from 1930, falling 17 per cent that year, a further 42 per cent the following year, before bottoming out in 1933 at a level barely one-third of the prices of 1920. Recovery was also slow to arrive, with rice prices not recovering beyond 50 per cent of the 1920 benchmark before the Second World War. Again, as noted in Chapter 2, all of this cut a swathe through Burmese agriculture, as tenants, landlords, millers and almost the entire paddy production chain went into serial default. This brought down the Chettiars as we have seen, and it brought about great losses at the banks. The National City Bank of New York made losses in each of the years 1930 to 1934, a pattern repeated at Lloyds Bank, the Chartered Bank and HSBC (Jones 1993: 177–188, Brown 2005a: 68–70, King 1988a: 60, Starr 2002: 30).

A logical response to these troubles for the banks *individually* was to reduce their exposure to the crisis by greatly curtailing their lending. A policy in play all over the world, in aggregate it only made matters worse, since the cessation in lending imposed a monetary contraction and a credit squeeze (on top of the loss of export income). Bank lending creates deposit money as we have seen, but when credit contracts, the money creation process shifts into reverse. The data on the size of the monetary contraction in Burma during the 1930s depression, alas, does not exist, but given the near universal story of financial retrenchment by all types of lenders it is unlikely to have been mild. Nevertheless, in the face of the scale of the disaster, and in the absence of an adequate response by the imperial and *global* monetary authorities, there was not much else the banks could do. One of the few novel efforts to drum up *new* business was a proposal by one of Lloyds Bank's managers in Rangoon. Noting the fierce competition for the declining trade of European firms, the manager proposed that Lloyds seek to diversify their lending by opening a sub-branch in Rangoon's Sooratee Bazaar, and targeting 'Mahemedon [sic] and Chinese merchants'. His proposal was not followed up on (Jones 1993: 187–188).

Naturally, the Chettiars were greatly affected by the sudden drying up of bank lending. In a splendid and highly detailed analysis of the interactions between the banks and the Chettiars at this time, Brown (2005a, *passim*) reveals that a tougher line was taken by the banks with the Chettiars well before the nadir of the crisis. He notes, for instance, that as early as 1929 most of the exchange banks had begun to copy the practice of the Imperial Bank in calling in Chettiar advances at the end of the cultivating season, instead of allowing moderate overdrafts to persist as they had in previous times in order to gain a competitive edge. Citing internal memoranda from within Lloyds Bank, Brown also reveals growing concern amongst the exchange banks that the competition between each other had caused advances to the Chettiars to rise to levels beyond which they 'could safely use'. As a consequence, in 1929 Lloyds and other banks 'reduced some lending ceilings' (Brown 2005a: 58–59). There also developed at this time an increasing perception that the Chettiars *as a group* were no longer the good risk they used to be. Brown (2005a: 59) notes that this was prompted by the failure of several leading Chettiar firms to meet loan commitments due in August 1929. In the past such troubled firms would have received help from the Chettiar community more broadly, but the tight collective discipline of the Chettiars was now beginning to unravel (see also BPBE 1930a: 213–221).

When the Depression really struck in early 1931 the exchange banks sought savagely to cut back their exposure to the Chettiars. Using Lloyds Bank once more as indicative, Brown (2005a: 68) found that the Bank's total advances to Chettiars fell from Rs 7.5 million in July 1931 (which was itself greatly down from the previous year), to Rs 3.0 million in July 1932. In subsequent years the Bank attempted to continue to reduce its exposure to the Chettiars, and distrust between both parties grew. Brown (2005a: 68) cites this description of Chettiar attitudes at the time by the manager of the Rangoon branch of Lloyds to his opposite number in Calcutta:

> I cannot sense any sincerity on the part of the Chettiars as a whole that it is their desire and intention to repay the Banks to the best of their means but I sense a very definite air of evasion at any time I interview any of them.

In fact, there was broad sympathy amongst most of the exchange banks for the position of the Chettiars, whose own problems with defaulting borrowers (detailed in Chapter 2) were far more extensive than the situation facing the formal banks. In any case, when it came to the crunch, there was little the banks could realistically do against defaulting Chettiars. Using the courts to seize Chettiar land was little compensation, since the banks could no more dispose of it for a reasonable price than the Chettiars could. The other alternative, of cultivating the land (and paying tax upon it), was as distasteful to the banks as it was to the Chettiars. Of course, legal action was also costly, and time-absorbing.

Dawson's Bank

Dawson's Bank was almost ruined by the Depression, and its experiences give us another window into the desperation facing Burmese cultivators during these years. We have seen that Dawson's Bank had quite a conservative policy when it came to lending, with an especially large 'collateral cushion' when it came to land mortgages. This was to prove no avail, however, as the Bank was overwhelmed by what Lawrence Dawson described as 'an extraordinary coincidence' of events – which not only included the collapse in paddy prices generally but, for Dawson's Bank, the added shock to land values in its Pyapôn heartland that came as a result of the 'Saya San' rebellion of January-February 1931.[10] By mid-1931, Dawson's portfolio of mortgaged properties was worth a mere 25 per cent of its pre-1931 value. Lamenting on the impact of this later, Lawrence Dawson recalled, it was

> to be of little or no use as an index of value, his situation may be likened to that of a sailing ship in uncharted seas or worse, sailing on seas that cannot be charted. And if large reserves vanish in a day, is this not like striking a hurricane, which has dismasted the ship, depriving it of the power to keep underway and exposing it to the elements?[11]

By the end of the year Dawson's Bank was forced into what was officially called 'voluntary liquidation' (but more accurately a form of voluntary restructuring), a strategy that became a necessity when rumours of the Bank's solvency caused a 'run' on its deposits in late 1931. It survived this panicked withdrawal of deposits, which totalled Rs 2.3 million (around 25 per cent of total deposits, more than enough to destroy most banks), but only because of its substantial holdings of reserves and liquid assets (GuB 1950: 12).

Dawson's Bank was able successfully to reconstruct itself after 1932, a task that involved the conversion of the bulk of its deposits into long-term bonds (repayable over 23 years at 5 per cent interest), and/or shares in the recreated company (Tun Wai 1953: 80). It emerged from voluntary liquidation in 1932, but throughout the ordeal it continued to credit interest on the deposits that remained with it. In 1936 it even resumed dividend payments. For the remainder of the 1930s Dawson's Bank was able to continue lending even as other sources dried up. Its activities were on a smaller scale than before the crisis, however, and meanwhile the Bank's sources of funds had changed. Deposits, especially of a long-term nature, were difficult to obtain in Burma in the 1930s and, as such, the Bank increasingly relied upon its bond holders and capital resources for renewed lending. By 1941 the Bank's deposit base had recovered somewhat but, at Rs 500,000, was still only 5 per cent of the total in 1930 (GuB 1950: 14). Very few new land mortgage loans were written, a function not only of previous experiences, but also of what Dawson's complained were problems in land title – and how this was being interpreted by the courts in a number of cases in which the Bank had sought repossession (GuB 1950: 14). With land mortgage lending greatly reduced, most of the loans granted by Dawson's Bank in the latter half of the 1930s were short-term cultivation advances. In an environment that was increasingly economically and politically risky, however, interest rates (at 18 per cent) were substantially higher than before the events of 1931. Recognising the new realities the Bank also started to accept repayment of crop loans *in kind*, and to this end built a number of 'godowns' for paddy in Pyapôn (GuB 1950: 13).

Finally, much of Dawson's Bank's activity in the latter half of the 1930s was concerned with managing the substantial lands the Bank had repossessed during the worst of the crisis. Such land was worth substantially less than the loans originally advanced on it, and the Bank was unable to sell even the best of it except at a substantial loss. Most of the repossessed land, accordingly, remained in the Bank's possession. Some was let out to tenants (often the original mortgagees), but a vaster amount simply remained out of cultivation (a fact exacerbated by the movement of Indian agricultural labourers out of Burma due to the political troubles). Dawson's Bank also kept many borrowers in possession of their land, even when in arrears, depending on the nature of the situation and the personalities involved. With the returns to agricultural production so low in the latter half of the decade, the Bank embarked upon a scheme whereby each borrower's situation was reviewed annually and a schedule of repayment calculated according to their 'capacity'. Under these arrangements the Bank levied an average of 7 per cent interest on its old mortgage loans, half the amount charged on the loans before the crisis (GuB 1950: 14). Another scheme initiated by the Bank to aid its borrowers who had their land repossessed was to enter into an agreement to sell it back to them, at a set price and within a set time.[12]

WAR

Flight of the Eagles

On March 7 1942 Rangoon fell to the forces of Imperial Japan. On 1 May Mandalay followed, and what remained of the Burmese colonial government evacuated Burma for the 'hill-station' of Simla, India – and exile.[13] In a matter of months British rule in Burma had come to an end. The British would, of course, return temporarily after the war, but a chapter of Burmese history had come to a close.

Despite the speed of the British collapse in Burma, the British and other exchange banks were relatively well-prepared. Months before the invasion the Chartered Bank had begun to duplicate all its records in anticipation of Japanese air attacks on Rangoon. In January 1942 the same bank 'took the lead in obtaining permission to send its securities to Calcutta by sea', a policy soon adopted by the other exchange banks (Mackenzie 1954: 290). Events soon overwhelmed orderly timetables, however, and with Rangoon soon to come under Japanese artillery, permission was granted on 17 February 1942 for a specially requisitioned train to evacuate the banks, most of their staff, their cash and bullion, and all of their important remaining records to Mandalay. The train finally left 'bedlamite' Rangoon on 20 February, and reached Mandalay the following evening (Mackenzie 1954: 291). This evacuation was not without its critics. As an anonymous memorandum written later for the Burmese government in exile recorded, albeit defending the evacuation, the banks 'were criticised in some quarters, and accused of precipitating panic, but it was conveniently overlooked that the exodus of Government Departments, and their staffs, was largely responsible for increasing the nervous tension so deplored. The fact (...) that the [general] compulsory evacuation order was issued the same day as the banks entrained, is sufficient evidence that the decision was a wise one'.[14] Interestingly, despite the dire situation, it seems that many of the banks did not really expect to have to leave Burma completely, remaining 'optimistic that the capital would not fall, and that the crisis was a temporary one'.[15]

One bank that did not join the train to Mandalay was the National City Bank of New York. The Bank's Rangoon manager, William Goldrick, closed the branch with the others on 17 February, but sought help from the United States Army in evacuating staff and the Bank's records. His request, surprisingly, was turned down, but Goldrick took advantage of the Bank's Chinese contacts, who provided three trucks and a jeep to take the Bank's records and staff to Lashio. The convoy arrived in Lashio four days later, after which Chinese Kuomintang planes flew the party to Calcutta via Kunming (Starr 2002: 73). Meanwhile at HSBC, a senior banker who happened to be in possession of much of the Bank's currency holdings missed the train to Mandalay but walked an extraordinary trek across Burma's northern border and into India – with all the money intact (King 1991, p.70). Lawrence Dawson of Dawson's Bank did not get the train to Mandalay either. E.C. Foucar, a logging merchant and miller similarly fleeing the Japanese, had this account of Dawson's efforts to hide his Bank's 'treasure' in Maymyo:

> Lawrence Dawson, managing director of an agricultural loan bank in Lower Burma, had brought with him to Maymyo a fortune in gold and jewels, security upon which cultivators had borrowed money from his Bank. He was much concerned about the safety of his treasure; and as he was due to fly to India shortly he could take with him no more than he could carry. The gold and jewels must be left behind.
>
> Dawson one day found an acquaintance digging a hole in his garden. On inquiry he was told by the digger that he was burying his plate and silver until he could recover it after the war. "Let me use the hole, too", begged Dawson. "I'll have it lined with bricks and properly cemented over". His acquaintance agreed, and the work was done. After the other's valuables had gone into the cache it was sealed up and the ground above it smoothed over. But Dawson's friend had not seen the Bank's treasure placed in the hole. In fact it had gone into the bare earth beneath the brick flooring provided by the banker.
>
> After the war a search showed the cavity to be empty. Dawson's friend lost all his belongings; but the floor was unbroken, and Dawson's Bank duly recovered its valuable securities (Foucar 1956: 137).[16]

For the bankers who did manage to get the evacuation train, the arrival in Mandalay was chaotic. All the staff of the evacuated banks and their records were lodged in a single building (belonging to Rowes, the famous department store of colonial Burma), which narrowly missed being destroyed in a fire-storm that followed a Japanese bombing raid on the night of 3 April. The Imperial Bank's branch in Mandalay was destroyed in this attack – a considerable problem since that was where all of the cash of the evacuated banks had been stored. The heat-affected safe doors had to be blown open by the British Army. Yet, notwithstanding the air attacks and the general chaos, the remaining banks actually opened for business in Mandalay.[17] Such 'business' was limited, however, essentially to that of handing out cash deposits. Of course, before long the time came to evacuate Mandalay too, and on 10 April the banks opened for three final days to allow depositors to withdraw their funds. Senior staff of the banks were subsequently flown out to Calcutta. Mackenzie (1954, p.292) tells us that the remaining records of the Chartered Bank went with its senior staff on a flight to Calcutta, and then to the Bank's 'Rangoon Evacuation Office' in Lahore, packed in a suitcase. More junior staff, which included most of the Indian employees of the banks, were left to join the caravan of Europeans, Indians (including many Chettiars, as noted in Chapter 2), on the long and deadly march to Assam (Bayly and Harper 2004: 167).

Banking Under the Japanese

Japan occupied Burma from 1942 and until the final months in 1945 of the Second World War. Scarcely three years, and too little time one might suppose to establish anything in the way of a viable financial system. Indeed, this was essentially the case. The Japanese, in collaboration with the puppet-government established under the pre-war premier of Burma, Ba Maw, did manage to create a number of symbolic monetary institutions. The purpose of these, however, together with that of creating an occupation currency, was essentially to extract resources from Burma without cost to Japan's financial system.[18]

One of the 'commercial' banks that did *re*-establish itself in Burma during the Japanese occupation was the Yokohama Specie Bank (YSB). Forced to close its doors in Rangoon following the outbreak of war, the YSB re-entered Burma in the wake of Japan's victorious army (with which, as noted above, it had become close in the late 1930s). Initially it was the YSB that was the issuer of Japan's occupation currency, but soon the primary function given to it by the Japanese Military Administration (JMA) was to act more or less as a replacement for the exchange banks. A somewhat strange and redundant task perhaps, given the absence of much in the way of 'exchange' activity. Nevertheless, it was into the YSB that the *outstanding* accounts of former depositors in the foreign banks were 'rolled'. A Japanese broadcast made early in the occupation ordered all holders of such accounts in 'enemy' banks to give a 'full report of them' to the YSB by August 1943 (Burma Intelligence Bureau [BIB] 1943: 70). Less ominously perhaps, the YSB latter offered to pay 'up to 10 per cent' on these deposits. Somewhat hopefully, it also requested that repayments on loans previously given out by the foreign banks continue to be made, but now to the YSB. As Andrus

(1948: 312) sardonically notes, 'Debtors and creditors alike ignored the request.'

The YSB took up the recently evacuated building of the Chartered Bank as its Rangoon head office, and established other branches in Bassein, Lashio, Mandalay, Maymyo, Mergui, Moulmein, Myingyan, Prome, Tanggyi, Tavoy and Toungoo. In the end, the state of Burma's economy during the war meant that the YSB was mostly involved in servicing Japanese corporations granted various 'concessions' by the JMA. It engaged in little that could be described as standard banking activity with the Burmese populace.[19]

A 'new' bank established during the period of Japanese occupation was the 'Peoples Bank of Burma'. Created in December 1942 as a 'joint-venture' between the JMA, the Burma Executive Authority (BEA, the then title of the Burmese puppet administration) and the YSB, it had at its core the confiscated 45 branches of the Bank of Chettinad, the largest of the pre-war Chettiar firms. The People's Bank was established with capital of 100,000 (Japanese military, 'JM') rupees, and was meant to form a key component of the BEA's efforts to revitalise agriculture. Its head office was in the former Central Bank of India building in Merchant Street, Rangoon.[20] As with so many institutions established during the Japanese occupation, real control of the Bank remained in the hands of the Japanese military. Andrus (1948: 312) speculated that the Bank 'may have had some success collecting interest on old loans by Chettyars', but otherwise made few loans, took in few deposits and conducted little in the way of real business.[21]

Other banks were also mooted by the BEA, but in the end they amounted to little more than 'might have beens' in Burma's dramatic banking and financial history. One of these was an institution called the 'Burma State Bank' (BSB), which would have been Burma's first central bank. Responsibility for creating the BSB was given to a committee headed by U Ba Maung, the former manager of the 'Pegu Central Cooperative Bank' and who was described by a contemporary British intelligence report as 'Burma's outstanding financial figure' (BIB 1945: 105). As a central bank, the BSB's primary function was to create and issue a new currency for Burma – a task that also reflected the growing concern of Ba Maw's government over what they regarded (rightly) as the 'reckless' magnitudes of JM rupees being printed by Burma's Japanese occupiers. An order was even placed in Tokyo in 1944 for the printing of Rs 3,000 million of notes bearing the imprimatur of the BSB. Of course, by then the war was turning very much against the Japanese and their allies and, beyond a few samples, the BSB notes never did see the light of day (Robinson and Shaw 1980: 117). Meanwhile, a proposal of the BEA's agricultural secretary, Thakin Than Tun, for 'farmer credit associations' in place of the pre-war cooperatives and even 'land mortgage banks' were similarly still-born (BIB 1943: 46–47).

Finally, two other Japanese-aligned banks that surfaced in Burma during the war years were the 'Bank of Chosen', and the 'Azad Hind Bank'. The Bank of Chosen was the supposed central bank of Korea. Korea had been occupied by the Japanese since 1910, and the Bank of Chosen was one of the vehicles through which Korea was converted 'into a supply base for the war' (Bagchi 2000: 421). From the early 1930s, the Bank of Chosen expanded its activities progressively with the advance of Japan's imperial conquests. It operated in Manchuria, Taiwan and Thailand, as well as Korea. Burma was never successfully converted into a 'supply base', and very little is known of the activities of the Bank of Chosen in the country. Very likely it facilitated, in minor ways, the Japanese military authorities as well as that 'swarm of Japanese business and manufacturing [that] invaded the country' throughout the war (Cady 1958: 459).

The Azad Hind (or 'Free India') Bank also had a branch in Rangoon during the Japanese occupation years. This bank, which was also sometimes known as the 'Indian National Bank', was established to fund the operations of the Indian National Army (INA) – the Axis-aligned force of Subhas Chandra Bose. The Azad Hind Bank had similar branches throughout Asia in countries under Japanese rule, but its operations were largely limited to that of supporting the INA. In Burma, the Azad Hind Bank was relatively successful in applying 'patriotic pressure' upon those Indians remaining to hand over valuable and fungible assets (not the increasingly worthless JM rupees) including gold, jewellery and *Indian* rupees (Chakravarti 1971: 175). Cady (1958: 477) reports that the Bank raised some 215 million Indian rupees in Burma in this way, including 150 million from Burmese-Indians alone.

The Return of the Exchange Banks

Meanwhile, throughout the war the exchange banks formerly in Burma cooled their heels – mostly in India (Lloyds in Lahore, the Chartered Bank in Calcutta, and HSBC in Simla) (Gotts 1973: 508, King 1991: 45). In exile they plotted their return, and even formed their own representative body, the 'Bank's Burma Reconstruction Committee' to discuss and lobby on such issues as debt moratoriums, and the question of whether or not to recognise transactions that had taken place under the Japanese (a case-by-case approach between individual banks and borrowers was judged best in the end).[22] Interestingly, since it was in contrast to the situation for the decade leading into the war, the relocated Burma branch of HSBC in Simla actually made a profit during the years in exile, mainly via its remaining investments in Indian government bonds (King 1991: 45).

At the end of the war the 'banks in exile' sought an early return to Burma, and to this end had a series of meetings (beginning in 1944) with both the Burmese government in exile, and the British government in London. Such was their eagerness, which was seemingly informed by a fear that other banks could arrive to take their pre-war place, that they created a 'recce party' to accompany the troops fighting in the field. Interestingly (and, as it turned out, ineffectually), the banks did not favour the demonetisation of the Japanese occupation currency. In 1944 they told the Bank of England that they thought that it was 'inconceivable that the reoccupying power would in effect create a position whereby the Burmese could not use the money in their pockets and banks to satisfy their needs'.[23] Consistent with their earlier expressed views, the banks also believed that questions of 'title transfers, debts and transactions' undertaken during the Japanese occupation be left up to the courts on a case-by-case basis. The banks views on honouring the Japanese occupation currency were not adhered to and, to the great distress of the many ordinary Burmese who held them, JM rupees were declared to be no longer legal tender by the returned British authorities from 1 May 1945.[24]

Demonstrating that they had at least maintained a sense of humour, Lloyds Bank code-named its return to Burma 'Operation Shylock'. The Bank arrived back in Rangoon in December 1945 and, with most of the other exchange banks, formally re-opened for business on 23 January 1946 whereupon, they claimed, 'we were soon helping to finance the rice crop and so get exports going again to earn the foreign currency the country so badly needed' (Gotts 1973: 510).

NOTES

1   The extraordinarily influential 'gentlemanly capitalism' thesis explaining the economics of the British Empire is most comprehensively stated in Cain and Hopkins (2001).

2   This transition is celebrated in Jones (1993). Of course, Wallace Brothers (via their ownership of the 'Bombay Burmah Trading Company') played an immensely

important role in the early history of colonial Burma. Indeed, their actions could well have precipitated the third and final Anglo-Burmese war of 1885. As Webster (2000: 1004) notes, however, this remains 'well-trodden but precarious territory', and it is not the purpose here to revisit these many controversies. Suffice to note, for these pages, is that amongst the many 'issues' that prompted the final conflict between the British Empire and the Burmese Kingdom was a mooted trade deal between Burma and France – a trade deal that included the establishment of the so-called 'Royal Bank at Mandalay'. This undertaking would have fulfilled the role of a central bank for Burma, and the provider of loans and funds to the Burmese king much along the lines as those originally performed by the Bank of England for the English crown. The evidence suggests that it was Wallace Brothers' representatives in Burma who 'tipped off' the British government about these moves. The British Government (in the person of Lord Randolph Churchill, the Secretary of State for India) were more than receptive to such news, which was consistent with their great anxiety over what they feared was an expansionist France. For more on the controversies over the final incorporation of Burma into the British Empire, and the possible role of Wallace Brothers therein, see Maung Htin Aung (1965), Keeton (1974), and (most importantly) Webster (1998 and 2000). For a comprehensive discussion of Wallace Brothers itself, see Pointon (1974).

3   List based on one created for the Bank of England, 6 March 1944, Archives of the Bank of England (BoE), Overseas Department (OV) 79/19.

4   Chartered Bank, Court (Board) minute, 1899, cited in Jones (1993: 126)

5   'Godown' was the label imperial officials used for the storehouses of primary commodities throughout Southeast Asia. It was a word brought across from India.

6   Letter, Lawrence Dawson to the Secretary to the Ministry of Finance, Government of the Union of Burma, 13 May 1948, National Archives of the United Kingdom (NAUK), Foreign Office (FO), Political Departments, General Correspondence 1906–1966, Burma, FO371/83144.

7   *Ibid.*

8   The Tatas and the Birlas were (and are) prominent 'business families' in India who, amongst many other enterprises, established their own banks and financial institutions.

9   A scam that continues to the present day. See for instance the testimony of one moneylender in Stephen Brookes, 'Black Market Banking in Burma', *Asia Times*, 18 April 2006.

10   Dawson cited in GuB (1950: 13). For more on the rebellion, see Maung Maung (1980).

11   Untitled memorandum by Lawrence Dawson, reproduced as 'Appendix B' in Binns (1946: 16).

12   *Ibid.*, p.1.

13   For details of the Japanese invasion of Burma, see Bayly and Harper (2004), Allen (1984) and Won Zoon Yoon (1973) – as but three of a large and growing literature.

14   'Account of the Evacuation of the Banks from Rangoon, February 1942', anonymous memorandum, 14 July 1942, Oriental and India Office Collection, British Library

(OIOC), Select Material, Private Papers, Anonymous, Accounts of the Evacuation of the Banks from Rangoon, 1942, Mss Eur D750.

15   *Ibid.*

16   Freda Dawson, Lawrence Dawson's niece, confirmed this story in personal correspondence with the author in November 2003.

17   'Account of the Evacuation of the Banks from Rangoon, February 1942', anonymous, 14 July 1942, OIOC, Mss Eur D750.

18   A splendid and comprehensive account of Japan's monetary arrangements is the subject of Longmuir (2002).

19   'Burma Economic Notes', 28 February 1945, Burma Military Intelligence Liaison Office, OIOC, Burma Office Private and Intelligence Files, Burma economic notes produced by Burma Intelligence Liaison Office and Civil Affairs Staff (Burma), September 1944–May 1945, IOR M/5/85.

20   'BIB Fortnightly Report, No.35', 16 February 1944, BoE, OV 79/19.

21   Tin Shwe, a 'thakin' who remained loyal to the British and who was inserted back into Burma as an agent for the famous 'Force 136', reported in 1944 that he had not heard of the People's Bank. 'Interrogation Report of Mr Lancelot [pseudonym of Tin Shwe] in Delhi in May 1944 by S.D. Jupp, Deputy Director, Intelligence Bureau, Government of Burma, Simla', in Tinker (1983: 67).

22   'Moratory and/or "Standstill" Legislation for Burma', Bank's Burma Reconstruction Committee memorandum. 31 January 1944, BoE, OV 79/19.

23   Minute by R.N. Kershaw of a meeting between the Bank's Burma Reconstruction Committee and the Bank of England, London, 6 March 1944, BoE, OV 79/19.

24   *Ibid.*

CHAPTER 6

Reconstruction, a Currency Board and the Union 'Banks' of Burma

A country, particularly a developing country, derives many benefits from having a highly professional, highly respected central bank

Stanley Fischer, 1994

In late 1944, British and Allied forces began a series of long-awaited offensives designed to re-take Burma from the Japanese.[1] In heavy and bitter fighting they reversed the sequence of events that had brought about their expulsion not yet three years earlier. By January 1945 Arakan had fallen, in the North-East Lashio had also been re-taken, while in the centre the British 14th Army had begun their push down the Irrawaddy. On 20 March 1945 Mandalay was back under British rule, but not before much of the former capital's most important cultural and historical sites had been destroyed. A few days before the fall of Mandalay the Burmese National Army (BNA) under Aung San signified that the end was near, turning against their Japanese overlords and joining their Karen, Kachin and other compatriots in fighting alongside the Allied forces. Finally, on 2 May 1945, Rangoon was recaptured. 'Mopping up' operations continued, especially in the Shan States, along the Martaban coast, and in the jungles and hills of the Irrawaddy and Sittang rivers. On 13 September 1945, 11 days after Japan's formal surrender and over a month after the dropping of the atomic bombs, Japanese forces in Burma laid down their arms.

In previous chapters we briefly examined the destruction of the colonial financial system in the wake of the Japanese invasion, and the flight from Burma of the Chettiars and the European exchange banks. In this chapter we begin by examining the efforts of the (temporarily) returned British colonial authorities to reconstruct Burma's financial system, and to craft a new set of institutions that would deliver financial stability. At the apex of the latter was Burma's 'Currency Board'. We also look at the companion institution to the currency board – the 'first' Union Bank of Burma. Nominally Burma's first central bank, this was in fact a simple institution with little in the way of real central-banking powers. The chapter then changes tack somewhat to briefly observe various laws against moneylenders that were rejuvenated by the 'interregnum' colonial government from Burma's pre-war legislatures. These laws were ineffectual amidst the chaos of the immediate postwar years, but their effects would be damaging to Burma's financial system in the long term. We then take up the story of the 'second' Union Bank of Burma, created in 1952 as a replacement for both the currency board and the first Union Bank, and Burma's first 'true' central bank. Finally, we investigate the performance of the Union Bank through the years of Burma's parliamentary democracy.

THE CURRENCY BOARD

In 1947 the war-inspired chaos of Burma's monetary arrangements came to an end with the establishment of the Burma Currency Board (BCB). For all practical purposes an 'invention of the British Empire', currency boards came to be the favoured instrument of monetary management throughout the Empire after the Second World War (Williamson 1995: 5). By the late 1940s there were around fifty currency boards operating around the world, most in various colonial dependencies. Within a decade the majority of these had made way for fully-fledged central banks, but they returned to fashion in the 1990s, primarily amongst a group of former Soviet-bloc countries anxious to establish new and credible domestic currencies. Currency boards were, and are, ideally suited to conditions in which the seeds of monetary stability must be planted in relatively inhospitable soil. As noted in the last chapter, this was precisely the circumstance that Burma found itself in as it attempted to recover from the monetary mayhem of the war years.

Traditional currency boards (of the sort created in Burma) are relatively simple structures whose purpose is narrowly confined to that of issuing and redeeming domestic currency against a specified foreign 'anchor' currency at an exchange rate fixed by law. Ideally they hold reserves of the anchor currency to at least 100 per cent of the domestic currency on issue, and must be ready to exchange the domestic currency to that of the anchor on demand. A traditional currency board is prohibited from acquiring domestic government or private securities, so (unlike central banks) they cannot conduct discretionary monetary policy, nor finance a government's fiscal policy through the purchase of bonds. Similarly, since they cannot take on any liabilities apart from note issue, orthodox currency boards cannot provide lender-of-last-resort facilities, or in other ways support commercial banks. Rather, at their purest, currency boards are essentially passive institutions that issue and redeem the domestic currency in response to movements in anchor currency reserves. Such reserve movements are in turn the simple function of the difference between a country's payments *to* overseas, and its income *from* overseas.

Given the features above, at first glance a currency board looks a most unattractive device. With a currency board, fiscal policy is limited to the amount of funds a government can raise via taxation or bond sales to the *public*, whilst a discretionary monetary policy is more or less completely unavailable. A currency board also imposes upon an economy a potentially in-built deflationary bias by restricting accommodative currency movements for economic expansion, unless this expansion is matched by an improving balance of payments. And, of course, a currency board system does not allow the exchange rate to vary – for policy or any other reasons. For a new country bent on reconstruction or creating a socialist state (as in Burma's case in the postwar era), one might wonder as to its appeal. Such wonderment need not be prolonged, however, for currency boards bring with them certain advantages too:

(1) Because of their passive role regarding monetary policy, currency boards are simple to administer and require a minimum of staff, expertise and other 'overheads'.

(2) By eliminating 'money financing' (government borrowing from the central bank), currency boards prevent the 'over-issue' of the domestic currency and, as such, minimise domestically-fuelled inflation while maximising trust in the currency.

(3) Since they guarantee convertibility of the local currency into its foreign anchor at a fixed rate, currency boards eliminate exchange rate risk for foreign and local investors, and deliver an extra degree of assurance in the credibility of the domestic currency.

(4) By issuing a domestic currency, but at the same time possessing anchor currency denominated reserves, currency boards earn 'seigniorage' revenue for a country, whilst eliminating the risk from the *excessive* pursuit of seigniorage.

(5) In theory, currency boards contain within them an 'automatic' mechanism for eliminating balance of payments disequilibria. If, for instance, there is an excessive outflow of funds from a country, its currency in circulation must contract (as the currency board's reserves decline), pushing down domestic prices and causing imports to fall, and its exports to rise.

(6) Whilst currency boards limit the ability of governments to 'create' money by simply borrowing from a central bank, they do not preclude the creation of *deposit money* by commercial banks. That is, currency boards limit the creation of *currency* on issue, but not explicitly the other forms of 'money' that, traditionally, economists have defined under such labels as 'M1' (currency plus current deposits in banks), 'M2' (M1 plus less-liquid deposits), and so on. Such money is a function of the familiar money-creation process through the deposit/lending dynamic described in Chapter 2, and its creation is unaffected by changes in currency board reserves except where commercial banks are at their own reserves/lending limits (which is unusual). Thus, there was invariably an 'elastic' margin in the broad definitions of the money supply in currency board countries – a margin that does not impose a monetary constraint upon the development and growth of the private sector.[2]

None of the above were irrelevant to the circumstances Burma found itself in during the early postwar years. The emerging victim of excessive currency issues during the war that had destroyed any semblance of monetary order, short of expertise and the other infrastructure required for more policy-active institutions, and with a general level of profound mistrust in money of all forms, Burma in 1947 was ripe for the benefits promised by a currency board. Longer term the *dis*advantages of a currency board arrangement might have become apparent. In 1947, however, the BCB was the right instrument at the right time.

Planning the Currency Board

The idea that Burma should have a currency board after the war, rather than a note-issuing central bank, was a decision made before the Second World War had ended. In February 1944, well before Burma had been retaken from the Japanese (and even before such an outcome was likely), Sir Otto Niemeyer, the famed Bank of England adviser who had investigated India's currency arrangements in the 1930s, wrote to the then 'Financial Adviser' to the colonial government of Burma, W.A. Iliffe, that whilst he believed there was no reason why Burma could not have its own currency after the war, 'the idea of a Central Bank of Burma was impracticable because Burma had not a sufficiently broad financial base to support a reserve bank'.[3] Niemeyer's counsel was consistent with a general scheme of advice then emerging from the Burmese (colonial) government in exile in Simla, increasingly anxious to devise mechanisms by which prewar commercial certainties in Burma (such as a trusted, stable currency), could be quickly restored. In any case, the Reserve Bank of India had indicated before the end of the Japanese occupation that they were unwilling to resume their functions as the bank of issue in Burma.[4]

Of course, what was also inescapable in all of this, though we have no direct evidence to the effect that the BCB was *specifically* seen in this light, was that a currency board arrangement was also highly consistent with Britain's emerging plans for Burma *politically* after the war. If 1944 was the year that Niemeyer and his colleagues in the British Treasury started to contemplate Burma's postwar monetary arrangements, it was also the year that the British government more broadly began to plan Burma's postwar political arrangements. As it turned out, these arrangements (informally expressed in a 'blueprint' issued by Britain's Conservative Party in 1944, and officially in a White Paper released in 1945), were temporarily to offer Burma a measure of sovereignty considerably less than that which had been offered even before the war (Thant Myint-U 2006: 241–242). The details and controversies need not detain us unduly here. Suffice to say, however, that the upshot of these documents was that Burma's 1937 Constitution would not come into force until 1948 – up until which time the country would be ruled by the Governor and his council. This period of direct rule was meant to be one in which Burma's productive capacities were restored, critical infrastructure was rebuilt and the conditions made ripe for the return and continued participation in the economic life of Burma of British capital. A currency board, located in London and by its very nature aimed at protecting the value of financial claims and ensuring convertibility, was an ideal institution to accompany these ends.

In May 1946 the Governor's Executive Council (five of whose members were Burmese, though none were associated with the dominant independence party, the 'Anti Fascist Peoples' Freedom League' [AFPFL] headed by Aung San) took the formal decision to establish the BCB.[5] A series of meetings in order to establish the BCB quickly followed between the Bank of England (BoE) and various colonial government officials. These meetings, and the 'drafting committee' that derived from them, were dominated, however, by Raymond Kershaw, the BoE's chief representative, who urged the creation of an institution that would resemble as much as possible the West African Currency Board – the model upon which almost all of the postwar colonial currency boards were fashioned. Very much the BoE's expert in the field of currency boards, Kershaw (a former Australian Rhodes Scholar) had been especially recruited as early as 1929 by the BoE's Governor, Montagu Norman, and given the 'new and formidable task' of equipping 'the emergent Commonwealth with the necessary financial machinery' it would need in the post-gold standard world (Boyle 1967: 284).

The most important policy question considered during the meetings of the drafting committee to establish the BCB concerned the question of reserves coverage. Under an orthodox currency board arrangement there was a simple answer to this (as noted above): reserves of the anchor currency (sterling, of course) had to be at *least* sufficient to cover 100 per cent of the domestic currency on issue. However, Burma's circumstances brought complications, primarily two; (1) what to do about the notes issued before the war which had escaped destruction during the conflict, and which were still circulating, and (2) what to do about the notes subsequently issued by the British Military Administration (BMA) during its tenure (which at the time of the BCB meetings had only just concluded)? Since these currencies, unlike the Japanese wartime scrip, were liabilities of the British crown there could be no question of outright demonetisation. And yet, should reserve coverage for such currencies be the responsibility of the proposed BCB, which might under the best of circumstances struggle to have sufficient reserves?

For Kershaw there was only one solution to the problem. Burma's currency board arrangements would have to depart from orthodoxy and contain within them a fiduciary (that is, 'unbacked') element. This element, which Kershaw labelled 'Y', he deemed as particularly necessary with respect to the prewar currency issues (known as 'Old Burma Notes'), the precise amount of which were extant was unknown. Curiously, however, Kershaw also initially called for an additional fiduciary element (which he referred to as 'X'), which would have allowed the BCB to extend currency to the commercial banks according to seasonal demands. He stipulated, however, that his proposed X element be both of a modest dimension, be capped at a fixed amount, and could in no way be used to finance the expenditure of the government. Providing 'backing' to any X issue would be ad-hoc government securities, created for this express purpose. The fiduciary element Y, on the other hand, was to be gradually whittled down under Kershaw's schema – using any sterling profits made by the BCB to 'buy it back' over time.[6]

Kershaw's 'X element' turned out to be a step too far from orthodoxy for the other members of the BCB's drafting committee. The British Treasury representative on the committee, Norman Young, urged a 'wait and see' approach on the issue of reserves since the question would 'depend on the fiduciary policy adopted for the whole sterling area'.[7] In the end, the Committee apparently decided to leave this clause of the Draft Bill (clause 29[2]) blank. As events would demonstrate (below), various agreements were at this precise moment being reached in confidence between the British Government and the likely leaders of the newly independent government of Burma that would allow for a fiduciary element with respect to 'old Burma notes', and *British* backing for the BMA issues.

A great deal of the BCB's drafting committee was spent in considering the composition of the board of the new institution. Kershaw regarded the creation of a responsible board of directors for the BCB as critical. Insisting that it be dominated by British officials lest it be 'captured' by local elites, but allowing for Burmese representation nonetheless, he proposed the BCB Board consist of:

(a) a Chairman;

(b) a representative of the Burma Office;

(c) a representative of the Bank of England;

(d) the Financial Adviser to the Government of Burma;

(e) two Burmese nationals;

(f) a representative of the British Treasury as an observer.[8]

Kershaw's proposed Board was a microcosm of the assumptions of the British official position on Burma generally which, under the so-called 'White Paper' on Burma issued on 17 May 1945, originally held back restoration of Burma's pre-war constitution until December 1948, and more or less left the Governor and his Executive Council in charge. Even limited to two individuals, Kershaw believed that the appointment of the Burmese nationals (though 'essential') 'presented some difficulty'. There were, he wrote, 'no persons of sufficient standing' in Britain [sic] and, as such, it would be necessary to send from Burma 'suitable persons with financial experience to act as the Burmese members'.[9] Later this aspect was solved by appointing Burma's London Embassy staff (led by the Ambassador) 'ex-officio'.

As can be seen from the above, there seems never to have been any question that the BCB be physically located anywhere but in London. Precisely where in London, however, generated a lot of discussion. One school of thought proposed that it should be based within the Bank of England itself – 'this might appeal to Burma's prestige and sentiments'.[10] Another, based upon the same reasoning of appealing to Burmese sentiment thought the reverse – that the BCB should be housed in premises of its own, and 'would thus appear to be running independently and unconnected in any way with His Majesty's Government'.[11] In the end an independent location was chosen on Chelsea's King's Road for the Head Office of the BCB. A 'representative office' was subsequently established in Rangoon. A fascinating 'might have been' that came in the deliberations of the drafting committee was Kershaw's proposal that the new currency to be issued by the BCB be called by the old Burmese name of '*kyat*' rather than rupee. Anticipating controversy, however, Kershaw withdrew the suggestion, minuting that he was 'not certain that this was acceptable'.[12]

The formal drafting of the law establishing the BCB commenced in August 1946. Kershaw was the principal author, but he was greatly aided in the process by U Tin Tut. The 'brightest Burmese official of his generation', U Tin Tut had been Secretary of Finance in 1939, had accompanied Prime Minister U Saw to London in 1942, but is perhaps most revered in Burma today as the principal author of independent Burma's first constitution (Thant Myint-U 2006: 252).[13] At the time of his work on the BCB, U Tin Tut was a member of the Burma Executive Council. A trusted adviser of Burma's revered independence hero, Aung San (though he was not a member of the AFPFL), U Tin Tut was Minister of Foreign Affairs and finally Inspector General of the Armed Forces in U Nu's first cabinet. U Tin Tut was assassinated in mysterious circumstances in 1948 (Mya Maung 1991: 73).

The Currency Board is Established

The BCB formally came into operation on 1 April 1947, just days before the elections that established the AFPFL's dominance of Burma's Executive Council, but still eight months before Burma's formal independence. Established under the *Currency and Coinage Act*, 1946 (*Burma Act* XLV of the British Parliament), its provisions more or less reflected the deliberations of the drafting committee. Its main features included:

(1) Currency – Under Section 10 of the Currency and Coinage Act (hereafter the 'Act') the Burmese rupee was created as the currency of Burma. The rupee was divided into 16 annas and was fixed against sterling at the traditional rate of 'one shilling and sixpence' (1s. 6d.). The chance to change the name of the currency to the kyat, and to decimalise it, was not taken up.

(2) The notes themselves came in denominations of 1, 5, 10 and 100 rupees and were designed 'by four eminent Burmese artists'. The notes featured the traditional Burmese 'chinthe' on one side and a peacock (as 'watermark') on the other. The notes bore the signature of the chairman of the BCB. Inscriptions on the front of the notes were entirely in Burmese, although the back of the notes bore the imprint 'Government of the Union of Burma' in English. Delays in producing the notes at the De la Rue works (in London) meant that the initial circulation of BCB notes was in fact Indian notes overprinted with the words 'Burma Currency Board, Legal Tender in Burma Only' (Burma Currency Board [BCB] 1948). Initially no coin was produced by the BCB, and Indian coins continued to circulate. In 1949, however, the order was placed at the Royal Mint in London for Burmese coin in one-half and one-quarter rupees, and in 2, 1 and one-half annas. The coins featured a chinthe (BCB 1949)[14]

(3) Conversion of Burmese rupees into sterling was guaranteed (under Section 15 of the Act) at the settled exchange rate in London or at the BCB's office in Rangoon.

(4) Reserves coverage – Under Section 25 (2) of the Act a fiduciary issue of 10 'crores' (100 million) Burmese rupees, backed only by securities

issued by the government of Burma, was allowed. This issue (equivalent to Kershaw's 'Y' element) was both limited in amount and purpose: specifically created to cover the Currency Board's liability to redeem 'outstanding issues of Old Burma and B.M.A Notes'. The precise amount of the former in circulation was unknown at the time (as shall be revealed below, 'Old Burma Notes' were redeemed in far larger quantities than guessed at in 1947).

(5) Beyond this Rs 100 million, the remaining issue had to be covered by sterling or sterling securities.[15] To bring this about the British government transferred sterling assets of £31.3 million and undertook 'to provide (...) such further sums as may be necessary to bring up the sterling held by the Board to the amount required to cover in full all notes in excess of 10 crores issued before 1st April 1950'. In its first annual report the BCB estimated that the fiduciary component would not exceed 20 per cent of the note issue – thus implying minimum sterling cover for the Burmese rupee of 80 per cent (BCB 1948).

(6) Hidden from contemporary external observers with regard to the 'coverage question' were the details of a 'confidential annexe' to the 1947 Financial Agreement between the British government and the government of Burma (the Act settling the financial arrangements between the departing British and the incoming Burmese government). Under this annexe, which was kept from all except the inner circles of both governments, the British 'agreed to provide full backing for new Burmese rupee notes issued against BMA currency handed in to the Currency Board before 1 April 1950, in excess of [the] fiduciary issue of 10 crores of rupees'. In other words, all BMA notes were covered by sterling reserves. The final redemption date was subsequently postponed by successive stages to 1 April 1952, and the final British liability agreed at £3.3 million.[16]

(7) The governing Board of the BCB was appointed by the Governor of Burma and consisted of five appointees. Consistent with Kershaw's proposal, two positions were reserved for 'persons born and domiciled within the dominions of His Majesty in Burma, of parents habitually resident in Burma, and not established there for temporary purposes only'.[17] The wording was to ensure non-European representation, but avoided the use of divisive racial categories. This issue caused the drafters of the Act some angst – Kershaw minuting at one point as to the problems

of using the label 'Burman' and favouring 'Burman native' as the 'least worst alternative'.[18]

(8) The first governing board comprised:

Sir Richard Hopkins (Chairman)
U Kaung (Burmese representative)
Saw Htin Lin Mya (Burmese representative)
W. Johnston (representative of the Secretary of State for Burma)
R.N. Kershaw (Bank of England).

Sir Sydney Turner, a former Accountant General of the India Office, was the Secretary of the BCB. U San Lin, a member of the Burma Civil Service since 1938 who had accompanied the Burmese government into exile in Simla during the war years, headed the BCB in Rangoon as its 'Currency Officer'. San Lin was to be a dominant figure in independent Burma's early monetary history. Simultaneously with his role at the BCB he was also (the first) General Manager of the Union Bank of Burma, a position he would hold until 1963. At the time of his appointment to both the BCB and the Union Bank, San Lin had just returned from training stints at both the BoE and the Reserve Bank of India.[19] The BoE performed the role of bankers to the Board (BCB 1948).

Performance of the Currency Board

The period of the currency board's tenure, 1947–1952, was, as will be examined further in subsequent chapters, one of great turmoil and disorder. Yet, as we shall see, even one of the BCB's harshest critics, Tun Wai (1962: 221–222), conceded that in the face of these convulsions the BCB presided over a period of extraordinary 'monetary stability'. Table 6.1 below paints the picture:

Table 6.1 Selected Monetary Indicators, 1948–1952 (Rs millions)*

Year*	International reserves	Government budget surplus/ (Deficit)	State board deposits with UBB	Money (M1)	Money + quasi-money (M2)
1948	358	(315)	30	499	526
1949	505	82	93	599	631
1950	556	67	200	551	589
1951	748	217	328	606	651
1952	941	173	495	599	641

* As at 30 September. Source: IMF (1966).

As can be seen from the data above, steady progress was the overriding narrative in the broad monetary sphere in Burma under the BCB. International reserves increased progressively, a function of the growing demand and high prices for paddy and other commodities. This same phenomenon (the result of the postwar commodities boom and the 'spike' in demand during the Korean war) was responsible both for the extraordinary growth in the earnings of Burma's state export boards (more on which in Chapter 7) and – via them – the strong surpluses recorded by the government. Of course, this latter phenomenon is critical to any assessment of the BCB. As shall be examined shortly, a principal criticism of the BCB was that its rigid reserve requirements would unnecessarily inhibit Burma's economic development by starving the state of resources. Yet, as is readily apparent, the state in Burma was *not* short of financial resources during the tenure of the BCB. It is true that the ambitious 'Two-Year Plan for the Economic Development of Burma', the seminal statement of Burma's economic aspirations announced at the time of Burma's independence, failed in implementation (also more on which in the next chapter). This failure, however, was not due to the lack of financial resources allowed to the state by the BCB, but simply to the fact that so much of the plan could *not* be implemented (as the government itself later admitted) in the face of the insurrections and disorder of these years (GoB 1961b: 1). During the BCB years a lack of 'money' was the least of the problems facing Burma's government.

One disappointing aspect of Burma's financial development during the BCB years, however, was the low level of deposit money creation by Burma's commercial banks. The problems these banks faced in postwar Burma will be discussed in later chapters, but the macroeconomic consequences of their inert condition is readily apparent in Table 6.1 above. It can be seen from the data, for instance, that whilst the growth of international reserves during the BCB years was strong, the creation of money both narrowly (M1) and more broadly defined (M2), grew more slowly and irregularly. Much of this can be explained by the actions of the state: the budget surpluses of 1948 to 1952 drew currency from circulation (as revenues exceeded spending), but the sluggishness of M1 and M2 growth was also a function of the failure of the banking system to create deposit money. Of course, the reason for this was hardly a mystery, and the failure of banks to lend in this period was more or less due to the same unsettled political circumstances that curtailed government spending. Nevertheless, the idea that banks themselves created financial resources in excess of the currency issued by a currency board (and therefore an argument that currency boards are not as limiting as sometimes supposed), was not particularly relevant in the case of Burma.

BMA and 'Old Burma' Note Redemption

If column inches in its annual reports are any guide, the BCB devoted almost as much time and effort into redeeming (and removing from circulation) the BMA and 'Old Burma' Notes during its existence, as it did with issuing its own currency. As noted above, the BCB's fiduciary issue of Rs 100 million was meant to account both for the BMA notes in circulation, as well as the Old Burma Notes. Of course, this figure was always something of an ambit, based on the following estimates of the distribution of *all* notes circulating in Burma (as presented in the first of the BCB Annual Reports [BCB 1948]):

	Rs
BMA Notes:	88,804,360
Old Burma Notes:	9,128,786
BCB Notes:	237,633,698
Total:	335,566,844

Redeeming the BMA notes did not pose any great difficulty. They were a known quantity and they were not only 'covered' by the fiduciary issue, but also by the 'confidential annexe' arrangements noted above. The 'Old Burma Notes', on the other hand, proved a more intractable problem. The original BCB estimate above, of Rs 9.1 million, proved far short of the mark, and in each and every year of the BCB's Annual Reports there were repeated attempts to explain dramatic variations in the notes that actually appeared for redemption. In 1950 the Burmese government even announced that henceforth they would 'demonetise' all remaining old notes. The government ultimately backed down from this threat in the face of public opposition, and that of the Chairman of the BCB, Sydney Turner, who minuted on 5 April 1950 that he thought there was 'a real danger of discrediting the whole of the currency if the notification is left in the form proposed by the Minister of Finance'.[20] A compromise was eventually reached in which redemptions could continue, provided that the bona fides of the people holding notes was established, and the reasons why they still held them.[21] In the end, the total number of 'Old Burma Notes' redeemed was Rs 38,345,750 – over 420 per cent above the 1948 estimates.[22] Of course, one implication of this was that the BCB's truly held reserves against the currencies on issue was rather less than appeared at the time.

One final consideration that must be addressed in this outline of the performance of the BCB is to note its profitability. Put simply, and with the exception of its final year when the costs of winding-up were booked, the BCB was an enormously profitable institution for the Burmese government, and a valuable 'earner' of foreign currency. Such profits derived from the fact that the reserves held by the BCB, and backing the note issue, were not primarily in the form of sterling 'notes and coin', but (as per standard currency board practice) government securities denominated in sterling. That this could be allowed was based on the simple idea that it was unlikely that little more than a small proportion of the holders of Burmese rupees would ever be seeking to exchange them for sterling 'cash' at any point in time (experience told that no more than a third of the backing needed to be in the form of currency notes) (Drake 2004: 154). Of course in theory such securities, as the liabilities of a sovereign state in the same way currency is, are also no more risky than currency, but bring with them the substantial benefit that they yield interest returns (seigniorage). In the case of the BCB the securities backing its rupee issues were British government treasury and 'war' bonds, but technically they could have included similar securities issued by a number of other 'sterling countries' such as Canada or Australia. Finally, in addition to its seigniorage earnings, the BCB generated revenue via the commissions it charged for currency exchange transactions.

Against the seigniorage and other earnings of the BCB were its expenses – administration, the purchase of paper and coin metals, printing and stamping costs, distribution and redemption costs, and so on. In the case of Burma such expenses were (the special circumstances of 1952 excepted) well short of the revenues it earned, yielding the following profits (in sterling) for each year of its tenure:

Currency Board Profits (£ sterling) [23]

1948	99,421
1949	42,298
1950	146,105
1951	67,874
1952	-40,922

Objections to the Currency Board

The relatively strong performance of the BCB in difficult times did not make it immune from criticism in Burma. Much of this, not surprisingly (and perhaps not unreasonably), had a nationalist flavour to it and which was as exercised about the BCB's location and the composition of its governing board as it was about monetary policy. Indeed, pressures to relocate the BCB to Rangoon were more or less present from the start.[24] As early as 1948, the (now independent) Burmese government considered a draft Bill which would have transferred control of monetary affairs in Burma not only away from London, but away from the BCB completely and in favour of (a new) Union Bank of Burma. Under the Bill, the Union Bank would take responsibility for the note issue, but in a nod to policy concerns (more on which below), there was proposed a sterling backing of just 60 per cent. The Bill was presented in a hurry for rapid implementation, authorising the Union Bank in Rangoon to take over the note issue by 1 November 1948. After successive postponements of the Bill, however, it was eventually decided to abandon the idea until a full scale reform of the *Union Bank of Burma Act* could be put through giving it full central bank powers.[25] Referring to the issue in his budget speech in 1950, the Finance Minister, U Tin, admitted defeat for the moment, but made clear where matters were heading;

> ...owing to continuance of unsettled conditions the Government is still unable to implement its decision to transfer the seat of the Currency Board from London to Rangoon. Besides, it will take some time for the draft of the necessary legislation and detailed arrangements for the making over of sterling backing for the currency from the Burma Currency Board, London, to be finalised. It is the intention of Government, however, to affect the transfer as soon as it is opportune'.[26]

However, it should be noted that eliminating the BCB and transferring control to Rangoon was not universally accepted. Around the time the draft relocation Bills were mooted, for instance, the *New Times of Burma* opined in an editorial that basing the BCB in London 'might be objectionable on sentimental grounds', but it gave Burma 'the solid advantage of the services of experts at very little cost'.[27]

Substantive *policy* objections to the BCB were voiced by Tun Wai (1953 and 1962), the chronicler of Burma's monetary affairs who, at the time of the BCB's operations, was a graduate student in Rangoon (but of Yale

University), and a keen observer of and commentator on government policy. Tun Wai had a number of objections to the BCB, most centering around the 'deflationary bias' of currency boards noted above. In Tun Wai's own phrase (1962: 148), 'a country could not expand money supply to increase output to pre-war levels, without putting aside hard-earned export proceeds to increase foreign reserves'. Not accumulating reserves condemned a country to the dilemmas posited by the famous 'quantity theory of money', which in its essence can be expressed in the equation familiar to economics students the world over, $MV = PT$; where M is the volume of the money supply, V is its 'velocity of circulation' (mostly assumed to be a constant and dependent on certain institutional features of a country), P is an index of prices in the economy, and T denotes real national output. From the equation it follows that if M is fixed (as would be the case under a currency board in the absence of reserves accumulation), and with V assumed to be constant, any growth in national output T must be accompanied by falling prices, P. The trouble was, according to Tun Wai (1953: 202), that prices (and wages) were 'sticky' in Burma. End result – simply that growth in national output *(T)* would not take place so long as there was no accumulation of reserves via a balance of payments surplus. If there was no surplus in a country's international accounts, there would be no economic growth or development.

Tun Wai's criticism of the BCB in this context, rendered here in an abstract way, but faithful to the abstract reasoning in the works (1953 and 1962) cited, contains a kernel of truth, but it falls down somewhat with regard to the specific circumstances of Burma during the BCB's tenure:

(1) As can be seen in Table 6.1 (p. 147), Burma *was* accumulating foreign reserves – and at a rather rapid rate. Stimulated by the surge in demand for commodities brought about by the Korean War, in the four years of the BCB's operations Burma's external reserves grew by 41 per cent (1948–49), 10 per cent (1949–50), 35 per cent (1950–51) and 26 per cent (1951–52). Even in its year of smallest reserves accumulation (1949–50), Burma was earning sufficient external reserves to meet the monetary needs of even the wildest estimates of its likely economic growth. Simply, the BCB did not impose a deflationary bias on Burma's economy.

(2) Tun Wai ignored that component of the money supply that is not so dependent on the accumulation of anchor-currency reserves – that is, the deposit money created by the commercial banks. Of course, to some extent here the *reality* of Burma's specific circumstances can

be employed in Tun Wai's defence – after all, we have already noted the desultory creation of money by the banks throughout the period of the BCB. Nevertheless, there is a further problem in ignoring the commercial banks in Burma in this context – to wit, at this stage most of Burma's commercial banks were branches of foreign banks with access to the resources of their parent banks offshore. In the past such banks were not inhibited in their financing by Burma's domestic monetary circumstances, but to circumstances relating to their own strategies and commercial decisions. In other words, should there have been profitable financing opportunities in Burma there seems no reason to believe these would have gone unfunded. Of course (and as noted in earlier chapters), foreign banks were under pressure to scale down their activities in Burma, but that itself is a story that is hardly consistent with the idea that Burma in this period was struggling under the lack of availability of funds.

(3) As noted by Drake (2004: 128), there was no reason at this time to assume that the velocity of circulation was, as implicit in Tun Wai's analysis, a constant. The spread and development of banking had led to rapid increases in currency note circulation throughout the Asia-Pacific in this period, and there is little reason to suppose, given the arrival of new indigenous banks and with more (government-owned) on the way, that this same phenomenon would not take place in Burma. A technical point perhaps, but as per the simple equation underlying this particular critique of currency board arrangements, one with far-reaching consequences.

(4) There were both implicit and explicit assumptions in Tun Wai's critique of the BCB that the reserves it employed (which earned profits, as noted) could have generated higher returns if used otherwise. According to Tun Wai (1962: 148), such reserves could have been used 'for imports to reconstruct the country after the war', and more generally to support the 'economic policy of establishing a socialistic economy through the nationalization of important sectors'. Again, Tun Wai's point here is fine in the abstract – the BCB could have been an impediment to Burma's acquisition of imports, and it could have constrained the government's nationalisation plans. Once again, however, the point must be made that this was not what actually took place in Burma under the BCB. The country's foreign exchange reserves were plentiful and growing, and

the government was not constrained by the BCB in either its foreign or domestic spending. Curiously, Tun Wai (elsewhere a great critic of what he saw as the waste and mismanagement associated with the spending of Burmese governments of this era), acknowledged the issue in the same (1962) edition of his book when discussing the failure of the government's early economic plans, despite the funds at its command:

> The windfall profits accruing to the government could not be spent quickly and usefully as there was no proper plan. The so-called two year development plan adopted in 1948 was merely a list of desired projects with no feasibility or technical studies. Therefore when the funds were set aside in the budgets for these projects, it was inevitable that they could not be spent (Tun Wai 1962: 222).

The End of the BCB

By 1952 the internal political situation in Burma had stabilised to an extent that the long-awaited plans for postwar reconstruction, and for the creation of a socialist state, could at last be implemented. These plans, culminating in the *Pyidawtha* Plan and its ambitions to double Burma's GDP between 1950 and 1960, sat rather oddly with the humble BCB. Its days were numbered.

The end of the BCB came in stages across 1952. In March of that year Burma's parliament passed an Act transferring to the Union Bank of Burma all the functions of the BCB, as well as its assets and liabilities. The Act came into force from 1 July 1952, although a section of the BCB's authorising legislation, the *Currency and Coinage Act* 1946, remained in force to allow the completion of one final annual report, and to allow an orderly wind-up (BCB 1952). On 31 December 1952, the BCB officially ceased to exist.[28]

MONEYLENDER AND USURY ACTS OF THE INTERREGNUM

An interesting series of early legislative developments in postwar banking arrangements in Burma was a rush of laws 'reintroduced' by the newly-returned colonial government from Simla, concerned, primarily, with various reform measures for agricultural finance that had been left in abeyance because of the Japanese invasion. Uppermost in this respect was *The Money Lenders Act*, 1945 (*Burma Act XXVII*, 1945), which was based on the draft *Usurious Loans Act* recommended in Part Four of the Land and Agriculture Committee's Report of 1938 (GoB 1938, noted in Chapter 3). This Act, fully incorporated into the law of independent Burma under the

Union of Burma (Adaptation of Laws) Order, 1948, was most far-reaching in its *formal* restrictions upon money lenders. Its prescriptions included:

(1) The compulsory registration of all moneylenders.

(2) The requirement that interest rates charged by moneylenders could not exceed 12 per cent per annum on secured loans, and 18 per cent per annum in the case of unsecured loans.

(3) The prohibition of 'compound interest', and the rendering void of any loan that specified it.

(4) The requirement that total interest payments on any loan could not, in aggregate across the life of the loan, exceed 100 per cent of the original principal of that loan.

(5) The outlawing of any attempt to 'molest' or intimidate a debtor for the purposes of collecting a loan. Breaches of this, and the other requirements of the Act could see a moneylender de-registered, fined and even jailed (GuB 1955b: 304–312).

Of course, the tone of the *Money Lenders Act* was redolent with the passions and crises of when it was drafted in the late 1930s. There were some unusual aspects to it, however, that go rather deeper than even the traumatic events of that era. The injunction upon total interest exceeding the original principal, for instance, and the related prohibition against compound interest, had contemporary relevance but also had deeper roots in far older cultural rules and norms. In the Burmese Kingdom of Pagan a well-known maxim rendered in English as 'the tree should not outgrow its roots' implied the same limitation of interest relative to principal.[29] Nevertheless, the inclusion of the injunction by the *British* authorities seems more likely to have derived from a similar *Hindu* concept of *'Damdupat'* – cited in the *Punjab Relief of Indebtedness Act* 1934, which, in turn, was something of a model for the members of Burma's Land and Agriculture Committee of 1938 .[30] Of course, this injunction was liable to unintended effects, since it implicitly outlawed many types of long-term loans. As always, however, there were (and are) ways around limits upon interest – in this case a simple expedient (widely practised wherever *Damdupat* has applied) of renegotiating a loan at regular intervals into 'fresh loans' that capitalise past interest within the principal.

Other laws were also introduced by the returned government with a similar objective of relieving the pressure on indebted cultivators. The *Accrual of Interest (War-Time Adjustment) Act* and the *Agricultural Debts Moratorium Act*, both enacted in 1947 by Burma's Governor, Hubert Rance, sought to dramatically scale back debts and interest accumulated during the war.[31] Meanwhile the *Burma Agriculturalists' Debt Relief Act* of the same year (which was based on its Punjab namesake, above) established the machinery for the compulsory renegotiation of loans exceeding Rs 10,000 – and incorporated a proviso that loans upon which interest of 100 per cent of principal had already been paid were automatically discharged (GuB 1955b: 315–323).

As it turned out, however, few of the laws above had much of an impact 'on the ground' during the 'interregnum' colonial government, which was almost devoid of any capacity to enforce them. Thant Myint-U (2006: 250) paints the context in which the returned colonial government functioned during its short tenure:

> ...political instability, the protests and strikes, the stillborn reconstruction, and the absence of any real law and order meant the country was a mess. Banditry was a problem almost everywhere in a country awash with guns and martial spirit and with a standard of living far below that of the 1920s. Rice was in short supply, with government price ceilings and diversion of part of the crop to famine-stricken India. The Irrawaddy Flotilla Company, the lifeline of many backwater towns, was forced to discontinue service in the delta because of fears over security. Armed guards had to be assigned to all trains, buses and boats (...) revolution was imminent.

THE UNION BANK OF BURMA, MARK I

The first Union Bank of Burma (UBB) was established on 1 October 1947 under the *Union Bank of Burma Act, 1947*. It was, of course, not a 'note-issuing' central bank, the currency issuing role being undertaken by the BCB. The UBB acted as the agency for the BCB in the distribution of notes, however, and handled the foreign exchange activities of the government beyond those pertaining to the sterling backing of the currency. The UBB acted as the government's banker, and could lend to the government, albeit with the significant proviso that such advances had to be short term, and repayable within 90 days. The UBB was also banker to the many government boards and corporations, as well as traditional government departments. It had authorised capital of Rs 40 million. The UBB had very limited powers over the commercial banks. It had no authority to require the banks to hold reserves with it, nor did it have power over the interest rates they could charge. In practice, however, many of the commercial banks *did* hold substantial deposits with it. The UBB's articles were based upon those of the Reserve Bank of India Act (1934), the broad features of which we examined in Chapter 4. The UBB differed from the Reserve Bank of India in important respects, however, including the term limits on its lending to government, its lack of enforcement powers over the private banks, and the fact that it was completely government-owned.[32]

The first General Manager of the UBB was San Lin who, as noted above, was also the BCB's chief officer in Rangoon. J.C. Reid of the Bank of England was appointed Chief Accountant, with Tin Tun as his deputy. At the opening ceremony of the UBB's head office in Rangoon (in February 1948) the Finance Minister, U Tin, announced that he 'regretted' that the Bank of England had been 'unable to spare us an officer for the post of General Manager'. This less-than supportive remark would not necessarily have perturbed San Lin, who told Raymond Kershaw of his 'immense relief' at the arrival of Reid since, he admitted, he was 'completely ignorant about central banking matters'.[33] In the same speech U Tin explained that Burma's search for 'foreign talent' was so as to ensure the country should 'not suffer from a lack of technical experience', and that eventually 'local talent' would be 'trained up'.[34]

During the first year of its existence it was Reid who most authoritatively put his stamp on the UBB. With San Lin, he wrote the internal rules and regulations governing the Bank (once again using the Reserve Bank of India as the template), and used it as the vehicle for establishing embryonic bond and money markets in Rangoon. The latter was comprised mostly of government-issued treasury bills.[35] Reid also used the UBB as the foundation for rebuilding the remittance system across Burma which, outside of the capital, was based on treasury offices in 180 townships linked by telegraph.[36]

Reid's experiences at the UBB would, in the end, prove disheartening, however, and he emerged from his time at the Bank a severe critic of independent Burma's early governments. His principal villain was the Ministry of Finance which, he wrote (in a lengthy memorandum drafted soon after his departure from the UBB), 'was without a single official with any experience of finance or monetary management'.[37] He referred to the first Finance Minister, the aforementioned U Tin, as 'an ex-journalist with no experience of finance' who, along with his Ministry, was also hostile to 'independent thought and criticism'.[38] Such thought and criticism was taken by Reid to be his own mandate, but it isolated him as a foreign 'expert' at the centre of an essential antagonism as 'the champion of the Union Bank and the Government's unwelcome guest'. The question of foreign involvement in Burma's financial system was more sensitive generally, of course, and Reid detected what he believed was a certain xenophobia within the Ministry of Finance and elsewhere. Reid's denunciation of this perceived tendency was bitter, describing a situation in which the UBB was

> ...subordinated to a Ministry [which was] knee-deep in prejudice against the moneyed foreigners and their banks...on whose assistance the economic progress of Burma depends, and which tended to resent the influence of the bank as a matter of prestige or professional jealously; to a Government administratively as well as financially bankrupt.[39]

Beyond governance and management issues, Reid's substantive policy complaints regarding the Ministry of Finance centred on what he regarded as its failure to coordinate the spending of other ministries which, together with the government's general profligacy, 'provided the greatest threat to the bank's stability'. Other specific issues also earned his attention and ire, including the widespread evasion of Burma's exchange control laws by 'an inefficient and corrupt import licensing authority'. This activity, coupled with a lack of cooperation from other government departments and the inexperience of its own staff made 'the UBB's exchange control responsibilities difficult' according to Reid.[40] A related affront, which Reid believed exemplified the lack of government support for the UBB, was the government's preference to keep its own foreign exchange earnings with Lloyds Bank rather than the UBB. Reid's one consolation amongst all of this was the satisfaction that, in the face of all of this, the UBB had 'stayed afloat'.[41]

In December 1948 Reid left the UBB and Burma, no longer willing, he said, 'to risk the good name of the Bank of England or my own reputation in appearing to play an active part in Burma's financial deterioration'.[42] Reid was replaced at the UBB by another foreigner, Paul Fitchen, who, prior to his appointment, had been the manager of the Cash Department at the Federal Reserve Bank of New York.[43] The appointment was made at the behest of the Burmese government, but Fitchen was made available to the UBB under the technical assistance program of the 'Economic Cooperation

Agreement' between Burma and the United States. Fitchen's appointment caused a degree of consternation amongst officials in the United Kingdom, with Sir George Bolton of the Foreign Office complaining that this was 'yet another case of the Americans muscling in on Burma'.[44] Some consolation, however, was taken from the fact that Fitchen was at least a central banker. Fitchen paid a visit to the Bank of England for 'advice and consultation' prior to taking up the appointment, in the light of which he was approvingly assessed as 'tough', 'no nonsense', 'realistic and (...) ideal for Burma'.[45]

Notwithstanding its many problems (so unsparingly set out by Reid), the first manifestation of the UBB had a number of virtues, not the least of which was its fearlessness in criticising government policy in its annual reports. In the first of these (1948, admittedly largely authored by Reid but published by the government without censorship), it was scathing regarding the difficulties created by various laws passed by the parliament. Highlighted was the *Transfer of Immoveable Property Act* (more on which in the next Chapter), which disallowed foreign lenders from taking land as collateral. According to the UBB report, this caused 'discouragement and uncertainty in the field of commerce' and, by inhibiting bank lending against property, had kept 'three to four crores of rupees in idleness'. Likewise the government's broad approach to the nationalisation of key sectors of the economy came in for criticism. This policy, the UBB argued, had begun too early, 'before the country's economic structure was completely repaired', resulting in losses and stretching the government's 'limited financial resources'. The UBB concluded its first annual report with a call for nothing less than a complete rethink of government policy:

> The time has come for a re-orientation of economic policy because of the extremely limited monetary resources of the country and insufficiency of technical ability, with a view to the better interests of the nation (UBB 1948).

THE UNION BANK OF BURMA, MARK II

The UBB as a 'true' central bank was established on 1 July 1952 under the *Union Bank of Burma Act* (1952), which conferred upon it all the 'powers and duties appropriate to a central bank with a view to strengthening the monetary and banking system of the Union of Burma and stimulating the sound growth of indigenous banking'. The same Act simultaneously disbanded the BCB, repealed the 1947 UBB Act and introduced a decimal currency system for Burma. Accompanying the UBB's broad new powers were equally broad responsibilities, which Section 4 of the Act established as:

(a) monetary stability in the Union of Burma;

(b) stability of the currency in relation to foreign currencies;

(c) development of the productive resources of the country and a rising level of real income.

To a modern observer trained to see the fight against inflation as the sole task of a central bank, the objectives as set out in the UBB Act appear extraordinarily broad. Such objectives were not unusual at the time, however, especially not for the 'new' central banks rapidly appearing across the de-colonising world. But nor were they uncommon amongst the central banks of the 'developed' world in this era, many of which were incorporating the ideas of the Keynesian 'revolution' in economic thinking. Indeed, counting amongst the latter was the Bank of England itself which was at the same time going through the throes (unthinkable just a few years earlier) of nationalisation. Of course, for the industrially advanced countries these broader central bank objectives usually entailed some sort of commitment to full employment. For the central banks of less-developed countries a broad commitment to development, and the nurturing of a financial system, was not at all unusual.

The authorised capital of the 'new' UBB remained at Rs (soon kyat) 40 million. The Bank's ultimate decision-making body also remained its seven-strong Governing Board. All directors had to be a citizen of the Union of Burma. The Board would be headed by a Chairman [sic] but, as with the 'first' UBB, day-to-day authority would be exercised by the General Manager (UBB 1952: 2–4). Both of these positions were filled by the incumbents from the 1947 version of the UBB, that is, U Mya and San Lin respectively.[46]

The UBB was given sole authority for the issuing of currency in Burma. In what was perhaps the most *visible* change in Burma's monetary affairs from the 1952 Act, however, the currency would now be based on a decimal system, and would be known by the ancient Burmese name of kyat. The value of the kyat remained the same as that of the Burmese rupee. The kyat in turn was divided into 100 *pyas*. Kyat notes were initially issued in denominations of one, five, ten and one hundred kyats. Coins were produced in denominations of one kyat, and 50, 25, 10, 5 and 1 pyas (UBB

1952: 5–6). The UBB assumed all liability for existing BCB notes, and other notes that remained legal tender at the time that the 1952 Act came into force.

Of interest, given Burma's previous experience with the currency board (and the controversies ahead) was the question of international reserve backing for the currency. In the end a figure of 'not less than 25 per cent' was arrived at. There was a considerable 'loophole' in this, however, for a further provision of the Act (Section 36) allowed the relaxation of this requirement, provided the approval of parliament was granted 'within fifteen days' (UBB 1952: 8). International reserves were defined for these purposes as 'gold', as well as the currencies and securities of foreign governments.

The UBB of 1952, in great contrast to its 1947 manifestation, was given wide parameters for the conduct of monetary policy. In this context the UBB could buy, sell, and rediscount government securities, bills of exchange and promissory notes, as well as make advances to scheduled banks and cooperative societies. The UBB was required to publish the rates at which it was willing to rediscount the various types of securities, as well as the interest rates it was willing to make advances at.

The UBB was given responsibility for managing Burma's fixed exchange-rate system, under which the kyat was formally listed at set parities against gold and foreign currencies (initially this was simply the previous Burmese rupee/sterling rate of K1:1*s*.6.*d*, K1:$US0.21). To this same end, the UBB was given the responsibility of authorising and supervising Burma's registered foreign-exchange dealers, and with ensuring that all trades took place at rates of between plus or minus one per cent of the fixed parities (UBB1952: 11).

Supervising and regulating the scheduled banks was, as it had been in the case of the 1947 version of the Bank, the responsibility of the UBB. Now, however, such supervision was made much more effective since, given the ending of the currency board strictures, the UBB could now require the banks to hold reserves with it, as well as function as a lender of last resort. The reserve requirements were established in the UBB Act as applying to demand deposits (of between 8 and up to 40 per cent), and time deposits (between 3 and 15 per cent) (UBB 1952: 11). In practice, such reserves against deposits were set initially at the minimums of these ranges; that is, at 8 and 3 per cent respectively. Initially also, such reserves had to be held in the form of cash deposits in the UBB (this was subsequently relaxed to include government securities). Beyond reserve requirements (and in great contrast to the first manifestation of the UBB), the general powers of the UBB over the scheduled banks were far-reaching. The UBB was responsible for licensing the scheduled banks, for undertaking on-site inspections of their activities, and its permission was required before the banks could open new branches. Significantly, the UBB had the power to fix minimum and maximum interest rates on bank deposits and loans. Under Section 52 of the Act, the UBB was also given qualitative and quantitative powers over bank lending, for specifying the type, volume and direction of lending to specified sectors and its timing (UBB 1952: 12–13).

Under the 1952 Act, the UBB remained the government's banker, fiscal agent, chief economic adviser and it was charged with the management of the public debt. Of great significance, however, the ability of the UBB to lend to the government was greatly liberalised under the 1952 Act compared to its 1947 predecessor. Ostensibly, the UBB was now authorised to lend directly to the government, provided that such lending did 'not exceed 15 per cent of the estimated revenues of the Government (...) for the financial year in which the advances are made'. There was, however, a very substantial loophole here too – one which would be promiscuously exploited in the years ahead. This was simply that, notwithstanding the '15 per cent' restriction on general advances, the UBB could purchase, essentially in any quantity, 'securities of, or guaranteed by, the Union Government of Burma' (UBB 1952: 15).

Drafting Controversies and Issues

Surprisingly perhaps, drafting the statutes giving the UBB full central banking powers had been undertaken by Raymond Kershaw at the Bank of England (architect, as we have seen, of the BCB). From July to November 1948 multiple drafts of his proposals made their way to San Lin in Rangoon for comment, to whom he explained his drafting philosophy:

> ...changes that were unavoidable; (2) to keep the principles and wording of the *Currency and Coinage Act* 1946 where applicable; (3) to follow the *Reserve Bank of India Act* for other necessary additions, but with the maximum possible degree of simplification. [47]

Kershaw left many important issues out of his drafts, including such contentious items as the 'reserve coverage' for the currency. This, he wrote, was an issue that 'only the Burmese themselves could decide'. He noted, however, that whilst the BCB level of 80 per cent reserve backing was on the high side for a central bank, he recommended that the Burmese Government 'be on the conservative side in choosing your percentage and not to set yourselves too low a target'.[48] In the end, as detailed above, a figure of 25 per cent reserves cover was chosen.

Kershaw was concerned throughout to keep the new UBB within 'orthodox' lines. For example, in response to a question from San Lin during the drafting process, he sought to pour cold water on the idea that the institution could be used to directly expand credit for crop loans, saying that the view of the Bank of England was that 'such a priority would be misplaced in an Act constituting (...) a Central Bank'. Further, he stressed that he 'knew of no precedent for such provisions (...) Direct crop financing is generally regarded as being completely outside the functions of a properly constituted Central Bank.' Of course, should the UBB become involved in crop lending there would be implications for the question of reserves coverage – any amounts lent implying 'a very considerable seasonal weakening of the reserve of sterling (...) upon which public confidence in the currency depends'.[49]

Meanwhile, within Burma there had developed around this time some agitation to vary the rate of exchange of the currency simultaneously with the introduction of the new UBB. Kershaw was anxious to hose such thoughts down, declaring that such a move would be 'undesirable in the present state of development of the Burmese financial mechanism'. Confidence in Burma's currency, he argued, depended upon a legislated *fixed* rate of exchange with sterling. Moving to a system in which the Burma rupee 'could be varied at will' would have 'unfavourable effects on public opinion (...) and would be regarded with suspicion by those interested in financial relations with Burma'. Pressing the point, he reminded San Lin that a move away from a fixed exchange rate would also pose implications for the 'Confidential Agreement' between Burma and the United Kingdom.[50]

The gestation period between Kershaw's original draft and the final emergence of the (new) UBB was a long one – and by the time of the bank's establishment in July 1952, Burma had moved considerably out of the British political orbit. Yet, notwithstanding this broader truth, the final drafts of the UBB and accompanying legislation (completed by San Lin and the new American adviser to the UBB, Paul Fitchen) were ritually sent to the Bank of England for comment.[51] From this august body the new UBB got a broad, but cautionary, tick. The Bank of England did not regard the *macroeconomic* aspects of the draft exceptional, but it did express concern over what it saw as the 'exceptionally broad powers' given to the UBB over the commercial banks. These powers were, according to the Bank of England, fine 'so long as there is sane management' at the Union Bank, 'but with a different management they could be dangerous both to Burma and to the British and other foreign banks'. These were to prove prescient remarks, but they were followed by an assessment that sadly was to prove even more so:

> It is very doubtful whether such far-reaching powers of control over almost every aspect of commercial banks are necessary, or whether Burma will in the foreseeable future be capable of using them wisely and efficiently. *They could provide an ideal framework for the regimentation of the Burmese economy along State socialist lines* (emphasis added).[52]

PERFORMANCE OF THE UBB

The UBB (Mark II) was established during a relatively prosperous time for Burma. The insurgencies that had destabilised the country since independence remained unresolved, but the central government had achieved a degree of control over the country sufficient to allow for something of a national 'economic space' to function. Above all, the crucial channels delivering paddy for export were open. Paddy prices were rising (in part because of the lingering effects of the 'commodities boom' driven by the war in Korea) and government finances grew fat on the back of the profits made by the State Agricultural Marketing Board (SAMB, more on which in the next chapter) on paddy exports. National output, which had been trending downward over the preceding three years, now began a strong recovery. Thus in the first few years of its existence the monetary situation facing the new UBB was a benign, even a promising one. As Table 6.2 (p. 166) shows, Burma's relative prosperity in the first half of the 1950s made for a less challenging monetary environment than the country had faced before, or than which it would subsequently confront.

Perhaps the most notable element of the monetary circumstances facing the UBB in the first years of its tenure was the absence of 'crowding out' pressure from the state. In 1951–1952 the government's strong fiscal position was a countervailing and stabilising presence against a money supply that was swelling from Burma's substantial trade surplus (the cause of the increase in foreign reserves across 1950–1953), and against the solid growth in lending to the private sector in the same years. A consequence of this benign climate, together with improving infrastructure and the increased availability of goods from abroad (both circumstances which kept costs down), was the substantial reduction in Burma's inflation rate. By 1952, as the near contemporary account of Tun Wai (1962: 173) put it, the government was feeling sufficiently prosperous to begin 'looking around for ways and means of spending'.

Such ways and means were not long in coming, and the establishment of the UBB as a fully-fledged central bank preceded by just one month the *Pyidawtha* Conference, at which (as will be dealt with more fully in Chapter Seven) the 'Eight Year Plan of Economic Development' was adopted. The *'Pyidawtha* Plan' (as it came to be known) was based on some very rosy assumptions that in turn came out of the favourable circumstances encountered by Burma above. Alas, such assumptions would provide no firm basis upon which to construct the world envisaged by the planners.

More Challenging Times

The most notable change after 1952 in the monetary circumstances of Burma was the reversal of the hitherto stabilising role of the state. Burdened by its spending responsibilities under *Pyidawtha*, the government engaged in a dramatically increased programme of spending which far outstripped both its ability to tax as well as the profits it accrued via the SAMB. Indeed, falling paddy prices (which fell 26 per cent between 1952 and 1960) greatly reduced the latter as a funding source, as well as severely dented Burma's foreign currency earnings throughout the eight year period of *Pyidawtha* (GuB 1961b: 58–59). As can be seen in Table 6.2 (overleaf), Burma's central government ran substantial budget deficits throughout the latter half of the 1950s.

These deficits were financed via the purchase, overwhelmingly by the UBB, of three-month treasury bills and 2 and 5 year treasury bonds. As noted earlier, the purchase of such bonds was a vehicle through which the UBB could avoid the provision in the UBB Act that limited its advances to the government to '15 per cent of estimated government revenue in the year in which such advances were made' (UBB 1952: 15). But there was also an extra motivation for the government to sell such securities to the UBB, since on treasury bills the government paid a yield that averaged a mere 1 per cent per annum, whereas direct UBB advances were charged at 5 per cent.

In addition to the government's own direct spending, were the demands of the many state 'boards and corporations' created to develop specific

Table 6.2 Selected Monetary Indicators, 1950–1962 (kyat millions)*

Calendar year	Total reserves ($US m)	Govt. budget deficit (-)/ surplus	Claims on private sector	Money	Consumer price index (1953 = 100)
1950	119.5	67	130	551	113.1
1951	160.0	217	159	606	108.9
1952	199.1	173	178	599	102.6
1953	212.4	−18	161	753	100.0
1954	125.0	−357	212	842	95.5
1955	75.0	−414	216	1,116	99.4
1956	115.1	−180	250	1,343	104.8
1957	85.0	−144	343	1,106	108.0
1958	109.8	−167	270	1,311	105.4
1959	132.1	−265	305	1,471	98.4
1960	121.7	52	379	1,451	105.8
1961	95.0	−170	436	1,485	105.4
1962	112.1	136	469	1,661	103.8

* Except where indicated. (Source: IMF 1966)

sectors of Burma's economy, and critical to *Pyidawtha*. Such boards, which included the SAMB, the 'Burma Railway Board', the 'Inland Water Transport Board', the 'Electricity Board' and so on, received government guarantees to allow them to borrow cheaply via the commercial banks. In practice, however, over 90 per cent of the securities issued by such boards were taken up by the UBB (GuB 1961b: 58–59). These, in turn, came to represent nearly a quarter of the UBB's assets by 1958 (Emery 1970: 18).

Together with the government's borrowing, the advances to state boards and corporations 'led to large injections of money by the Government (...) during the eight years' of *Pyidawtha* (GuB 1961b: 58) The inflationary impact of these, however, depended upon the extent to which the resultant expansion in spending power was 'mopped up' by imports. In the early independence years, the 'liberal' import policy of the government meant that any excess demand for goods was met by an increased supply of goods from abroad, and therefore inflation was kept in abeyance. Of course, the obvious downside to this was that Burma accordingly began to run down its international reserves (both facts being apparent in Table 6.2). In March 1955 the government, increasingly concerned about its international reserves position, undertook what it called 'drastic action' to restrict imports. But with no concomitant reduction in the rate of growth of the money stock (indeed, across the proceeding year there was a significant expansion) inflation accelerated.

At various times throughout its tenure the UBB attempted to slow the increasing financial demands of the state. In a representative meeting in October 1954, for instance, between the UBB, various government departments, the heads of the various state boards, and staff from the US economic consultancy firm advising the government ('Knappen Tippetts Abbett Engineering' [KTA], more on which in Chapter 7), the UBB objected that its 'forced' lending to the government breached 'the *spirit* of the Union Bank legislation (Section 61) that placed specific and effective limits on government borrowing from the Bank'. Remarkably, the UBB's suggestion was rebuffed at the meeting not by the government departments or boards, but by the representatives of KTA, who (correctly if unhelpfully) insisted that 'these limits were related to general advances, not the purchase of securities'.[53] The UBB kept up the pressure to limit government spending, however, primarily via statements in its Annual and other reports, and in private representations to the government throughout these years.

Meanwhile, accelerating inflation from 1956 brought about the first effort by the UBB to actively 'tighten' monetary policy via an increase in the reserve requirements of the commercial banks. From August 1957 the banks were required to hold reserves equivalent to 16 per cent of demand deposits (up from 8 per cent), and 6 per cent against time deposits (up from 3 per cent). The rate the UBB offered the banks to rediscount government securities also rose from 2 to 3 per cent (GuB 1961b: 59). Somewhat diluting this, however, was the fact that the UBB would now allow the banks to hold a proportion of these reserves (50 per cent) in the form of government securities. Given that many of the banks held large tranches of government bonds, in lieu of lending, this softened the impact of the reserves increase upon banks' ability to lend to the private sector. In a further tightening move, in 1958 the UBB stopped making seasonal advances to the banks – even at the seasonal peaks (Emery 1970: 18). Taking into account the usual monetary policy lags, these 'tightening' moves brought about the intended outcomes, and in 1959 (see Table 6.2) Burma experienced sharp improvements in both inflation and its reserves position.

As shall be examined in more detail in Chapter 7, from October 1958 to April 1960 Burma experienced its first episode of military rule under what became popularly known as the '*Bogyoke* (roughly 'General's') government'. This regime, rather more benign than those that would follow in the years ahead, embarked upon a rapid and large expansion of rural credit. As can be seen from Table 6.2, sharp increases in inflation and equally large falls in Burma's external reserves were not slow to follow. In an effort to correct both, once more the UBB – in what would be the last hurrah of any semblance of its independence – sought to dampen lending volumes by increasing banks' reserves. In July 1961 reserve requirements against demand deposits increased again to 20 per cent and those required against time deposits to 7.5 per cent (UBB 1962: 16). Once more, however, the reserves increase was not quite as restrictive as it looked, since the banks could now include in its calculation of reserves an even greater proportion (up to 60 per cent) of their holdings of government securities (UBB 1962: 14). By 1962 these measures had started to make their impact but, as we shall see, the coup in March of that year was to make such conventional concerns little more than irrelevant.

Other Functions

In addition to its broad 'macroeconomic' function, the UBB undertook a number of other 'routine' activities which it overwhelmingly carried out well. One of these was to 'smooth' monetary conditions against the seasonal variations in bank lending to the agricultural sector. The typical pattern of these seasonal fluctuations was a great expansion in lending in February and March, retrenchment across the remainder of the year until November, whereupon lending increased again with the arrival of the new paddy season. The banks themselves dealt with this cycle primarily by running their stocks of government securities up and down. They also borrowed and lent to each other in the interbank market. From 1953 the UBB greatly aided the banks by making regular seasonal advances to them during the seasonal lending peaks, 'against the collateral of Government and other Trustee securities' (UBB 1962: 17). When the banks became subsequently flush with funds when seasonal loans were repaid the transactions were reversed, and the UBB became a net seller of securities to the banks.

Of course, as noted, the UBB was also the regulator of Burma's commercial banks and the stability of the financial system generally. It's 'Bank Supervision Department' undertook on-site inspections of the banks, a somewhat innovative measure not adopted by most other central banks around the world until much later. During the life of the UBB very few individual bank problems emerged, and there was nothing even close to any systemic failures. From time to time there were minor problems; for instance, in early 1962 when one scheduled bank 'failed to maintain the statutory minimum reserves for one week and had to be penalised [with a fine]' – but this and other such episodes were easily dealt with by the UBB (UBB 1962: 17). Commercial bank failures were relatively common throughout the developing world then, as now, and it was to the considerable credit of the UBB that not a single one occurred in Burma during the entire period of parliamentary democracy.

NOTES

1   There is a vast and (rapidly) growing literature on the Burma campaign, and one that suggests that the oft-used label the 'forgotten war' is a tad exaggerated. For a most comprehensive examination of the battles and issues mentioned in this paragraph, however, see Allen (1984) and Bayley and Harper (2004).

2   For further discussion of these and other attributes of currency boards, see Nevin (1963: 513) and Drake (2004: 123–130).

3   Niemeyer to Iliffe, 9 February 1944, BoE, OV 79/1.

4   'Burma Currency Board', memorandum by P.L. Hogg, 30 December 1953, BoE, OV 79/2.

5   The 'council of moderates' as described by the Governor, Sir Reginald Dorman-Smith (Collis 1956: 258). The Burmese members of the Executive Council were led by Sir Paw Tun, who had briefly been (colonial) Burma's war-time Prime Minister. The AFPFL (led by Aung San) was at this time demanding that *they* should pick the nominees for the Executive Council, and choose their portfolios. This demand had been refused by Dorman-Smith, which then led the AFPFL temporarily to refuse to participate in the Council (Tinker 1957: 19, Tucker 2001: 111–112). 'Burma Currency', R.N. Kershaw, 4 June 1946, BoE, OV 79/1.

6   'Minutes of the 14th Meeting, Draft Currency Bill', 3 July 1946, BoE, OV 79/1.

7   *Ibid.*

8   'Burma Currency Board', R.N. Kershaw, 19 August 1946, BoE, OV 79/1.

9   *Ibid.*

10   *Ibid.*

11   *Ibid.*

12   'Burma: Draft Currency Law', R.N. Kershaw, 14 June 1946, BoE, OV 79/1.

13   U Tin Tut's family was especially prominent in the early history of Burma after independence, and he was just one of four brothers who each became brilliant barristers, judges and civil servants.

14   Colour plates of the BCB note issues can be found in Robinson and Shaw (1980).

15   Including cash, cash on deposit in banks authorised by the currency board, in British Government treasury bills or other securities and in securities of the Government's of other British Dominions.

16   The 'Confidential Annex' is included in the memorandum 'Burma Currency Board', by P.L. Hogg, 30 December 1953, BoE, OV 79/2. Instructions to the effect that the Annex had to be kept from members of the Commonwealth is contained in a British

Treasury memorandum, 'Burmese Financial Position', 5 February 1949, NAUK, Treasury Documents, 'Burma Currency Board, 1947–1949', T236/3557.

17   Burma Currency Board (1947).

18   Minute by R.N. Kershaw, 4 June 1946, BoE, OV 79/1.

19   San Lin to R.N. Kershaw, 3 March 1948, BoE, OV 79/14.

20   Memorandum by Sir Sydney Turner, 'Burma Currency Board', 5 April 1950, BoE, OV 79/2.

21   *Ibid.*

22   Author's calculations based on BCB Annual Reports, BCB (1948–1952).

23   Profits compiled from BCB Annual Reports, BCB (1948–1952).

24   Such discussion was noted in an untitled memorandum of 29 November 1948 by C.E. Loombe of the Bank of England, BoE, OV79/2.

25   'Burma Currency Board', memorandum by P.L. Hogg, 30 December 1953, BoE, OV 79/2.

26   Budget Speech, Minister of Finance, Government of the Union of Burma, 1 September 1950, BoE, OV 79/2.

27   As noted in 'Burma Currency Board', memorandum by P.L. Hogg, 30 December 1953, BoE, OV 79/2.

28   The replacement of the BCB was viewed as desirable by most of Burma's politicians, as indicated throughout these pages. But its passing was reportedly noted with regret by one unexpected admirer. Kyaw Nyein, one of the Burma's leading socialists figures, a one-time leadership contender with Aung San, and in 1952 the Secretary-General of the AFPFL, confided to the Bank of England 'his full realisation of the dangers of tampering with the currency and said that for that reason he himself had been a little dubious about the wisdom of transferring the note issuing powers from the Currency Board to the Union Bank'. Diary note of visit of U Kyaw Nyein to the Bank of England, 6 June 1952, BoE, OV 79/2.

29   The author is grateful for this information to Andrew Huxley, Michael Aung-Thwin, Michael Charnley and other correspondents to the Burma research online discussion group hosted by the School of Oriental and African Studies, University of London.

30   For more on *Damdupat,* see Oak and Swamy (2005). Of course, nor is the concept unknown within 'Western' law. 'Justinian's Code' (*Corupus Iurus Civilis*), the effort of Emperor Justinian to codify Roman law in the 6th century, likewise includes a prohibition against total interest payments exceeding the original principal (Johnston 1999).

31   Both of these Acts can be found in GuB (1955b: 313–315).

32   'Comparison Between Reserve Bank of India Act 1934 and Union Bank of Burma Act 1947', R.N. Kershaw, undated memorandum, BoE, OV 79/1.

33   San Lin to R.N. Kershaw, 3 March 1948, BoE, OV 79/14.

34   Souvenir booklet, 'Opening Ceremony of the Union Bank of Burma', 3 February 1948, BoE, OV 79/14.

35   The market for Treasury Bills was functioning before the end of 1948 (UBB 1948).

36   J.C. Reid, UBB, to R.N. Kershaw, Bank of England, 24 May 1948, BoE, OV 79/14. The telegraph-linked network was completed by 1951 (UBB 1951).

37   'Union Bank of Burma', memorandum by J.C. Reid, 7 April 1949, BoE, OV 79/14. Reid's views were largely shared by P.L. Hogg of the British Foreign Office, who visited the UBB at around this time and who left his impressions in an untitled memorandum of 6 January 1955, BoE, OV 79/2.

38   J.C. Reid, UBB, to R.N. Kershaw, Bank of England, 18 May 1948, BoE, OV 79/14.

39   'Union Bank of Burma', memorandum by J.C. Reid, 7 April 1949, BoE, OV 79/14.

40   Reid's accusations with regard to evasions of exchange controls are supported by other scholars of the era – see, for instance, Walinsky (1962: 163–184).

41   Of course, in some ways Reid's criticisms of Burma's early independence governments were unfair. The lack of expertise in monetary and financial issues within the ministries and the UBB was, for instance, scarcely to be wondered at – not least given that indigenous Burmese had been largely excluded from decision-making over such matters throughout the colonial era.

42   'Union Bank of Burma', memorandum by J.C. Reid, 7 April 1949, BoE, OV 79/14.

43   Memorandum by P.J. Keogh, Foreign Office, 4 April 1951, BoE, OV 79/14.

44   Handwritten annotation to the memorandum of P.J. Keogh, 4 April 1951.

45   Anonymous Bank of England memorandum, 3 July 1951, BoE, OV 79/14.

46   The full Governing Board of the UBB as newly-constituted in 1952 comprised:

U Mya (Chairman)
Dr U Set (Deputy Chairman)
U Po Byaw
U Tun Myint
Sydney Loo-Nee
U Ba Aye
U Kyin.

47   R.N. Kershaw, BoE, to San Lin, UBB, 6 August 1948, BoE, OV 79/14.

48   *Ibid.*

49   R.N. Kershaw, BoE, to San Lin, UBB, 25 November 1948, BoE, OV 79/14.

50   *Ibid.*

51   'Revised Union Bank of Burma Statutes', memorandum by C.E. Loombe, BoE, 18 January 1952, BoE, OV 79/14.

52   *Ibid.*

53   Diary note, 16 October 1954, Louis Walinsky, Louis Walinsky Papers, Collection no. 4874, Division of Rare and Manuscripts Collections, Cornell University Library.

CHAPTER 7

Agricultural and Commercial Banking in the Parliamentary Democracy Era

We have been in a hurry and we are in a hurry. We have waited for so long and we feel we must accomplish a great deal in a short time.

U Nu, 1955

We are modifying somewhat our ideas of what Socialism is...No longer is socialism necessarily identified with government ownership of the means of production...Socialism and nationalization in every field are not equivalent terms in our thinking any longer

U Nu, 1957

Burma regained its independence on 4 January 1948, and almost immediately the country descended into chaos. Ethnic separatism, a multi-faction communist insurgency and general political upheaval and unrest meant that economic development and institution building initially took a back seat to the economics and politics of civil war. As we have seen, however, beginning in 1952, Burma's economic and political circumstances began to turn for the better. The boom in commodity prices precipitated by the Korean War resulted in a dramatic increase in the price of rice and this – coupled with military circumstances that allowed Burma's rice exports to recommence in volume (even while the civil war still raged) – swelled the country's foreign-exchange reserves. The long-awaited plans for Burma's economic development, now as an independent nation, could at last be implemented.

These plans were ambitious. Fuelled by nationalist sentiment and the conviction that 'democratic socialism' provided the short-cut to prosperity, plans for the wholesale transformation of Burma's political economy were formulated in earnest. The revolutionary nature of these plans was especially apparent with regard to the financial system. Centred upon the creation of great state-owned institutions, soon there would emerge a state agricultural bank, a state commercial bank, a network of state-controlled pawnshops, and a reconstructed cooperative movement. The centrality of the state as the principal actor was obvious and deliberate. More than any other sector of the colonial economy, the financial sector had been the province of private *foreign* interests. Public ownership and 'Burmanisation' would now be the order of the day.

Burma's 'parliamentary democracy era' is often portrayed as a period of lost opportunity and squandered hopes. In fact, the country's economic performance in this period was rather better than critics then or since have allowed. Nevertheless, it is certainly true that mistakes were made. The reigning orthodoxy in so much of the developing world, that state-ownership and national planning provided the elixir for sustainable growth, would prove a particularly costly illusion. Nor would Burma's state-owned financial institutions prove to be immune from the inefficiencies and corruptions of government-directed credit. Yet, by the end of the democratic era, Burma at least had a set of stable financial *institutions* from which much could have been expected with the incremental reforms that were even then in play. Alas, by then the sun was fast setting on democracy in Burma, and such reforms would be far from the minds of a new set of 'revolutionaries'.

In this chapter we chart the course of Burma's financial sector development in the parliamentary democracy years. We depart, however, from strict chronological ordering by considering in turn developments in agricultural finance, and then commercial banking. Within these two broad divisions, the chapter is divided into nine sections, beginning with an examination of the allure of 'planning' as it related to a proposed 'state agricultural bank'. The chapter looks at the practical manifestation of these plans under the so-called *Pyidawtha* programme, the institutions created out of it, and their subsequent performance. We then turn our attention to the realm of commercial banking, with a focus upon the creation of Burma's state commercial bank in 1954. The chapter also considers the private commercial banks, and the performance of the commercial banking sector as a whole. Reasserting the demands of chronology, the chapter then outlines the changes wrought to both agricultural finance and commercial banking during the so-called *Bogyoke* government, and the late evening of Burma's parliamentary democracy.

AGRICULTURAL FINANCE

The Planning Allure

Burma's post-independence governments were divided by a great many things, but on one issue there was near unanimity – that the state should take the lead in pursuing the country's economic development. This was clear even in the country's new (1947) Constitution. Section 41 of the Constitution, for instance, explicitly stated that the 'economic life of the Union shall be *planned*' (GuB 1948a: 8). Socialism was not mentioned in the Constitution by name, but its presumptions were everywhere in the document. Section 44 made clear that the operation of public utilities and the exploitation of Burma's natural resources were to be the preserve of the state, or of 'people's co-operative organizations'. The latter were given special status indeed for, although Section 23 of the Constitution guaranteed the rights of 'private property and of private initiative', under Section 42 the state was directed to render 'material assistance to economic organisations not working for private profit' and to render preference 'to co-operative and similar economic organizations'. Section 30, which was revealingly titled 'Relations of the State to Peasants and Workers', was perhaps the most avowedly socialist component of the Constitution. Its stipulations regarding land tenure (below), however, would prove particularly problematic. Later implemented in the form of the 1948 *Land Nationalisation Act* (amended 1953), this dilution of property rights would hamper the development of viable financial institutions in Burma in the years ahead:

(1) The State is the ultimate owner of all lands.

(2) Subject to the provisions of this Constitution, the State shall have the right to regulate, alter or abolish land tenures or resume possession of any land and distribute the same for collective or co-operative farming or to agricultural tenants.

(3) There can be no large land holdings on any basis whatsoever. The maximum size of private land holding shall, as soon as circumstances permit, be determined by law (GuB 1948a: 7).

Burma's embrace of socialism in its early post-independence years was not difficult to fathom. State planning was the 'prevailing orthodoxy' amongst the great majority of countries then emerging from colonialism, and even amongst their former colonial masters. Britain was itself then in the middle of a programme of nationalisation that brought many of its great institutions into the state sphere, and planning (albeit with Keynesian overtones) was *de rigueur*. In Burma's case, however, this general and global fashion was shaped by two other factors. Firstly, many of Burma's post-independence leaders (especially the dominant *'thakins'*) had spent their formative years before the war reading and absorbing the (sometimes banned) Marxist–Leninist literature that was made available via the numerous left-wing 'book clubs' then prevalent in the country (Maung Maung 1980, *passim*).[1] Burma's Prime Minister at independence (and for 10 of the 12 years of Burma's parliamentary democracy era), U Nu, was himself a founder of one of the most prominent of these, the 'Naga Ni [Red Dragon]' Book Club. For most of Burma's post-independence leadership then, socialism was no passing fancy. Secondly, but perhaps most importantly of all, for a great many of Burma's political elite, 'capitalism' and 'imperialism' were more or less one and the same. The capitalism brought by the British had created the 'plural society' in which the Burmese were at the bottom, while British, Indian, Chinese and other foreign 'capitalists' enjoyed the fruits of Burma at the top (Myat Thein 2004: 15). Socialism was the rejection of the colonial economic order and thus it went hand-in-hand with nationalism.

In April 1948 Burma's government released its avowedly socialist 'Two Year Economic Plan for the Development of Burma'. It was to be the first of many such documents, but this inaugural plan was more 'an enunciation of the economic aspirations of a newly born state', than a detailed policy document (GuB 1961b: 1). Its enduring fame perhaps is due to the fact that it emerged from the so-called 'Rehabilitation Conference' held at Sorrento Villa in Rangoon in 1947 and was hosted by Burma's independence hero, Aung San (who was assassinated just a few months later). But the 1948 Plan was also distinctive in the centrality that it gave agriculture – a logical emphasis given that 80 per cent of Burma's population was then engaged in agriculture, but an emphasis that would be greatly neglected in subsequent plans. Within this emphasis there was also a recognition of the importance of agricultural credit, a cognisance of the failures of the past, and a firm conviction that *state* provision of agricultural credit was 'imperative'. The latter conclusion was reasoned thus:

(a) Credit is almost universally needed by the cultivators;

(b) Lightening of its cost will be of benefit to the rural community;

(c) Provision of private credit has led to (...) land alienation;

(d) Existence of foreign capital in the past resulted in heavy losses to the country of profits remitted abroad;

(e) The private credit system has more or less broken down;

(f) It is unsound that agricultural credit should remain dependent on private enterprise;

(g) Higher rates of interest for agricultural credit results in undesirable diversion of capital from industry to agriculture.

Accordingly: 'The policy of the government in regard to agricultural credit shall be directed to provide, as far as possible, state credit for agricultural finance' (emphasis added, GuB 1948a: 11).

FURNIVALL'S COMMITTEE FOR A STATE AGRICULTURAL BANK

The chaos in Burma during the early years of independence robbed its new government of the ability to implement its practical plans for economic development, and the Two Year Plan was only one of the documents made redundant by the turn of events. Nevertheless, a number of important foundations were laid under its auspices. One of these was the commissioning of a committee of inquiry into the creation of a 'state agricultural bank' for Burma. This committee (hereafter SAB committee) was slated to report within three months, with the intention that the proposed bank would commence operations in 1949.

The SAB committee contained an eclectic mix of individuals that included two politicians, Thakin Ba Han (who had served as head of the 'Planning Department' under the Japanese occupation administration of Ba Maw) and Thakin Tun Yin, both of the All-Burma Peasants Association (ABPA). The ABPA was a socialist organisation with strong grassroots support in rural areas, but was aligned to the ruling AFPFL (Maung Maung 1989: 202). Predominantly, however, the SAB Committee was comprised of 'experts', most numerous of which was a contingent from the cooperative credit movement (which at this time was largely moribund). They included the greatly respected and experienced U Ba Maung (Manager of the Cooperative Bank at Pegu, and who had served on the Burma Provincial Banking Inquiry Committee in 1929)[2], U Ba E (Manager of the Cooperative

Bank at Prome), and U Aung Soe (the then Registrar of all cooperative credit societies). Also on the committee was Hla Myint. The most eminent economist Burma has produced, and who would later make a number of seminal contributions to economic theory, at this time Hla Myint was Economic Adviser to the National Planning Department.[3]

The most influential member of the SAB committee, however, and the principal author of its final report, was the Committee's chairman (and only non-Burmese member), the venerable J.S. Furnivall. Furnivall had arrived in Burma as a member of the ICS in 1902, afterwards marrying a Burmese woman and establishing a family. He also fell in love with Burma as a whole, and came to hold an 'idealised' conception of pre-colonial Burmese society. Furnivall established the Burma Research Society and its eponymous journal in 1910, and through these and other fora he exercised an extraordinary influence upon the country's emerging political class. Furnivall retired from the ICS in 1923 and in 1931 he returned to England. In 1948, however, Furnivall returned to Burma at the invitation of the new Burmese government (and at the urging of Hla Myint), to take up the position of 'Planning Adviser'.[4] Apart from his idealisation of pre-colonial Burma, Furnivall was a Fabian Socialist and a constant critic of what he saw as 'the unbridled capitalism of British business in Burma', a force that had produced in Burma a 'plural society' that served the interests of 'markets' rather than the community (Pham 2005: 323). Throughout his professional life Furnivall 'actively promoted a mild form of socialism in Burma', and to this end established the Burma Book Club which was to become an important vehicle for the dissemination of socialist ideals to many young Burmese nationalists (Pham 2005: 327). Furnivall's seminal work, *Colonial Policy and Practice: A Comparative Study of Burma and Netherlands India*, appeared in 1948, the same year he penned his SAB proposal.[5]

Furnivall's Committee proposed a tripartite structure for the SAB, at the base of which would be 'Village Banks'. At the next level, performing a supervisory role and as lenders in their own right for purposes deemed beyond the village institutions, were the 'District Banks' – branches of the SAB proper. At the apex of it all was the 'Central State Agricultural Bank', with a head office based in Rangoon. Of course, given the make-up of the SAB Committee, the fact that this structure resembled the *ideal* of Burma's colonial cooperative system was no accident. The principles upon which the SAB would be founded, and which were regarded by the Committee as essential if the mistakes of the past were to be avoided, included:

(a) The Bank must rest on foundations in the village;

(b) The procedure for making and recovering loans must be so simple that it asks nothing beyond the capacity of the ordinary villager;

(c) The procedure within the village should so far as possible be conducted on democratic principles;

(d) Both on grounds of expense and with a view to educating the people in their financial responsibilities (...) Supervision should be indirect by strict insistence on the punctual repayments on loans, rather than direct supervision by instruction, inspection and reprimand (GuB 1949: 11).

Village Banks

The Village Banks were the 'face' of the SAB, but were technically owned by the village they served. Each Village Bank was controlled by a village committee that comprised the 'headman' of the village as chairman, as well as a minimum of two members who occupied land, and two members representing landless labourers. The primary function of the Village Bank committee was to manage lending: deciding and distributing loans, and ensuring the necessary repayment processes were in place (GuB 1949: 18). Each inhabitant of a village was entitled to elect the committee members, the only exceptions to this universal franchise being *pongyis* and those of 'unsound mind' (GuB 1949: 17). Accordingly, the Village Banks were 'democratic' structures – but they were supposedly predicated on an entirely contrary philosophy to that which had informed the cooperative movement of colonial Burma:

> We regard co-operation as a key to social welfare, but hold that the first step towards the enhancement of social welfare is to satisfy the hunger for credit. The co-operative credit society [by contrast] looks to character as a condition for granting credit: *we regard the provision of credit as a condition of improving character* (emphasis added, GuB 1949: 11).

Village Banks were designed to accept deposits, but since these would take time to accumulate, lending in the early years would proceed via capital provided by the government and allocated by the District Banks. Village Banks provided funds for short terms only – and initially only 'self-liquidating' crop loans. The SAB committee's stance on interest rates was that they should be 'as low as may be consistent with the solvency of the bank'. They suggested that District Banks charge their village affiliates a rate of 6 per cent per annum for funds, and that Village Banks lend out at 12 per cent. The margin was viewed as the 'necessary minimum' for institutional sustainability (GuB 1949: 14).

Given the failure of Burma's credit cooperatives between the wars, designing a mechanism to ensure loans were repaid would be one of the greatest challenges for the Village Banks. The cooperatives had relied on the unlimited liability of members for the debts of their society, but the inability to apply this in practice had rendered this 'discipline' meaningless. In the place of unlimited liability, Furnivall's Committee came up with 'joint security' – what the microfinance movement today would label a 'group-lending contract'. In the specific case of the Village Banks, this was implemented in the form of an arrangement that each loan was to be secured against default by 'the joint personal security of *three* landowners or tenants'. In other words, each loan was effectively guaranteed by the borrower and two other cultivators in the village up to the value of their land, occupancy rights, crops and all other property. Of course, accessing such security in the event of default would require the application of law. As Furnivall's Committee noted, it was 'easy to make rules but difficult to enforce them' (GuB 1949: 35).

A further device designed to ensure that the widespread default of the cooperatives was not revisited upon the Village Banks was a requirement that 'no village bank should be eligible for an advance unless all outstanding loans to the District Bank have been repaid' (GuB 1949: 21–22). Of course this measure effectively did for banks as a whole what group-lending did for the individuals within them. According to the SAB committee, the restraint upon defaulting institutions was quite straightforward, since the 'whole village would exercise pressure on potential defaulters and this should gradually inculcate a greater share of personal responsibility for the repayment of debts' (GuB 1949: 22). It also greatly reduced the costs of supervising the Village Banks by aligning compliance with their ability to fund future activity. Such a simple device for self-compliance was infinitely preferable to close supervision:

Supervision weakens responsibility. If we aim at building up the character of the cultivator and imbuing him with a sense of responsibility for the payment of his debts, we must so far as possible avoid direct supervision, and teach him by experience that if he does not pay up his debts he will not receive loans (GuB 1949: 36).

To give impetus to the savings mobilisation role of the Village Banks, as well as to a 'savings culture' more generally, Furnivall's committee recommended a regime of *compulsory savings*. Such a scheme was necessary, it concluded, since Burma was not only a country of 'no capital', but its people were 'not in the habit of saving' (GuB 1949: 51). The enforced saving took the form of a 'Five-Year Savings Plan' under which cultivators were required to 'subscribe annually towards the Village Bank an amount equal to one-tenth of the revenue due on the land'. For non-cultivators, enforced savings would apply if they were borrowers from the Village Bank, as a proportion of earnings or as deductions from wages. Since it was the village headman who already had responsibility for collecting land revenue, the responsibility for collecting savings would fall on their (overburdened) shoulders too. The SAB committee recommended that the savings be treated as 'share capital' in the Village Bank, rather than as deposits. So long as a Village Bank was profitable a dividend on the shares could be paid in lieu of interest. True to the name of the scheme, such shares could only be sold or 'cashed out' after a minimum of five years. Of course, together with accumulated earnings, this capital from forced savings would add to the ability of Village Banks to stand alone in funding their activities (GuB 1949: 51–53).

Initially designed purely as financial institutions, the SAB committee had a broader vision that ultimately the Village Banks would be

> ...a means of organising not only the credit of the cultivators but their capital, so that each Village would be able to provide for its own requirements without looking for outside support; it would be financially autonomous. We regard the Bank (...) as a foundation not only for the organisation of the credit and capital, but for a superstructure on co-operative lines that would promote the social and economic welfare of the Village in all its aspects (GuB 1949: 13).

District Banks

What the SAB Committee called the 'District Banks' were the branches of the SAB proper – one in each of Burma's (then) 36 districts. They had three functions. First, they were the supervisory agency for the Village Banks affiliated to them. This would be a relatively simple task provided the mechanism of self-compliance noted above worked. Secondly, they were to be lenders in their own right. The District Banks were to be the providers of the medium-term loans (especially cattle-loans and loans for land improvement) that the Village Banks could not be. Since it would take some time for Village Banks to be established across the country, the District Banks were also to lend in villages without their own bank. Finally, and as already noted above, the District Banks were the providers of funds to the Village Banks: exclusively in the immediate period before savings and deposits could be mobilised. In providing funds to the Village Banks, the District Banks would apply a simple formula that allocated to each village a set rate per acre multiplied by the number of acres under cultivation (GuB 1949: 7–8).

The Central State Agricultural Bank

At the apex of the SAB was what the SAB committee called the 'Central State Agricultural Bank', but which can more meaningfully be simply regarded as the SAB head office. This allocated funds to the District Banks in much the same way as the District Banks allocated money to the villages. Likewise, it also performed a supervisory function over the operations of the District Bank branches.

One of the most difficult tasks facing the SAB committee was deciding upon how much capital the bank required. Given that eventually the objective of the SAB was to be the sole provider of the credit needs of agriculture in Burma, it was important that the number was sufficiently large. Interestingly, the SAB committee thought that the borrowing needs of Burma's cultivators would be smaller than they had been before independence. The reasoning was that the foreshadowed tenancy, land nationalisation and land redistribution laws would reduce the size of land holdings and, as a result, both the need and ability to raise credit. Events were to prove this reasoning wrong. But drawing upon it, and upon earlier estimates of the credit needs of cultivators by the Burma Provincial Banking Enquiry Report and other sources, the SAB committee eventually decided upon a 'desired' figure of Rs 75 million, with Rs 50 million as a minimum. In the view of the SAB committee the 'bulk' of this capital should be supplied by the government, but Burmese nationals should be 'allowed' to subscribe up to 40 per cent (GuB 1949: 7–9). Another vexing question facing the SAB committee was deciding upon the relationship between the SAB and its Village Banks, the Cooperative Department and the surviving credit cooperatives. Burma could not 'afford to maintain two separate organizations dealing with agricultural credit' and 'unnecessary duplication' had to be avoided (GuB 1949: 47). Accordingly, it recommended that, 'in the first instance', village banks should *not* be formed in villages where a cooperative credit society existed and was functioning well. Beyond the short-term, however, it regarded the days of cooperative credit as numbered. The war, the destruction of the records and accounts, the new environment of land nationalisation and other reforms would transform the rural economy of Burma in ways that the cooperative credit system would be unlikely to adapt to. Better, the Committee concluded, 'to transfer the provision of agricultural credit (...) to the State Agricultural Bank' (GuB 1949: 48).

PYIDAWTHA AND THE KTA REPORT

The SAB Committee estimated that the SAB could not realistically commence operations until January 1950 (GuB 1949: 45). In fact, it was not until June 1953 that the SAB was finally established. In the meantime the civil war and an overstretched political leadership and bureaucracy meant that scant progress was made in the establishment of new financial institutions.

As noted in the introduction to this chapter, however, by 1952 events had turned in favour of Burma's new government. In charge of little more than Rangoon and its suburbs at critical moments during the 'civil wars', in August 1952 U Nu was sufficiently in charge, and Burma sufficiently prosperous, for the launching of what has come to be known as the 'Pyidawtha Plan'. *Pyidawtha* (translated literally as 'royal pleasant country') became both a slogan and something of a talisman for U Nu's efforts to construct in Burma both a democratic socialist state, and one coloured by 'his ideals of peace, prosperity, and morality based on Buddhism' (Mya Maung 1991: 75).[6] Central to *Pyidawtha* was the industrialisation of Burma, and the efforts to shed the 'colonial extractive economy' constructed under British rule. Agriculture was not ignored, but the emphasis clearly was on industry and the 'balance' it would provide an economy otherwise dominated by a mono-crop. Of course, an emphasis on industrialisation was as ubiquitous as planning to most post-colonial and developing nations at the time, synonymous indeed with what was popularly understood as 'economic development' itself (Golay *et al* 1969: 229).

Pyidawtha was the great objective of U Nu's government, but underlying *Pyidawtha* as an 'operating template' was the celebrated 'economic and engineering' development plan for Burma written by the economists of

Robert R. Nathan Associates, an economic consultancy working under the supervision of the Knappen, Tippetts and Abbott (KTA) Engineering Company. Engaged initially under a US foreign aid grant (later they were employed by the Burmese government itself, following its rejection of US aid on account of perceived US support for *Kuomintang* incursions into Burma), KTA had been commissioned to come up with a multi-faceted development plan for Burma. With KTA itself concerned mostly with physical projects, the economic components of the plan were subcontracted to the Nathan company, within which Robert Nathan himself, and the firm's chief economist, Louis Walinsky, were the leading lights. Nathan had been a prominent 'New Dealer' with strong links with the Roosevelt and Truman administrations, and a pioneer in the establishment of national income accounting by the US government. His firm had already carried out similar work to that which they would undertake in Burma in the postwar reconstruction plans of France, Korea, Iran, Indonesia, Nigeria and Thailand (Galbraith 1987: 508). According to Walinsky (who would be the 'point man' in Rangoon for the company throughout their tenure in Burma, and a trusted confidante of U Nu), Nathan's 'support for the economic positions and policies of organised labor in the United States made him (...) more acceptable to the socialist-oriented Burmese leaders than would otherwise have been the case' (Walinsky 1962: 84). KTA produced a 'preliminary report' in January 1952 and a 'comprehensive strategy' in August 1953. The preliminary report had the objective of doubling Burma's real GDP between 1950 and 1960. U Nu's (1955) recollection of the circumstances behind the commissioning of the KTA Report eloquently illustrated the hopes and constraints of the times:[7]

Since the time when we, as politicians, were struggling for independence, we were particularly enamoured of the various projects being implemented in other independent countries. We had built castles in the air after reading about such projects. We vowed we would draw up similar projects once independence was achieved. But, on the eve of independence our leaders fell in one swoop at the hand of the assassins, and barely three months after independence multi-coloured rebels started widespread insurrections. We were therefore, constrained to wave aside whatever projects we had in mind and we were only set on the restoration of law and order. While we were thus engaged in the suppression of the insurrections, my attention was drawn to a news item in which I had been all along interested. It appeared in one of the English newspapers and it was on Iran. According to that news, the Government of Iran entrusted to a foreign firm the task of surveying and reporting on the economic resources of that country, and that firm, after a detailed survey, submitted a report to the Iranian Government. It was then that I asked Secretary U Hla Maung to find a suitable firm worthy of being entrusted with the task of submitting a similar report on the economic resources of the country (U Nu 1955: 107–108).

The KTA Report was in many ways a remarkable document. Above all it was a quintessential example of the self-confidence of a generation of economists who, convinced that they had the right 'toolbox' of theories for solving economic problems, sought to apply them across all circumstances and in all places. The 'toolbox' was self-described by Walinsky as 'Keynesian' (Walinsky 1962: 84). In truth the philosophy underlying the KTA Report was better labelled as 'hydraulic Keynesian' in the vernacular of theoretical economists. Thus it envisaged the economy as a giant mechanism, open to mechanical solutions that involved 'pumping' funds in this direction, 'pulling' a policy lever in another, opening a 'valve' in yet another. In particular it was a philosophy that believed that if only information flows were good enough, economists and other technicians could 'plan' an economy's trajectory and smooth its path. National accounts, which had only been regularly tabulated in rich industrial countries in the wake of the Second World War, were thus of critical importance. The KTA Report, over two thousand pages in its comprehensive edition, was essentially an attempt to construct a vast table of accounts for Burma, and to apply the development policies its authors were convinced were implied in the numbers.

But the KTA Report was also deeply flawed. The self-confidence of its authors was simultaneously their *over-confidence*, and notwithstanding the undoubted scholarship and sincerity of their work, the complexities both of the specific circumstances of Burma, and that of economic policy-making more generally, would prove overwhelming. KTA's assumptions regarding Burma's export income had particularly been far too optimistic. These had been formed with the (Korean War) boom years of 1950–52 in mind and, as circumstances would soon demonstrate, these were quite anomalous years. However, this shortcoming highlighted a further one – the general lack of concern in the report for financial matters and, in particular, the importance of creating in Burma a sustainable financial *system*. As shall be examined in the pages below, KTA paid some attention to the financial and credit needs of industry, and it nodded to the creation of new financial institutions in agriculture (the SAB as noted). This would not be enough, however, and it would be telling.

The SAB is Established

Establishing the SAB was a centrepiece of the 'Five Year Plan for Agricultural Self-Sufficiency and Development' that came as part and parcel of *Pyidawtha*, but the Bank that came into being in June 1953 was closely based upon the blueprint offered by the SAB committee and KTA. Perhaps the most conspicuous way in which *construction* differed from *conception* was in the terms of 'membership' of the Village Banks. As we have seen, the SAB committee proposed that membership of Village Banks be open to all villagers, but the SAB that emerged required that a member of a Village Bank be a shareholder – 5 shares at 1 kyat each being the designated minimum subscription. Prospective members were also vetted by the relevant 'Village Bank committee'. Village Banks charged borrowers 12 per cent per annum on loans, from funds the banks in turn borrowed from the SAB at 6 per cent. At the time of repayment of their loans, borrowers were required to make a compulsory savings deposit of 1 per cent of the value of their former loan. Such deposits, together with the funds from share subscriptions, voluntary deposits and profits, were deposited with the SAB, which invested the funds 'in order that the deposits might be built up to such an extent as will enable Village Banks to *dispense* with financial assistance from the Bank in course of time' (Revolutionary Government of the Union of Burma [RGUB] 1963: 26, emphasis added).

Another difference between conception and construction was that the SAB could theoretically make long-term loans (5 to 15 years) for land improvement. In practice, however, this difference mattered little since, as Tun Wai (1962: 181) later observed, the SAB did not make long term loans. With an authorised capital of 80 million kyat (50 million of which was paid up), the SAB was resourced more or less exactly at the levels deemed necessary by the SAB Committee and KTA. Taking the age-old banker's adage to hasten-slowly, the SAB was initially established in just four districts (Insein, Henzada, Mandalay and Pegu). By 1963, however, the SAB had 33 district branches which dispensed loans through 2,669 village banks across the country (RGUB 1963a: 25–26).

OTHER INSTITUTIONS INFLUENCING AGRICULTURAL CREDIT

Cooperatives

The SAB was the most important rural financial institution established in the parliamentary democracy era, but it was not the only one that, for good or ill, was to yield influence upon Burma's agricultural credit regime. One of these 'other' institutions was a re-created system of agricultural cooperatives that would dispense credit. Such cooperatives were not part of the vision of the SAB committee, which had recommended the winding up of the remaining pre-war credit cooperatives. But cooperatives of all sorts *were* very much central to the government's vision of the economy more broadly. Given special domain in Burma's 1947 constitution as we have seen, cooperatives were highly attractive to Burma's new government in that they combined the promise of a more egalitarian distribution of economic power, while limiting that of traditional elites (such as foreign banks and moneylenders).

There was, therefore, a qualitative difference between the systems of cooperative credit in the years of parliamentary democracy, and that which had existed in the pre-war years. In the colonial period credit cooperatives were, more or less, the only cooperatives of any significance in Burma. In the post-war era, by contrast, cooperatives were a dominant form of organisation in all corners of the economy. In the context of agricultural production, such cooperatives were meant to be of the form of 'multi-purpose producers' cooperatives' (popularly known as 'ProCos'), into which would be rolled a number of activities (such as marketing and distribution) for which it was felt a cooperative approach would be appropriate (GuB 1952: 33–35).[8]

To make all of this concrete, in 1950 a 'National Convention on Co-operation' adopted a 'Five Year Cooperative Scheme' for the spread of multi-purpose cooperatives across the country. These were meant to supply credit, however, only when and where a village bank had yet to be established. Such credit as provided by the ProCos came initially via the Cooperative Societies Department (CSD). The CSD charged individual cooperatives 6.25 per cent, who on-lent to member cultivators at rates that ranged from 10 to 12 per cent. Loans were restricted to K10 per acre per family up to a maximum of K500 with no collateral security, and K1000 with collateral (GuB 1952: 35).

State Pawnshop

The creation of a network of state-owned pawnshops had been a recommendation of both the SAB Committee, as well as the KTA Report (and, indeed, of the BPBE two decades earlier). As Furnivall himself noted, the need for villagers 'to borrow a few rupee for petty day-to-day requirements' would not go away but, given the focus of the SAB on crop and other agricultural loans, this was not a demand that could be met by Village Banks (GuB 1949: 59). Yet, traditional sources of petty loans such as village moneylenders and *private* pawnshops charged 'too high interest rates' and provided 'too insecure' storage facilities for pawned items (KTA 1953: 71).

Consistent with the reports of its expert committees then, Burma's government decided in 1949 to establish a system of state-owned pawnshops. Based upon a Javanese model advocated by Furnivall (a government team was sent to Indonesia in 1950 to examine the operation of its system of state pawnshops), a 'pilot' scheme was established at Insein in November 1952. By the time of the KTA Report's publication this had been 'progressing favourably' – enough, certainly, for KTA to urge its replication in townships across Burma (KTA 1953: 71). By 1962 there were 99 state-owned pawnshops in Burma, as well as two 'sales depots' in Rangoon and Mandalay at which auctions of unredeemed articles took place. Administered initially by the Cooperative Ministry, in March 1955 management passed to the 'State Pawnshop Management Board' (SPMB). As shall be examined below, under the SPMB Burma's state-owned pawnshops began to make inroads into the business of the privately owned pawnshops, the licenses of which continued to be held overwhelmingly by ethnic Chinese. In late 1955, in a further effort to supplant the private Chinese operations, the Government brought down the 'State Pawnshops Management Board Order', under which the SPMB was authorised to assume the licences of all private pawnshops as they expired (Golay *et al* 1969: 257).

The procedures for obtaining credit from Burma's state-owned pawn-shops were simple. Almost any item of worth was acceptable for pawning (including, for instance, cooking utensils and work tools), against which advances of up to 80 per cent of the value of the pawned item were made. The initial term of the pawn loan was five months, after which the borrower was expected to repay the principal of their loan and redeem their pawned article. Should the borrower wish to extend the term of the loan, a fresh mortgage contract was meant to be drawn up. If, in the end, the borrower failed to discharge and redeem his pawned article, the item would be auctioned. Any balance realised that was over and above the original principal plus interest was paid to the borrower (RGUB 1963: 110).

GA Loans

Two Acts of the colonial era, the *Agriculturalists Loans Act* of 1883 (as amended 1947), and the *Land Improvement Loans Act* (1883), allowed for the Burmese government to make direct advances to cultivators via township and divisional officers, and without the intermediation of a bank, cooperative or any other institution. The first of the laws was designed to be used primarily in emergencies, the second to make long-term loans that were difficult for cultivators to get from other colonial-era institutions. In practice, however, the volume of funds supplied from the government via these Acts was, during the colonial years, trivial (Tun Wai 1953: 83–85).

This was not the case, however, in the post-independence era, when these two Acts provided the legal basis for a relatively large programme of government loans to cultivators (especially in the early independence years, and then again towards the end of the 'democracy era'). In common parlance the loans made under the two Acts were referred to as General Administrative (GA) loans, and they were made at the pre-war interest rate of 6.25 per cent, and via the same administrative procedures (Tun Wai 1962: 169).

The Chettiars

One 'institution' of Burma's pre-war rural credit system that did not feature prominently in the post-war period was the Chettiars. The harrowing scenes that accompanied the flight of the Chettiars from Burma following the Japanese invasion in 1942 were not ameliorated, as they were for others, by any triumphant return in 1945.[9] In the years thereafter a few Chettiars did attempt to return and resume both their business and their lands, but most did not. Burma's new government, though in many ways a natural ally of the similarly newly-independent Congress government in India, made apparent their hostility to any large scale return of the Chettiars. Of course, in this they were simply reflecting the undoubted will of the Burmese electorate, who saw the Chettiars as on-going and living symbols of colonial exploitation. Moreover, this hostility was made manifest (if thinly disguised) in legislation that aimed to ensure that Burma's agricultural lands would never again fall into the hands of alien moneylenders. Two laws were particularly written to this end, the first of which, the *Burma Agriculturalists Debt Relief Act* of 1947, cancelled completely all debts that were incurred before 1 October 1946. The second was to have even more profound effects on the Chettiars, and on Burmese cultivators thereafter. The *Land Nationalisation Act* (1948, but rewritten in a more effective form in an Act of the same name in 1953) put into action Section 30 of Burma's Constitution that made the state the ultimate owner of all agricultural land. Under the *Land Nationalisation Act* all agricultural land in the hands of absentee landlords was nationalised by the state, with the intention of redistributing it to Burmese cultivators (many of whom would be on the land already as tenants) up to a maximum of fifty acres per family. In practice, many abuses and petty corruptions accompanied the efforts of land nationalisation, but by 1958 some 3.4 million acres of land had been nationalised, around 17 per cent of Burma's total of land under cultivation (GuB 1958b: 79). For most of this land it was the Chettiars who had held the title deeds.

The Chettiars themselves were not generally enthusiastic about returning to Burma in any case after the war. As Cooper (1959: 94) noted, they were under no illusions about what they would face in Burma should they try to return, and realised that conducting business hereafter on the basis of 'land as security' was, in fact, no 'security' at all. Nevertheless, they *were* interested in compensation for their reclaimed land and, throughout the 1950s, Chettiar representative groups kept up the pressure on the Indian government to seek amelioration from Burma. These efforts initially ran into opposition in Burma, and as late as 1953 U Nu was to rhetorically ask:

> Who is the real owner of the land? Is he the Chettyar with the bloated abdomen (...) No! The ownership of the land is held by the constitutionally elected Government of the people (...). In such a case, it is perfectly legal and morally right to take back our land and there is no obligation at all to pay compensation for the expropriated land (U Nu 1953: 113).

Notwithstanding such sentiments, in the face of Chettiar persistence in lobbying both the Indian and Burmese governments, machinery for apportioning compensation for nationalised land was finally set in place via the 1953 version of the *Land Nationalisation Act*. This contained a directive that compensation would be paid for 'resumed land irrespective of race or creed to each and everyone without any discrimination' (GuB 1958b: 63). Such compensation was at a dramatic discount to the value of the land resumed, however, and it was calculated according to a decreasing scale. Thus compensation of 'twelve times' annual land revenue (taxation) was to be paid on the first 100 acres, but just one year's land revenue would be paid on holdings in excess of 1,100 acres. This formula valued compensation to the Chettiars at a mere Rs 15 million, compared to an estimate of Rs 900 million that was the 'market value' of their land (Chakravarti 1971: 178).[10] Progress in actually making payments was slow, moreover, and in the end the Chettiars saw little in the way of compensation payments before the whole arrangement was suspended, and then cancelled, when Burmese democracy itself came to an end in 1962 (Siegelman 1962: 299).

Dawson's Bank

Also greatly affected by postwar legislation was Dawson's Bank. The *Land Nationalisation Acts* severely dented Dawson's ability to make seasonal and other agricultural loans based on land collateral, and the Bank was also chronically short of capital following the losses it suffered during the war. In 1945 it had approached Lloyds Bank for a credit of £4.5 million 'for financing seed loans and for other agricultural purposes in Burma'.[11] The initiative ultimately did not go anywhere, and it was not helped by the intervention of the Bank of England (BoE). The BoE's Deputy Governor, B.G. Catterns, wrote to the Chief General Manager of Lloyds in April 1945 advising that, whilst there was nothing intrinsically objectionable about the proposal, the plan was 'premature' and Lloyds should 'go slow on the matter'.[12]

By the early 1950s Dawson's Bank had transformed into something akin to a large, but respectable, pawnbroking operation. Most loans were secured against gold and precious stones. The Bank continued to take in deposits, but by the end of Burma's parliamentary democracy years these amounted to little more than around K120,000 (of course, Burma had made the switch from the Burmese rupee to the kyat in 1952). Loans and advances were equally modest – around K340,000 in total, a mere K50,000 of which had been lent by Dawson's for the purchase or improvement of property.[13]

By the end of the 1950s Dawson's Bank was also very much a Burmese rather than a European concern. The Dawson family gradually moved out of the business over the decade, and by 1962 there was just one European on the Bank's Board.[14] By this time the Bank had moved its head office to Rangoon too, though it maintained a sizeable branch in its traditional home of Pyapôn.

The State Agricultural Marketing Board (SAMB)

In addition to the formal financial institutions, a range of state trading enterprises, government boards and corporations engaged in lending activities throughout the parliamentary democracy years. By far the most significant of these was the State Agricultural Marketing Board (SAMB), the near-monopoly buyer and seller of Burma's rice crop. Though an institution in sympathy with the nationalist and socialist ethos of Burma's independence government, the SAMB in fact was established (in 1946) by the British Ministry of Food to aid the distribution of Burmese rice to other parts of the Empire.[15] The SAMB mainly lent to millers, both short-term for the purchase of paddy, and long-term for the construction of mills, paddy-storage facilities and other capital and maintenance works. Since the SAMB paid a price for paddy that was below that which could be got on the open market, forward selling of paddy to the SAMB meant that cultivators implicitly paid an 'interest rate' on advances received. Nash (1965: 231) reckoned this to the equivalent of about 8 to 12 per cent per annum across the democratic era. This was more costly than some other sources of government finance (GA loans for instance), but was considerably below the rates charged by moneylenders. The SAMB was not short of problems or critics – a fact that was to become increasingly apparent after 1954 when government investigations uncovered wide-spread corruption, unqualified staff, and an absence of accounting and other systems of good governance (Silverstein 1977: 150).

The SAMB was exclusively involved in the trade in paddy, but there were other state bodies that that provided financing of various forms for particular agricultural sectors, including government 'boards' such as the 'State Timber Board' and the 'Town and Country Development Board'. Another state enterprise that was involved in providing a certain amount of rural finance was the Agricultural and Rural Development Corporation (ARDC). Its creation a recommendation of the KTA, the ARDC was accompanied by an 'Industrial Development Corporation' and the mineral 'Resources Development Corporation'. Each received funds from the Government for on-lending in their respective spheres, but they also raised funds through the issuing of bonds and debentures (Golay *et al.* 1969: 231). The role of these corporations was set out by the Government thus:

Each, operating as a company, on a business basis, and outside the frame-work of government departments and procedure, would be the instrument of

Government for the development programme in its field. The major functions visualised for each development corporation include the establishment, financing, and supervision of subsidiary companies to develop and operate governmentally-owned projects; establishment and financing of joint ventures; granting of financial aid to privately-owned enterprises on a sound credit basis; operation of training and research programmes and other services to mining or industry (GuB 1952: 26).[16]

AGRICULTURAL CREDIT: PERFORMANCE IN THE PARLIAMENTARY DEMOCRACY ERA

As detailed above, Burma established an array of rural credit institutions in the early years of its re-found independence. Yet, and notwithstanding the care and thought that had gone into their creation, the actual performance of these institutions would prove, on the whole, disappointing. A number of problems would emerge, some structural and organisational, and some reflective of pathologies that lived on from the colonial era. Above all, however, was a more profound dilemma that persisted through the parliamentary democracy era: simply, formal financial institutions did not provide *enough* credit to meet the needs of the Burmese cultivator.

Estimating the credit needs of Burmese agriculture was something that a number of the architects of Burma's postwar economy and its institutions attempted to grapple with. In 1946 the Secretary of the Reconstruction Department of the returning colonial administration, Sir Bernard Ottwell ('B.O.') Binns, came up with a figure for seasonal loans of Rs 100 million (Binns 1946: 28). This was half the estimate of the BPBE in 1929 (which calculated that Lower Burma needed Rs 165 million and Upper Burma Rs 30 million in short-term cultivator loans). Binns's lower estimate was made on account of a number of factors, including the idea that pre-war, pre-depression estimates of credit needs were based upon high paddy prices that were not likely to be repeated, and Chettiar lending that (he believed) was more liberal than prudent.

A much higher estimate of Burma's seasonal credit needs was calculated by Aye Hlaing (1958: 5). A member of the Economics Department of the University of Rangoon in the 1950s, Aye Hlaing had served on the colonial government's 'Land and Agriculture Committee' in the late 1930s. Writing a decade after Binns, and basing his calculations on acreage extrapolations from Burma's 1953/54 census, Aye Hlaing put Burma's annual agricultural credit needs at K350 million. Aye Laing's reasoning for the higher number was based on a number of considerations, including the fact that agricultural labourers now demanded cash payment, rather than the large element 'in kind' they used to accept before the war. Most important, however, was inflation, which in his estimate had driven agricultural prices up by 3 times prewar levels in Lower Burma, and 5 times in Upper Burma (Aye Hlaing 1958: 5–6).

Whichever estimate of Burma's agricultural credit needs we take, what is unambiguously apparent is that the supply of agricultural credit in the parliamentary democracy years came nowhere close to filling the demand for it. The total amount of credit provided by the government from 1945 to 1962 (through all of its outlets, including the SAB, the cooperatives and GA loans) came to no more than around K900 million.[17] Richter (1968: 105) came to an even lower estimate of K730 million. Either way, and it is not really possible to be any more precise, this represented an annual average that was well below even the 'minimum' estimated need of Binns above of K100 million – and clearly well short of the estimates of the BPBE and Aye Hlaing. Even the 'peak' year of 1960/61 saw only K88 million in agricultural loans (Richter 1968: 105).

The shortage of formal institutional lending for Burma's agriculturalists in the parliamentary democracy era was not without cost to the country. Most obviously, the absence of institutional credit pushed Burma's farmers into the hands of moneylenders. Of course, with the Chettiars gone these were mostly 'local', but this was no comfort in terms of lower interest rates. Indeed, as noted in Chapter 2, the interest rates charged by indigenous moneylenders mostly greatly exceeded those of the Chettiars, and reports of interest rates in excess of 250 per cent (on an annualised basis, though most loans were for shorter periods) were not uncommon.

Beyond high interest rates were other costs that had the effect of sapping the productivity of Burmese agriculture. The lack of affordable credit to cultivators of paddy was, for instance, the principal cause of the increasing use of the broadcasting method to sow paddy rather than the more expensive transplanting approach. Broadcasting, a technique 'which had almost disappeared in Lower Burma after the labour-scarce mid-nineteenth century', produced yields per acre that were far below that achieved via the transplanting method (van Schendel 1991: 214–215). Contemporary estimates by Aye Hlaing put the increases in yield from transplanting at up to '10 baskets per acre as compared with broadcasting'. Yet, despite this, there had been 'a distinct trend towards more and more broadcasting in recent years' (Aye Hlaing 1958: 7). The reason for this seeming self-defeating strategy on the part of cultivators was simple. In the absence of available formal rural credit there was only the moneylender, whose high interest rates 'wipe out any advantage of using the transplanting method' (Aye Hlaing 1958: 7).

The neglect of agriculture generally in the parliamentary democracy years was the ultimate 'cause' of the scarcity of affordable rural credit in Burma. But there were other contributing factors as well, not least the confusion that extended from the proliferation of agencies involved in dispensing rural credit. A near-contemporary analysis of Mya Maung (1965:333) noted that not only did the 'overlapping, often conflicting, roles and functions by different government agencies in the same field of socio-economic action' breed a certain chaos, but it also greatly stretched the available administrative expertise. Richter (1968: 105) came to a similar conclusion, noting 'in particular the shortage of qualified staff to administer loans and insure repayment at the village level' – across all the agencies. Richter also identified other obstacles to the provision of the necessary credit to Burmese agriculturalists, including (1) the departure of the Chettiars; (2) postwar price controls that reduced the returns to agricultural production, and therefore both the ability and the incentives to expand production; (3) the nationalisation of the export of rice under the SAMB, which removed the traditional role of commercial banks in financing the trade; (4) the land nationalisation laws – which removed from cultivators the ability to pledge their land as collateral in order to finance technological and other improvements, and; (5) government controls on rents chargeable on agricultural land (under the *Tenancy Standard Rent Act* of 1950), which, in other ways, reduced the opportunities for profitable investment in agriculture.[18] Richter's list, though not exhaustive, amounts to what might be regarded as a general consensus of the ills causing, and caused by, Burma's chronic shortage of rural credit in these years that had promised so much. Myat Thein's (2004: 35) analysis of the parliamentary democracy era is certainly consistent with the consensus, but he also offers a succinct statistic that is surely a summary of all of the above: paddy production in 1960/61 of 6,682 million tons was only 89 per cent of the 7,426-million-ton average of 1936–1940.

INDIVIDUAL INSTITUTION PERFORMANCE

The overall performance of Burma's rural credit institutions was disappointing as noted, but this broad fact disguises considerable variation of performance amongst particular institutions. Below we examine the performance of the major formal dispensers of rural credit in Burma during the parliamentary democracy era, before taking up the perennial standby – the moneylender. Meanwhile, Table 7.1 presents the relevant summary magnitudes:

Table 7.1 Agricultural Loans and Repayment Rates by Institution, 1949–1962 (kyat millions)

	Loan Volumes	Repaid	Repayment Rate (%)
State Agricultural Bank	267.3	263.9	98.7
General Administration	422.0	234.1	55.5
Cooperatives	78.6	54.3	69.1

Source: Author's calculations based on *Economic Survey of Burma*, various years 1953–1964

The SAB

The Burmese government's ambitious plans for the SAB were not realised in terms of the volumes of loans it disbursed, but in many other respects the SAB was one of the institutional success stories of the parliamentary democracy era. Above all, its methodologies for ensuring that loans were repaid (which protected the Bank's capital and maximised what funds *were* allocated by the government) demonstrated that the perennial problem of defaulting borrowers, a phenomenon that had bedevilled and *was bedevilling* other institutions, could be surmounted by good organisational design. The SAB's nearly 99-per-cent repayment rate was not only extraordinary, but (as detailed earlier) it was based on a sound and plausible 'peer lending' methodology that would later form the basis of successful 'microfinance' schemes around the world.[19] Of course, sound methodologies are often undermined by poor or inappropriate implementation (as had been the case with the colonial-era cooperative credit schemes), but the 'practices' of the SAB seem to have matched design, at least in this era. Walinsky (1962: 290) was particularly enamoured with the work of SAB 'field workers' who, he wrote, 'studied each [loan] applicant, visited the farms during the growing season and made the collections'. To Walinsky, the only thing holding back the expansion of the SAB was the shortage of such competent loan supervisors. Good as they were, they were short on the ground, a situation that meant it would be 'many years before a major part of the total credit needs of Burma's cultivators can be met at reasonable rates of interest' (Walinsky 1962: 291).

Walinsky's assessment, coming as it did from the senior representative of KTA in Burma, was that of someone 'from the top'. His judgement, however, was backed up by assessments closer to the ground. David Pfanner, a Ford Foundation training fellow and anthropologist who was based in the village of Mayin in 1959–60 (in Pegu District), was able to closely study the operations of 'Mayin Village Bank' (which was affiliated to the Pegu District branch of the SAB). The Bank, which had commenced operations in August 1957, was relatively large with loans outstanding at June 1960 of K35,000. Even so, Pfanner estimated that this met 'only about 23 per cent of total credit requirements for the village of Mayin'. Pfanner was impressed, however, with what he regarded as the 'superior organisational principles' of the SAB, which included a system of accounts that did 'not permit the irregularities which occurred in the cooperatives' (Pfanner 1962: 256). As important, he thought that the superior organisation of the SAB attracted to it equally superior staff and a quality of leadership that 'fostered an esprit-de-corps among members' that precluded the abuses and anomalies that plagued other rural institutions. His account of those in charge of the Mayin Village Bank eloquently made the point:

> The Mayin village bank leadership is of high quality, performs its work efficiently and has never had its integrity brought into question. Meetings are relatively frequent and cultivators are informed of the bank's plans and activities and their own responsibilities. There is always opportunity to raise questions with the leadership on any issue. The bank president (...) is especially aware that the success of the bank depends upon the mutual efforts of all members and identifies village progress with an increasingly active role on the part of the village bank. He regards its membership as a core of accredited cultivators and contrasts this group with the "discredited" members of the cooperative society or non-members who may have defaulted on government loans in the past. His speeches to the membership are frequently peppered with moral exhortations based on the Buddhist scripture which he quotes at length in Pali (Pfanner 1962: 253).

Pfanner's assessment of the performance of the Mayin Village Bank was matched by what he regarded as the equally good performance of the Pegu District branch of the SAB. Like the Village Bank, Pfanner regarded the Pegu SAB as exceptionally well run and headed by a 'hard working, popular and dedicated former Township officer' (Pfanner 1962: 251). Also like its smaller village affiliate, the Pegu SAB enjoyed exceptional repayment rates and a record generally that offered 'one of the few really encouraging signs in the organization of credit in the agricultural economy' (Pfanner 1962: 254).

Of course, the story of the SAB in its formative years was not a totally sanguine one. Clearly, however, its biggest problem was that of the relatively modest size of its advances relative to need. What Tun Wai (1962: 182) described as the SAB's 'slow and understandably cautious' beginning was reflected in very small advances in the first five years or so of its operations. The slow growth in SAB advances reflected a number of factors, including the shortage of experienced staff noted above, and the cautious way in which new village banks were established. In order to be awarded a village bank, at least four conditions had to be satisfied: (1) the village had to be free from insurgent activity; (2) the village could not be subject to chronic climactic and other vagaries causing frequent cop failure; (3) the village had to have a satisfactory record of loan repayments in previous years, from all sources; (4) there had to be 'good morale' amongst the village's cultivators (Tun Wai 1962: 183). Such conditions were criticised at the time as being too restrictive. Tun Wai (1962:183) acknowledged they were 'conservative' but, as he reasonably noted, it was 'better to err on the side of conservatism than liberalism, at least at the beginning'.

A worrying aspect of the SAB's lending – a problem common to all such institutions everywhere – was that of its 'capture' by wealthy borrowers who took out loans only to on-lend them to borrowers who could not access loans from the Bank themselves. David Pfanner noted that, in Mayin, borrowers from the SAB were primarily prosperous farmers who had no real need for SAB funds to finance their own crops, but took loans nonetheless simply in order to re-lend them at substantially higher rates to their less credit-worthy peers. In this they provided something of a service 'to those ineligible for membership in the SAB who need credit' but the overall effect of the situation was, as Pfanner evocatively put it, 'that those most in need of credit are often denied it and are thus forced to borrow from those who get credit but do not need it' (Pfanner 1962: 259).

Cooperative Credit

The broadly positive organisational narrative of the SAB in the parliamentary democracy years was not replicated in the experience of credit-issuing cooperatives. As noted, these were central to the government's nationalist and socialist agenda, and by the end of the 1950s they were dotted all around the country. The extension of rural credit within the cooperative movement was concentrated primarily in the 'ProCos' discussed above, of which there were over 7,500 by 1961. Their numerical growth and geographical spread, however, disguised a less flattering reality – since around 3,400 of these (44 per cent) were officially classified as 'non working' (Mya Maung 1965: 330–331).

The volume of credit actually extended by cooperatives was modest. As Table 7.1 revealed, the cooperatives were the smallest of the three major rural lenders of the parliamentary democracy years, and their record of securing repayment was considerably worse than the SAB. That they failed to develop in the ways hoped, however (and with a repayment rate of less than 70 per cent they can only be regarded as a failure), was perhaps less important than the nature of their failure which was, astonishingly, an almost precise replay of what had happened to the cooperatives of the colonial era. In a later study of the cooperative movement in Burma, Khin San Yee (1997: 83) offered the following diagnosis. It could easily have come from the Calvert report six decades earlier:

> ...the cooperatives have not been permitted to evolve from below. Instead of organising the cooperatives with the members' interests and member goals, the cooperatives were formed to serve government interests. Cooperative development was promoted through a top-down or blue print planning and implementation with close and strong government control.

Khin San Yee's assessment carries the benefit of hindsight, but it was entirely consistent with near-contemporary judgements such as that of Mya Maung, who wrote a series of papers on the cooperative movement in Burma in the 1960s. This, from 1965, is both representative of his views, and damning of the cooperative apparatus generally. Once more too, it could have easily been written for the circumstances of the 1930s as much as for the 1950s:

> The manifest function of agricultural co-operation in independent Burma is characterised by a large gap between the intended ends and the actual realisation of such ends. The agricultural co-operative movement, like many other state socialist endeavours in independent Burma, exemplifies the above gap in that the intended ends of the successive socialist governments have not been realised in the rural economy and different

purpose-rationality prevails in the agricultural co-operative societies. It is not to suggest that the empirical structure of the Burmese social system does not permit effective modern co-operation *per se* but to assert that the propensity to co-operate on the part of the cultivators cannot be assumed *a priori* as innately given in the traditional cultural system (Mya Maung 1965: 322).

But even worse was the way in which the cooperative movement actively *stifled* a true cooperative and enterprising spirit. Mya Maung again (1965: 323):

> The passive role and function assumed by the co-operators in the rural economy of Burma have been directly *conditioned and caused* by the continuous doling out of credit and other support without effective supervision and organization by the government [emphasis added].

The above analyses were entirely consistent with contemporary assessments on the ground. David Pfanner who, as noted above, was so enamoured of the performance of the SAB in Mayin village, was damning of the performance of the credit cooperative there. The accounts of the village cooperative, he wrote, were 'hopelessly tangled' and less than 50 per cent of its loans had been repaid. By 1959 it had 'virtually suspended all activities' and its organising committee had come under investigation for fraud. Manning Nash, another anthropologist (and also funded in part by the Ford Foundation), who was based in the villages of Nondwin and Yadaw in 1960, found a similar situation with the credit cooperatives in these villages. Members and 'office holders' in the cooperatives, he wrote, were mostly merely 'names on paper', and the cooperatives themselves '... are never operational, but are only to show, if an official asks, that the offices are filled. No official is naïve enough to ever ask' (Nash 1965: 85).

Cooperatives were initially largely funded by the SAB, which used the network as a distribution vehicle while it was still building its own complex of Village Banks. The great expansion of the latter by the late 1950s, together with the problems noted above, caused the SAB to cease funding credit cooperatives in 1958.

GA Loans

Worse than the performance of the cooperative system, however, was the great wastage of government funds provided as General Administrative (GA) loans under the *Agriculturalists Loans Act*. This system had proved useful during the early postwar years, when desperate need was aligned with one of the few administrative networks still functioning. Beyond this period, however, the system was clearly the vehicle for much corruption. District and township officers were formally in charge of loan disbursement but, as Walinsky (1962: 290) noted, they 'had little contact with the villagers and could not visit their farms prior to loan issue, maintain contact with them during the life of the loans or follow through effectively in collections'. In practice, district and township officers were far too busy to closely supervise the GA loans, and tended to simply follow the advice of the 'Land and Tenancy Committees' that had been established in most villages (originally as the devices via which land nationalisation was supposed to proceed). These Committees were highly politicised entities, and were dominated for the most part by members of the (AFPFL) government-linked 'All Burma Peasants Organisation' (ABPO). Contemporary reports were full of stories of 'lavish' funds being provided to ABPO members and supporters, and to the intercession of ABPO leaders 'on behalf of borrowers, both to obtain loans for them and to request leniency in cases of non-repayment' (Tinker 1957: 231, Walinksy 1962: 290). Quite quickly there developed a widespread view that GA loans were little more than government grants which need not ever be repaid. Such a view was reinforced, moreover, by the unfortunate awarding of amnesties by the Government itself – most significantly in 1952, when all unpaid debts contracted before 1949 were cancelled. By 1954 the level of GA loans in arrears amounted to over K100 million (out of a total of GA loans advanced to that point of around K260 million), a situation that prompted the Prime Minister U Nu to declare before an ABPO conference of that year: 'Frankly speaking, if the situation does not improve, things cannot go on at this rate for long. It will be the painful duty of the Union

Table 7.2 GA Loans to Agriculture, 1945/46–1961/62 (kyat millions)

Year	Loans	Repayments	Year	Loans	Repayments
1945/46	28	1	1954/55	27	23
1946/47	34	12	1955/56	17	17
1947/48	28	20	1956/57	18	18
1948/49	8	2	1057/58	23	12
1949/50	20	4	1958/59	27	22
1950/51	30	22	1959/60	30	23
1951/52	36	30	1960/61	30	26
1952/53	42	38	1961/62	88	35

Source: Author's calculations based on various issues of the *Economic Survey of Burma*, 1951–64.

Government to put a stop to the whole process.'[20] As Table 7.2 reveals, however, the situation was never really resolved satisfactorily.

Moneylenders

In the absence of adequate *formal* rural credit, Burmese agriculturalists relied, as they had always done, upon local moneylenders. Of course, the very nature of such credit means that there is very little in the way of hard data on moneylender aggregates. Nevertheless, there is equally little doubt that private and informal moneylenders provided the bulk of credit to Burmese agriculturalists throughout the parliamentary democracy years. Basing his estimates upon the government's 'Agricultural Census' for 1953 and 1954, Aye Hlaing (1958: 21) concluded that government-originated credit accounted for only around 30 per cent of credit ultimately obtained by agriculturalists in these years. Tun Wai (1962: 176) used the same censuses and came up with a similar result in terms of moneylender share of total agricultural credit. However, he also extracted data on moneylender interest rates, both for money loans and traditional *sabape* and other loans in kind:

Table 7.3 Moneylender Credit and Interest Rates, 1953/54 Census Data

Loan source	Share of seasonal loans (%)	Average amount borrowed per agriculturalist (kyats)	Interest rate charged (% p.a)
Government	35.3	105	7.0
Moneylenders (cash)	40.6	260	51.0
Moneylenders (in kind)	24.1	130	56.5
Total	100.0	395	36.9*

* Weighted average, all sources. Source: Tun Wai (1962: 176)

Micro-analyses of particular situations and places support the conjecture of the ubiquity of moneylender borrowing by Burmese agriculturalists, but they also give us insights into the nature of such moneylenders and of their status in village life. Manning Nash who, as noted above, spent some time in the village of Yadaw in 1960, observed that moneylending was the common practice of heads of prominent families – as he notes, the men of 'pon' (Nash 1965: 26).[21] Of course, all of this was a change since the days of Chettiar dominance, but the pattern reflected other, negative forces as well. Principal amongst these was the way in which the government's new land laws (the lack of clear title, the nominal restriction to 50 acres) reduced the returns and therefore the incentives to invest in land improvement and agricultural modernisation. As a consequence 'wealthy' farmers turned to moneylending and petty commerce, and the end result was a less efficient agriculture.

According to Nash, in the village of Yadaw, government credit (of all types) provided at most between K35 to K40 per acre, against cultivation costs of around K100 per acre. The 'gap' was financed by the local moneylenders of the type noted above – usually 'in kind' (primarily *sabape*) at an implicit per annum interest rate of around 35 per cent. Nash noted that moneylenders bore little risk, since they knew their borrowers well, knew the land and market conditions and got their cut of the paddy crop before the borrower got theirs. In all of this there was system enough to keep agricultural production going, but there was a 'treadmill' aspect to the predicament of borrowers that was hard to hide:

> The continual cycle of need to borrow, pay off with interest, need to borrow, both to live and to produce, results in a debt burden that is never discharged, nor is it expected to be discharged. Debt is built into the system and, without the provision of credit by a whole host of moneylenders, the rice would never be grown (Nash 1965: 231).

In her memoir on Burmese family life, Mi Mi Khaing (1956: 89) painted a rather more benign picture of moneylenders in the guise of retired civil servants. According to her, such 'pensioners' got a 'fat income' from moneylending, even if they did not like to admit to it. But such income was not the product of avarice. Rather, the income derived from a service that was a common enough episode of the cycle of life. Moneylending, she wrote (1956: 89),

> ...was connected with the ability to discharge the duties of a parent and a good Buddhist during one's last years, to have sufficient means to settle children into a good marriage, which is one of the duties laid down to a good parent, and to make many donations to pagodas, rest houses and monasteries, all as a foundation for a rebirth into a better existence.

COMMERCIAL BANKING

In terms of commercial banking, Burma's post-independence governments had two objectives. Firstly, they wanted a financial system that could foster and support the country's industrialisation. Secondly, they wanted the system itself to be transformed from one dominated by foreign banks to one in which indigenous institutions would take the lead. But, as with agriculture and almost every other sphere of economic activity, the private sector was not seen as the likely vehicle to bring this about. Thus, just as agriculture was to be serviced by the SAB, so would industry and commerce be facilitated by a 'state commercial bank'.

As with the SAB, the creation of a state commercial bank had been a key recommendation of the KTA Report, which noted that at the dawn of Burma's independence 'few individual small-scale enterprises have enough capital to finance ordinary operating costs, much less expansion and improvement in capital equipment'. Given this, and the fact that hitherto Burma's (foreign-owned) commercial banks had been confined to external trade, Burma's nascent industrial enterprises had relied upon 'loan sharks', the 'middlemen who provide raw materials on credit and often as a condition (...) obtain the finished product'. Such 'middlemen' charged 'exorbitant' interest rates that kept 'small operators in a state of virtual peonage' (KTA 1953: 812).

KTA asserted that it was 'imperative that commercial banking expand in scope' as at least a partial solution to the cost and availability of credit to small-scale industry (KTA 1953: 71). However, on this KTA was once more in step with the presumptions of the Burmese government, since it regarded such an expansion as being the responsibility of the state, rather than of private enterprise. Noting that the failure of private commercial banks 'from premature establishment would retard the future development of banking', KTA instead urged that the 'Government should carefully consider the establishment by *it* of commercial banks' (KTA 1953: 70, emphasis added).

Besides acting as a vehicle for the promotion of Burma's industrialisation, the proposed state commercial bank was also seen as the means through which to 'Burmanise' the country's financial sector in the same way that institutional and legal changes in other sectors had placed 'economic gains originating in Burma into the hands of the Burmese' (Asian Economic Research Institute [AERI] 1961: 392). This was, of course, a long term objective of both the government and KTA, but the issue in relation to banking had become more sensitive in the early independence years, not least because of a perception (most vocally espoused by U Kyaw Nyein, the then Secretary-General of the AFPFL) that the newly-returned foreign banks had 'not assisted' Burma as much as they could. [22] That the criticism was in many ways unfair (since the passing of the *Immoveable Property Act* of 1947, the foreign banks were more or less confined to their traditional foreign exchange activities) did little to temper the passion with which it was advanced, nor the potency of its effects.

The State Commercial Bank (SCB)

Established under an eponymous Act of Parliament (promulgated on 1 June 1954), the SCB had an authorised capital of 50 million kyat, 10 million of which was fully paid up at the time of its founding. All of this was contributed by the government, but a provision allowed for the remaining authorised capital to be sold to the public should it be issued. Whatever the degree of private ownership of the share capital, however, 'the majority of directors [would] always represent the Government' (GuB 1954: 79). As outlined in the Act, the purposes of the SCB was to: (1) accept deposits in order to mobilise savings for productive purposes; (2) grant credit for commercial, industrial and agricultural purposes; (3) support the introduction of new productive techniques; (4) supplement the services of existing commercial banks by providing different types of credit and by providing broad financial facilities; (5) foster the habit of utilising commercial banking activities. [23]

As a Japanese Government study noted, this was more or less the remit of a 'development bank' (AERI 1961: 391). A distinguishing feature of the SCB compared to the plethora of development banks then mushrooming across the developing world, however, was its emphasis on providing short-term and working capital – with less emphasis on the long-term capital traditionally supplied by this type of institution. Of course, in the case of Burma much of the latter came directly from the public purse to state-owned corporations and boards.

Governing the SCB was a seven-member board of directors, all of whom were in essence government appointees. The Chairman and Deputy Chairman (no women were to fill these posts in the life of the SCB) were directly appointed by the government, though by convention the position of Deputy Chairman came to be filled by the Chairman of the Union Bank of Burma (UBB). The first Chairman of the SCB was Kyaw Nyein, who, as noted above, had been a strong critic of the (foreign) private banks, and was otherwise at this time the Minister of Industry (and acting Foreign Minister). U Tin Tun, who had been J.C. Reid's understudy at the UBB, was the SCB's first General Manager. Tin Tun had good relations with the Bank of England, and sought its help in the early years of the SCB in recruiting staff. [24] The first branch of the SCB was in Rangoon, but a programme of rapid branch expansion was put in place from the outset. In establishing new branches, the practice adopted by the SCB was to open a sub-branch first (where only lending business was conducted), and then if business conditions proved profitable, the sub-branch was transformed into a full branch (GuB 1961b: 60). By 1963 the SCB had 40 branches across Burma, including an office at Rangoon airport. By this time it also employed around 2,000 people (Emery 1970: 21).

Not surprisingly perhaps, the hitherto dominant British exchange banks were worried about the implications for them of the creation of the SCB. In a report to the then British Foreign Secretary, Anthony Eden, the British Ambassador to Burma, P.H. Gore-Booth, wrote that 'British banking interests here are apprehensive' about the new SCB, not just because the Government promised that the new bank would lend at lower interest rates than existing banks, 'but also because they think that pressure of various kinds will be put on Governmental and quasi-Governmental organisations to transfer their business (which is both safer and more profitable than the general run of banking here) to the new bank'.[25]

The exchange banks did not receive a sympathetic hearing from the Ambassador, who told Eden that he believed that there was

> ...no case for an official protest or scope for any other action on our part to preserve for British banks the virtual monopoly which they have so far enjoyed. It was only to be expected that, sooner or later, the Burmese would take some sort of step of this kind, and provided that there is no gross discrimination calling for diplomatic protest, the only defence of the British banks against this competition lies in the integrity of their record and in the service they offer.[26]

The foreign banks' concern about unfair pressure being wielded in favour of the SCB was accorded some unexpected support, however – from Burmese business which, so reported the British Embassy in Burma, was 'not enthusiastic' about the SCB. According to the Ambassador, Burmese business owners 'feel that they are likely to be subjected to pressure to transfer their dealings from the existing banks to the new one'. Of even greater concern, they suspected the government had an ulterior motive too – that, via their possible involvement with the SCB, 'the Income Tax Department and the Bureau of Special investigation will be able to find out a great deal that they would prefer should remain hidden'. The Ambassador thought their suspicions well-founded: 'I suspect the Burmese [government] had this point very much in mind when they planned the new bank.'[27]

As events turned out, both the fears of the British banks and of the Burmese businesses were prescient, and on 2 March 1955 the Burmese government issued a directive to all government departments, boards, corporations and companies in state joint ventures 'to deal exclusively' with the SCB. Likewise, most import licenses would now only be issued on the proviso that SCB bills of exchange and other trade instruments were exclusively used. More ominously perhaps was the tone of the directive, which concluded with the assertion that foreign banks posed 'dangers to the economic condition of the State'. [28] The British Embassy was sanguine about the directive, however, noting that the Government's policy was, whilst discriminatory, 'normal enough'. It took umbrage at the reasons stated, however, calling the claims of the dangers of foreign banks 'outrageous'.[29] Hogg of Britain's Foreign Office also noted similar accusations by Burma's Finance and Revenue Ministry, which was accusing the foreign banks of 'exercising all-out pressure on the nation's economics'.[30] Elsewhere, the Embassy reported a general feeling of 'uncertainty and anxiety' of foreign business in Burma.[31]

As a consequence of these and other policies, within a few years the SCB would win the major share of commercial banking in Burma, and the role of foreign banks would whither. We shall examine the latter phenomenon in detail presently, but what must also be remarked upon is the emerging structural pattern of the SCB's lending:

As Table 7.4 (opposite) reveals, the SCB would prove a remarkably conservative lender, and in many ways a captive institution to the credit needs of the government and state-owned boards and corporations. The SCB undertook only a modest amount of direct lending in the form of loans and advances, and a substantial proportion of its assets comprised 'investments' (mostly government securities). Lending to enterprises was primarily in the form of guarantees and endorsements of bills issued by state boards and corporations. In terms of the *types* of activities funded by the SCB, 35 per cent went to manufacturing and processing, 29 per cent for distribution and marketing, 17 per cent to construction, 14 per cent to retail trade, and 5 per cent to international trade (SCB 1963: 14). The SCB provided little in the way of financing for new ventures, usually lending only to established enterprises that could pledge immoveable property as

Table 7.4 State Commercial Bank: Selected Assets and Liabilities, 1955–1962 (kyat millions)

As at 30 June	1955	1956	1957	1958	1959	1960	1961	1962
Assets								
Cash	67	71	69	102	139	149	155	138
Loans and Advances	7	23	59	72	74	107	144	148
Investments	142	151	152	285	362	323	277	286
Acceptances, Endorsements and Guarantees	73	108	255	99	189	179	184	143
Liabilities								
Deposits	214	183	235	409	481	523	535	522

Source: SCB (1963)

collateral. Throughout its existence the SCB lent almost nothing against new capital equipment or other 'moveable' property except in the case of very short-term inventory loans (Emery 1970: 23).

Private Commercial Banks

The overriding narrative of private banks in the parliamentary democracy years is one of retrenchment and decline with respect to the foreign-owned institutions, and unfulfilled promise in the case of the indigenous Burmese banks that might have taken their place.

We have noted at various places above the generalised hostility towards foreign banks on the part of the Burmese government. Extending from this were the favours granted to the SCB, but there were other factors in play that also conspired against them. One of these, which told against the hitherto dominant *British* banks, was simply the economic decline of Britain itself during the period. The exchange banks had relied upon the strength and stability of sterling, but in the post-Second World War era this was an increasingly doubtful proposition. The huge debts accumulated by Britain during the Second World War left the country short of foreign exchange and unable to guarantee the convertibility of sterling throughout the 1940s and 1950s. Various exchange crises over the period, and sterling's substantial devaluation in 1949, consolidated the displacement of sterling in favour of the US dollar as the world's 'reserve currency'. The exchange banks were increasingly unable to offer 'exchange' at a profit, and sometimes barely at all. Of course, a related issue was the decline of British firms generally in the region. Such firms – the trading companies, the millers, plantations, mines and utilities – were the traditional customers of the exchange banks, but they were setting with the Empire they had once served.

Circumstances within Burma were likewise not favourable to the established foreign banks. Some of these have been alluded to in general terms already, but amongst the most significant included the *Immoveable Property Act* of 1947. This law, passed immediately prior to independence as a sop to nationalist sentiment (by the British interim administration), prohibited foreigners from securing title over immoveable property. This had enormous implications for the ability of foreign banks to expand their lending beyond simple trade transactions (even if they had wanted to), since collateral for long-term lending in the traditional form of title to land, buildings, mills and so on was no longer useable. The UBB itself estimated in 1948 that this Act alone 'kept in idleness about K30 to K40 million of banking funds'.[32]

Other events in Burma told against the foreign banks. The creation of the government 'boards' with a monopoly over the trade of many of Burma's principal commodities removed almost completely the foreign exchange business derived from commodity exports. Providing foreign exchange for imports remained a viable activity to some extent, but even this greatly declined from the prewar situation. By 1960 half of all imports were bought by the government, for which it drew upon only the UBB and SCB (Tun Wai 1962: 199–200). The government boards (principally the SAMB and the State Timber Board) did still further damage to the foreign banks when later they turned to on-lending government funds to private sector firms (rather than simply being the recipients of funds for their own operations). In this context Tun Wai noted (1962: 169) that government funds supplied in this way became 'more important than the lending activities of the commercial banks'.

Finally, on top of all these obstacles were physical ones. For the 're-turning' foreign banks much of the immediate postwar period was spent reconstructing physical infrastructure destroyed in the war. This reconstruction was largely limited, however, to Rangoon. The foreign banks had always been concentrated in the capital, of course, but the political unrest of the early independence years inhibited any desire they might have had to extend (or rehabilitate) their operations into the country broadly, or even to the major provincial cities. In 1949 there were 20 bank offices of which 18 were in Rangoon (the other two were in Akyab and Maymyo). By 1957 this had grown to 37 offices, 10 of which were beyond Rangoon but the bulk of these were branches of the SCB (Tun Wai 1962: 190). Burma's political unrest, and the other difficulties noted, caused some of the prewar commercial banks to not return to the country at all after independence. The most notable of these were the National City Bank of New York and Lloyds Bank, both of which, as noted in Chapter 5, had been prominent in the colonial era.

The declining presence of foreign banks in Burma was especially apparent amongst those originating from Britain, Western Europe and the United States. With respect to Indian banks the picture was a more nuanced one. Some banks had greatly scaled back their presence because of the exigencies above (notably the State Bank of India, the new name of the Imperial Bank), while some had not returned following the war (such as the Mohaluxmi Bank and the Indian Bank). These moves were partly offset, however, by the arrival of new Indian banks in Burma. Prominent amongst these was the 'United Commercial Bank' (UCB), described by the British Ambassador to Burma as 'a go-getting Indian concern' which, in its early years, even managed to snare a substantial amount of government business.[33] The UCB had been established in 1943 by G.D. Birla – the famed Indian industrialist, friend and adviser to Gandhi, and a leader of the 'Quit India' movement.[34] The Bank itself was conceived by Birla as a 'truly Indian bank', and its strong connections with the government of newly-independent India gave it a certain cachet in Burma. The UCB opened its first Burma office in Rangoon in 1947 but, in great contrast to almost all other foreign banks, specialised in agricultural lending. It had four branches 'up-country', and its operations were described by the British Ambassador as being reminiscent of a 'streamlined version of the Indian bania' (the Indian moneylending caste, originally from the Punjab, but never greatly active in Burma).[35]

The UCB's Rangoon head office was located in the old Yokohama Specie Bank building, and its opening occasioned one of the most ostentatious (secular) public spectacles of the parliamentary democracy era.[36] Attended by leading politicians and Burma's ruling elite more broadly, the event attracted 'very favourable' press coverage – no better exemplified than by the *New Times of Burma's* description of the UCB as 'the altruistic friend of the cultivator and a leading contributor to the welfare state'. This was all too much for the British Ambassador, who noted sardonically that the 'state welcome accorded by the Government of a professedly socialist country to one of the foremost manifestations of Indian capitalism is odd, to say the least'.[37] The early prominence and success of the UCB meant that it was perhaps the most affected of the Indian banks by the subsequent creation of the SCB and, according to one British observer, was 'moving heaven and earth to get the brakes put on their new rival'.[38] In this, of course, it did not succeed.

Most of the other Indian banks were limited in their operations in Burma, primarily being engaged in the financing of trade between the two countries, and in extending loans to Indian-owned businesses in Burma. One of these was the Indian Overseas Bank, the institution founded simultaneously in Rangoon and Tamil Nadu in 1937 by Shri M.Ct.M. Chidambaram Chettyar, head of the grandest and most powerful of all the Chettiar banking families. By 1962, Indian banks held about 10 per cent of all deposits of commercial banks in Burma, and extended around 4 per cent of all loans advanced (Indian Institute of Bankers 1963: 78).

Table 7.5 Private Commercial Banks in Burma in March 1963

Burmese Banks	Foreign Banks
• Ava Bank	• The Central Bank of India
• Burma Economic Development Corporation	• Chartered Bank
• Union of Burma Co-operative Bank	• Habib (Overseas) Bank
• Burmese National Bank	• Hongkong and Shanghai Banking Corporation
• Upper Burma Bank	• Indian Overseas Bank
• East Burma Bank	• Mercantile Bank
• Rangoon Bank	• National and Grindlays Bank
• Export-Import Bank	• Netherlands Trading Society
• Burma Economic Bank	• Overseas Chinese Banking Corporation
• Tavoy Bank	• Punjab National Bank
• Burma Central Commercial Bank	• United Commercial Bank
	• Bank of China
	• Bank of Communications
	• State Bank of India

Source: Banerji 1963: 106

Table 7.5 above lists all of the foreign banks that survived through the parliamentary democracy years, and to the eve of nationalisation. Also listed are the indigenous Burmese banks created in these years – a group to which we now turn.

Indigenous Burmese Private Commercial Banks

Indigenous Burmese banks did not have to contend with the *Transfer of Immoveable Property Act*, but in every other respect they confronted the same difficult environment as that faced by the foreign banks in the parliamentary democracy era. By the end of this era (as per Table 7.5) there were 11 of these banks, not counting the state-owned banks elsewhere dealt with. Most were small operations, and today would be completely forgotten by history, were it not for a certain immortality occasioned by the internet – and the brisk market that has developed therein in the share certificates of little-known banks.[39]

The first, and probably the largest of the Burmese private banks formed after independence was the 'Burmese National Bank'. Created in 1948 by U Po Sa, the Bank began with capital of K2 million, and by 1956 had attracted K30 million in deposits (U Po Sa 1955). U Po Sa found fame as a writer and interpreter of Buddhism, but he was also very much a member of that part of the Burmese elite who had found success and esteem in the old colonial order. He was well qualified to start a bank – his career in the colonial years as a district commissioner and magistrate being capped during the war years as the government's Finance Secretary. The dominance of the Burmese National Bank over the other indigenous banks is noted by a number of contemporary sources, including the British Embassy, which declared it the 'most active of the Burmese private banks'.[40] The Bank was also celebrated by Tun Wai (1962: 191) who noted its high profitability (K1.3 million of profits in 1956, a return on capital of a remarkable 65 per cent), the cause of which he concluded was the confidence it had inspired amongst the Burmese. As the decade wore on, however, the Burmese National Bank faced harder times and increasing competition – primarily (as with all the other private banks) from the SCB, but also from the aforementioned (Indian) 'United Commercial Bank' with its strong government connections. According to the British Embassy, the growth of the latter was 'largely at the expense of the Burmese National Bank', especially with respect to government business.[41] Later the Burmese National Bank was to complain about the fickleness of Burmese business, and 'the lack of support it received from the public'.[42]

The 'Union of Burma Cooperative Bank' (UBCB) was a creation of the cooperative movement. Formed in October 1954, the UBCB's share capital was owned by both cooperative societies and private individuals. The UBCB's borrowers were mostly limited to cooperative institutions. By June 1956 the UBCB had deposits of K18.4 million and loans of K11.2 million – testimony to what Tun Wai (1962: 188) rightly notes was the Bank's 'rapid progress'. Despite its unique ownership structure and other features, the

UBCB had to meet all the requirements for commercial banks set down by the UBB. Great hopes (not realised) were held for the UBCB 'as the link between cooperative credit societies and commercial banks in Burma' (Tun Wai 1962: 188). Another indigenous bank for which optimistic hopes were held was the 'Burma Central Commercial Bank'. Formed in August 1950 and with (a relatively large) capital base of Rs (subsequently kyats, K) 2.5 million in paid-up capital, the Bank was initially seen as a strong competitor to the Burmese National Bank. The Burma Central Commercial Bank never really lived up to expectations, however, and the scale of its activities were relatively modest.[43]

A surprising and positive aspect of Burma's emerging indigenous bank cohort was that a number of them originated from outside Rangoon. Two of the most prominent in this respect was the 'Bank of Upper Burma', which was formed in Maymyo, and the 'Tavoy Bank', established in the city of the same name in 1951. The Bank of Upper Burma was a small bank – indeed, its capital of Rs(K) 400,000 was not sufficient to be regarded as a 'scheduled' bank under the UBB's regulations. It was a subsidiary of Hamid and Company, an Indo-Burmese trading enterprise long resident in Burma. Tavoy Bank had capital of K1 million. All of its directors and principals were Burmese, and all from Tavoy.[44]

Towards the end of the parliamentary democracy era, two other banks emerged that may have had a greater impact on Burma's financial system had nationalisation not arrived in 1963. These two, the 'Ava Bank' and the 'Export Import Bank', were both subsidiaries of the military-owned 'Defence Services Institute' (DSI). The DSI had been established in 1952 as a military-owned company to operate 'canteens' and various welfare and ancillary services to the military. Though it expanded its range of activities throughout the democratic era, it enjoyed spectacular growth during the later 1950s (under the *Bogyoke* government', more on which below), and by 1960 ran shops, hotels, agricultural and fisheries concerns, a shipping line, Rangoon's bus system and the country's largest export/import business (Callahan 2003: 168–169). In 1961 the DSI was re-named the 'Burma Economic Development Corporation' (BEDC) to reflect its expansive role (Steinberg 2005: 54). The DSI's creation of Ava Bank came simultaneously with its purchase (in 1959) of the venerable stockbroking firm A. Scott and Company (Tun Wai 1962: 161). The Ava Bank was subsequently used as the financing vehicle for *Tatmadaw* officers to participate in DSI businesses (Callahan 2003: 191). Ironically, perhaps, the rise of Ava Bank was aided by the granting of a substantial sterling loan in November 1960 by one of the grandest and oldest of the British exchange banks – HSBC (King 1991: 204–205). The Export Import Bank, meanwhile, was established in 1961 by what was now the BEDC. Allocated a relatively large K10 million capital base, it was founded by the BEDC upon the apparent hope that it would eventually emerge as the primary provider of foreign exchange services in Burma. Of course, this would have put it in direct competition with the SCB. The coming nationalisation of the banks undid such ambitions.

COMMERCIAL BANK PERFORMANCE

As was the case with respect to agricultural credit, in the sphere of commercial banking the years of parliamentary democracy were disappointing ones. Modest advances were recorded in terms of institutional *creation* (as per the above), but the potential of these was scarcely realised before they would be swept away along with democracy itself in 1962. Also consistent with the experience in agriculture, a general shortage of credit was the most apparent manifestation of the sector's problems but, much more obviously than was the case for agriculture, the problem of credit *allocation* was to the fore. Credit for small to medium enterprises was Burma's most pressing need in the 1950s but it went unfulfilled – mostly, as recounted below, because what financial resources were created by Burma's commercial banks were diverted to the needs of state-owned enterprises, and to the state itself.

Table 7.6 (overleaf) demonstrates the essential problem. As can be seen from the data here, Burma's commercial banks made steady, if not remarkable, progress in terms of their relative size to the economy as a whole. By the end of the 1950s the ratio of commercial banks' assets to Gross National Product (a useful measure of 'financial depth') stood at almost 17 per cent. The ratio moved about somewhat according to fluctuations in both bank lending and GNP itself, but it was a ratio that was comparable to countries at similar stages of economic development. Malaysia, for instance, had a ratio of commercial bank assets to GNP in 1960 of 19.5 per cent, Ceylon (Sri Lanka) 17.1 per cent, Pakistan 13.3 per cent and India 15.7 per cent.[45] Of concern, however, was the *allocation* of these assets in terms of the relative shares of commercial bank funds that were lent to the private sector, as opposed to the state. As Table 7.6 reveals, here the situation appears less sanguine, as funds advanced to the government (mostly in the form of bank purchases of government securities) grew rapidly, especially from the mid-1950s, beyond which the state's 'claims' on the financial resources of commercial banks began to exceed those available to the private sector.

Table 7.6 Measures of Commercial Bank Development, 1950–1962

Year	Commercial bank assets % of GNP	Commercial bank claims on private sector (kyat millions)	Commercial bank claims on government (kyat millions)
1950	8.1	130	27
1951	7.4	159	81
1952	8.0	178	22
1953	7.0	161	62
1954	10.2	212	155
1955	13.6	216	289
1956	15.5	250	358
1957	12.7	343	240
1958	16.4	270	475
1959	17.9	305	578
1960	16.7	379	512
1961	15.6	436	467
1962	16.4	469	497

Source: IMF (1966).

The state, in short, became a significant *competitive* source of demand for funds in Burma, and to this extent 'crowded out' private entrepreneurs.

Finance for Small to Medium Enterprises

The biggest casualties of the diversion of commercial bank funds to the financing needs of government were Burma's small to medium businesses. According to Khin Than Kywe ([1960: 112], using data from the census of 1953/54), there were around 2,500 of such 'industrial enterprises' in Burma, defined as having between 10 to 50 employees, and concentrated in small-scale manufacturing and processing firms, food and beverages, textiles and clothing, tobacco and wood products.[46] With much large-scale industry in the hands of the state under *Pyidawtha*, these enterprises had a particular hunger for *borrowed* capital. Equity capital could not be raised effectively in the absence of a stock market and, in any case, a majority of Burma's small industrial firms were sole proprietor and partnerships. They sourced their initial capital from internal resources (their own funds, borrowing from friends and relatives), which was usually tied up in the fixed assets of the enterprise. Working capital, however, was primarily sought through credit. This was not unusual for small-scale enterprises anywhere, but in Burma at this time the demand was heightened by unreliable raw materials supplies (necessitating the holding of higher stocks) and a workforce that demanded pay in advance (prompted by their fears of not being paid) (Khin Than Kywe 1960: 127–128).

Unfortunately, the demand for capital from Burma's industrial enterprises was not matched at any time in the democratic era by its supply. Amongst the three primary sources of 'outside' capital, commercial banks, the government and 'private' sources (principally moneylenders), only the latter was available in any great volume, and this only on unfavourable terms. Of course, commercial banks were the primary sources of working (and other) capital for industry in most countries, but in Burma they were unequal to the task. Indeed, as can be seen from the table below, they were the least significant suppliers of capital to Burmese industry. Their lending to the smallest enterprises was especially paltry. Only for large enterprises (in excess of 250 employees) did they constitute the most important source of finance.

Table 7.7 Size Classification and Source of Outside Financing to Burmese Industrial Enterprise, 1953/54

Employees	No. of enterprises	Govt. %	Banks %	Private %	Mixed funding
10–24	448	12	3	79	6
25–49	185	19	6	66	9
50–74	86	20	17	57	6
75–99	28	21	29	43	7
100–249	63	24	27	33	16
250–499	18	6	72	16	6
>500	1	-	100	-	-
Percentage	100	15	10	68	7

Source: Khin Than Kywe (1960).

The Burmese government was not indifferent to the credit needs of commercial enterprise (even though it increasingly competed with it for finance), and in September 1955, in an effort to improve the quantity of finance available for the purchase of new *capital equipment*, it established the Industrial Loan Board (ILB). A division within the Industrial Development Corporation (IDC), the ILB offered what was in effect a 'hire purchase scheme' to Burmese industrial firms (Golay *et al.* 1969: 256). In

1956–1957 the ILB financed K13.4 million worth of machinery under hire purchase to 136 enterprises. Its success, however, was short-lived. Subject to 'drastic economy measures' during the period of the military caretaker government (below), thereafter it appeared to do little but recover the old loans advanced (Golay *et al.* 1969: 256–257).

THE BOGYOKE INTERLUDE AND THE FINAL YEARS OF BURMA'S DEMOCRACY

In April 1958, a growing political crisis in Burma manifested itself in a split in the ruling AFPFL into two bitterly opposed factions – the so-called 'clean AFPFL' led by the Prime Minister, U Nu, and the 'stable AFPFL' whose members had strong links to the military. The conflict between the two coloured many contentious issues in the country and divided most of its key institutions, and throughout 1958 rumours of a military coup became increasingly intense. On 28 October 1958 the head of the *Tatmadaw* (as Burma's armed forces were, and are, known), General Ne Win, took power in an affair that was dressed up at the time as a 'voluntary' hand-over of power by U Nu to a 'caretaker' military government. In fact there was little that was voluntary about the hand over, and the event is more appropriately to be regarded as the first coup of the Burmese military against the civilian government (Callahan 2003: 190–191). Of issue here, however, is that this caretaker government (popularly known as the *'Bogyoke'* [General's] government) took a number of initiatives that foreshadowed the momentous changes soon to engulf Burma's financial system, and the country more broadly.

In terms of commercial banking, these changes were manifest in the emergence of new institutions and yet, simultaneously, in the growing dominance of the SCB. The latter phenomenon reflected increasing government control of the economy generally, and by the end of the brief *Bogyoke* rule the SCB accounted for 49 per cent of all bank deposits in Burma. Over this 18-month period the Bank's assets expanded by 36 per cent, driven by greater lending to industry, though much of this came from the decision to reduce the role played by the SAMB in funding paddy millers. The SCB's financing of Burma's foreign trade also increased, helped by the ever-increasing share of the country's exports and imports that passed through the hands of government agencies (GuB 1960b). Amongst the 'new' institutions created during the *Bogyoke* period included the Ava and Export-Import Banks – both owned by the military's Burma Economic Corporation as noted, and both of which enjoyed something of a 'bonanza' during the 18 months of this first experiment in military rule in Burma (Callahan 2003: 191).

In April 1960 the military 'returned to barracks' and, following elections conducted in February, a new civilian government, once more led by U Nu, took back power. In the realm of commercial banking the trend of growing state control more or less continued, however, and in October 1961 a new state-owned bank, the 'Industrial Development Bank' (IDB), was created to 'enhance the economic development of the Union of Burma (...) by providing finance in the form of long or medium term loans or equity participations'. The IDB had authorised capital of K50 million, and paid-up capital of K20 million. The government contributed K10 million of the latter, the SCB and the Union Insurance Board K 5 million each (Banerji 1963: 107). The IDB undertook little in the way of its intended activities, however, before the second military coup.

It was in agriculture that the most dramatic changes were instigated under the *Bogyoke* government, including a greatly expanded program of GA loans. A dramatic 50 per cent increase in these was authorised, though actual disbursements would subsequently fall short of this. Even more dramatic, however, if rather more destructive in its implications, the *Bogyoke* government also announced what amounted to a limited amnesty of past loan defaulters in seeking *new* loans. As one of the few disciplines under the previous arrangements, defaulters had been precluded from seeking fresh loans from government bodies (including the SAB) until their arrears had been cleared. Under the new arrangements, the *Bogyoke* government waived this prerequisite for three categories of defaulters: (a) those who had been rendered ineligible through acts of fraud or misappropriation committed by the [Village Loan or Co-operative] Committee; (b) those who were unable to repay because of loss of cattle or crop failure due to drought, flood or other causes beyond their control; and (c) those of a group of borrowers to whom loans had been granted on collective security bond, who had fully repaid their respective loans, and of whom only one or two had defaulted (GuB 1960b: 159).

Of course, to some extent these appeared reasonable, even 'fair', but provisions (b) and (c) especially were nevertheless corrosive of good financial practice and sufficiently 'flexible' to allow for almost any sort of argument. It might also be noticed that (c), however equitable-sounding, more or less removed in one stroke the entire discipline principle of 'peer lending' that was such a celebrated feature of the SAB system. In an environment in which loan default was endemic it was all just one more unfortunate development.

The brief return to civilian rule in 1960 brought with it certain administrative changes with respect to the GA programme, the most significant of which was that henceforth it would be administered by the SAB. Beyond that, the SAB's own lending was to be given priority. Under what became known as the 'Four-Year Plan' for the SAB, the Bank was charged with expanding both its short-term cultivation loans, and with establishing a modest new programme of 'special' and long-term loans for cultivators. The latter were particularly designed to encourage new tea, orange, rubber and coffee plantations. There was also a modest proposal (compared to what would follow in the wake of the military coup) to expand the number of Village Banks. The Four-Year Plan called for the SAB 'to form Village Banks in every village-tract in Tharrawaddy District in 1961–62, in Shwebo and Henzada districts in 1962–62, in Sagaing and Myaungmya districts in 1963–64 and in Monywa and Prome districts in 1964–65' (GuB 1961b: 102). The overall volume of loans predicated under the Four-Year Plan, and the various categories within which they were to be made, is revealed in Table 7.8:

Table 7.8 Credit Programme, Four-Year Plan for the SAB (kyat millions)

Year	SAB Short-Term Cultivation Loans	Special and Long-Term Loans	GA Loans (administered by SAB)	Total
1961–62	80	10	35	125
1962–63	95	10	34	139
1963–64	110	10	32	152
1964–65	130	10	30	170

Source: GuB (1961b: 102)

Administering the GA programme, and the problems created by the *Bogyoke* government's expansion and amnesty policies, were to prove the greatest vexations for the SAB for these last years of Burma's democracy. Manning Nash, the American anthropologist based in the village of Nondwin and Yadaw in 1960, noted the programme's ill-effects 'on the ground' in the two villages. As always, and despite the expansion of the programme overall, there was insufficient credit available to the villagers. What *was* new, however, were that loans available in the villages were contingent 'upon the political relations of Nondwin to the national government through village performance in elections' (Nash 1965: 58). The loans available under the GA programme were, in short, a 'political weapon' (Nash 1965: 99). In the case of Nondwin, all was well for the village as a whole since it had voted overall in favour of the candidate from U Nu's victorious *Pyidaungzu* (Union) party. The disbursement of funds *within* the village, however, was more problematic, and Nash wrote of the process taking on an 'acrimonious tack of bickering and favouritism' according to which political party a potential borrower was seen to support (Nash 1965: 99). Nash's assessment of the overall effect of the loan programme of the *Bogyoke* government is worth citing more extensively, since it distils both the political imperatives of the schemes, and the problems left unsolved:

> The loan program is in part an attempt to fill the gap left by the flight of small private capital and, also, to lessen the burden of small holder debt. It is not a program to spur innovation, to demand new behaviour from villagers. It is only a modest underwriting of the usual agricultural activity. It did not have the resources, the personnel, the tools, or the vision to significantly affect, let alone transform, the life of Nondwin villagers (...) [it] was not massive enough, not sustained enough, not placed enough in the villagers' hands to make any sort of impact on the economic structure of the community or its image of the modern world. Its chief yield to the peasants of Nondwin was symbolic; there was in existence a national government of Burmans, dedicated to the welfare of Burmans, and perhaps, with luck, it might even be really useful (Nash 1965: 99–100).

As we shall see in the next chapter, soon this 'national government' would itself be utterly transformed.

NOTES

1   The title 'thakin' meant 'sir' or 'master' in Burmese, and its use by young Burmese nationalists in the 1930s to address each other was a calculated act of defiance to the British imperial authorities. The thakin 'movement' (the 'Dobama Asiayone' was its political organisation) included Aung San, U Nu, Kyaw Nyein, Thein Pe, M.A. Raschid and other young men who were to be prominent in Burma's post-independence governments. Of course, the depiction above greatly simplifies the intellectual and ideological influences upon the thakins which, in addition to Marxism, included readings of Nietzsche, Hitler, Mussolini, Nehru, Sun Yat-Sen and tracts from the Irish Sinn Fein movement. On top of all of these was their own 'lived experience' of Burmese history and culture, imperialism, and the spiritual influence of Buddhism. Certainly for U Nu personally, reconciling Buddhism and Marxism was the great

intellectual quest of his youth (Butwell 1963: 26–27; Silverstein 1977: 45; Maung Maung 1980, *passim;* Thant Myint-U 2006: 257–289).

2   As noted in Chapter 5, U Ba Maung was also the nominated chief of the proposed 'Burma State Bank' of Ba Maw's wartime government.

3   For more on Hla Myint, see Bauer and Meier (1994).

4   Memorandum by Walinsky of conversation with Hla Myint, 19 Dec 1958, Walinsky Papers, Cornell University Library, Box 4.

5   Furnivall's central role was not well received by some, however. The former financial adviser to the Government of Burma, A.K. Potter, who was now ensconced at the British Embassy in Rangoon, despaired of Furnivall's role in a letter to the Bank of England. Thinly veiling his target's identity, Potter referred to the 'one European adviser to the Government, an ex-Indian civil servant who retired from service in Burma many years ago and is now aged over seventy. He is a theorist of leftist views and works mostly with the National Planners'. Potter reported that U Kyin [Secretary of the Department Of Finance] had told him that Furnivall's 'head [was] in the clouds most of the time'. A.K. Potter to Bank of England, 19 August 1948, BoE, OV 79/1.

6   As Cady (1958: 616) notes, more often than not *Pyidawtha* is simply translated as 'welfare state'. As he also rightly indicates, however, it had a different flavour for its Burmese audience than this rather anodyne label suggests. Cady's amended translation of 'cooperation between the people and government for the happiness of the country' is, thus, a truer rendering of how it was understood in Burma at the time.

7   According to Walinsky, the 'Government of Burma had not attempted in overt and specific ways to influence the formulation or composition of the development program'. Untitled memorandum by Louis Walinsky, 7 January 1959, Walinsky Papers, Box 3.

8   Mya Maung (1965: 332) notes that the 'multi-purposeness' of the ProCos was more apparent than real, and that to most of their members the expressions 'cooperative' and 'credit' remained inseparable.

9   For more on the flight of the Chettiars from Burma, see Bayley and Harper (2004: 230–244).

10   Boquérat (2001: 5) has an estimate for the market value of Chettiar land of Rs 700 million, and compensation of Rs 10 million. The difference hinges upon a number of factors (including the exact magnitude of Chettiar land holdings) for which it is impossible to be precise. Nevertheless, that the magnitudes are broadly similar is instructive. The Government of India attempted to negotiate an increase in the compensation payments, but its entreaties in this matter were continuously rebuffed by Burma (Boquérat 2001: 5).

11   Untitled memorandum, J. Fisher (Bank of England), 29 March 1945, BoE, OV 79/1.

12   B.G. Catterns, Deputy Governor of the Bank of England to S. Barnes, Chief General Manager, Lloyds Bank, 23 April 1945, BoE, OV 79/1.

13   'Report of the Directors, Dawson's Bank, to Shareholders', 29 February 1964, OIOC, Papers of James Douglas Stuart, Mss Eur D1239.

14   The Managing Director of the Bank was Khin Maung Hla and, apart from James, the other directors included Daw Saw Myint, Soe Myint, and Htoon Min. *Ibid.*

15 Hla Myint to Louis Walinsky, 4 February 1960, Walinsky Papers, Box 3.

16 Details of KTA's planning regarding the ARDC and the other corporations can be found in the Walinsky Papers, Box 4.

17 Author's calculation based on various issues (1951–1964) of the government's *Economic Survey of Burma*.

18 The *Tenancy Standard Rent Act* limited maximum rent payable on agricultural land to twice the land revenue payable (Tinker 1957: 230).

19 Richter (1968: 108) estimated a repayment rate at the SAB of 97 per cent.

20 U Nu's speech was made in June 1954, and is here cited from Tinker (1957: 232).

21 'Pon' is that mystical power or charisma possessed, according to Burmese folklore, in varying quantities by all men (Ardeth Maung Thawnghmung 2004: 28).

22 Diary note of visit of Kyaw Nyein to the Bank of England, 6 September 1952, BoE, OV 79/2.

23 Article 5, Section 2 of the State Commercial Bank Act 1954, reproduced in Asian Economic Research Institute (1961: 391).

24 See telegram, U Tin Tun, Deputy General-Manager of the Union Bank of Burma, to Bank of England, 17 December 1953, BoE, OV 79/2.

25 British Ambassador to Burma, P.H. Gore-Booth to Secretary of State for Foreign Affairs, Anthony Eden, 5 January 1954, BoE, OV 79/2.

26 *Ibid.*

27 Letter, British Ambassador, Rangoon to J.M. Patterson, South-East Asian Department, Foreign Office, 10 April 1954, BoE, OV 79/2.

28 Memorandum by P.L Hogg, Foreign Office, 6 January 1955, BoE, OV 79/2.

29 B.C. Cook, British Embassy, Rangoon, to Foreign Office, 4 March 1955, BoE, OV 79/2.

30 P.L. Hogg, British Embassy, Rangoon to D.M. Butt, HM Treasury, 29 April 1955, BoE, OV 79/2.

31 British Ambassador, Rangoon, to Harold Macmillan, Secretary of State, Foreign Office, 24 May 1955, BoE, OV 79/2.

32 UBB cited in Tun Wai (1962: 191).

33 British Ambassador, Rangoon, to J.M. Patterson, South-East Asian Department, Foreign Office, 12 February 1954, BoE, OV 79/2.

34 The UCB lives on to the present day as the 'UCO Bank'. A brief history of the Bank can be found at its website, <www.ucobank.com>.

35 *Ibid.*

36 The event is described in detail in the letter from the British Ambassador to J.M. Patterson, 12 February 1954, BoE, OV 79/2.

37 *Ibid.*

38 Untitled memorandum by P.L Hogg, Foreign Office, 6 January 1955, BoE, OV 79/2.

39 Any casual perusal of online auction sites will reveal the trade in such certificates, a component of a broader collector's market for antique financial securities. The share certificates of the Burmese private banks tended to be highly colourful with

exquisitely drawn Burmese motifs. The certificates of the Burmese National Bank and Tavoy Bank seem to be especially sought after.

40   Memorandum by the British Embassy, Rangoon, to the Bank of England, 1 September 1951, BoE, OV 79/2.

41   British Ambassador, Rangoon, to J.M. Patterson, South-East Asian Department, Foreign Office, 12 February 1954, BoE, OV 79/2.

42   The complaint was made at the Annual General Meeting of the Bank in 1951, and reported to the Bank of England by Lloyds Bank, which also reported its view that it was 'reasonable to expect that any new institution will take some time to become firmly established'. The General Manager Lloyds Bank to the Bank of England, BoE, OV 79/2.

43   Memorandum by the British Embassy, Rangoon, to the Bank of England, 1 September 1951, BoE, OV 79/2.

44   The information here on the Bank of Upper Burma and the Tavoy Bank is derived from that contained in their operating certificates – original copies of which are preserved at the Library of the Institute of Southeast Asian Studies, Singapore, and accessed by the author.

45   Calculations made by the author, from data provided in IMF (1996).

46   In 1953 and 1954 the Government of Burma attempted to conduct a census of the country. The 1953 iteration was limited to urban areas and covered about 15 per cent of Burma's towns. The 1954 version was meant to cover rural areas, but the continuing unrest in the country meant that the census included only 'accessible' parts of the country, comprising around 2,000 village tracts and an (estimated) 14% of the population. Together, about one-sixth of Burma's population was covered in the 1953/54 census (Khin Than Kywe 1960: 108).

CHAPTER 8

The Road to Ruin:
Credit and Banking under Military Rule

The special privileges and power that they cornered in the economy caused the military managers to believe that they were truly efficient and more capable of running the society, polity, and economy of Burma.

Mya Maung (1991: 93)

He admitted that he didn't know anything about economics. But he said every economist he talked to told him something different, and he didn't know what to do.

U.S. Ambassador Henry Byroade, recalling a conversation with Ne Win[1]

On 2 March 1962, Burma's parliamentary democracy era firmly closed when the tatmadaw once more left its barracks, this time in an explicit *coup d'état* that suspended the country's 1947 Constitution and placed in its stead a 'Revolutionary Council Government' led by the previous 'caretaker' prime minister, General Ne Win. The political philosophy of this new regime was styled 'the Burmese Way to Socialism', a sometimes uneasy mix of doctrinaire socialism and extreme nationalism that was articulated in an ideological tract of the same name published in April 1962.[2]

The impact of the 1962 coup on Burma's monetary and financial system was immediate, profound and, ultimately, deeply destructive. Within a year the country's commercial banks would be nationalised, and before too long they were agglomerated (together with the pre-existing state-owned banks) into the 'Peoples' Bank of the Union of Burma' (PBUB), a monstrosity inspired by other such unitary banks that had emerged throughout the socialist world. In agriculture, an initial vast expansion of rural finance was followed by both chronic credit scarcity and the demolition of

223

many of the institutions created since Burma's independence. Of course, most spectacular of all were the surreal 'demonetisation' episodes that characterised this era of Burmese history. Beginning in 1964, these moments of reflexive monetary folly became one of Burma's trade-marks, a source of almost comic interest, but whose causes and consequences would prove as tragic as they were bizarre.

In this chapter we examine the travails endured by Burma's monetary and financial system from 1962 to the eve of the 1988 uprisings – uprisings that were themselves partly driven by the country's unfolding monetary miasma. The chapter is divided into seven sections, beginning with an examination of the nationalisation of Burma's commercial banks (foreign and domestic) soon after the coup, and their fashioning into serially numbered 'peoples' banks' of various specialisations, before their ultimate fusion into the monolithic PBUB. We then explore the changes made to rural finance, and the serial expansions and contractions in agricultural credit and the institutional volatility whose legacy to Burma would be a barely functioning rural financial system. Following this we investigate Burma's 1964 demonetisation experience: a misguided effort to curb inflation and catch speculators off guard, but which would establish a dangerous precedent. We then return to the perennial question of rural finance in Burma, noting in particular the emerging dominance of 'advance purchase' as the main vehicle for state-provided credit. The chapter considers the series of banking 'reforms' launched in 1975. These reforms broke up the PBUB into four specialised banks – one to deal with foreign exchange transactions, another agriculture, a general 'commercial' bank and, finally, a reconstituted 'Union of Burma Bank' as the central bank. Private banks remained prohibited. The chapter concludes with an account of yet another demonetisation round which took place in two stages in 1985 and 1987. The latter episode proved uniquely damaging, not least to the military regime itself, and it was to presage the dramatic political events just around the corner.

THE NATIONALISATION OF THE BANKS

Burma's private commercial banks (foreign and domestic) were out of favour from the outset of the installation of Ne Win's 'Revolutionary Council' (RC) government. This was partly ideological, as banks and bankers (and other 'parasitic classes') were generally held to be inconsistent with the Burmese 'way to socialism'. Ideology was never omnipotent in the counsels of the RC government, however, and the coming hostility to Burma's financial institutions had undoubtedly deeper roots – central of which was the still-festering wounds and grievances of Burma's recent financial history.

The 'solution' to the banking problem perceived by the RC government was simply to 'nationalise' the private banks. This was not only time-honoured in countries professing some form of socialism, but it was consistent with the broad nationalisation program of the RC government, which had commenced with the nationalisation of the Burmah Oil Company on 1 January 1963. On 15 February Ne Win had announced that henceforth 'no new private industry would be allowed', which itself was sufficient to prompt a 'run' on the banks by nervous depositors (Steinberg 1981a: 31). Finally, on 23 February 1963, it was announced that the banks themselves would be nationalised. This announcement, codified under the 'Nationalisation of Banking Business Ordinance No. 1 of 1963', followed the convening of a peremptory 'Bank Nationalisation Committee', chaired by the new Home Minister, Colonel Kyaw Soe (Banerji 1963: 106). To give it some semblance of expertise, people such as San Lin, the venerable General Manager of the UBB, were pressured to sit on the Committee (UBB 1963: 24). The reasons put forward for nationalisation also revealed the RC government's perceptions as to the centrality of the banks in Burma's economy:

> Through their power of mobilising excess funds, private savings and the all-powerful weapon of credit expansion, the banking sector exerted a controlling interest upon the economy. Moreover, foreign trade was largely financed by the banks (...) Thus the banks controlled the greater part of the nation's financial resources, and it was necessary for the State to transfer this power into its own hands (RGUB 1963: 159).

The same statement also contained a revealing glimpse into the government's intentions towards the banks as funding vehicles for its own activities:

> In previous years Government had to borrow money from the Union Bank when it was in need of funds. This was done by selling Treasury Bills and Bonds to the Union Bank which in turn sold some of these securities to other banks and purchased the balance by printing new currency notes. This undesirable practice of issuing new currency notes can lead to inflation as it means that there has been an increase in money supply without a corresponding physical increase in goods at that particular period of time. In future, it is expected that this form of borrowing can be eliminated or

greatly reduced as Government can borrow directly from the banks (RGUB 1963: 161).

Of course, the last aspect of the above was also indicative of the government's profound ignorance of monetary matters, as government borrowing from the banks would be just as inflationary as 'issuing new currency notes' whenever the demands of the state exceeded the economy's productive capacity to meet them. Such ignorance was, alas, never to be remedied throughout the tenure of Burma's military governments.

At the time of nationalisation there were 24 private banks operating in Burma, 14 foreign, and 10 local. They were nationalised simultaneously, after which their individual names disappeared to be replaced by serially numbered 'Peoples' Banks' (1 to 24) (UBB 1963: 6). Table 8.1 illustrates the decidedly un-poetic consequences:

Table 8.1 The Nationalised Banks

Original Name	Name from February 1963
Central Bank of India	People's Bank No. 1
Chartered Bank	People's Bank No. 2
Habib Bank	People's Bank No. 3
Indian Overseas Bank	People's Bank No. 4
Mercantile Bank of India	People's Bank No. 5
United Commercial Bank	People's Bank No. 6
Punjab National Bank	People's Bank No. 7
State Bank of India	People's Bank No. 8
Hongkong and Shanghai Banking Corp.	People's Bank No. 9
National and Grindlays Bank	People's Bank No. 10
Bank of Communications	People's Bank No. 11
Bank of China	People's Bank No. 12
The Netherlands Trading Society	People's Bank No. 13
Overseas Union Banking Corporation	People's Bank No. 14
Ava Bank	People's Bank No. 15
Export–Import Bank	People's Bank No. 16
Union of Burma Cooperative Bank	People's Bank No. 17
Rangoon Bank	People's Bank No. 18
Burmese National Bank	People's Bank No. 19
East Burma Bank	People's Bank No. 20
Burmese Economic Bank	People's Bank No. 21
Central Commercial Bank of Burma	People's Bank No. 22
Tavoy Bank	People's Bank No. 23
Upper Burma Bank	People's Bank No. 24

Source: RGUB (1963: ii)

At the time of nationalisation, the private banking sector in Burma held deposits of K637.1 million (444.2 million with the foreign banks, 192.9 million with the local institutions), loans of K515 million (353.2 million foreign, 161.8 million local) and had capital employed of K23.7 million (13.4 million foreign, 10.3 million local) (Banerji 1963: 106). The shareholders of the nationalised banks were given assurances by the RC government that they would be compensated for the capital they contributed, as well as the value of buildings and other fixed assets 'within 90 days' (Emery 1970: 26). There was a sting in the tail for the 14 foreign banks, however, since their capital contribution would be returned to them, in their own currency, but only for the amount originally brought into the country. For the European and Indian banks that had been in Burma for many years (some for around a century), this implied a considerable capital loss (Indian Institute of Bankers 1963: 79). Meanwhile, compensation for the *assets* seized was decided by a specially established 'Compensation Commission'. The work of this Commission continued in a desultory fashion for a number of years, but few of the former shareholders in the nationalised banks saw much in the way of recompense (UBB 1963: 6).[3] In the end, K1.4 million was paid in compensation to the private foreign banks, K2.7 million to the private domestic banks (Emery 1970: 27).

Almost immediately upon nationalisation the government assigned military officers as 'general managers' of the banks, 'assisted' by transferred staff from the UBB and SCB as 'managers' (Emery 1970: 26). Lower-level staff of the nationalised banks were initially assured 'of continuance of service, rights and privileges' but, as Myat Thein noted (2004: 66), within a short while 'the pay scales of bank personnel were revised downwards in order to bring them in line with other government employees'.

Burma's bank nationalisation policy caused barely a ripple amongst the 'international community'. The biggest reaction came from India, from where a majority (seven) of the foreign banks originated. India's Finance Minister, Morarji Desai, issued a statement shortly after the nationalisations had been announced in which he expressed concern over the treatment of Indian bankers and their assets. He also sought to make the point that 'Indian banks and money-lenders have played a notable part in assisting the growth and development of the Burmese economy' (Banerji 1963: 106). The Indian Institute of Bankers was similarly anxious to ensure the well-being of Indian nationals in Burma. Whilst acknowledging that it was not 'their place' to question the internal policies of a friendly foreign government, they feared that 'many Indians, permanently settled down in business in Burma, may now find it difficult to secure regular credit for their business' (Indian Institute of Bankers 1963: 79). A quite different response came from the People's Republic of China (whose Bank of China was nationalised) which, as a gesture of solidarity and 'friendship' to its socialist neighbour, waived the return of the Bank of China's capital as well as compensation for its assets (Silverstein 1977: 156).

The RC government assigned 'special functions' to eight of the nationalised People's Banks: People's Bank No.1 was directed to specialise in industrial credit; No.2 and No.3 in savings deposits; No.4, certain services to government previously carried out by the UBB; No.5, servicing the government boards and corporations; No.6 and No.7 'private accounts'; No.8, banking services to facilitate 'Union of Burma Insurance Board' (Emery 1970: 29). Later the banking functions of the post office, and its postal savings accounts, were rolled into People's Bank No.19. These assignations appear to have been made without any apparent logic, as there was nothing in the past histories of these banks to suggest they had any particular expertise in the areas they were supposed to specialise in. Indeed, such was the disjuncture between their new areas of specialisation and their former roles that one is drawn to the inescapable conclusion that the banks so selected were chosen simply because they were the first '8 numbers' in the series of People's Banks.

Beyond being nationalised, a new series of regulations and restrictions were also imposed upon Burma's banks. Principal amongst these were strict interest rate controls – controls that held the rates banks could pay on deposits, and receive on loans, well below the rate of inflation (an extremely damaging policy that, as shall be examined in subsequent chapters, continues to the present day). The interest rate floors and ceilings imposed in September 1963 were as shown on Table 8.2 (opposite):

In addition to the interest controls were a veritable web of other measures, most of which were designed to 'police' the activities of Burma's citizens as depositors. Bank depositors were, for instance, only permitted to hold one account in one bank; could not deposit more than K10,000 per month or more than K50,000 per year; could not make more than two withdrawals from their account per week; could not withdraw more than 10 per cent of their deposits in one transaction; and could not withdraw less than K5 per

Table 8.2 Allowable Bank Interest Rates, 1964 (per cent per annum)

Loan and Deposit Type	Minimum	Maximum
Rates on Loans:		
Against government securities	4.0	7.0
Against title deeds of immoveable property	5.5	9.0
Against stock inventory	4.5	9.0
Against gold ornaments and precious stones	5.0	9.0
Rates on Deposits:		
For three months	0.25	2.5
For six months	0.5	2.5
For nine months	0.5	3.0
For one year	0.75	4.0
Inter-bank rate	2.0	2.0

Source: UBB (1964: 9)

transaction. As Emery (1970: 43) rightly noted, such regulations did 'not appear to be designed to encourage the use of savings deposits'.

The nationalisation of the banks was complemented by other developments which ensured the progressive marginalisation of banking in Burma's economy. The most significant of these were the extension of the nationalisation programme, and of the role of the state in a myriad of other ways, into *all* sectors of the economy. Between 1962 and 1964, 14 major socialist economic 'laws' were promulgated to allow the state to appropriate businesses and assets. In October 1963, for instance, the private sector was prohibited to import, and from April 1964 Burma's entire export trade was nationalised (UBB 1964: 2). Of greatest visual impact was the nationalisation, in March 1964, of all 'wholesale trade, including shops, broking houses, departmental stores and cooperative stores' (Mya Maung 1991: 122). By the end of the decade all large and medium-sized enterprises had effectively been taken over by the state. Of course, with each of these strokes went the customers and the business hitherto serviced by the banks.

The decline of Burma's banks, by almost every indicator except that of loans provided to the state, was precipitous. Demand deposits in the banks, for instance (notwithstanding the restrictions on withdrawals), fell by a fifth between 1963 and 1964, and by a further 30 per cent between 1964 and 1965. Time deposits likewise dramatically declined, as did the volume of cheque clearings (Roberts 1968: 300). These contractions caused financial distress to a number of the 'People's Banks', and some 'had to resort to emergency overdraft facilities from the Union Bank' (UBB 1963: 9). Even more dramatic, however, was the decline in lending to the private sector, and the creation of quasi(bank)-money, as Table 8.3 below testifies:

Table 8.3 Private Lending and Quasi-Money Creation, 1962–1968 (kyat millions)

Year	Bank loans outstanding to Private sector	Quasi-money
1962	469	197
1963	343	145
1964	214	95
1965	145	53
1966	172	63
1967	155	45
1968	179	45

Source: IMF (1989).

The fall in bank lending in Burma could be traced across the various sectors of the economy in roughly the same order that each came under government control. Thus, in 1963 the biggest falls came in lending to transport and public utilities (76 per cent), food and raw materials (57 per cent), and export–import trades (52 per cent) (UBB 1963: 7). Nor did the pre-existing state-owned banks escape the carnage. For the SCB, lending fell by 60 per cent from mid-1962 to mid-1965, a fall Emery (1970: 24) ascribed to the disruptive effects generally of the coup. There was also a dramatic fall in deposits at the SCB – from K625 million at 30 June 1963 to K319 million at 30 June 1964. *This* decline was mostly due to the consolidation of the accounts of state boards and corporations into a single 'Union Government Consolidation Fund Account' at the UBB. The government argued that such boards and corporations individually 'held unnecessarily large balances' and so, after consolidating them, took the opportunity to transfer the bulk of the money to the UBB for its own use (Emery 1970: 22–23). Meanwhile, lending by the only recently created Industrial Development Bank fell to a miserly K0.5 million in 1963 and to K0.3 million by 1964 – after which it essentially ceased to function (UBB 1963: 9).

In 1966, the RC government ruled that 'no new bank credits should be extended to the private sector and old loans should not be renewed' (Emery 1970: 30). For state-owned enterprises (SOEs) the banks likewise became increasingly irrelevant. For the larger SOEs direct access to the government's 'cash consolidation fund' functioned as something of a substitute for bank funds, while for smaller SOEs (especially manufacturing concerns) necessary inputs were increasingly sourced 'interest free' from government trading organisations. Of course, 'interest' *was* implicitly extracted – deducted from the price of the finished goods when delivered (Emery 1970: 30).

The People's Bank of the Union of Burma

The denouement of what had once been Burma's diverse banking system arrived via the process, which concluded in 1970, of merging each of the serially numbered 'People's Banks', as well as the original state-owned banks (including the UBB), into a single entity – the 'People's Bank of the Union of Burma' (PBUB). Reminiscent of the 'Gosbank' of the Soviet Union, this monolith was actually inspired by the 'People's Bank of China' which had been created in similar manner in 1948 (Emery 1970: 11). The rationale of the PBUB, as set out in the preamble to the eponymous Act of 1967, was described thus:

> It is desirable to have the various existing undertakings on banking, money lending, currency and credit, savings banking, foreign exchange, insurance, and so forth, grouped together into one, and placed under a single institution to assist in the development of the socialist economy (RGUB 1967: 4).

The giant merger of Burma's banks into the PBUB was completed in two stages. In November 1969 the UBB, the Industrial Development Bank, the People's Loan Company (the re-named State Pawnshop), the Burma Insurance Board and the People's Banks 5, 11 and 19 were joined. At the moment of the UBB's absorption the *Union Bank of Burma Act* (1952) was repealed. Finally, in February 1970 the second round of mergers that completed the creation of the PBUB took place. This brought into the monolith the SAB, the SCB and all the remaining People's Banks. At this moment the *State Commercial Bank Act* (1954) and the *State Agricultural Bank Act* (1953) were likewise repealed.

Thus created, the PBUB fulfilled all banking functions in Burma. It was the central bank that conducted monetary policy, regulated the note issue and was banker to the government; it was Burma's sole commercial bank, sole agricultural bank, sole foreign exchange bank, and sole savings bank. It was also Burma's only finance company, insurance office and pawnshop. These functions were administratively divided within the PBUB into 11 divisions – thus, for instance, the SAB became simply the agricultural finance 'division' of the PBUB (Myat Thein 2004: 230). The PBUB was initially capitalised at K200 million. Worthy of note is that the capital of all of the banks merged into the PBUB amounted to K600 million – the 'excess' capital being subsequently transferred into the government's general accounts (Emery 1970: 12). There was a provision for the capital of the PBUB to increase by the annual transfer of 25 per cent of its annual profits into a capital reserve fund, up to the point that this equalled the original capital subscription. Subsequently, any profits would be paid to the government. At the time of its creation the PBUB had over 7,000 employees, 54 branch offices, 50 sub-branches and 139 smaller agencies (in addition to the network of village banks) (World Bank 1972: 77).

The operations of the 'central bank' division of the PBUB were supposedly constrained by the maintenance of the 25 per cent international reserves/currency requirement which had applied throughout the life of the UBB. In practice, however, this was hardly a constraint since, under Section 15 of the PBUB Act, the government had the power to suspend the requirement 'for a specified period'. This was precisely what happened in March 1971, albeit the 'specified period' was 'indefinite'. Nominally, the only other major restriction imposed on the PBUB in the interests of 'sound' central banking was a limit on the amount of funds it could *explicitly* lend to the government (likewise a carry-over from the days of the UBB). This limit was originally set at a maximum of 15 per cent of budget revenues but this was easily eroded by the simple (and already exploited) expedient of selling government *securities* to the PBUB in *any* amount. In practice, the PBUB's central banking functions would amount to little more than a government cash-box, and 'the executive arm of the Ministry of Finance' (World Bank 1972: 77).

A final instalment in the story of Burma's 'monobank' that warrants recording at this point is to note the rapid change to its name. On 30 April 1972, the 'People's Bank of the Union of Burma' became the 'Union of Burma Bank' (UBB*). Rendered into English this was a slight variation of the old 'Union Bank of Burma' (UBB), but there was no variation in the Bank's *function* with respect to the PBUB.[4] Interestingly, at around this time the decision was also made to print (for the first time) Burma's currency *in Burma*. In the colonial era, and in the parliamentary democracy years, Burma's currency notes had been produced in Britain, whilst since the coup in 1962 they had mostly been sourced from East Germany (as were Burma's famous *aluminium* coins of this era). In 1972, however, note-printing equipment was purchased from what was then West Germany, and installed at Burma's new note-printing facility at Wazi (Robinson and Shaw 1980: 146–147).

Agricultural Credit, 1962–1965

In the wake of the nationalisation of the banks, the RC regime embarked upon a great expansion in the funds the government made available to agriculturalists. Partly, no doubt, in response to demonstrable need (as outlined in Chapter 7), partly to curry favour with the rural population, this great expansion was announced on the eve of the Burmese New Year in April 1963. At its centrepiece was a promise that K700 million would be made available to agriculturalists that coming year, an effective tripling of that made available in the immediate preceding years, even taking into account the erosion of spending power through inflation. Moreover, complementing this direct expansion of funds from the government, were measures designed to stimulate the lending into the sector by the (now nationalised) banks. These included a dramatic reduction in the required reserve to deposits ratios of the banks: from 20 per cent to 8 per cent for demand deposits, and from 7.5 to 3 per cent for time deposits (RGUB 1963b: 93). Of course, this was a reversal of the 1961 measures designed to reign in excessive monetary growth.

The K700 million total had been arrived at by aggregating increases in allowable loans at the crop/cultivator level. Lending for paddy, for instance, increased to K25 per acre (up from K8 per acre), while for higher-cost crops such as groundnuts, up to K40 per acre was declared. In addition, a general credit allocation of K250 was announced (regardless of crop) as being available 'to each agricultural family' (RGUB 1963b: 102). Impressive increases, but still not sufficient. According to the near contemporary account of Richter (1968: 111), the costs per acre of the more efficient 'transplanting' method of paddy sowing was itself K20 per acre (while K10 for 'broadcasting'). Counting the costs of other inputs (not least increasingly expensive fertiliser), the increased credit still 'offered no inducement' to employ best, but more expensive, agricultural practices and technologies.

The largest proportion of the expanded rural credit programme (around K500 million of the K700 million total) was classified as General Administrative (GA) loans, advanced under the *Agricultural Loans Act* (as detailed in previous chapters), but now distributed through so-called 'District Security and Administrative' committees. The remaining K200 million was to be disbursed through the SAB (before its later absorption into the PBUB). The SAB was itself expanded, receiving a funds injection of K120 million (K40 million supplied by the government, K80 million subscribed by the UBB) and a greatly enlarged network of Village Banks.

In 1962/63, 2,444 Village Banks were added, bringing the total to 4,961. There was also a promise 'to provide each of the village-tracts with a village bank and thus to open 5,313 *additional* banks during 1963/64' (UBB 1963: 9). The SAB almost hit the target on this; in 1963/1964, 5,150 new Village Banks were allegedly opened, bringing the total to an astonishing 10,111 by the year's end (UBB 1964: 9).

Yet, and notwithstanding the admirable targets, the RC government's 'big push' on rural finance fell well short of its lofty ambitions. In part this was a result of administrative capacity. Simply, the GA system of loan distribution, especially as restructured via the new 'Security and Administrative' committees, was unequal to the task of distributing the large volumes of credit made available. Corruption, nepotism and political favouritism became the practical distribution mechanisms, and in the end the volume of funds distributed across 1962/63 totalled around K450 million rather than the K700 million proposed (Richter 1968: 107, World Bank 1972: 82).

Beyond administrative incapacities were other problems, which in the longer run were even more destructive of Burma's rural credit arrangements. Principal amongst these, however, was a decision in March 1963, legally manifested in the *Farmers' Rights Protection Law*, which amounted to a legal amnesty to indebted cultivators who were in loan arrears. The Law, which extended the injunction against the seizure of land as collateral to the protection of borrowers' '*persons* against arrest for debt and all their other working property, such as cattle, tools, and produce', had, in practice, the effect of perpetuating the idea that *new* loans under the GA arrangements did not need to be repaid. The upshot was wide-scale, dramatic default – so much so that the World Bank estimated as late as 1971 that '68 per cent' of the GA loans from 1963 had not been repaid (World Bank 1972: 82). Of course, credit available in subsequent years was reduced by the same magnitude.

The RC government attempted a number of strategies in an effort to stem the administrative problems of its rural lending program, one of which was simply and futilely to exhort 'peasant leaders' to change human behaviour. More constructive, but in the end no less ineffectual, was the return to a policy of channelling more of the GA loans through the SAB and its village bank network. This strategy fell foul, however, of the growing politicisation of the SAB system, which increasingly came under the sway of the 'Security and Administrative Committee' apparatus. The

RC government's own *Economic Survey* for 1963, for instance, spelt out a Byzantine lending process that required managers of District branches of the SAB 'to inform the District Security and Administrative Committees (SACs) the names of the village banks, the amounts of loans to be granted, and the dates on which these loans would be issued (...) only when the District SACs approved the proposal did the District Managers issue loans to the village banks concerned' (RGUB 1963: 25–26).

The corruption of the SAB network reversed the hitherto good relative repayment record of Village Bank borrowers, which led to the imposition of measures in an attempt to lift repayment rates. Principal amongst these was an effort to reintroduce the 'joint liability' methodology which had largely fallen into abeyance since the years of the *Bogyoke* government. Clearing past arrears was also re-emphasised, and in order to get new loans a village tract (the responsible unit) would have to repay a minimum of 75 per cent of the previous year's outstanding loans, and undertake to repay the remaining 25 per cent within two years (Emery 1970: 35). It was not enough. The coup and the advent of military rule, on top of the conflict and disruptions of preceding years, had greatly weakened traditional village authority structures throughout Burma, which were accordingly unable to bring the peer pressure required on recalcitrant borrowers. Indeed, as Richter (1968: 113) noted, such 'village tract joint liability' may even have exacerbated matters 'because those farmers in defaulting villages capable of repaying did not do so, knowing that they would be disqualified from receiving fresh loans in any case'. A final, desperate, effort to recover the situation in the Village Banks came with a scheme instigated by the RC government to allow Village Bank committee members to receive a 10 per cent commission on recovered loans. This led to much browbeating of distressed borrowers, many threats of violence and an unusual number of fraudulent Village Bank books – and little discernible impact on loan defaults.

Monetary Policy, 1962–1966

The RC government's dramatic expansion of agricultural credit impacted greatly on Burma's broader monetary policy which, of course, was formally overseen by the UBB. As we have noted, the credit expansion was less than projected, but it still accounted for 'one-half of the Government's net cash disbursements in 1962–63' (UBB 1963: 2). Significantly, and as can be seen in Table 8.4 (overleaf), the increased lending was exclusively financed by government borrowing from the UBB – which rose nearly 70 per cent in financial year 1963. This likewise more than accounted for the growth in 'money' (M1) across the same period, which rose by 43 per cent (offset by smaller increases in demand deposits at the banks).

Table 8.4 UBB Lending to Government/Money Supply, 1962–1966 (kyat millions)

Year	UBB Claims on Government	Money
1962	723	1,661
1963	1,228	2,372
1964	1,719	2,208
1965	1,401	2,064
1966	1,331	2,221

Source: Author's calculations, IMF (1968)

The effect of this monetary expansion did not take long to be felt. But not, however, in *officially* recorded price inflation. The coming of the RC government had brought with it controlled prices, rationing and exclusive state distribution of critical commodities. These were the standard accoutrements of a socialist–planned economy, and they rendered orthodox measures of inflation meaningless. What such devices did bring, however, was another standard set accoutrements of a socialist–planned economy – including commodity shortages and a substantial 'black market'. The latter was the principal venue through which many commodities were only really available and, in this market, price inflation was rampant. According to Roberts (1968: 302–303), the price of rice quickly grew to five times the government-set price across 1962–1963, and the prices of cooking oil, clothing and other household products rose up to ten times. Meanwhile, by this time a swelling black market in foreign exchange likewise took hold. In 1963 the black market exchange rate of the kyat ranged from K8.75 to K20 to the US dollar, against an official exchange rate of K4.76:$US1. Hedging against the kyat soon became a national habit, one that would only grow in the decades ahead.

In response to these inflationary pressures (suppressed or otherwise) and other strains on the currency, one might have expected strong action from the UBB – or, at the very least, an expression from it of concern. Sadly, by now the UBB had lost any semblance of real independence from the government and the candour the UBB had once displayed was gone forever. In its Annual Report for 1963 the UBB was content to simply congratulate the RC government on its success 'in curbing speculation and hoarding activities' (not true), and on the measures it alleged had brought about this happy state of affairs, including what would later become the notoriously inefficient and corrupt 'civil stores' committees. The loss of the UBB's independence had another deleterious effect upon the country's financial system, moreover, and one that would prove costly in the years ahead: the loss of many of its most experienced and expert staff. One of these was San Lin, the venerable General Manager of the UBB. A central figure in Burma's monetary system since the Second World War as we have seen, San Lin escaped in September 1963 to the International Monetary Fund (UBB 1963: 24). A not unrelated development was the dramatic change in the 'model' the UBB looked to for the training of its staff. Eastern Europe was the new ideal and, in November 1963, fifteen staff of the UBB were sent to Czechoslovakia to undergo training in 'socialist banking' (UBB 1964: 22).

The 'Demonetisation' of 1964

Although the UBB might have sought to disguise it, the swelling black market that grew with the oppressive economic controls imposed by the RC government was not long in becoming painfully conspicuous. A reasonable response to this might have been a pause for reflection, even an easing in the headlong drive to the wholesale nationalisation and suppression of private enterprise in favour of the state. This was not, however, the response of the RC government. Rather, a measure which would sadly become a characteristic device of Burma's governments now and in the years ahead was given its first outing: 'demonetisation'.

Conducted under the *Demonetisation Act, Revolutionary Council Law No.7,* the demonetisation order of May 1964 declared that, from 7 p.m. on 17 May 1964, all K100 and K50 notes would no longer be legal tender. Such notes were to be surrendered to 'receiving centres' established by district and village SAC's (supposedly overseen by the UBB) and, so long as this was done within a week, reimbursed in various gradations. For the first K500 to be handed over, reimbursement in the form of lower denomination notes was meant to be complete and carried out on the spot. For amounts between K500 and K4,200, reimbursement was also meant to be total, but the issue of new notes in exchange was delayed and had to be undertaken at a local bank branch. Notes handed in totalling above K4,200 were meant to require a special scrutiny of the individual concerned, and the application of an escalating 'special tax' (Mya Maung 1971: 140).

The 1964 demonetisation was justified as a device to remove 'the purchasing power of the vast sums of hidden money which could be used to embarrass the Government and the economy, by unsocial acts of hoarding and speculation of essential commodities' (UBB 1964: 2). Its aims, targets and dispensations were set out by the RC government thus:

1. The primary target of demonetization is the indigenous and foreign capitalists who have for many years unfairly accumulated the people's money with which they now oppose the Burmese Way to Socialism (...).

2. In order to avoid harming the innocent or honest savers and the poor, the value of surrendered notes up to K4,200 will be completely redeemed.

3. On the basis of humanitarian considerations, the same amount of redemption will be made according to size even to the savers of large sums of money through dishonest means.

4. With the aim of national unity, those who committed the crimes in connection with these illegal tenders will be granted either a complete amnesty or light sentences.[5]

Mya Maung (1971) was one of a number of commentators (including the World Bank [1972]) who were sceptical as to whether the 1964 demonetisation truly captured the 'indigenous and foreign capitalists' targeted by the RC government. As he rightly noted (1971: 146), in a predominantly 'cash economy' such as Burma's (made more so following bank nationalisation) the targeting of currency notes cast a wide net indeed, and one which captured far more farmers, workers and 'legitimate' business people than it did 'capitalists', 'hoarders' and 'speculators'. Mya Maung was likewise sceptical regarding the motivation behind the 'humanitarian' and 'national unity' considerations of items 3 and 4 of the justification above, which he thought were driven by 'the lack of know-how, apparatus and resources to enforce and control the Demonetisation Law and, most important of all, the social and political necessity of not harming the relatively well-off class of military political elite and sympathisers' of the regime itself (Mya Maung 1971: 146).

As with most of the other major 'policy' changes instigated by the RC government, the implementation of the 1964 demonetisation was surrounded by much chaos, corruption and general inefficiency. An account of the process in Rangoon by Balwant Singh, the recent (forcibly) retired Commissioner of Pegu Division, captured both this and the 'human side' of the 1964 demonetisation:

Centres for surrendering the notes were designated. One was the Students' Christian Centre, next to our house. As all notes were to be turned in within a week of the announcement, a huge crowd formed. The press was so heavy that the brick pillar of the Centre's gate gave way. Crowds at other locations all over Rangoon were equally large and the arrangements equally poor. The public was hurt and resentful, and tempers boiled over. Fear alone kept the people under control (...). It was pitiful to see so many waiting their turn in the hot sun – a turn that never came! By evening, it was clear that only a small number were going to get to turn in their notes for the promised exchange. The doors of the Centre were closed and the crowd told to disperse. An announcement was made that next day's note-changing venue would be the Teachers Training College.

The next day, I got up at 2.30am to hand in my hoard of K11,000. When I reached the place, the gates were locked, so many of us climbed the iron railing – a humiliating experience. There were twenty people already in the queue for K1,000 and over depositors. The line for those depositing K1,000 or less was longer (...) By 10am I had handed in my treasure and gone home. (Singh 2001: 153)

As might be apparent from the above, the logistical requirements of the 1964 demonetisation were overwhelming for the agencies and individuals tasked with managing it. The 'on the spot' reimbursement limit of K500 had to be lowered on 18 May (just a day after it commenced) to K200, and on 20 May immediate reimbursement ceased altogether. Particularly troubled was the UBB which was not only overseeing the process, but had also been tasked with 'examining the surrendered notes and scrutinising various returns from the SACs relating to deposits, refunds and recoveries of Government revenues and debts' (UBB 1964: 21). Altogether the UBB claimed it scrutinised 5.5 million K50 notes, 7.3 million K100 notes and 1.4 million bank deposit books (UBB 1964: 21). On 13 June the government issued a statement to explain that the delays in reimbursement came from the need 'to distinguish between capitalists and bona fide working people' (Robinson and Shaw 1980: 143). By the conclusion of the redemption period (which extended to September) K555 million worth of K50 and K100 notes had been surrendered – around 78 per cent of those on issue prior to the demonetisation (Mya Maung 1971: 142).

In the end, as a device for stemming state-created monetary growth, the 1964 demonetisation was a dismal failure. The state's ever-present demand for funds, coupled with the (less than complete) reimbursement policy resulted in a situation in which the disappearance from circulation of the K50 and K100 notes was more or less evenly matched by the 'appearance' of new notes of other denominations. As Table 8.5 reveals, the denominational composition of kyats on issue had changed, but the total *volume* in circulation was remarkably constant:

Table 8.5 Currency in Circulation, 1963–1964 (kyat millions)

Denomination	As at 30/9/63	As at 30/9/64	Percentage change
1 Kyat Notes	64	102	+ 59
5 Kyat Notes	109	218	+ 100
10 Kyat Notes	311	604	+ 94
20 Kyat Notes	284	680	+ 139
50 Kyat Notes	210	–	- 100
100 Kyat Notes	703	–	- 100
Notes in Circulation	1,681	1, 604	- 4

Source: UBB (1964: 4).

Of course, one unambiguous consequence of the 1964 demonetisation was the first serious jolt to confidence in holding the kyat. From this time on the people of Burma increasingly returned to older methods of holding wealth – gold, silver, precious stones – as well as more modern forms such as consumer goods. There was even a substitution of notes for coins which, as Robinson and Shaw pointed out (1980: 144), were promptly 'hoarded, resulting in a shortage of small change'. Scares and rumours of further demonetisations likewise became endemic, beginning a cycle of distrust that was greatly destructive of Burma's financial institutions in the years ahead.

DEVELOPMENTS IN AGRICULTURAL CREDIT, 1966–1973

By the mid-1960s the great expansion in agricultural credit that had accompanied the installation of the RC government had petered out, after which acute scarcity of rural finance resumed its place as a characteristic feature of Burmese agriculture. This lack of finance was just one of a number of chronic problems that beset agriculture throughout the years of the RC government, whose policy to the sector was centred upon the compulsory procurement of many commodities (rice above all), severe restrictions on domestic trade, and a complete state monopoly over the export trade. The state also had a monopoly over processing, domestic marketing and the provision of agricultural inputs. It gave administrative directions to cultivators on their choice of crops, and imposed a myriad of other measures consistent with state intervention on a hitherto unprecedented scale. The end result would be falling agricultural incomes and production, a near collapse of paddy exports, and an agricultural sector of low incentives, low productivity and overall stagnation (Myat Thein and Mya Than 1985: 212–213).

Up until 1973, the SAB (the agricultural finance 'division' of the PBUB from 1970) and its network of Village Banks remained at the core of Burma's rural credit system. By 1972 there were over 11,000 Village Banks, supposedly serving 1.9 million rural households (World Bank 1974: 34). The latter number was less than half of Burma's total number of such households, the remainder of whom were left to seek informal credit of various forms. Importantly, even those with access to the SAB and its Village Banks were unable to borrow anywhere near enough for their needs. The size of loans advanced by the SAB depended on a rigid formula that allocated a set amount of kyats per acre as determined by the Ministry of Agriculture and Forests. For paddy this remained K25, with higher limits set for costlier crops such potatoes and onions (K70), and lower allocations for lower-cost crops such as beans and pulses (K10–15) (World Bank 1972: 35). These amounts were far less than was sufficient, however, with the K25 allocation for paddy representing a mere 11 per cent of average cultivation costs in 1972/73 (Mya Than and Nishizawa 1990: 89). According to the World Bank (1974: 33), the average 'credit allocation to cost ratio' across *all* crop categories was 'less than 5 per cent'.

It was not only in terms of kyats per acre where SAB lending was deficient. The total funds available, in aggregate and to any one borrower, likewise fell far short of need. The maximum amount a Village Bank could lend to a single borrower was capped at K1,200, paid in three instalments, two during cultivation (of K500 each) and a final draw-down of K200 at harvest. In practice, however, such a limit was irrelevant since most Village Banks had nothing like the financial resources necessary to make loans of this size. Indeed, across the RC government era the average size of a Village Bank loan was a mere K80 (Steinberg 1981b: 131). Another restriction, with significant implications for the current and future productivity of Burmese agriculture, was that the limiting of Village Bank loans to very short terms only (nothing beyond a season) solidified during the RC government years – and no loans were available for land or other productive capacity improvements.

Freedom of speech was a virtue largely noted by its absence in the RC government era, but during the early years of its reign voices of complaint against the poor provision of rural credit were occasionally heard. Mostly such complaints resulted in little more than trouble for the complainant. Occasionally, however, they did reach powerful ears even if, as below, cold comfort was all that was promised in return. The following was the response of General Ne Win himself, to a meeting of villagers from Dauk-U township in May 1963. Ne Win admitted that the loans provided by his government were insufficient, but,

> ...we have lent you money to give you a start. Use it as capital. Don't squander it. I am asking you to be frugal because I have heard that a shop which was opened here yesterday sold about 4,000 kyat worth of goods last evening. Our loan is insufficient. Work hard and put up with austerity for a couple of years.[6]

Unfortunately, Ne Win's 'austerity' would last more than 'a couple of years', as would the shortage of credit at the Village Banks. The diversion of financial resources from the SAB and the rural sector generally by the RC government was a significant reason for this, but so was the growing phenomenon of loan default which (as is clear from Table 8.6 below), increased dramatically following the brief expansion of rural credit in 1963/64.

Table 8.6 SAB and Village Bank Loans and Repayments, 1958–1967 (kyat millions)

Year	Loans granted	Loans repaid	Cumulative net debt
1958/59	38	38	54
1959/60	53	53	54
1960/61	69	66	57
1961/62	64	63	58
1962/63	21	18	61
1963/64	302	172	191
1964/65	236	215	212
1965/66	128	153	187
1966/67	113	102	198

Source: Emery (1970: 34)

This denied the SAB and its Village Bank network internally generated funds that could have been the basis of greater levels of lending in the future. In an effort to try to redress matters, in 1967 the RC government announced that any borrower in arrears would not be able to access new loans from the Village Banks. As with other measures introduced earlier, this did little to induce an increase in loan repayments, and by the end of 1967 cumulative loans outstanding to the SAB and its Village Bank network came to K198 million (Emery 1970: 36). The real problem behind the loan arrears was not, of course, a lack of *incentives* to repay, but a lack of borrower income. The cause of this, in turn, was not laziness or malfeasance on the part of the Burmese cultivator, but government policy – policy that fixed compulsory crop procurement prices of rice at levels that barely covered production costs. As Emery (1970: 37) noted, at this time it was often difficult for the cultivator *'not* to default' on loans received.

Greatly damaging to Burmese agriculture in the RC government era were other decisions by the authorities that *deliberately* starved agriculture of funds for credit. One measure, mild sounding but as crippling as low repayment rates in negating financial self-sufficiency for the Village Banks, was a directive issued in 1965 that Village Bank 'savings, share capital, and profit deposits in the [PBUB] could not be used for lending purposes' (World Bank 1972: 37). Inexplicable is perhaps the only way to describe this directive. The idea that capital cannot be used for lending and, to a degree, that a portion of retained profits should be set aside in the form of reserves is entirely consistent with prudence. The prohibition against the re-employment of savings through lending, however, is truly mystifying. Such financial 'intermediation' between savers and borrowers is the primary role of a financial institution, and the ordinary source of its profits. The prohibition against this core activity removed the major long term source of finance for Village Banks and left them dependent on disbursements from the government. Of course, this may well have been the intention of the measure.

Consistent with its ideology, the RC government also imposed a series of other devices that limited available credit and impaired the efficiency with which it could be used. Such devices included 'an on again off again' prohibition against the granting of credit to farmers who 'employed labour' (Richter 1968: 109). More generally, there was a lack of consideration in allocating credit according to how productively it could be used, to the differing climactic, geographical and other circumstances of farmers, to the expense and availability of required inputs, and so on. Rather, rural credit in the RC government era, when available, performed an ideological function rather than one concerned with productive investment. Yet, even on this score the RC government's rural credit policies can only be adjudged a failure. Silverstein's (1977: 75) portrayal of this aspect is wonderfully illustrative of a system that did not succeed on its own (ideological) terms:

The farmers accepted (...) the easy loans, and other benefits bestowed upon them by the soldiers in power, but they did not change their outlook or life style. They farmed and marketed as before, and when consumer goods were not available or government demands seemed unacceptable they sold their produce on the black market, withheld their crops from the government buyers, and continued to live in their traditional unsocialistic ways.

Advance Purchase

In April 1973, Burma's system of allocating rural credit via the Village Banks was replaced by a regime in which the bulk of 'credit' available was channelled to cultivators by way of 'advance purchase' of their output by the state. Compulsory procurement of major crops by the state had been in place for some time as noted, but the decision to use it also as the vehicle through which to implicitly distribute credit was foundational to a new plan, 'Guidelines for the Economic Plan of the Union of Burma', which was adopted at the 'First Congress of the Burma Socialist Programme Party' in 1973. For agriculture broadly, this Plan formalised a number of practices and policies well established by the RC government, including the planned production of most crops, state control of trade and state provision of inputs (World Bank 1974: 45).

The body administering the advance purchase program was 'Trade Corporation No.1', the former SAMB. It paid 70 per cent of the value of a cultivator's contracted output, at a common price determined by the government, but which was significantly below that prevailing in what remained of the free market. This payment was initially made in three instalments – 40 per cent at the outset for land preparation, 15 per cent for the transplanting of crops and a further 15 per cent immediately before harvest. Later the whole 70 per cent advance was given in one lump-sum before land preparation. The final 30 per cent of the procurement price was paid upon delivery of the crop (World Bank 1974: 39).

The 'Trade Corporation No.1' had a limited number of purchasing stations (mostly confined to the divisional capitals), necessitating a network of other establishments to actually make the 'advance payments' and receive the product. These establishments were provided by a reinvigorated cooperative system, under which newly constituted 'Agricultural Multi-Purpose Cooperatives' (AMPCs, replacements for the 'ProCos' discussed in Chapter 7, which by now had largely fallen into disuse in their credit dispensing role) were created at the village level. The AMPCs were very different animals to their forebears in the colonial and parliamentary democracy eras, however. Established under a new *Cooperative Law* (1970), the role of the state in their formation and operation was explicit. Under the Law, one third of a cooperative's committee members were appointed by the state and, in practice, the remaining members likewise had to meet the approval of state authorities (Khin San Yee 1997: 93).

Advance purchase relieved cultivators from paying interest on advances, but this did not mean that the 'credit' they received was free from cost. Indeed – quite the opposite. There had long been a substantial 'gap' between the government's procurement price and that prevailing in the market, but following the installation of the RC government this became a chasm. Of course, this gap represented the cost to the cultivator of providing their crop to the state and, in this sense, was akin to an 'interest rate' that might be otherwise levied on loans. The analogy is not exact – for instance, quality differences in product meant that a single and precise 'market price' could not be assigned – but it is meaningful enough to give an idea of the real cost to the cultivator of the advances they were given. Table 8.7 displays the implicit costs to cultivators of their provision of funds via advance purchase, calculated according to the official government procurement

Table 8.7 Advance Purchase, Procurement Price/Market Price, 1972–1989 (kyats per ton)

Year	Govt. procurement price	Open market price	Implicit annual cost to cultivator %
1972/73	204	582	185
1973/74	431	729	69
1974/75	431	744	73
1975/76	431	679	58
1976/77	431	579	34
1977/78	431	732	70
1978/79	446	1132	154
1979/80	446	1211	172
1980/81	472	1253	165
1981/82	472	1833	288
1982/83	472	1986	321
1983/84	472	2291	385
1984/85	472	2444	418
1985/86	472	2521	434
1986/87	472	2597	450
1987/88	472	2879	510
1988/89	472	3834	712

Source: Author's Calculations on Price Data in Mya Than and Nishizawa (1990: 97)

price per ton (of paddy) and an estimate of the 'average' free market price of the same quantity. Quickly apparent is not only the dramatic escalation of this implicit cost, but also the increasing pauperisation of Burma's rice farmers.

As can be seen from Table 8.7, with the exception of all but the first few years of the scheme, advance purchase as a vehicle for credit delivery became as costly to cultivators as funds drawn from moneylenders. Indeed, by the early 1980s it was considerably *more* expensive than the historical cost of most moneylenders. Occasional adjustments to the procurement price were made, but these came nowhere close to tracking either inflation or the increasing market price of paddy.[7] Nor, moreover, was there any 'science' behind the procurement prices selected. As Mya Maung (1991: 124) notes, price setting was an entirely arbitrary process with 'no scientific explanation or econometric model' behind it. The procurement price was not 'fair and equitable' as argued by the government and it is hard not to agree with Mya Maung's general assertion that, via the advance purchase scheme, 'new state carpetbaggers' had simply replaced the 'capitalists' that allegedly were earlier engaged in the exploitation of the Burmese cultivator. In this light it was hardly surprising, as the World Bank subsequently reported (1974: 40), that cultivators did all that they could to 'minimise their participation in the advance purchase program', and to employ all manner of devices to beat the system.

But if the cost of rural credit became increasingly burdensome under advance purchase, then no less a burden was the perennial problem that it remained wildly insufficient relative to need. One outcome of the low official procurement price was that it exploited cultivators, but another was simply that it meant cultivators were provided with too little funds. The serious implications of the continuing chronic lack of credit in Burma was noted by the World Bank, which in its 1974 report on agricultural development and credit in Burma bemoaned the lack of rural finance, especially over the medium to long term. This discouraged land improvement, the use of implements and even the use of draft animals. Of course, it also greatly inhibited technological innovation that would otherwise create the virtuous circle of raising 'output and income and provide the means for repaying loans' (World Bank 1974: 43).

Moneylenders and Other Sources of Credit

Private moneylending was officially banned by the RC government. Despite this, the practice continued to flourish. Indeed, given low procurement prices and the diminution of financial institutions such as the SAB and the other formal banks, it became *more* prevalent relative to the situation in the parliamentary democracy years. Of course, precision in estimates of the informal economy such as this are impossible, but there is rough consensus as to the increasing necessity of accessing moneylenders throughout the tenure of Burma's military regimes. According to Emery (1970: 39), 75 per cent of credit provided to agriculturalists was supplied by moneylenders, a figure upon which the World Bank (1974: 37) roughly concurred. The interest rates charged by moneylenders varied. Emery (1970: 39) noted a wide range of rates charged – from 2 to 4 per cent *per month* (27–60 per cent per annum) against collateral, to 5 to 10 per cent per month (80–314 per cent per annum) on unsecured loans. Meanwhile the World Bank (1974: 37) believed that what it called a general 'gentlemen's agreement' on moneylender interest rates limited them to about '10 per cent per month'. Of course, on top of borrowing from dedicated moneylenders, most Burmese accessed credit in other time-honoured ways, especially via shopkeepers and suppliers of all varieties. Finally, and not unexpectedly, the efforts by the military governments to stamp out private moneylending came to naught. This was just as well. To the extent that restrictions on moneylenders were sincerely motivated to protect borrowers then they were self-defeating. Making lending a clandestine activity made it more risky and, as a consequence, required an increased risk premium in the form of higher interest rates. It was (and is) the poor who, excluded from the formal financial system by their poverty, ended up paying.

Beyond simple legal prohibition, the RC government sought other strategies to eliminate the moneylender. One of these was a programme, launched in 1963, that allotted K100 million for a credit programme for 'landless farm labourers' to purchase food. The credit made available (up to K200 in *value* per person) was 'in kind' only, and could only be accessed in instalments to a value of no more than K20 per month. An additional requirement was that such loans had to be guaranteed by the borrower's employer. Regarding this condition, General Ne Win himself declared that it was included to ensure that farm labourers 'did not become indolent (...) and squander their money on unnecessary things' (World Bank 1974: 42). This program proved a dismal failure, however. In its first year of operation only K300,000 had been lent out, mainly because of the 'strings attached' to the scheme (World Bank 1974: 43). It was quietly dropped soon after.

A more serious competitor to the local moneylender (particularly in urban areas) was the state's own pawnshop operations. As examined in Chapter 7, these had been established under the 'State Pawnshop Management Board' (SPMB). With the creation of the 'monobank' this became simply the 'Small Loans Division' (SLD) of the PBUB/UBB*. The SLD functioned through the years of the RC government – and even doubled its lending from 1961 to 1971 in nominal terms (from K83 million to K180 million) (World Bank 1972: 83). Of course, in real terms this nevertheless was a reduction in funds available.[8] The SLD charged differential interest rates according to the amount borrowed. These ranged from 5 per cent per month (80 per cent per annum) on loan amounts from K1 to K20, 3 per cent (43 per cent) on loans from K21 to K250, and 2 per cent (27 per cent) on loans in excess of K250 (Emery 1970: 41). Roberts (1968: 301–302) was one contemporary observer who thought that the state pawnshop operations had made inroads into the informal moneylending market, especially 'those small private pawnshops still in the hands of the Chinese'. This view is very much an outlier, however, and most commentators (including the author of this book) have concluded that the efforts of the state in this area scarcely dented the pervasiveness of the traditional moneylender in Burma. Of course, the private moneylender was but the tip of a very large iceberg that was the informal economy of Burma at this time – an economy that Mya Maung (1991: 210) observed was the 'real economy of Burma'.

THE END OF THE MONOBANK

On 3 January 1974, the 'Socialist Republic of the Union of Burma' came into being and formal political power was transferred from the Revolutionary Council to a reconstituted *Pyithu Hluttaw* (People's Assembly). Notwithstanding these constitutional changes, however, real leadership of the country remained in the hands of 'active and retired military commanders' (Mya Maung 1991: 147). Ne Win remained at the top of this cohort, but now as Chairman of the ruling party (The 'Burma Socialist Programme Party', BSPP) and of the Council of State (and therefore effectively President of the Republic).

Under the new BSPP government there were a number of changes made to economic policy-making in Burma, driven by what Myat Thein

(2004: 60) called the growing 'recognition of the link between the country's economic isolation and its poor economic performance'. The changes were not dramatic, but there was a definable tilt towards a greater use of market processes and decentralised decision-making. Many of the changes were outlined in (yet another) seminal manifesto, in this case the *Long-term and Short-term Economic Policies of the Burma Socialist Programme Party,* which had been issued (just before the new constitutional arrangements had come into place) in January 1973. The manifesto set out a new long-term agenda for Burma's financial system thus:

(a) To issue loans and advances to State Economic Enterprises (SEE) through People's Banks and to charge appropriate interest on the loans and advances given.

(b) To instruct public corporations, co-operative societies and registered private businesses to open accounts at People's Banks.

(c) To change the focus of People's Banks from an administrative to a commercial viewpoint.

(d) To evaluate the performance of SEEs according to national financial plans.

(e) To increase socialist accumulation of capital by raising the bank rate and by providing requisite facilities to the people.

(f) To operate SEEs in both domestic (kyat) and foreign currencies.[9]

By the time this plan came to be applied the 'People's Banks' had been renamed once more, but the broad thrust of the above remained in place more or less throughout the 'BSPP period'. As is apparent from the above, SEEs were supposed to be subject to more financial 'discipline' than hitherto, but the continuing emphasis on state and cooperative enterprises (with but a passing mention of *registered* private businesses) spoke volumes regarding the persistence of the 'Burmese way to socialism'.

The *Bank Law* of 1975 (*Pyithu Hlyttaw Law,* No. 9 1975) was the practical expression of the changes the BSPP government wished to make to Burma's financial system. Its most noteworthy feature was the end of the monobank – and the breaking up of the UBB* into functional constituent parts. This move, variants of which were being enacted across the socialist world, was a badly needed one. The 'PBUB/UBB*' was little more than a device for channelling funds decided upon by the planners, and was structurally incapable of acting as a device for screening projects, allocating capital and ensuring loan repayments – in short, acting like a 'bank' in the ways deemed now to be needed.

Under the *Bank Law* the PBUB/UBB* was broken up four ways: into a dedicated central bank, and three other banks with specific responsibilities. The central bank retained the label 'Union of Burma Bank' (hereafter simply 'UBB' once more to distinguish it from the monolith), and its parameters of operations were formally set by merely dusting off the *Union Bank of Burma Act* of 1952. As such, the UBB was officially responsible both for the conduct of monetary policy, and for supervising the other banks. In practice it had little to say, and even less influence, on monetary policy. This remained the preserve, as Myat Thein (2004: 67) noted, of the 'ruling oligarchy'.

The three other banks established under the *Bank Law* were the Myanma Economic Bank, the Myanma Agricultural Bank and the Myanma Foreign Trade Bank. All three banks operated under instruction from the UBB, and the Ministry of Planning and Finance. Something of a direct substitute for the former State Commercial Bank of the parliamentary democracy era, the Myanma Economic Bank (MEB) was delegated to provide long and short-term credit to state-owned enterprises, cooperatives and regional authorities and agencies 'for all non-agricultural activities' (Bunge 1983: 149). It was also the vehicle for the deposits of all state enterprises and for the savings of the broader populace. In April 1975, in an effort to encourage more savings with the MEB, the allowable interest rate it could pay on deposits was raised to 6 per cent (from the 3.5 per cent of the PBUB/UBB*) and then to 8 per cent in November 1977. Such interest rate increases did little to encourage savings, however, or instil much of an institutional savings 'culture'. In an unpublished paper produced within Rangoon's Institute of Economics in the early 1980s, Khin Maung Nyunt (1990: 141) set out some cogent reasons as to why this might have been the case, which included:

(a) inadequacies in providing deposit and withdrawal services due to an absence of computerisation and banking skills amongst bank staff;

(b) interest rates that still lagged considerably below the rate of inflation;

(c) perceptions that holding wealth in the form of 'jewellery, gold, land and buildings' was considerably safer and more profitable than accumulating kyat savings in a bank;

(d) the 'over-supervision by authorities' of deposits – including the requirement for 'documents of rightful possession' for deposits in excess of K100,000;

(e) Burma's poor economic performance meant that most people had little 'wealth' to save in any case.

Such pathologies would sadly live on. Meanwhile, the role assumed by the MEB as the primary financing vehicle for state enterprises, as well as the continuing lack of interest in what remained of the private sector, is amply apparent from Table 8.8.

Table 8.8 MEB Lending to State Enterprises and the Private Sector 1975–1986 (kyat millions)

Year	MEB lending to private sector	MEB lending to state enterprises
1975	790	1,151
1976	1,336	2,518
1977	1,743	1,089
1978	2,363	2,758
1979	2,009	7,025
1980	2,131	10,158
1981	2,540	15,202
1982	2,470	21,020
1983	2,628	25,734
1984	2,396	31,678
1985	2,762	35,926
1986	3,009	41,939

Source: IMF (1989)

As established in 1975, the MEB had capital of K80 million, double that of the next of the four new banks created under the *Bank Act,* the Myanma Foreign Trade Bank (MFTB). As its name implied, the MFTB was charged with handling the foreign exchange business of government departments, state agencies and the very limited number of cooperatives and enterprises allowed access to foreign currencies. Private individuals were mostly forbidden from holding foreign currency, and the only people allowed to open foreign exchange accounts in the MFTB were those who could demonstrate that they had earned foreign funds 'legally'. In practice this meant that such accounts were essentially limited to Burmese seamen. An important limitation even on them, however (which greatly reduced the attractiveness of such accounts), was that, whilst deposits could be made in foreign currencies, withdrawals could only be made in kyat at the (overvalued) official exchange rate.

The Myanma Agricultural Bank (MAB) was likewise capitalised initially at K40 million. Though in many ways a re-creation of the old SAB,

251

its particular focus was meant to be upon medium and long-term lending rather than the provision of seasonal credit. For seasonal lending, advance purchase via the former Trade Corporation No.1 (from 1974 known as the 'Agricultural and Farm Produce Trade Corporation' [AFPTC]) continued to be the primary distribution vehicle. The mechanics of procurement changed somewhat, however, with the implementation of a new system whereby farmers were individually assigned a procurement target (based on the size of their land holding, likely yield per acre, family size, and so on), beyond which any excess production could be sold in local markets or otherwise consumed (Mya Than and Nishizawa 1990: 102–103). In practice the new system was deeply corrupt, with the method by which procurement targets were set being particularly open to abuse. Mya Than and Nishizawa (1990: 102–103) and Ardeth Maung Thawnghmung (2004) are just two studies pointing to circumstances where small farmers had to purchase production on the open market in order to meet their quotas assigned by the AFPTC's assessors. In 1973/74 the procurement prices for paddy were raised to K35 per acre (K25 for land preparation and planting, K10 for harvesting), but they remained woefully insufficient both as 'credit', and relative to fast appreciating market prices (as per Table 8.7, p. 245).

THE DEMONETISATIONS OF 1985 AND 1987

On 18 September 1988, after months of urban unrest, upheaval and the mass killings of civilians, an internal military coup brought about an end to BSPP rule in Burma, and its replacement by that of the State Law and Order Restoration Council (SLORC). These events were amongst the most tragic in the history of modern Burma, but they were triggered, at least in part, by yet two more demonetisation episodes, in 1985 and 1987. As with the 1964 experience, the motivation behind these episodes was said to be the desire to check speculators: in the words of the then Deputy Prime Minister and Minister for Planning and Finance, Tun Tin, 'to collect taxes from those who engaged in the unscrupulous economic activities and to prevent the rising prices of foodstuffs and personal goods brought by those who, holding black money, were manipulating the market' (cited in Mya Maung 1991: 217).

The 1985 demonetisation concerned the K100, K50 and K20 notes which, under the *Currency Notes Demonetisation Bill,* were declared to be no longer legal tender beyond November 3.[10] As with the 1964 affair, a period

Table 8.9 Money Supply and Inflation, 1984–1989

Year	Money (kyat millions)	Consumer price index (1985=100)
1984	12,777	93.6
1985	11,551	100.0
1986	16,337	109.3
1987	9,474	136.4
1988	15,668	158.3
1989	21,317	201.3

Source: IMF (1991)

of time was initially set (11 November to 31 December) for exchanging the notes, and a maximum that could be exchanged (one person per household only) of K5,000. Also like the earlier experience, however, this period was later shortened and downgraded, until eventually only 25 per cent of the value of surrendered notes would be reimbursed (Mya Maung 1991: 217). Simultaneous to the demonetisation order was the introduction into circulation of K25, K35 and K75 notes. As Table 8.9 reveals, these were ultimately issued in such numbers that the money-supply contracting efforts of the demonetisation orders were rendered ineffectual within a year. Inflation likewise continued to accelerate.

The most destructive of all of Burma's demonetisation experiences was that which took place in 1987. Announced on 5 September at the behest of General Ne Win, but seemingly without the knowledge of the Central Committee of the BSPP, all K25, K35 and K75 notes – the same notes that had been first issued less than two years earlier – were declared to be no longer legal tender. Unlike all the previous demonetisation episodes, however, no exchange or compensation was provided. Later up to K100 could be converted, mainly for the purposes of allowing students with funds to travel home, and away from the fast-developing strife in Rangoon (Steinberg 2001: 5).

But there was one more, bizarre, twist to the 1987 demonetisation. In an infamous follow-up to the declaration of 5 September was another, on September 22, of a new series of currency notes in the decidedly strange denominations of K45 and K90. Perhaps no event in Burma's monetary history has been as oft-commented upon as this peculiar action, nor the motives for which the subject of so much speculation. Most prominent of these speculations, and with the passing of time and events increasingly the most likely, were the theories suggesting that it was prompted Ne Win's belief in the mythical virtues of the number '9' – both generally, and as particularly auspicious to him personally. As Ardeth Maung Thawnghmung (2004: 208) notes, not only are the numbers '90' and '45' divisible by 9, but the addition of their integers likewise sums to 9. Of course, looking for signs of providence, via astrologers and other mediums, is an on-going trait of Burma's government to the present day. That said, final proof of the origins of Burma's '9 series' notes remains elusive.

As with the 1985 episode, the 1987 demonetisation did nothing to arrest Burma's trend of monetary growth (driven by the desperate money-financing of the state), nor the country's galloping inflation rate. As Table 8.9 above reveals, there was a dramatic contraction in the money supply during fiscal year 1987, but with the issue of the new notes Burma's money supply thereafter continued its upward trend. Likewise for inflation as measured by the consumer price index. This latter measure, based on IMF estimates on Burmese official data, is likely to significantly understate the true rate of inflation in a country whose currency had become so greatly compromised. After 1987 the kyat essentially ceased to function as a store of value, even if it continued to serve as an imperfect means of exchange. Steinberg (2001: 131–132) wrote of its descent:

> No one wanted to hold cash for fear of further demonetizations, and economic chaos resulted. Farmers held rice, their only major marketable asset, and urban dwellers bought any non-perishable commodities with whatever cash was available. There were four major results: increased inflation; a drop in the black market value of the Burmese currency: a precipitous rise in the price of rice in urban areas; and a dramatically increased demand for consumer (thus smuggled) goods.

NOTES

1   Recollection cited from Thant Myint-U (2006: 299).

2   And, in somewhat more detail, in the regime's *The System of Correlation of Man and His Environment*, published in January 1963.

3   Amongst these included the former shareholders of Dawson's Bank. As noted in Chapter 7, by 1962 Dawson's Bank was little more than a large pawnshop and, as such, its assets were seized and sold up by the government, rather than being nationalised within the banking system. Funds thus realised were 'locked-up' in Burma until 1973, however, their repatriation persistently denied for a decade by the Controller of Foreign Exchange. This experience was not atypical. 'Report of the Directors, Dawson's Bank, to Shareholders', 29 February 1964, OIOC, Papers of James Douglas Stuart, Mss Eur D1239.

4   Following the lead of Myat Thein (2004: 67), we have used the 'asterix' here to differentiate *this* UBB from its central bank forebear. In Burmese the difference in names between the two banks was that the word 'daw' was missing from the title of the new UBB (Robinson and Shaw 1980: 146).

5   This four-point statement of the RC Government was reproduced in 1965 in a publication of its economic policies, 'The Economic Affairs of the Burma Socialist Program Party no.1'. It is here cited from Mya Maung (1971: 140).

6   Cited from Ardeth Maung Thawnghmung (2004: 76).

7   For a detailed examination of these adjustments, and their inadequacy, see Mya Maung (1991: 172–174).

8   Using the consumer price index estimated by the IMF (1979) for the period 1961–1971, the 'real' value of the SLD's lending in 1971 represented 60.9 per cent of its 1961 equivalent.

9   'Long-term and Short-term Economic Policies of the Burma Socialist Programme Party', cited from the translation by Khin Maung Nyunt (1990: 11).

10   The K100 and K50 notes had been quietly re-introduced after the 1964 demonetisation.

CHAPTER 9

'Reform' under the SLORC/SPDC

I admit that it is not easy to reform the inefficient and corrupt adminis-trative system of a developing country, even without politicians throwing a spanner in the works.

Hla Myint, 2001

Years of incoherent policies, inept official measures, burgeoning inflation and falling real income had turned the country into an economic shambles.

Aung San Suu Kyi, 1995

The 'internal coup' that brought the State Law and Order Restoration Council (SLORC) into power in September 1988 came at a time when Burma's economy was near collapse. The monetary chaos of the previous year was but the latest in a long line of policy-inspired disasters that not only brought Burma's macro-economy to the brink, but also destroyed the institutions that would be necessary if the country was to achieve any measure of prosperity in the future. Infamously, and revealingly, a year before the advent of the SLORC, Burma's government requested, and was granted, the assignation of 'least developed country' status by the United Nations.

Burma's dire economic circumstances, and the need for the SLORC to craft at least a semblance of legitimacy, gave rise to a programme of economic reform that, imperfectly and with considerable backsliding, continues to the present day. The objective of this programme was the achievement of four economic objectives for Burma, each of which was boldly printed (daily) on the front page of the government's mouthpiece, *The New Light of Myanmar*:

1. Development of agriculture as the base and all-round development of other sectors of the economy;

2. Proper evolution of the market-oriented economic system;

3. Development of the economy inviting participation of technical know-how and investments from sources inside the country and abroad;

4. The initiative to shape the national economy must be kept in the hands of the state and the national people [sic].[1]

The above was made manifest, in words at least, amidst a variety of new laws that were supposed to clear a space for market-oriented economic reforms. Some of the more important of these laws (in areas other than banking) included the *Union of Myanmar Foreign Investment Law* (1988), the *State-Owned Economic Enterprise Law* (1989) and the *Private Industrial Enterprise Law* (1990). Critically, other laws were repealed – the most significant of which (in March 1989) was the 1965 *Law of Establishment of the Socialist Economic System*. Finally, and of importance symbolically, was the change in Burma's formal name from the 'Socialist Republic of the Union of Burma', to simply the 'Union of Burma' (later, the 'Union of Myanmar') (Mya Than 1997: 105).

The extent to which the SLORC (re-named the 'State Peace and Development Council' [SPDC] in November 1997) fully understood the process they set in motion via the above laws, and other initiatives, is still hotly debated. In their behaviour in the years since, and in the subsequent performance of Burma's economy, there is much evidence to suggest that they did not. History has demonstrated that the first three 'economic objectives' sought by the SLORC above have often, even mostly, taken a back seat to the fourth – which in reality was the maintenance of power and privilege in the hands of Burma's military leadership. In any event, and whatever laws were passed, the reforms set in place by the SLORC/SPDC did not bring about the creation in Burma of the fundamental institutions necessary for a functioning market economy.

In the field of banking, however, a triumvirate of laws promulgated in 1990 appeared which transformed the sector and wiped away many of the remnants of the socialist era. The *Financial Institutions of Myanmar Law* allowed, for the first time since 1963, the creation of private banks. The *Myanmar Agricultural and Rural Development Bank Law* promised at last a solution to Burma's chronic shortage of rural credit. Finally, the *Central Bank of Myanmar Law* gave Burma a modern central bank with all the formal powers necessary to conduct monetary policy, and to regulate the country's financial system according to the best international practices. That reality would turn out rather different from these promises is the principal subject of this chapter.

The chapter begins then with an account of the 'revolution' yielded by the *Financial Institutions of Myanmar Law* and the appearance in its wake of Burma's first private banks for a generation. We trace the rise of these banks, who was behind them and what they did, up until the moment they reached their collective apogee in the closing months of 2002. In this section we also examine (up to the present day) the re-formed state commercial banks under the new Law, and some new *state* institutions that were created along the way. Following this, we explore the creation and subsequent performance of the 'Myanmar Agricultural and Rural Development Bank' (MADB). A name change in 1997 saw the label 'Rural' dropped, but beyond that the Bank continued as the primary vehicle through which Burma's farmers and cultivators were meant to be able to meet their credit needs. Our findings reveal, however, that the MADB failed as comprehensively as its forebears in the task. The chapter examines the establishment and performance of the Central Bank of Myanmar (CBM). Armed with all the formal devices needed by a modern central bank, the CBM likewise failed as both a system regulator, and as the device for the conduct of monetary policy in Burma. The chapter concludes at the end of 2002, and immediately before the CBM was put to its most gruelling challenge.

THE RETURN OF THE PRIVATE BANKS

Banned since 1963, private commercial banks reappeared in Burma following the promulgation of the *Financial Institutions of Myanmar Law* (FIML, SLORC Law no.16/90) in July 1990. The FIML allowed private banks to offer more or less a full range of traditional banking services (set out in Article 25 of the Law), with the exception of foreign exchange activities which, as shall be examined below, remained for the most part the exclusive domain of the state-owned banks.

Financial institutions defined under the FIML had to be licensed by the CBM, but for banks this was the final stage in a procedure that involved firstly the creation of a limited liability company under the Myanmar

Companies Act (originally the Burma Companies Act, 1914), the Special Company Act, 1950, and the submission of a 'feasibility study' (outlining the market to be served, the likely community benefits, profit estimates and owner/management qualifications). For commercial banks, minimum capital was set at K10 million (later K30 million). The liberalisation of private banking in Burma was supposed to take place in three stages:[2]

Stage 1. Establishment of private domestic commercial banks. Also allowable at this stage was the opening of foreign bank 'representative offices'. Such offices, authorised under Section 13(b) of the FIML, had to be vetted by the CBM and were not permitted to 'perform any of functions prescribed for financial institutions'.

Stage 2. Domestic private banks were to be permitted to form 'joint ventures' with foreign banks. Such foreign banks had to first establish a representative office.

Stage 3. Foreign banks could set up in their own right.

No timetable was ever announced for this three-stage process which, in practice, became frozen at Stage 1. Stage 1 was successfully implemented to the extent that domestic private banks were indeed established, but the modest openings for foreign banks envisaged at this point proved less than fully successful. At their peak (in the mid-1990s), nearly fifty foreign bank representative offices had set up in Burma but, faced with the limitations on their activities and Burma's under-performing economy, most departed within a few years. By the end of the century barely fifteen remained. Most that did so primarily functioned as 'liaison offices' for parent banks that were involved in offshore financing of Burma-based projects. Stages 2 and 3, however, proved to be steps too far. As shall be revealed in more detail below, four joint venture proposals of the sort envisaged in Stage 2 *were* announced at various times, but only two of these proceeded to the point that the approval of the CBM was sought. Its approval was not given. Meanwhile no progress was made under Stage 3 at all.

But, as noted, 'private' commercial banks did arise in Burma in the wake of the FIML, with the first of them taking up business in June 1992. By 2002 some twenty-one banks had been established.[3] Table 9.1 (overleaf) lists the twenty banks that remained in business in 2002, in order of the date they commenced operations. The final column of the table gives some indication of the relative size of each as originally conceived in terms of initial paid-up capital. Capital data for the banks that could be regarded as 'semi-government' (more on which below) was (and is) mostly unavailable:

Table 9.1 Burma's Private and Semi-Private Banks, Foundation Dates and Initial Capital (kyat millions)

Bank	Date commenced operations	Initial paid up capital
Myanmar Citizens Bank	2//6/1992	110
Cooperative Bank	21/8/1992	50
Yadanabon Bank	11/9/1992	100
First Private Bank	6/10/1992	507
Myawaddy Bank	4/1/1993	n.a.
Yangon City Bank	1/4/1993	n.a.
Yoma Bank	14/8/1993	268
Myanmar Oriental Bank	18/11/1993	170
Myanmar Mayflower Bank	9/6/1994	480
Tun Foundation Bank	14/6/1994	70
Kanbawza Bank	1/7/1994	15
Asia Yangon International Bank	18/10/1994	40
Myanmar Universal Bank	24/1/1995	80
Asia Wealth Bank	30/4/1995	664
Myanmar Industrial Development Bank	15/2/1996	1,208
Myanmar Livestock & Fisheries Development Bank	15/2/1996	680
Cooperative Promoters Bank	6/7/1996	n.a.
Cooperative Farmers Bank	6/7/1996	n.a.
Sibin Thayar Yay Bank	4/7/1996	650
Innwa Bank	28/11/1997	n.a.

Source: Data derived from World Bank (1999), Wajima (1999: 243), and author's sources.

The nature, background, scale and ambitions of Burma's new commercial banks varied widely. The first two new banks (Myanmar Citizens Bank, the Cooperative Bank), as well as roughly a third of those that followed them, were either significantly state-owned, or 'state-connected' in various ways. Amongst the remainder were also a number of banks that were essentially moribund from the start – their creation reflecting primarily a desire amongst their entrepreneurial owners to enjoy the prestige of possessing 'a bank' as much as anything else. There were, however, a core of private commercial banks that became both highly active and uncommonly prominent. Of these, a so-called 'big five' (Asia Wealth Bank, Yoma Bank, Myanmar Mayflower Bank, Kanbawza Bank and the Myanmar Universal

Bank) especially stood out. Each built a substantial branch network and ostensibly seemed to be concerned with building broad banking operations that extended from retail and consumer products, to the provision of an array of business services. All five shared a number of traits including being a part of larger conglomerates, being headed by 'flamboyant' executives and enjoying strong ties with Burma's influential ethnic-Chinese business community. The latter feature was particularly notable, and of the top five banks, only one (Kanbawza Bank) was *not* founded by a Sino-Burmese.[4] For some of the five, widespread suspicions that they were involved in money-laundering and other unsavoury activities were also never from the surface.

Archetypal of the new private banks, and in embodying all of the traits above, was the Asia Wealth Bank (AWB). Created only in 1995, the AWB's rise seemed unstoppable. By 2002 it was not only Burma's leading and largest private bank but, in terms of assets, was the largest of *all* banks in Burma, even though the state-owned MEB continued to have more branches. By 2002 the AWB had K170 billion in assets, 3,000 staff, 39 branches, '1,000 computers', and claimed a market share of bank-lending in Burma of 45 per cent.[5] The most aggressive in pursuing retail customers, in 1996 the AWB became the first bank in Burma to issue credit cards. Over 15,000 of these had been issued by 2002. In 2001, AWB also became the first Burmese bank to offer an 'online' banking facility.[6]

AWB claimed that its lending portfolio was distributed to manufacturing and industry (40 per cent), traders (30 per cent), agricultural services (8 per cent), construction (6 per cent), hire purchase (6 per cent), and consumer loans (10 per cent). It conducted 50 per cent of its business in Rangoon, 20 per cent in Mandalay and the rest elsewhere – including 5 per cent in 'border areas'.[7] More generally, the AWB was especially popular with Burma's ethnic Chinese business community. At its peak, the AWB was extraordinarily profitable, reporting a return on equity of 54.56 per cent for 2000–2001, and 'non-performing' loans of a mere 1.29 per cent of its portfolio.[8]

The founder and 'front man' of AWB was Aik Htun, a shadowy figure who emerged in the early 1990s from Kokang, an area near-synonymous with Burma's opium trade. Stories linking him to Burma's narcotics trade emerged early and never went away, and he was said to have deep and long-standing links with the Kokang 'national race leader' Pheung Kya-shin.[9] As we shall see in the next chapter, such stories were later given weight when specific charges were laid by both the United States Treasury and the Burmese government itself. For all that, Aik Htun maintained an elaborately constructed public image that belied the stories of his links to narcotics, and in numerous public appearances and press profiles he affected a 'rags to riches' story that chronicled his rise from being the son of a small-farmer from Mon Kaing in the Shan State. The narrative even included the vignette that he walked two miles to school each day, after which he completed his chores on the farm. Aik Htun maintained that he grew rich via a succession of enterprises, beginning with a 'tiny biscuit shop' in downtown Rangoon. He admitted that 'real riches' came to him, however, via his aggressive pursuit of 'border trade' following the 1988 economic reforms. Upon such trade he subsequently founded the 'Olympic Group', one of Burma's leading trading and property development conglomerates which was active in investing in residential property and hotel developments in Rangoon.

Beyond the AWB itself, Aik Htun was the most prominent 'face' of Burma's private banking sector throughout the late 1990s, and up to the bank's demise in 2005. He often publicly complained of the restrictions imposed on the commercial banks, especially with respect to the prohibition on conducting foreign exchange business. He once said that his business model was based upon targeting the top ten per cent of Burma's population, and he expressed a desire to 'go public' with the bank.[10] Aik Htun sometimes chafed at his fellow private bankers, telling one interviewer that he didn't 'know why they all closed their mouths about calling for reforms'.[11]

The AWB's closest competitors for both prominence and retail 'presence' during the first decade of private banking in Burma were the 'Yoma' and 'Myanmar Mayflower' banks. The former was established in August 1993 by Serge Pun, an ethnic-Chinese business figure who headed 'First Myanmar Investment Company' (FMI), one of Burma's largest conglomerates with interests ranging from real estate to gem trading. By 2002, Yoma Bank had 43 branches (the most of any of the private banks), concentrated in Rangoon (15 branches) and Mandalay (5 branches). In the same year Yoma had assets of around K160 billion, total loans outstanding at K85 billion and deposits of K128 billion. Yoma paid interest on deposits on the basis of their minimum monthly balance, but *calculated* interest on loans according to what it called the 'Daily Rest Method'. Of course, this was simply daily compound interest, and the wording reflected ancient injunctions in Burma against the compounding of interest charges (see Chapter 6). Published interest rates paid and charged were otherwise in accordance with CBM limits (more on which below), but the *effective* rate of interest applicable to loans was increased by a compulsory 'Loan Acceptance Fee' of 1 to 2.5 per cent per annum. Yoma also charged various other fees to effectively increase its return on loans – for example, in levying collateral assessment fees and the like. As with AWB, Yoma issued a credit card, 'Yoma Card', which by 2003 had 25,000 cardholders and a claimed 6,000 outlets accepting it. Yoma identified a key business in providing firms with automatic salary payment systems (which would later cause problems during the 2002/03 crisis).[12]

For a time Yoma Bank provided funds to the United Nations Development Programme's 'Dry Zone' microfinance project (examined in Chapter 11). Under the arrangement, which was brokered by the Food and Agriculture Organisation of the UN, and local NGOs, Yoma provided the microfinance scheme with funds at a rate of ten per cent per annum, allowing the scheme to profit from its on-lending. Yoma was ordered to cease this activity by the CBM in 2002 presumably, as discussed below, because of the general injunction against the private banks lending to agriculture. At the time of cessation Yoma had extended loans to the project of K3.33 million. Yoma admitted that its involvement in the scheme was initially for public relations purposes, but later came to value the link as a precursor to future possibilities for agricultural lending.[13]

Yoma typically did not feature in stories linking various of Burma's private banks with money-laundering, and there was 'no evidence that Yoma was knowingly associated with narcotics-trafficking money'.[14] That said, Yoma's banking practices did not approach orthodoxy in a conventional sense, and the Bank lent considerable sums to entities 'connected' with the Pun family and other associates. Yoma was a large lender to various prominent real estate projects in Rangoon, including FMI City and the Pun Hlaing Golf Estate.[15]

In contrast to Yoma, the Myanmar Mayflower Bank certainly did feature in the swirling money-laundering allegations. So much so, indeed, that the bank was colloquially known for most of its history as the 'Poppy Flower Bank'. Mayflower was established in June 1994 by Kyaw Win, another leading ethnic-Chinese business figure and 'former Baptist lay-preacher'.[16] Kyaw Win was long linked with interests believed to be connected with the narcotics trade, and in 1997 he bought Yangon Airways, before selling it again in 2000 to the United Wa State Party.[17] One of the most innovative and fastest growing of the private banks, from the outset Mayflower had a strong retail focus, and it introduced Burma's first 'automatic teller machine' in

November 1995. At its peak Mayflower was the third-largest bank in Burma, and immediately before the 2002/03 crisis had K156.7 billion in assets, of which loans outstanding amounted to K129.1 billion. Deposits stood at K50.9 billion, shared amongst a claimed 190,000 depositors. Mayflower had 24 branches throughout Burma, and just over 1,000 employees.[18] Much of Mayflower's lending portfolio was made up of loans to 'leaders of national races' and, as such, were perceived of as enjoying a degree of government guarantee.[19] A mis-step in a story of otherwise inexorable growth came in July 1996 when rumours swept Rangoon that Mayflower was on the verge of insolvency. The rumours, which were not true, centred on a story that the Bank's directors had all resigned and that Kyaw Win had fled to Singapore. The rumours and subsequent panic were sufficiently serious for Burma's then Minister of Finance, Brigadier-General Win Tin, to publicly deny the rumours. He also declared that the Bank was 'operating in accordance with relevant banking laws and rules' – a claim a later Finance Minister would do a *volte face* upon.[20]

The two remaining members of Burma's 'big five' private banks were the Kanbawza Bank and the Myanmar Universal Bank. Kanbawza, which was part of the 'Myanmar Billion Group' conglomerate, was founded in 1994 in Taunggyi, the capital of Shan State. Its founding chairman, Aung Ko Win (also commonly referred to as Saya Kyaung) was long rumoured to be a protégé of SLORC/SPDC Deputy-Chairman, Maung Aye, and for this and other reasons the Bank was regarded as 'close' to the ruling regime. Marketed throughout Burma usually as 'KBZ Bank', Kanbawza's retail focus saw it offer a number of consumer and small business products, including its own credit card. Kanbawza also strongly pushed its (intra-Burma) remittance services and, to this end, was at the centre of a consortium of banks – which also included Tun Foundation Bank, First Private Bank, Cooperative Bank and Myawaddy Bank – that allowed remittance payments to be made between each other's branches.[21] Kanbawza Bank was especially prominent in lending in the Rangoon property market, but it was also more active than most of the other private banks in lending to small manufacturing and trading firms. Kanbawza Bank was famed for its largesse in many areas, not least for its sponsorship of Burma's national football team.[22] Kanbawza was also involved, along with Yoma Bank, in providing finance to the UNDP's Dry Zone microfinance project. This involvement ended, along with Yoma's, under the direction of the CBM.[23]

Myanmar Universal Bank (MUB) was another of the large private banks founded by a Sino-Burmese, in this case a businessman who went by the name of Tin Sein (purportedly a resident of Shan State). As with the AWB and Mayflower banks, the MUB came to be the subject of money-laundering accusations, with strong rumours that it was associated with Wei Hsueh-kang, a Chinese-born business figure (via the Hang Pang Company) who had been indicted for narcotics-trafficking in both the United States and Thailand.[24] The MUB was established in 1995 and at its peak in 2002 had total assets of K19.1 billion, total loans outstanding of K13.0 billion, total deposits of K12 billion and 125,000 depositors. The MUB had a mixed retail/business focus and had 26 branches and around 1,500 employees. It claimed that its lending was mostly to traders of various types (53 per cent), with the remainder to a mix of small manufacturers, service and transport enterprises, hire purchase and consumers generally.[25] One of the 'innovative' ways that the MUB tried to attract customers in the early days was to run a 'lucky draw' scheme for regular customers every six months, with prizes of televisions, refrigerators and washing machines.[26]

Beyond the 'big five' were a cohort of smaller private banks, some of which conducted little in the way of banking activity, but also some others that were to rise to greater prominence after Burma's 2002/03 financial crisis. Examples of the latter included the Tun Foundation Bank and the First Private Bank. Both of these banks were headed by particularly influential principals, U Thein Tun and Dr Sein Maung respectively, who were vocal proponents of economic reform in Burma and who were prominent spokespersons for private enterprise. Myanmar Oriental Bank was likewise an active but small bank which was to take advantage of the fall of some of its larger rivals following the 2002/03 financial crisis. Asia Yangon Bank and Yadanabon Bank (which was based in Mandalay) were both very modest operations for whom the label 'bank' was probably an overstatement of their status.

Amongst the state-owned, state-connected banks were institutions no less varied in their scale and scope. Two of the most notable of these was the Myawaddy Bank and the Innwa Bank. Though both formally 'private' banks, each was owned by conglomerates inseparable from Burma's military leadership. In the case of the Myawaddy Bank this was the 'Union of Myanmar Economic Holdings Company' (UMEH), the share capital of which was held jointly by the Directory of Procurement of Burma's Ministry of Defence, and by various armed forces' cooperatives, regimental associations and veterans organisations. The Chairman of the Myawaddy Bank was (and is) typically a senior military officer (and usually a member of the SLORC/SPDC). Befitting its central status in the circles of power, Myawaddy Bank's Rangoon head office was in the former Union Bank of Burma building. Prior to the 2002/03 crisis, however, Myawaddy functioned as little more than a 'corporate treasury' for UMEH, whose companies were almost its only clients. Innwa Bank was founded by the 'Myanmar Economic Corporation' (MEC), the other major conglomerate owned by serving and retired military officers. Founded only in 1997, like Myawaddy it functioned for the most part as a finance vehicle for MEC subsidiaries and affiliates.[27]

Amongst the other new state-connected banks were some that were more explicitly arms of the state. Most obvious in this respect were the three cooperative banks (the Cooperative Bank, the Cooperative Farmers' Bank and the Cooperative Promoters' Bank) – which were later (2004) merged into simply *the* 'Cooperative Bank'. These institutions were apex bodies of the cooperative credit system more broadly, and they operated under the direction of the Ministry of Cooperatives. They conducted very little banking business as stand-alone entities prior to the 2002/03 financial crisis. Also essentially moribund institutions, at least prior to 2003, were the Yangon City Bank (owned by the Rangoon municipal government), the Sibin Tharyar Yay Bank (controlled by the 'Ministry of Border Area, National Races and Development Affairs') and the Myanmar Industrial Development Bank (MIDB). Despite its ownership, Sibin Tharyar Yay Bank had only one office, in Rangoon and far away from the 'border areas'. The MIDB was initially a 'pilot' for what was originally planned as a series of industrial development banks to be located in various 'industrial zones' across Burma. Created in 1996 and initially financed by a K2 billion loan from the CBM, the MIDB established branches at Rangoon, Mandalay and Meikhtila, but these did little business prior to 2003 (FAO 2004b: 1).

Designed to undertake a similar developmental role in agriculture was the Myanmar Livestock and Fisheries Development Bank (MLFDB). Created in 1996 and operating under the direction of the Ministry of Livestock and Fisheries, the MLFDB was given a limited mandate centred upon the provision of finance for the livestock and fisheries industries in Burma. Within a few years of its founding the MLFDB had established eight branches, mostly in coastal and inland fisheries townships, but including one in Chin State which was at the centre of a programme to extend cattle-raising loans.[28] In contrast to other official sources of agricultural credit in Burma, the MFLDB generally enjoyed a good reputation amongst its clientele.[29]

The Regulation of Private Banks in Burma

The CBM was the responsible agency in Burma for 'licensing, inspecting, supervising and regulating financial institutions', and for generally ensuring their soundness and solvency (Article 57, Central Bank of Myanmar Law [CBML]). Such a supervisory role was assumed by most central banks around the world, and it was primarily to international regulatory templates that the CBM adhered. The most important of these was the CBM's adaptation of the Basel Capital Accord. Originally designed through the Bank for International Settlements (BIS) for the banking systems of the rich, industrial world (and specifically the so-called G-10 countries), the Basel Capital Accord quickly became the accepted benchmark for all banks everywhere.

At the heart of the Basel Capital Accord was the idea that capital (ultimately the net worth of a bank and, accordingly, the funds committed to it by its owners) acts as a 'buffer' against excessive risk-taking and the losses that might result from this. In the words of the World Bank (2002: 80), '[o]ne way of ensuring that owners retain prudent risk-taking incentives is to require them to have a significant amount of their own money at risk'. Of course, should the worst occur, the existence of capital can also allow a bank to continue to operate until problems are resolved, and provides a degree of assurance that it will honour obligations to depositors and other creditors.

The Basel Capital Accord established that banks should meet a capital-to-risk-weighted-assets ratio of 8 per cent – a ratio calculated by dividing a bank's capital base by its *risk-weighted* exposures (assets). Risk-weighting of assets was specified, according to various categories, to reflect (largely) the relative risk of the counter-party involved. The higher the risk, the higher the risk-weight, and the more capital a bank had to set aside. Under the standard Basel Capital Accord, *maximum* capital has to be set aside for exposures to private sector borrowers and individuals, but lower risk weights were granted to governments and state-owned enterprises. Of course this was just one area where what might work for the G-10 countries may not have been so relevant universally, and in situations (such as Burma's) where the state and its agencies might be the least trustworthy of borrowers.

As noted, the CBM applied the Basel Capital Accord in its supervision of Burma's private banks. Article 31 of the Financial Institutions of Myanmar

Law (FIML) specified that the 'relation between the risk-weighted assets and the capital and reserves of a financial institution shall not exceed ten times'. In language more similar to that of the Basel Capital Accord, this implied a minimum capital adequacy ratio of 10 per cent. This was a more stringent requirement than that specified by Basel's 8 per cent, but not an inappropriate one in a more risky financial environment such as Burma's. Details of the risk weights applied by the CBM have not been made publicly available, but given its approximation to the Basel Capital Accord more broadly, it is reasonable to assume that they vary little (formally) from international norms.

In addition to the basic Basel Capital Accord requirements, the CBM imposed other regulations on banks, many of which were in keeping with core international standards of bank supervision, but some of which were peculiar to Burma. The most important of the bank regulations were:

(1) *Liquidity.* Under Articles 58–59 of the CBML, banks in Burma were required to hold liquid assets against liabilities of a ratio of not less than 20 per cent. Such liquid assets could include currency, cash on deposit at the CBM, government bonds, gold, and cash held in current accounts at other banks.

(2) *Reserve requirements.* Under Article 58 of the CBML, banks in Burma were required to set aside 10 per cent of demand deposits, and 5 per cent of time deposits, as reserves. 75 per cent of these reserves in turn had to be deposited with the CBM, whilst the remaining 25 per cent could be held as cash.

(3) In addition to these liability reserves, Article 11(d) of the FIML included the requirement that banks set aside 25 per cent of their net profits each year 'in a general reserve account until this account reaches 100 per cent of its paid-up capital'.

(4) *Limits on individual borrowers.* Under Article 32 of the FIML, banks in Burma were not permitted to lend in excess of 10 per cent of their capital to any single borrower (enterprise, individual or group). As a further limit upon large exposures, the same Article stipulated that no single borrower should 'account for more than 30 per cent' of a bank's total loan portfolio.

(5) *Connected lending.* Under Articles 39–43 of the FIML, a number of restrictions were imposed on Burma's banks in making loans to 'related

parties' (defined as employees of a bank; companies and individuals with an equity stake in the bank that equaled or exceeded 10 per cent of its share capital; other companies owned by a bank's principal shareholders). Such restrictions included the requirement that the express permission of a bank's Board of Directors be given before a loan was granted, and a general requirement that such a 'related' loan not exceed 5 per cent of a bank's capital. Meanwhile, Article 42 outlawed the granting of 'special privileges' to related parties, including the provision of loans that 'would not be carried out (...) with other customers', and the charging of interest rates below those available to unrelated parties.

(6) *Branches.* Banks in Burma had to get the permission of the CBM to establish new branches. Likewise, changes to the location of existing branches had to be given prior sanction (Article 19, FIML).

(7) *Interest rate ceilings.* Amongst the most controversial of all the controls upon banks in Burma were those regulating maximum and minimum interest rates that could be charged and paid. Under Article 61 of the CBML, minimum interest rates that banks could pay on deposits could not be less than 3 per cent below the Central Bank rate, whilst the maximum interest rates they charged on loans could not be greater than 6 per cent above the Central Bank rate. In April 2006 the Central Bank rate was raised to 12 per cent (from 10 per cent), implying minimum and maximum deposit and lending rates of 9 and 18 per cent respectively.

Most of the formal regulations above were reasonable, indeed prudent, for a country such as Burma. Burma's adoption of a 10 per cent minimum capital adequacy ratio for banks was, as noted, above that of the Basel Capital Accord but it was appropriate in a financial system as underdeveloped and as volatile as Burma's. Such a premium above the Basel minimum was also consistent with most developing countries, and with the practices of Burma's neighbours. Likewise the specification of a formal liquidity ratio (20 per cent), a practice abandoned in many highly sophisticated financial systems, was entirely appropriate in an environment such as Burma's where confidence in banks was fragile, and where cash transactions dominated. The reserve requirements on various deposit categories, the limits on exposures to single borrowers, and the restrictions on connected lending were all similarly consistent with 'best practice' in financial settings such as those in Burma and/or were entirely suitable to its circumstances.

Such an assessment could not be made, however, for certain of the other measures, whose effect was to greatly inhibit sustainable banking in Burma while yielding little or nothing in the way of prudential safeguards. The requirement, for instance, that banks hold 25 per cent of annual profits up to the point that they accumulated to match capital, was a particularly regressive requirement, which not only effectively 'doubled' the capital requirement on banks, but disproportionately punished the (most prudent) banks with the greatest capital. A 'gearing ratio' limiting capital to deposits that was introduced later had a similar effect on the profits reserve. This measure, introduced in the wake of Burma's 2002/03 financial crisis, shall be examined fully in Chapter 10. Finally, the efficacy of bank regulations (like all such rules), depends upon how well they are understood, implemented and enforced. Few countries have poor banking regulations on paper, but what happens in practice is invariably the critical element. Burma's banking regulations were, for the most part, well-formulated and in accordance with international practice. As we shall see in Chapter 10, understanding, implementation and enforcement were much less so.

PERFORMANCE OF BURMA'S PRIVATE BANKING SECTOR, 1992–2002

During their first decade of existence, Burma's new commercial banks enjoyed what can only be described as stellar growth. As can be seen from Table 9.2, 'onwards and upwards' could describe most of the financial

Table 9.2 Private Bank Loans and Deposits, 1992–2002 (kyat millions)

Year	Reserves & other claims on CBM	Claims on central government and SOEs	Currency outside banks	Claims on private sector	Demand and time deposits	Price index
1992	26,581	8,541	54,429	19,173	23,083	48.8
1993	29,928	9,728	68,663	23,076	29,851	64.4
1994	33,721	11,326	90,659	28,262	43,125	79.9
1995	41,239	8,741	119,207	45,956	65,993	100
1996	48,506	9,290	159,608	75,346	97,747	116.3
1997	49,395	14,225	205,509	115,505	128,544	150.8
1998	76,756	16,964	256,605	155,761	196,145	228.5
1999	80,741	66,420	272,679	188,149	288,666	270.1
2000	94,438	105,317	344,728	266,466	455,320	326.8
2001	123,823	113,323	494,521	416,776	656,909	512.7
2002	138,612	112,410	713,633	608,401	831,827	700.3

Source: IMF (1999, 2004, 2006), and author's calculations.

aggregates coming out of the sector. Deposits across the decade grew by 3,500 per cent and loans to the private sector a scarcely less spectacular 3,000 per cent. Taking into account inflation (prices rose roughly fourteen-fold across the decade), these numbers would revert to a more modest (!) 2,100 and 1,600 per cent respectively. On the face of it, Burma's banking reforms seemed to have created the financial system the country had been in desperate need of for decades.

And yet, even at what would prove to be this moment of apogee, Burma's private banking system was not what it seemed. Proof of this would soon arrive in spectacular fashion as 2002 drew to a close. Even before the crisis described in the next chapter arrived in all its vividness and force, however, for those *who wanted to see*, the situation of Burma's private banks was troubling. The problems were manifest, and they included the following:

(1) For all the growth in many of the statistical indicators, Burma's commercial banking sector remained in an extraordinarily primitive state, even by 2002. A particularly effective indicator of this was the 'cash to deposits ratio', a system-wide measure that expressed the volume of currency outside the banks as a proportion of deposits (of all types) held within the banks. Deposits, 'bank money', was that component of the money supply that was a creation of the banking system, and an indicator of the extent to which banks were responding to the financial needs of the public. Currency, on the other hand, was simply the liability of the CBM, and ultimately the 'money' created by *and for* the state. Burma's cash-to-deposit ratio in 2002 was 86 per cent. Certainly this was a better figure than that of a decade earlier, but it still compared very poorly to the ratios of countries that ordinarily might have been regarded as Burma's peers. In 2002, Thailand and Indonesia (countries that had not long before experienced their own financial system problems) had cash-to-deposits ratios of 8 and 9 per cent respectively.[30]

(2) With respect to the sectors most chronically short of credit, agriculture and productive private enterprise, Burma's new banks provided little in the way of assistance. For agriculture the reason for this was unambiguous – simply, and astonishingly, the private banks were *forbidden* to make agricultural loans. A prohibition which, as the FAO (2004a: 137) later noted, was 'difficult to understand or justify' was even extended to such nominally 'rural' banks as the Cooperative Farmers Bank. The ruling was also behind the (noted) cancellation of the nascent

efforts of the Yoma and Kanbawza Banks to extend credit to the UNDP's microfinance schemes.

The relationship between the new private banks and productive private enterprise more generally was not so clear cut. Much anecdotal evidence suggested, however, that despite the many claims to the contrary, bank loans to private enterprise unconnected either to the banks, their owners or to the government were both expensive and hard to come by. Surveys of Burmese business owners conducted by the author indicated that the private banks were generally wary of lending to new enterprises that could offer little in the way of collateral. The collateral required, moreover, was steep: a 'rule of thumb' adopted by many of the banks was a demand for fixed asset collateral of around 200 per cent of the value of a loan.[31] Such collateral could really only be offered by 'connected' borrowers with larger business groups standing behind them, and/or parties with links to government and military enterprises. These same surveys revealed that 'unconnected' borrowers were typically asked to pay hefty 'establishment fees' for loans. Such fees functioned as recompense for the 'capped' interest rates charged by the banks, but they also had the effect of greatly increasing the credit costs to borrowers. The fees were sometimes informal by way of simple bribes paid to individual loan officers, but often they were imposed with the full knowledge of the management of the banks, albeit leaving little in the way of a paper trail.[32]

The high collateral requirements and the other high costs of loans brought about a situation in which lending by the private banks was predominantly to enterprises and individuals who were able to generate both high and quick returns. Such enterprises tended to be involved in highly speculative activities: in particular, hotel and real estate speculation, gold trading, jade mining, fishing and logging concessions and (for a brief period), garment factories. Sometimes too they functioned as 'quasi venture capitalists', taking equity positions in a project as yet another way of getting around the interest rate restrictions. In this context a 'cap' on interest mattered little when the bank shared in the returns of the project overall via their ownership stake. Hawke (2004) noted that an extra 'return' could be got if the loan recipients were the so-called 'leaders of national races' who often enjoyed extra privileges by way of special access to high-yielding natural resource sectors as well as government guarantees.[33] Of course, sometimes a bank partnered particularly 'connected' individuals on no terms at all – writing off their contribution as 'political insurance'.[34]

The few studies that have attempted to examine the activities of Burma's private banks generally support the perception that enterprises generating returns in the medium to long term, such as manufacturers, received little bank finance (Dapice 2003: 10, Myat Thein 2004: 143, Mya Maung 1998: 92). A particularly significant study is Mieno (2006), which surveyed some 167 small to medium enterprises (SMEs) in Burma in early 2003. Mieno found that most of these relied upon 'self-financing', and on funds available from friends and family, rather than bank loans. This was true even for working capital and trade (supplier) finance, which set the Burmese experience apart from that commonly observed for SMEs in other countries. Mieno also drew attention to the fact that most of Burma's new banks were at the centre of conglomerates and, in this context, demonstrated a bias in their lending to related entities. Such 'connected' lending (whatever the legal injunctions against it) had many causes, not least as a vehicle to 'cope with default' in a scenario in which 'the function of law in Myanmar seems to be very limited' (Mieno 2006: 158). In a similar vein to both this latter aspect and to general perceptions, Mieno (2006: 168) likewise found that 'entrepreneurs rooted in the private sector (...) have less access to bank loans than entrepreneurs from public sectors like government or state-owned enterprises'.

(3) Beyond self-financing, the moneylender remained for many enterprises a preferred source to the private banks. The ubiquity of the moneylender in Burma has been highlighted throughout this book, but it seems that the emergence of formal private banks in the 1990s did little to dent their importance. Especially dominant was *ne pyan toh* ('one-day lending'), usually provided to market traders by moneylenders (mostly women) according to a common formula of a K80 loan in the morning, and a (usurious) K100 repayment the same evening. Such moneylending activity was also an significant source of competition for bank deposits since, as one moneylender explained:

> Most people with money keep it as far away from the banks as they can. With inflation running over 20 per cent [sic], you'll lose money in a regular savings account. And why settle for 10 per cent a year when you can get three or four times that, with probably the same amount of risk, in the private money market?[35]

Of course, such moneylending remained illegal in Burma, which meant that documentation was kept to a minimum. Typically a written document was exchanged between borrower and lender, stating that the sum of money was being given in trust, and making no mention of any interest charges.[36]

(4) In place of productive lending to private enterprise, Burma's banks lent in considerable volume to the state and to state-owned enterprises. As Table 9.2 reveals, even by 2002 bank funds allocated to the state in various ways (including reserves held with the CBM) amounted to just over 40 per cent of funds advanced to the private sector. The lending or 'parking' of such funds with the state and its agencies was characteristic across all of the private banks in varying degrees – including the most 'entrepreneurial' of the banks such as the AWB (for which government bonds comprised 46 per cent of its assets in 2002).[37]

(5) Much of the lending that *was* made to the private sector by Burma's new banks was highly risky. It has been noted already that a good deal of it made its way into speculative activity of all types, but the banks themselves seemed to behave in ways that were outside banking ortho-doxy. One measure of this was the 'gearing' (or 'leverage') the banks took on in deciding on lending volumes, usually measured as a ratio of a bank's total assets relative to its capital. Such a ratio was a rough indicator of how active a bank was in using its capital to generate lending and other activity. If a bank was too highly geared then it was likely that it had insufficient capital to absorb the risks it was taking on – in other words, it was taking on too much business relative to its capacities. On the other hand, if the gearing ratio was too low, a bank might not be making the most of its opportunities to generate self-sustaining returns. In 1995, US bank regulators came to the consensus that a desirable gearing ratio was around 18, and that ratios greater than 20 probably signified that a bank was undercapitalised. The issue of capital adequacy in banking is a complex one, of course, and the history of finding appropriate benchmarks remains contentious. Nevertheless, the US regulators' standards were, and are, widely applied globally, and especially in Asia (Hempel and Simonson 1999: 324–329).

How did Burma's private banks score in the leverage stakes? Not surprisingly, system-wide data on the issue is problematic, but a rare World Bank study undertaken in 1999 estimated that most were very highly leveraged. The largest bank, AWB, had the highest gearing (ratio of assets/capital of 31), but most of the other major banks also had gearing ratios in excess of the 'undercapitalised' benchmark. These included Yoma Bank (ratio of 23), Myanmar Oriental Bank (28), Myanmar Citizens Bank (22), Myanmar Mayflower Bank (20) and Myanmar Universal Bank (20).[38] On the other hand, the same study revealed that some of the other banks were barely active in leveraging their capital and, as a consequence, were scarcely functioning as 'banks'. Included amongst this cohort was Yadanabon Bank (ratio of 1), Myanmar Industrial Development Bank (2), First Private Bank (4) and the Asia Yangon International Bank (5). Of course, some of these would greatly expand their business in subsequent years.

Over and above such statistical measures was a general perception that some of the new banks were lending imprudently. Sometimes such criticism even came from within banking circles. Thein Tun, chairman and founder of Tun Foundation Bank, recalled that the larger private banks had become hubristic, their lending policies 'too generous' and their procedures 'high risk'.[39] More typical were the contentions that the banks were not just engaged in speculative and risky activities, but actual criminality. The money-laundering question is examined below (point 6), but the broader extra-legal nature of some of the activities of the banks did not escape notice. According to an Australian government report in 1997, for instance, 'most private banks [in Burma] have found creative ways to conduct business, including using growth in [bank] equity values to private depositors with a return and providing hire purchase and illegal services such as conduits for illegal foreign equity inflows' (Government of Australia 1997: 130). Amongst Burmese commentators such problems were well known. Amongst those able to voice his concerns was the venerable Mya Maung (1998: 94):

> The question then is, how are these newly formed private banks surviving without going bankrupt? The answer to this puzzle lies in the fact that, like many government relations, the banking regulations either are not strictly enforced by the monetary authorities or are successfully evaded by private banks through bribery, connection, and engagement in illicit or underground banking activities to earn abnormal profit.

(6) Most ominously of all the allegations swirling around Burma's private banks were those asserting their involvement in laundering the substantial funds generated by the narcotics trade. These allegations

were extraordinarily widespread, and made their way even into travel and other general narratives about the country. Typical is this abstract, from Marshall's (2002: 164) travel journal (cum biography of Sir George Scott), concerning the strange ubiquity of banks in Taunggyi, the capital of Shan State:

> As I wandered up the main street it struck me that Taunggyi was oddly blessed with banks. They were all shiny and new, as if they had been built only yesterday, and I never saw a customer in any of them. To drum up trade, one bank had stationed pretty girls in red miniskirts at its doorway, which lent it the appearance of an expensive brothel. A plethora of new banks with links to either the Burmese military or ethnic drug lords had opened in Burma in the previous decade. Their primary function, it was suspected, was laundering drug money.

Of course, throughout this period Burma vied with Afghanistan as the world's largest producer of opium, and the issue of how the substantial funds from this trade were able to be 'laundered' exercised more than a little discussion in international and official circles. In June 2001 the Financial Action Task Force on Money Laundering (FATF), an international body established in 1989 by the G7 countries and partnered with the Organisation for Economic Cooperation and Development (OECD), declared Burma to be one of sixteen jurisdictions it deemed to be 'non-cooperative'.[40] The same label was applied in every year in which lists of non-cooperating countries and territories were issued by FATF up to 2006. Being so listed was a serious matter since it obliged FATF member countries (which included all the major financial centres in Europe, the Americas and Asia) to adopt special measures against financial transactions involving listed countries, on the not unreasonable grounds that such transactions were 'more likely to be suspicious'. In the wake of the terrorist attacks on the United States in September 2001, however, the issue of money-laundering became an even more serious one. Identified as a source of finance for terrorism, the existence of substantial money-laundering activity had become something of a 'red letter' issue in judging a country's standing as a responsible global citizen.

But FATF was not the only body to highlight the shadow cast by money over Burma's financial system. The US State Department, in its 'International Narcotics Control Strategy Report' also regularly drew attention to the issue, noting in its 2002 Report that:

There is reason to believe that money laundering in Burma and the return of narcotics profits laundered elsewhere are significant factors in the overall Burmese economy (...) Burma has an under-regulated banking system and ineffective laws to control money-laundering.

In the same year, the US Treasury outlined what it said were the systemic problems in Burma's approach to money-laundering specifically:

(a) Burma lacks a basic set of anti-money laundering provisions.

(b) Money laundering is not a criminal offense for crimes other than drug trafficking in Burma.

(c) The Burmese Central Bank has no anti-money laundering regulations for financial institutions.

(d) Banks licensed by Burma are not legally required to obtain or maintain identification information about their customers.

(e) Banks licensed by Burma are not required to maintain transaction records of customer accounts.

(f) Burma does not require financial institutions to report suspicious transactions.[41]

In response to the international pressure on it, in May 2002 Burma's government promulgated the *Law to Control Money and Property Obtained by Illegal Means* which, on paper, met many of the objections regarding money-laundering noted by the US Treasury above. Of course, passing a law and enforcing it are two very different things as was, indeed, the government's intent of the law and its ostensible purposes. As Ko Cho reminded (2002), '[a]nti-corruption purges in the past in Burma have typically been carried out to neutralise potential threats to the ruling clique, rather than to clean up the way the country does business'.[42] In fact the implicit 'watering-down' of the Law, and the signalling that it was not intended very seriously came in a series of press briefings issued by the government itself in early June 2002. These came in the wake of what appeared to be a panic sell-off of the kyat (for the first time breaching 1000 kyat/$US1) by individuals seemingly fearful that their transactions might invite scrutiny. At these briefings the government

... have taken pains to reassure Burma's leading financiers – some of them, like AWB Vice Chairman Aik Htun and MMB [Myanmar Mayflower Bank]

Chairman Kyaw Win, with deep involvement in the narcotics business – that they should not feel threatened by the new law.[43]

As we shall see in the next chapter, the failure of the Burmese government to implement its own laws with respect to money laundering would have dire consequences.

Fate of the 'Joint Ventures'

Stage 2 of the banking reforms that were meant to transform Burma's financial system called for the allowance of 'joint ventures' between Burma's new private banks and foreign banks that had established a representative office in Burma. Consistent with this concession, at least six such joint schemes were publicly announced. These included a proposal from the Asia Wealth Bank to enter into a joint venture with 'Thai Farmers Bank' in 1996, another between Mayflower Bank and Thailand's 'Siam City Bank' the same year, and two proposals put forward by the Myanmar Citizens Bank (in 1996 and 1997) with the Siam City Bank and the 'Public Bank of Malaysia'.[44] Credible sources have also written of two other joint venture proposals, between Yoma Bank and Japan's 'Fuji Bank', and between the Myanmar Livestock and Fisheries Development Bank, and the 'Global Commercial Bank' of Cambodia (Tin Maung Thet 2000: 96). Some of these proposals (it is uncertain which) made their way to the CBM for formal approval, but all were rejected. Stage 2 of Burma's private banking reforms, in short, was stillborn.

REFORMING THE STATE BANKS

Burma's pre-existing state-owned commercial banks were likewise given new legal identities, and to a degree transformed, by the FIML and other laws. These, together with the Myanmar Small Loans Enterprise and a new bank formed in 1993, the 'Myanma Investment and Commercial Bank', currently (2008) make up Burma's (explicit) state-owned commercial financial sector. It is to these banks that we now turn:

Myanma Economic Bank

Burma's state-owned 'general-banking' enterprise, the Myanma Economic Bank (MEB), took on a new legal identity under the *Financial Institutions of Myanmar Law* (Articles 62–73, which superseded the relevant Articles of the *Bank Law* 1975). Its activities continued more or less as before, but with greater emphasis on making loans to private enterprises and individuals. Much of these were made to traders of various kinds, particularly of agricultural commodities (around 75 per cent of the loan portfolio) (FAO 2004b: 17). The MEB provided essentially a full range of traditional banking services, including limited foreign exchange transactions in specially designated branches (most of which were in 'border trade areas').[45]

In 2005 the MEB had over 300 full branches and around 40 sub-branch 'saving agencies'.[46] The MEB was long regarded by the government more or less as an arm of policy, and its activities were greatly distorted by its role as a vehicle for the extension of concessionary loans and other forms of largess. The MEB was the principal provider of finance to state-owned and 'cooperative' enterprises, and had a number of 'social responsibility' roles, including the provision of interest-free housing loans to government employees (via a division of the MEB that went under the name of the 'Government Employees Bank', but which was not a separate bank as such). The MEB also lent on government instruction to both the Myanma Agricultural Development Bank and the Myanma Small Loans Enterprise. Loans to both of these institutions were levied at the concessional interest rates of 10 and 11 per cent respectively (FAO 2004b: 17).

Much of the growth in the private banks in the last decade came at the expense of the MEB. The MEB provided relatively poor service, and its staff were underpaid (causing many to leave to join the private banks). Yet, notwithstanding this, the closure of some of Burma's largest private banks in the wake of the 2002/03 financial crisis probably reinstated the MEB as Burma's largest bank in terms of assets. As at July 2003 (the latest data available) the MEB had around 35,000 loans outstanding for a collective value of around K122 billion. Surprisingly, the MEB admitted to a default rate in its loan portfolio of around 18 per cent (FAO 2004b: 17). Such a default rate underlines the likely unsustainability of the MEB's operations, and its equally likely technical insolvency.

Myanma Foreign Trade Bank

Formed alongside the MEB under the *Bank Law* in 1975, the Myanma Foreign Trade Bank (MFTB) was also re-established as a legal entity under the FIML in 1990 (Articles 62–73). For most of its existence the MFTB had exclusive control of ('legal') foreign exchange business in Burma, but from July 1996 to July 2001 a selection of the private banks were permitted to deal in foreign exchange. Upon the revocation of this authorisation (for which no reasons were given, but the presumptive cause was yet another slide in the value of the kyat), most authorised foreign exchange business (with the exception of that undertaken by the Myanma Industrial and Commercial Bank, and the small amount carried out by the MEB) reverted to the MFTB.

Under the SLORC/SPDC, the MFTB had been attempting to broaden its activities beyond exclusively dealing in foreign exchange-related activities. To this end it began to accept deposits and make advances to individuals and enterprises beyond foreign exchange matters. Foreign exchange accounts, however, were restricted to the following categories of individuals, institutions and enterprises: foreign embassies and their staff; United Nations, its agencies, and their foreign staff; other international organisations and their foreign staff; foreign firms and their foreign staff; foreign nationals; Burmese firms and nationals with a justified reason [sic] to be a recipient of foreign exchange; joint venture enterprises; government ministries and state-owned enterprises (KPMG 1995: 51–55).

The MFTB had the largest network of correspondent relationships with banks around the world of any of Burma's banks. Because of this, it was the bank most affected by US and European Union (EU) sanctions against Burma (in the case of the US, these included the suspension of all correspondent accounts with US banks – more on which in the next chapter).[47] Notwithstanding its efforts at diversification, the MFTB was primarily concerned with the foreign exchange business of government, government agencies and state-owned enterprises, leaving private sector foreign exchange business to the Myanmar Investment and Commercial Bank.

One area of 'private' business in which the MFTB was dominant in Burma was in the provision of financial services for expatriates in the country. Such expatriates, which included UN agency and foreign embassy staff, personnel of international NGOs as well as private business people, were required (as the recipients of 'offshore' income) to use the MFTB, at least as the vehicle for their initial payments (after which the use of local and informal foreign exchange dealers was very much the norm).[48] As with the MEB, the MFTB had a poor reputation for customer service, and numerous horror stories abounded.[49]

Myanmar Investment and Commercial Bank

The Myanmar Investment and Commercial Bank (MICB) was initially created in 1989 as a unit of the MEB, and only formally became a separate entity under the FIML. The MICB was designed to supply investment and commercial funds to private sector entities during what was predicted to be a 'transition' period prior to the new private banks being able to take on such a role. Branches were limited to Rangoon and Mandalay. The MICB had an almost exclusive 'business focus', providing kyat loans to private domestic businesses and to foreign and joint venture enterprises. The MICB expended some effort to cultivate deposits, but with little success. Just one reason for this was that the government imposed an 'automatic' tax of 10 per cent on all foreign currency deposits.[50] At one point the MICB had correspondent relationships with banks in 65 countries but, like the MFTB, the MICB's international dealings were subsequently greatly restricted by US and EU financial sanctions. The MICB once operated the foreign exchange booths where tourists were required to buy 'Foreign Exchange Certificates' (FECs, more on which below) at Burma's international airports in Rangoon and Mandalay.[51]

The Myanma Agricultural Development Bank

The Myanma Agricultural Development Bank (MADB) was created under its own law, the Myanma Agricultural and Rural Development Bank Law (1990), as a replacement for the MAB of 1975. It had a broader focus than the MAB. The latter, as we saw in Chapter 8, was ostensibly focused upon medium and longer term lending, with seasonal credit to cultivators supposedly being delivered via the advance purchase system. Under the new arrangements, however, all this would now change, and the MADB would become the primary source of short term and seasonal loans for agriculture. Medium and longer term 'developmental' loans remained in the MADB's mandate but, as we shall see, in practice little of such lending would be made. In 1997 the Law Amending the Myanma Agricultural and Rural Development Bank Law was promulgated. The most important change made under this Law was the placing of the MADB under the Department of Agriculture and Irrigation, rather than the Ministry of Planning and Finance. A cosmetic change under this Law was the removal of the word 'Rural' from the MADB's name. The MADB was technically exempt from the Financial Institutions of Myanmar Law, but in practice it deviated little from this Law's key provisions, including with respect to the interest rates the Bank paid and charged. By 2004, the MADB had 204 branches throughout Burma (of which 16 were regional 'head offices'), and 48 (sub-branch) agencies (FAO 2004b: 3–4).[52]

The re-emergence of the MADB as the primary vehicle for seasonal agricultural credit came off the back of changes in Burma's paddy procurement system. This was a long and tortured story of reform and counter-reform. Put simply, however: compulsory rice procurement was suddenly abolished in 1987, returned in 1989, and was abolished again in 2003. Importantly, the system of procurement between 1989 and 2003 was a considerably shrunken vehicle from that which had existed since the 1970s. Instead of a per acre procurement quota of between 30 and 40 baskets, a quota for paddy producers of between 10 and 12 baskets was set.[53] As a consequence, the state's 'take' of Burma's paddy production was decreased by two thirds, potentially liberating cultivators to produce more for the free market, but providing them with significantly less in the way of advance purchase payments. The MADB was meant to fill this gap. Of course, many of the anomalies and injustices of the advance purchase system remained. The state retained its monopoly over paddy exports, and the government procurement price for paddy remained set at about only 50 per cent of the prevailing free market price (Fujita and Okamoto 2006: 8–10).

Consistent with its broad mandate, the MADB made three types of loans: cultivation loans of up to one year; short term loans of 1 to 4 years, and long term loans of 4 to 20 years. In practice, however, the number of 'term' loans was negligible; in 2003–2004 a mere 1,615 loans were advanced, to a value of K234 million (FAO 2004b: 5).

The MADB claimed around 1 million active borrowers in 2004 (17 per cent of rural households), divided amongst 150,000 'borrowing groups'. Formed in place of collateral for seasonal loans, they were 'joint liability' groups (of the type once employed by the old State Agricultural Bank), and had around 5–10 members. To be effective, however, such groups rely upon a degree of social capital amongst their members, and a genuine sense of 'grass-roots' cooperation that may not have been present in the circumstances the MADB operated in. Contrary to best practices, the method by which the MADB disbursed loans was a highly centralised process involving approval instructions being passed from the MADB's head office to each State or Division Office; from there to the branches in the townships; and from these to each 'Village Tract Advisory Committee' (VTAC). Membership of the VATCs comprised the 'Village Tract Peace and Development Council' (local branch of the SPDC) Chairman, the secretary of the village borrowing groups, and the local representatives of the 'Myanma Agricultural Service and the Land Records Department'. Each VATC was the final arbiter of loans to individual borrowers (FAO 2004b: 6).

The size of loans was meant to be in proportion to demand and the capacity of borrowers to pay and, in principle, the MADB aimed to meet 30 per cent of agricultural production costs. In practice it fell well short of this modest target. The MADB lent (2004) between K2,000 to K8,000 per acre for paddy, while production costs for the same crop averaged between K50,000–65,000. Given the inadequate size of individual loans, the FAO reported (2004b: 6) that it was sometimes the case that two or more borrowers pooled their loans, taking turns to use the money in alternate loan periods. Over 80 per cent of all seasonal loans in Burma were for paddy. Table 9.3 below lists the principal seasonal loans extended by the MADB on various crops, together with the magnitude of these loans (per acre), juxtaposed against the indicative per acre costs of production of each:

Table 9.3 MADB Seasonal Loans, 2003–2004 (kyats per acre)

Crop	Loan size available	Estimated production costs	Available loans as proportion of production costs (average %)
Paddy	2,000–8,000	50,000–65,000	9
Peanuts	2,000–4,000	60,000	5
Sesame	1,500–3,000	50,000	5
Mustard	1,500	50,000	3
Maize	1,500–3,000	50,000	5
Pulses	1,000–2,000	50,000	3
Sugarcane	2,000	100,000	2

Source: FAO (2004b: 6), and information privately supplied to author

The MADB's lending had been declining in recent years in terms of the number of loans issued – from 1.66 million in 1998/99 to 1.23 million 2003/04. Loan volumes had increased across this same five-year period – from K10.4 billion in 1998 to K20.2 billion in 2004 – but this increase disguised a 'real' decrease in funds available when adjusted for the very high inflation over the period. Table 9.4 (overleaf) reveals the *real* decrease in MADB loan disbursements, and the average size of these loans from 1998/99 to 2003/04:

Table 9.4 MADB Seasonal Lending (1999–2004)

Year	Number of loans	Total loans disbursed (kyat millions)	Average loan size (kyat)	Inflation (% p.a)	Real decrease (-) /increase(+) in loans disbursed (%)
1999/00	1,470,665	11,186	7,606	49	-44.9
2000/01	1,444,341	12,124	8,304	11	-3.5
2001/02	1,395,557	12,740	9,129	21	-17.0
2002/03	1,168,413	12,015	10,283	57	-59.4
2003/04	1,233,815	20,150	16,331	37	+22.4

Source: FAO (2004b: 7), and author's calculations. Inflation estimates are from EIU (2006)

For financial year 2004/05, the MADB announced a substantial increase in lending, to K33 billion.[54] The number of borrowers was not disclosed, but the MADB claimed seasonal loans had risen to K27 billion and that 'term loans' (that is, non-seasonal loans given for capital investment) had increased dramatically, to K5.7 billion. This latter figure was dominated, however, by a very large advance (K3.7 billion) to a small number of oil palm producers in Tanintharyi Division.[55] All term loans from the MADB had to be secured against collateral. A liberal array of items were accepted as collateral, except of course the principal asset in the possession of cultivators – land. Notwithstanding other reforms that had taken place in Burma in recent years, agricultural land remained the property of the state, and could not accordingly be formally pledged as collateral. All term loans also had to be secured by the pledges of *two* personal guarantors. Table 9.5 below reveals the very small size of term lending by the MADB – in aggregate and to individual borrowers – the result of which partly explains, as the FAO noted (2004b: 8), the low-level of mechanisation in Burmese agriculture:

Table 9.5 MADB Term Lending (1998/99 – 2002/03)

Year	Aggregate term lending (kyat millions)	Number of term loans	Average loan size (kyats)	Average loan size ($US)*
1998/99	121.25	802	151,185	443
1999/2000	90.57	473	191,480	383
2000/01	62.60	290	215,862	348
2001/02	277.48	1,321	210,053	217
2002/03	233.83	1,615	144,786	151

* At market exchange rate. Source: FAO (2004b: 8), Bradford (2004a), EIU (2006) and author's calculations.

The final column in Table 9.5 has been included since, considering that Burma itself produces little in the way of capital equipment, the international purchasing power of MADB loans is perhaps a more relevant measure. Merely a cursory glance at the figures in this column is sufficient to indicate the difficulties Burmese cultivators would face in attempting to move to more capital intensive modes of production. Even fertiliser was beyond the reach of most borrowers reliant upon MADB loans, one consequence of which was that fertiliser is now seldom used in Burma – a phenomenon that has the effect of reducing agricultural yields, and income, all round (Dapice 2003: 9, Myat Thein 2004: 143). Aung Din Taylor painted the immediate human cost of this in the wake of her own observations in 2002:

> ...farmers are using less and less fertiliser, families are abandoning farming and becoming landless, yields of key crops like paddy and sesame are declining and rice prices are rising...more children are dropping out of school, large numbers of people appear to be criss-crossing the country in search of paid work, and farm families are going hungry on one meal a day consisting of rice gruel (Aung Din Taylor 2002: 22).

And in the longer term the cost to Burma's future agricultural productivity:

> When farmers can't improve their land or soil, they eventually wear it out. For example, in the Dry Zone region where sesame is grown, farmers haven't been able to rehabilitate their soils for years. So soils have become degraded and fragile. In fact, there's very little organic matter going back into them, because villagers have resorted to burning crop wastes and even cow dung as fuel, to cope with the shortage of firewood and other fuels. By converting natural fertilizer into fuel, the ecological cycle is being cut short. I recently saw farmers tilling rows of sesame in what looked like sand at the beach! Farmers in that township said their sesame yields had dropped in half in the last few years (Aung Din Taylor 2004: 23–24).

The constraints on MADB lending were a function of the MADB's precarious capital and funding position generally. Of its available loanable funds for 2003/04 of K20.8 billion, K15 billion came from a loan from the central government (at 10 per cent, and via the CBM and the MEB), whilst K4.6 billion came from deposits and K1.2 billion from capital and reserves. The MADB claimed to have 2 million depositors in Burma, but deposits themselves were greatly constrained. This was almost entirely due to inept government policies which (in addition to the sector-wide interest rate caps), further discouraged any prudent depositor via a policy, announced in March 2003 (at the tail-end of the banking crisis of 2002/03), of not allowing depositors to withdraw their deposits in all but 'exceptional circumstances', and only then on condition they forfeit all borrowing privileges and leave the Bank (FAO 2004b: 5). Table 9.6 below details the sources of MADB loanable funds, and the real (inflation adjusted) level of deposits:

Table 9.6 MADB: Source of Funds, 1998–2004 (kyat millions)

Year	Deposits (nominal)	Deposits (real)*	Funds provided by CBM/MEB	Capital and reserves
1998/99	1,374	1,025	6,000	656
1999/2000	1,963	1,317	6,750	843
2000/01	2,404	2,166	7,250	1,004
2001/02	2,837	2,345	7,250	1,084
2002/03	3,730	2,376	5,500	1,150
2003/04	4,616	3,369	15,000	1,206

* Inflation estimates as per Table 9.4. Source: FAO (2004b: 5) and author's calculations

The MADB's shortage of capital was likewise a function of poor government policy. In this context, however, the most crippling was a provision of the Act establishing the MADB – a provision that required the Bank to allocate (at least) 25 per cent of any profits each year to a reserve fund, and transfer the balance to the government in the form of a dividend. In fact, as can be seen from Table 9.7 (opposite), in practice considerably more of the Bank's profits were transferred to the government. Paid-up capital was also limited by law – currently (2008) to K1 billion. At around just $US1 million (at the market exchange rate), this was grossly inadequate for a bank with the responsibilities given to the MADB. Normally, paid-up capital is augmented by transfers to reserves from any net profits but, as a consequence of the 'dividend' the MADB was required to pay to the government, such capital accumulation through retained earnings was greatly limited. Table 9.7 illustrates the MADB's precarious capital situation, and the dilution of its declared profits:

As with the interest rate it paid on deposits, the interest rates charged by the MADB on its loans were consistent with the limits imposed on the other banks (in 2003, 15 per cent maximum). This was well below Burma's true inflation rate, meaning again that the Bank's capital position was eroding via a loan portfolio that was losing money in real terms, year by year. In short, with very little capital to begin with, the MADB was (and is) being progressively 'decapitalised'.

The operational and financial self-sustainability of the MADB must, however, be further called into question when the Bank's treatment of loan defaults is taken into account. Astonishingly, the MADB has recorded a 100 per cent repayment rate since 1991 – a performance that would be worthy of the most extraordinary accolades were it not for the fact that it was simply due to a policy, likewise (and not coincidentally) adopted in 1991, that 'no loans shall be written off' (FAO 2004b: 10). Assuming any reasonable level of loan' losses would quickly eliminate the MADB's declared 'profits'. Selecting a *very* conservative loan–loss provision of 5 per cent would make the MADB only 80 per cent operationally self-sufficient, while a 10 per cent provision would reduce this to 57 per cent.[56] Thailand's 'Bank for Agriculture and Agricultural Cooperatives' (BAAC), which might be regarded as a 'peer' of the MADB, has for several years made loan–loss provisions of around 17 per cent of its portfolio.[57] Assuming a similar default provision for the MADB would reduce its operational self-sufficiency ratio to below 25 per cent. Factor inflation into the story, and the MADB's resultant *financial* self-sufficiency drops to a disastrous 18 per cent.[58]

In addition to all of the financial inadequacies of the MADB above, the Bank was also greatly hampered by a number of practical problems on the ground. Unlike many other agricultural banks around the world, for instance, the MADB had no 'mobile banks', thus requiring many agriculturalists to travel great distances to MADB branches (FAO 2004a: 134). Coupled with a reputation for corruption and 'red tape' in accessing

Table 9.7 MADB Profits, Capital and Reserves, 1997/98 – 2002/03 (kyat millions)

Year	Net profit	Govern-ment 'dividend'	Allocation to reserves	Paid-up capital	Total capital + reserves	Total capital + reserves (inflation adjusted)
1997/98	586	439	146	560	656	490
1998/99	748	561	187	560	843	566
1999/2000	648	486	161	560	1,004	905
2000/01	322	242	80	1,000	1,084	896
2001/02	263	196	66	1,000	1,150	732
2002/03	225	169	56	1,000	1,206	880

Source: FAO (2004b: 10–11), EIU (2006) and author's calculations.

loans, and the small size of loans ultimately disbursed, there was very little incentive for the Burmese farmer to seek to do business with the MADB.

The MADB suffered from a severe shortage of staff trained in rural banking. This was partly a consequence of the low salaries on offer, but it was mostly as a consequence of poor recruitment. The MADB enjoyed little independence in recruitment policy. Instead, all key positions were decided by the government-appointed 'Public Service Selection and Training Board'. There was no recruitment of experienced bankers at senior operational levels, nor even 'business and accounting majors at the entry level' (FAO 2004b: 15). Skill gaps in risk management, credit analysis, accounting, auditing, asset valuation, and marketing were chronic within the MADB, and there was little understanding in the Bank of modern rural banking methodologies.

Staff problems and shortages in the MADB were matched, moreover, by a lack of modern infrastructure and communication systems. The MADB's large and dispersed branch network was not connected by a common computer system (in 2004 only 30 branches had 'a' computer), and the Bank was unable to transfer funds to or from its head office and branches (for this it relied upon the MEB). Communication between the MADB's branches relied upon Burma's (erratic) postal system, a situation that only exacerbated the delays caused by the Bank's cumbersome and overly-centralised decision-making process generally (FAO 2004b: 9).

Myanma Small Loans Enterprise

Burma's state-owned 'pawnshop' had been a creation of Burma's democratic government of the early independence years but, as revealed in past chapters, it had been through a number of manifestations down the decades, finally as the 'Small Loans Division' of the People's Bank (and subsequently the MEB). It was recreated as a stand-alone entity in August 1992 under the name 'Myanma Small Loans Enterprise' (MSLE), with an initial paid-up capital of K10 million. By 2003 it had become a network of 185 pawnshops across Burma, with around 120,000 loans outstanding to a total of K5.4 billion.[59] The MSLE charged 3 per cent per month on its loans (equivalent to around 43 per cent per annum), the 'term' of which averaged around 6 months. The size of the MSLE's loans were set to a maximum of 40 per cent of the market value of the pledged collateral (half of that made available by the MSLE's predecessor in the 1950s). Valuations of articles were made according to a scale determined by the MSLE's head office. Though nominally independent, the MSLE continued to be financed by the MEB, from which it had an overdraft facility to a maximum (in 2004) of K6 billion. The MEB charged only 11 per cent per annum on the facility, implying that the MEB part subsidised the MSLEs operations in 'real' (inflation-adjusted) terms (FAO 2004b: 31–32).

Notwithstanding the existence of the MSLE, private pawnshops remained ubiquitous across Burma. They charged higher interest rates than the MSLE, on average around 5 per cent per month (80 per cent per annum). They typically granted larger loans than the MSLE, however, and up to around 50 per cent of the value of the pledged collateral. Private pawnshops were supposed to be 'licensed' but, not surprisingly, a large number were not. Amongst the latter were traders and shops of various kinds, for whom pawnbroking was incidental to their main business. The pawnbroking industry in Burma remained disproportionately dominated by Sino-Burmese and, increasingly, by Chinese nationals.[60]

The MSLE and its private counterparts provided a large source of financing for many farmers and rural people generally in Burma, upon which, naturally, data is lacking. Private surveys in selected locations across Burma, however, indicated that between 10 to 20 per cent of agriculturalists had loans outstanding with pawnshops (FAO 2004b: 31–32).

THE CENTRAL BANK OF MYANMAR

The Central Bank of Myanmar (CBM) was established on 2 July 1990 under its own Act, the *Central Bank of Myanmar Law* (CBML), 1990 (State Law and Order Restoration Law No. 15/90). This Law of establishment had the effect of repealing the relevant central bank articles of the *Bank Law* 1975, that had recreated the UBB, and gave the CBM 'all the powers generally conferred upon a central bank'. The CBM was established with an authorised capital of K500 million and paid-up capital (contributed solely by the state) of K200 million (Article 14, CBML). One curious aspect of the CBML was the extension of the profits reserve requirement for commercial banks (noted above) to the CBM itself. Under Article 18 of the CBML, each year 25 per cent of any profits made by the CBM had to be allocated to a 'general reserve' up until that time the reserve reached 100 per cent of the paid-up capital of the Bank. Beyond this, all net profits of the CBM were to be paid to the government (Article 19). Formally, ultimate authority within the CBM rested with a Board of Directors of seven members, consisting of the CBM Governor, Deputy Governor, one member appointed by the Ministry of Finance and Revenue, and four other members appointed by the government (Article 25, CBML).

The first and primary aim of the CBM was set out in Article 5 of the CBML: 'to preserve the internal and external value of the Myanmar currency'. More or less the primary aim of all central banks, this was to be made manifest via the achievement of two objectives that followed as Article 6:

(a) to promote efficient payments mechanisms, and the liquidity, solvency, and proper functioning of a soundly based financial system;

(b) to foster monetary, credit and financial conditions conducive to the orderly, balanced, and sustained economic development.

Amongst central bank theorists and practitioners, these objectives are loosely aggregated into the 'microeconomic' and 'macroeconomic' roles respectively of central banks. The former, which is practically expressed via the prudential regulations central banks impose on commercial banks, has been dealt with above (and is again in the next chapter). With respect to the role of the CBM in fostering *macroeconomic* stability in Burma, it is worthy of note that the CBML was given great *formal* powers. Articles 75 and 76 gave the CBM most of the requisite 'toolbox' of monetary instruments necessary for the successful application of monetary policy, including the ability to set the 'discount rate' on government securities, the powers to conduct open market operations in government securities and foreign exchange (buying and selling these to influence financial asset prices), determining the exchange rate of the currency, and being the government's principal adviser on monetary policy – while 'assisting' the same with respect to the state budget.

In practice however, most of the formal monetary instruments and powers held by the CBM were rendered ineffective by Burma's underdeveloped financial system (which made irrelevant much of the toolbox above), and by the CBM's overriding role as the 'financing arm' of the state. The latter was especially critical, and more or less entirely negated the ability of the CBM in controlling inflation. Table 9.8 provides the relevant data regarding the CBM's role as a 'cash-box' for government spending, and its consequences:

Table 9.8 CBM Lending to Government, Banks and Inflation, 1989–2002 (kyat millions)

Year	Central Bank claims on government	Bank lending to private sector	Money supply (M1)	Consumer price index (1989=100)
1989	42,740	2,801	21,317	100
1990	51,813	3,262	30,587	117.6
1991	60,870	7,208	43,495	155.6
1992	74,710	19,173	58,708	189.8
1993	91,399	23,076	73,459	250.1
1994	116,131	28,262	98,288	310.4
1995	142,023	45,956	125,957	388.6
1996	182,431	75,346	167,971	451.8
1997	214,392	115,505	220,006	586.0
1998	281,383	155,761	282,177	887.9
1999	331,425	188,149	345,765	1050.6
2000	447,581	266,466	464,968	1050.0
2001	675,040	416,776	701,153	1270.5
2002	892,581	608,401	1,009,471	1995.5

Sources: IMF (1995, 1998, 2006), and author's calculations.

The CBM's claims on the government (column 1 above) was the primary driver of the country's rapidly increasing money supply which, in turn, was a principal cause of the country's high and chronic inflation through the period.[61] Article 49 of the CBML contained provisions for the financing of the government by the CBM – provisions that included limits and safeguards for such a role. As with past central banking legislation in Burma, the CBM advances were meant to be temporary and guaranteed by short-dated government securities (maturity no greater than 184 days). A very significant provision (under Article 49 (c)) required that the 'total of the loans and advances extended within any given year shall not exceed 20 per cent of the Government receipts of the previous year'. This was simply an update on a similar injunction (albeit at 15 per cent) included the 1952 *Union Bank of Burma Act* and the 1975 *Bank Law*. It was also similarly easily avoided since, in place of lending directly to the government, the CBM could simply purchase securities issued by the government – in any quantity.

Exchange Rate

Article 75 of the CBML gave the CBM responsibility for determining the exchange rate of the kyat. This formal, fixed, exchange rate regime pegged the kyat at a value of 1 kyat to 8.5085 of the IMF's 'Special Drawing Rights', which yielded a more or less constant K6:$1US throughout the period under examination here. The kyat was not legally tradable nor negotiable outside Burma, and strict exchange controls limited the ability of people to legally possess foreign exchange. As noted above, day to day (legal) dealing in foreign exchange was concentrated with the MFTB, but under the supervision of the 'Controller of Foreign Exchange' within the CBM.

The management of the exchange rate was (and remains) the most *conspicuous* failure of the CBM in its management of Burma's monetary system. The yawning gap between the 'official' exchange rate determined by the CBM, and the 'unofficial' rates at which the kyat traded illegally and informally was the most visible sign of the declining trust the people of Burma came to have in their own currency. The collapse in the value of the kyat is dramatically revealed in Table 9.9:

Table 9.9 Burma's Exchange Rates, 1988–2002 (kyat/$US)

Year	Official exchange rate kyat/$US	Approximate unofficial exchange rate kyat/$US*
1988	6.4	30
1989	6.5	45
1990	6.1	50
1991	6.0	60
1992	6.2	85
1993	6.2	100
1994	5.9	120
1995	5.8	115
1996	6.0	150
1997	6.4	240
1998	6.0	335
1999	6.2	340
2000	6.5	500
2001	6.8	650
2002	6.3	960

* Author's sources and estimates. *Source: IMF (1995, 1998, 2006)*

Foreign Exchange Certificates

Declining trust in a currency is often manifested in 'currency substitution', a situation in which the citizens of a country disavow their own currency in favour of one that is a more reliable store of value. This was (and is) certainly the case in Burma, where the possession of US dollars was especially prized (and, in particular, new and 'crisp' US $100 bills). Throughout the 1990s and beyond, the 'dollarisation' of Burma's economy in this way accelerated with the country's worsening political and economic crisis, and in lock-step with the collapse of the kyat.

The dollarisation of important parts of Burma's economy was given official sanction in February 1993 with the introduction of 'Foreign Exchange Certificates' (FECs). A Burmese copy of a Chinese device designed to both capture foreign exchange from tourists, and track it through the domestic economy, FECs were issued in denominations of 1, 5 and 10 US dollars. They were sold by the MFTB, the MICB (principally at the official counter set up for the purpose at Rangoon's Mingaladon international airport), the MEB, and via a small number of officially authorised agents. FECs functioned essentially as a 'tax' on tourists, who were 'forced' to exchange foreign currency for them upon arrival in Burma. The compulsory exchange was initially set at $US200, rising to $US300 in March 1994. Unspent FECs could not be redeemed back into foreign currency by tourists. Burmese citizens in receipt of FECs, on the other hand, could open an account denominated in them at either the MFTB or MICB (minimum $US100), but such accounts were subject to a 10 per cent 'service charge'. Moreover, 25 per cent of individual accounts could only be withdrawn in kyats.[62]

The credibility of the FEC system rested on the commitment that each FEC issued was 'backed' by an equivalent amount of foreign currency handed over in its place. In this sense the FEC arrangements represented a type of 'currency board' (similar to that which had existed in Burma from 1948 to 1952), and the FECs as a more credible 'currency' than the kyat. Alas, as with the kyat, Burma's authorities proved unable to resist temptation, and it soon became apparent that FECs were being issued in significantly greater volumes than the foreign exchange 'backing them'. By 1995 FECs had begun to sell in secondary markets at a significant discount to their face value. They lingered on for some time thereafter (and can still be found circulating), but the compulsory tourist exchange program ended in August 2003.

NOTES

1 Cited from Mya Maung (1998: 65).

2 These stages were set out in a document issued by Burma's Ministry of Finance and Revenue, 'The Financial Sector Development in Myanmar' which first appeared on the Ministry's website, and that of Burma's UN mission in Geneva, in the mid-1990s.

As at February 2007 it continued to live online, even though much of the information it contained was obsolete. It remains a document of great interest, however, in illustrating the early optimism that surrounded Burma's financial sector reforms. The document can be found at <http://mission.itu.ch/MISSIONS/Myanmar/t&b/finance.html>, accessed 15 December, 2007.

3   One bank created under the FIML did not survive until 2002. This was the 'Prime Commercial Bank', a shadowy operation whose 'front man' was a certain Colonel Kyaw Myint, reputedly a Sino-Burmese business figure who was also allegedly 'deputy finance minister' of the United Wa State Party. According to Hawke, the bank 'was so ostentatiously drug-linked that it had become an embarrassment even to the junta'. Bruce Hawke, 'Burmese banking: The Yangon laundromats' burnout explained', *The Irrawaddy*, April, vol. 12, no. 4, pp. 17–21.

4   The extent to which these ethnic-Chinese bank chiefs were linked into broader Chinese economic networks throughout Southeast Asia is much speculated upon, but very difficult to determine with anything like certainty. Of course, the issue is clouded by communal tensions long evident in Burma and, not least, the occasional efforts of the SPDC (and its predecessors) to stoke them.

5   'The man with the money', *The Myanmar Times*, 23–29 December 2002, vol. 8, no. 147.

6   *Ibid.* Information here was also gleaned from the AWB's website <http:www.e-commerce.com.mm/AWB>, which was subsequently 'taken down' following the bank's suspension of operations in 2003.

7   *Ibid.*

8   *Ibid.*

9   Bruce Hawke, 'Burmese banking: The Yangon laundromats' burnout explained'.

10   Aung Kyaw Tha, 'Credit cards usher in online shopping', *The Myanmar Times*, 23–29 December 2002, vol. 8, no. 147.

11   'The man with the money'.

12   Information on Yoma Bank derived from Yoma's former (now inoperative) website, and that provided confidentially to the author.

13   Information provided confidentially to the author.

14   Bruce Hawke, 'Burmese banking: The Yangon laundromats' burnout explained'.

15   *Ibid.*

16   *Ibid.*

17   *Ibid.*

18   'The nation's top 20 banks', *The Myanmar Times*, 4–10 March 2002, vol. 6, no. 105, and information privately acquired by the author.

19   Bruce Hawke, 'Burmese banking: The Yangon laundromats' burnout explained'.

20   *Myanmar Perspectives*, vol.2, no.8, online edition <www.myanmar.gov.mm/Perspecutive>.

21   Information based on confidential interviews with bank staff.

22   *Ibid.*

23   Information provided confidentially to the author.

24   Bruce Hawke, 'Burmese banking: The Yangon laundromats' burnout explained'.

25   'The nation's top 20 banks', and information privately acquired by the author.

26   The scheme was outlined in the commercial web pages of the Embassy of Myanmar in Geneva, <http://mission.itu.ch/MISSIONS/Myanmar/t&b/finance.html>.

27   Information based on confidential interviews with bank staff.

28   Thein Linn, 'Bank provides cattle loans', *The Myanmar Times*, 19–25 June 2006, vol. 17, no. 321.

29   An assessment apparent in discussions with MFLDB customers by the author.

30   Author's calculations based on data in IMF (2006).

31   See also May Thander Win, 'Banks claim a solid recovery', *The Myanmar Times*, 31 July–6 August 2006, vol. 17, no. 327.

32   This assertion is based on interviews with borrowers from the banks by the author.

33   Many of these leaders were those that had made ceasefire agreements between the groups they represented, and the SLORC/SPDC. Bruce Hawke, 'Burmese banking: The Yangon laundromats' burnout explained'.

34   *Ibid.*

35   Stephen Brookes, 'Black market banking in Burma', *Asia Times*, 18 April 2006, online at <www.stephenbrookes.com>. These testimonies are consistent with other sources in correspondence with the author.

36   *Ibid.*

37   AWB website, op. cit.

38   The World Bank's ratios are replicated in Wajima (1999: 243).

39   Thein Tun cited in Moe Zaw Myin, 'Banking sector shows sign of recovery after troubled year', The Myanmar Times, 22–28 December 2003, vol. 10, no. 197.

40   The original FATF report naming Burma can be found at FATF's website, <www.fatf-gafi.org>.

41   United States Department of the Treasury, Financial Crimes Enforcement Network, FinCEN Advisory, 'Transactions Involving Burma (Myanmar)', April 2002, <http://www.ustreas.gov/fincen/advis28.pdf>.

42   Ko Cho, 'Junta introduces money laundering law', The Irrawaddy, 9 June 2002, online edition.

43   *Ibid.*

44   'MCB, Public Bank of Malaysia sign MOU to establish joint-venture bank', The New Light of Myanmar, 8 March 1997.

45   Some of these broad institutional details regarding the MEB are outlined on the website of Burma's Ministry of Finance and Revenue, <www.myanmar.com/Ministry/finance>, accessed 15 December, 2007.

46   The latter are located typically in smaller townships, and offer a smaller array of products and services. Ibid.

47   For details of these sanctions, see Turnell (2006a, 2006b).

48   Information provided privately to the author.

49   See, for instance, the account of Michael Vatikiotis reproduced in Myat Thein (2004: 130).

50   US Department of State, Doing Business in Burma: A Country Commercial Guide for U.S. Companies, 2007, <www.buyusainfo.net>, accessed 15 December, 2007.

51   Certain basic details of the MICB can be found at the website of Burma's Ministry of Finance and Revenue, <www.myanmar.com/Ministry/finance>, accessed 15 December, 2007.

52   Some institutional detail of the MADB can be found at various official government websites, including that of the Ministry of Agriculture and Irrigation at <http://mission.itu.ch/MISSIONS/Myanmar/e-com/Agri>, accessed 19 February, 2008.

53   The modern 'basket' of paddy employed in this context equals 20.9 kilograms (Fujita and Okamoto 2006: 9).

54   Win Nyunt Lwin, 'Bank lends K33b to help boost agricultural sector', The Myanmar Times, 9–15 May 2005, vol. 14, no. 265.

55   *Ibid.*

56   A financial institution is said to be operationally self-sufficient when its income is equal to or greater than its operational expenses plus provisions. A ratio of 100 per cent or more indicates a financial institution is profitable and therefore operationally self-sufficient, a ratio below 100 per cent indicates an entity that is making losses. The ratios calculated here are based on the data for financial year 2001–2002.

57   Information on the BAAC's loan-loss provisioning can be found at the Bank's website, <www.baac.or.th>.

58   To be *financially* self-sufficient, a financial institution must not only earn sufficient income to cover operational expenses and provisions, but also the real (inflation-adjusted) cost of its capital.

59   Basic details of the MSLE can be found at the website of the Ministry of Finance and Revenue, <www.myanmar.com/Minsitry/finance>, accessed 15 January, 2008.

60   Information provided confidentially to the author.

61   The inflation estimates in Table 9.8 are indicative only. They are likely to understate the true rate of inflation in Burma since they are estimates of increases in the price of consumer goods in Rangoon only.

62   For more on the FECs, see Turnell (2001).

CHAPTER 10

$\mathcal{T}he$ $Crash$

The people are not to trust the rumours about the private banks and to do business with the banks with confidence.
Kyaw Kyaw Maung, Governor, Central Bank
of Myanmar, 11 February 2003

On account of the rumours, something that should not be done was done. People have experienced mistakes. The Secretary-1 cautioned the people that if the banks suffer losses due to the rumours spread by destructionists, the country will also suffer.
The New Light of Myanmar, 16 February 2003

In late 2002, Burma began to experience what became a prolonged banking and financial crisis. Triggered by the collapse of a series of informal finance companies (in reality mostly 'ponzi' and 'pyramid' schemes), the crisis quickly extended into the country's private banking sector. Subsequent 'runs' on the banks stripped them of reserves and prompted the adoption of measures to restrict withdrawals. In the panic a flight to cash led to a shortage of the kyat, and a liquidity crisis. Liquidity support, had it been rapidly and appropriately supplied by the Central Bank of Myanmar could have limited the contagion. Such liquidity support from the CBM, however, was too little and too late. Worse, the CBM's orders endorsing restrictions on withdrawals and the recalling of loans from borrowers greatly impaired trust – the indispensable ingredient of financial stability. Burma's private banks, which superficially had appeared to be performing strongly before the crisis (Chapter 9), were irreparably damaged.

Of course, as we have seen in these pages, financial crises are not new to Burma. What distinguished this latest drama, however, was that its genesis lay in the *private* sector. This meant that whilst its immediate impact upon the greater populace was perhaps not as great as the government-inspired disasters of the past, its longer term effects, not least in sowing distrust in the market economy, were great indeed.

In this chapter we examine this latest financial crisis in Burma, critique the policy responses to it and consider the condition of Burma's financial system in its wake. The chapter is divided into five sections – first taking up the narrative of the crisis as it unfolded chronologically, a difficult if necessary task in the opaque world of Burma's political economy. We then outline what might be regarded as international 'best practice' responses to banking crises, and how the efforts of Burma's monetary authorities fell far short of this ideal. Following this, we examine the climax of the money-laundering question in Burma. Developments here were a partial trigger of the bank crisis, and money laundering suspicions in the aftermath of the crisis were to bring down the biggest names in Burmese banking. Finally, the chapter looks at what was left. Our narrative here takes us to the present day, to the winners and losers amongst the private banks, and the continuing distortions that plague Burma's monetary and financial system.

THE UNFOLDING CRISIS

The precise origin of Burma's latest financial crisis was shrouded in myth, rumour and innuendo. What was undoubtedly true, however, was that its immediate trigger lay in the collapse of a succession of 'informal finance enterprises' (the so-called *A-kyoe-saung lou-ngan*) through the second half of 2002. These enterprises promised investors very high rates of return. 'Interest' rates of three to four per cent per month were typically promised and, while no precise data were available, such returns (vastly in excess of the ceilings imposed on the banks) attracted a large number of investors. Generating returns as high as this in legitimate and productive activity is scarcely possible even under the most favourable of circumstances. In the case of Burma's informal finance sector they were at best a function of highly speculative investments in real estate, construction and commodity trading, at worst they were only made possible by a sector that was in large part made up of little more than gambling syndicates and ponzi schemes.[1] It is the nature of such schemes, and such strategies, that failure is never far away. Much of the activity of the informal finance enterprises was similarly 'extra-legal' on the liabilities side. They were not, for example, authorised deposit-taking institutions under the FIML, and as such could not legally accept deposits. A commonly adopted loophole was to describe depositors as 'shareholders'. A blind eye seems to have been turned by regulators until very late.[2]

Exacerbating the crisis in Burma's informal finance sector were two potential crisis triggers involving the banks themselves. The first of these concerned the vexed question of money-laundering, and the Burma government's efforts to 'deal' with the problem. As we have seen, Burma's banks (and their principals) had long been rumoured to be involved in money-laundering. This, and the lack of systematic anti-money-laundering provisions in the country's banking laws, had led to Burma being consistently named by the OECD's 'Financial Action Task Force on Money Laundering' (FATF) as a 'non-cooperative' jurisdiction.[3] In its annual 'International Narcotics Control' reports the US State Department too consistently highlighted both the significance of the narcotics trade in Burma's economy, as well as the lack of laws dealing with the laundering of the funds that flowed from it.[4] Meanwhile, the US Treasury had long required all US banks and financial institutions to 'give enhanced scrutiny to any transaction originating in or routed to or through Burma, or involving entities organised or domiciled, or persons maintaining accounts, in Burma'.[5]

In the wake of these and other pressures, the government of Burma gave appearances of at last coming to grips with the issue and (as noted in Chapter 9) in May 2002 it promulgated the *Law to Control Money and Property Obtained by Illegal Means.* On paper this met many of the hitherto objections of FATF and the US State Department. Certainly for a while the customers of Burma's banks took the Law seriously, and in June 2002 there was something of a flight of funds away from the banks and a sell-off of the kyat, which for the first time breached 1000 kyat/$US1. Matters were sufficiently serious, indeed, for a series of 'briefings' by government officials to assure Burma's banks that they should 'not feel threatened by the new law' (also as noted in Chapter 9).[6] With depositors in the banks being placated for the while, operations returned more or less to normal. Rumours persisted, however, of large-scale withdrawals by certain 'sensitive' depositors. Such rumours were given credence in statistics supplied to the IMF by the CBM that showed declining reserves and demand deposits in Burma's banks during the final quarter of 2002 (IMF 2003). Of course, within six months of the promulgation of the anti-money-laundering law crisis and panic would descend upon Burma's banking system with greater force. Meanwhile the vulnerability of the banks had been laid open.

The second potential 'bank-centred' trigger for Burma's banking crisis was a political scandal that brought about the resignation of Burma's Finance and Revenue Minister, Khin Maung Thein. This occurred on 1 February 2003, just as fears of contagion from the finance scheme collapses were reaching their peak. The reasons for the Minister's resignation were never publicly revealed beyond reports that he was being 'investigated' over his role in the crisis. More damaging to the banking system was that the rumour mill linked the scandal to the Asia Wealth Bank (AWB) – as we have seen, then the largest and most prominent of Burma's private banks. Simultaneously other rumours circulated telling of large losses on investments in China, likewise concerning the AWB (Zaw Oo 2003). Whatever the truth or otherwise of the rumour mill, tales surrounding Burma's banks were given credence enough such that, in early February, queues of anxious depositors formed outside all of the active private banks. Principal amongst these were those banks which had shown extraordinary growth in recent years, including the 'big five' of the aforementioned AWB, Yoma Bank, Kanbawza Bank, Mayflower Bank and Burma Universal Bank.

The transformation of what might have been a localised crisis (limited perhaps to one or two banks) into a systematic bank 'run' took only a matter of days. On 11 February the Chairman of the CBM, Kyaw Kyaw Maung, attempted to reassure depositors with the statement that 'all 20 private banks established according to the Financial Institutions laws have firm financial standing and have the backing of the Central Bank'.[7] To no avail. Indeed, the statement by the Chairman of the CBM may even have exacerbated matters since, in a country in which unpleasant truths rarely featured in state-controlled media, 'ordinary citizens feared the worst'.[8] Not surprisingly the banks soon found themselves running short of liquidity and, as a consequence, all manner of devices emerged in the attempt to maintain reserves by limiting depositor access to their funds.[9] Initially these were *ad hoc*, and differed not only between banks, but even between different branches of the same bank. A degree of uniformity emerged, however, when on 17 February all banks (with the blessing of the CBM) imposed a withdrawal limit of 500,000 kyats per customer, per week. As the crisis continued this limit drifted downwards, and within a week some banks had reduced the maximum to 100,000, and then 50,000 kyats, per account.[10]

The crisis manifested itself in some unexpected ways. None more so perhaps than in the strengthening of the unofficial (market) exchange rate of the kyat.[11] This had been declining for many years, but had precipitously fallen to a low of around 1,100 to $US1 immediately before the crisis. At first glance this seems perplexing. Financial crises are usually times of great turmoil for the nation concerned, all of which was usually reflected in the 'price' of its currency. Of course, it is also true that banking and currency crises tend to go together. The reasons for the kyat's appreciation, however, were prosaic. Simply, and notwithstanding the little faith that the people in Burma had in the currency as a store of value, the kyat as a *means of exchange* remained indispensable, especially for everyday (small value) transactions. As a result there was a ready demand for it. With the onset of the banking crisis, moreover, a flight to currency (normally, as noted, not particularly valued as a safe haven – but now much safer than kyat denominated bank *deposits*) ensued. This flight led to a physical shortage of kyat supplies. With kyats scarce, their 'price' (exchange rate) appropriately rose. Of course all of this signified something else too – Burma's systemic banking crisis had now become a problem of systemic illiquidity too.

Less unexpectedly, Burma's financial crisis also manifested itself in more typical, damaging, ways. One of these was that the means of exchange created by banks (cheques, remittance facilities, credit and debit cards, electronic transfers and the like) quickly ceased to function and on 26 February the CBM ordered banks to stop 'all account transfer transactions'.[12] No explanation for this directive was given, but presumably it was aimed at ensuring that withdrawal limits were not evaded by the transfer of funds into different accounts, different banks or even different branches of the same bank (the latter a function of the lack of centralised account-keeping records by Burma's banks).[13]

Most serious of all was the way in which the banking crisis was now impacting upon the real economy. Data is lacking, but there can be little doubt that the vast array of anecdotes pointing to *severe* disruptions to production and distribution captured the essential truth.[14] It was, of course, the case that most people in Burma still did not have bank accounts in any form. Many employers and businesses, however, did – and this was the source of most of the damage. Simply, from the onset of the crisis, a great many workers in Burma – in textiles and footwear factories, in construction, in fisheries, in almost all market-related activities – went unpaid for considerable periods.[15] Suppliers and distributors were likewise materially affected. So too were contractors and transport providers. Saving the economy from complete seizure was the ever-ready fall-back to informal payment mechanisms and, undoubtedly, the resilience of the Burmese people in the face of persistent economic distress. Such a fall-back, however, was hardly ideal and only entrenched Burma as a cash and barter economy.

The attempt at soothing words early in the crisis was supplemented on 21 February by what was purported to be more concrete actions by the CBM. According to reports, on this day the CBM provided a 25 billion kyats loan shared amongst the Asia Wealth Bank, the Yoma Bank and the Kanbawza Bank (Zaw Oo 2003: 2; EIU 2003a: 17). Attached to the loan was an interest charge of 4.0 per cent, and the loan was made against lodged collateral (of Burmese government securities). The loan represented a mere 3.5 per cent of total deposits in the banks (as at June 2002), however, and was a figure decidedly insufficient for the scale of the crisis at hand. By way of comparison, liquidity support provided by the Indonesian monetary authorities to its banks during the 1997/98 banking crisis amounted to 15 per cent of pre-crisis deposits (Enoch *et al.* 2003: 87).

In the on-going absence of sufficient, concrete and credible support, Burma's authorities attempted to assuage the crisis with yet more soothing words. On the same day the CBM loan was made, then Secretary-1 of the SPDC, Khin Nyunt, declared that there was 'no safer place' for frightened depositors 'to keep their money than in the banks'.[16] Less helpfully, a few days later Brigardier-General David Abel, then Minister for the Office of the Chairman of the SPDC, was recorded as saying that some of the private banks had been found 'to be not operating in line with the Financial Institutions Law' in their lending practices.[17]

A concrete, but most unwelcome, plan emerged from the authorities a few days after these comments in the form of CBM endorsement of efforts by a number of the private banks to 'recall' loans.[18] Such recalls, which were first made in early February, were a direct reflection of the banks' (by now) dire liquidity position. The recalls ranged from 20 to 50 per cent of loan balances outstanding, with most banks tending toward the latter as the crisis dragged on. The CBM-endorsed timetable for the loan repayments required that they be completed by the end of March. Government exhortation to this end was less than successful, and the deadline was later extended to the end of May 2003.[19] This deadline too passed, but the repayment orders remained in place.

Coming on top of the restrictions on deposit withdrawals, there was much evidence to suggest that the loan recall announcements (even if widely evaded) did great damage to private enterprise in Burma. Once more there were no official or even plausible data on what followed, but much contemporary reporting told of attempts by Burmese firms and individuals to meet loan calls by selling assets, and otherwise downgrading businesses and lifestyles. Representative of these were tales of home borrowers being given just days notice to return 25 per cent of the value of their home loans, of asset price deflation (especially for items such as motor vehicles and other durables – sold to meet loan calls), of job losses, of continuing difficulties for firms in meeting wage and supplier commitments and even of falls in the prices of some commodities.[20]

In May 2003, with no seeming end to the crisis and no greater ability of depositors to access their funds, reports emerged of a growing 'secondary market' in frozen bank accounts. The going price was said to be between 60 and 80 per cent of face value. Meanwhile in the ongoing absence of adequate official support, the banks themselves continued their efforts to acquire liquidity. The Yoma Bank, then Burma's second-largest private bank, was reported to be attempting to sell its fleet of cars in order to raise kyats.[21]

THE POLICY RESPONSE

Banks are inherently brittle institutions. They take in deposits (liabilities) which they promise to repay in full on demand, and use them to make longer-term loans (assets). Should all the depositors in a bank insist on repayment simultaneously, the bank would be unable to redeem its promise and it would fail. Moreover, the mere fear that a bank might fail tends to becoming self-fulfilling. As was the case in Burma in 2002/2003, once a panic starts it makes perfect sense for individual depositors to try and get their money out. Once sowed, fear is rarely limited to a single institution and systemic crisis is never far away.

The inherently risky nature of banking, and indeed the history of its fragility, has prompted the creation of a host of measures designed to mitigate against the worst of these risks. There is disagreement amongst economists and bankers on the margins of what can and should be done to alleviate the risks in banking. But upon the fundamentals, and especially upon the role of a central bank in a crisis, there is broad consensus.[22] The most crucial function a central bank must perform in a bank crisis is to ensure that problems in individual institutions do not make the transition into a systemic banking panic. Prompt, credible and *visible* liquidity support is the key to stopping this transition. In the early stages this involves the central bank coming to the aid of illiquid but not insolvent banks. Such assistance involves anything from coordinating a rescuing consortium of peer banks, to shifting government deposits to troubled banks, to acting as the time-honoured 'lender-of-last-resort'. Should the cross-over point be reached, and a bank crisis become a full scale systemic bank panic (as was the case in Burma) then there is really no option but for the monetary authorities to establish full depositor protection via a deposit guarantee. According to Frydl and Quintyn (2000: 11):

> Such a blanket guarantee aims to stabilize the banks' funding and prevent, or stop, bank runs. As such, it is mainly a confidence booster. In addition, announcing a blanket guarantee buys the government time while the restructuring work is being organized and carried out.

A deposits guarantee delivers to the monetary authorities a potentially large contingent liability. But, as Frydl and Quintyn (2000: 21) note, it was 'possible that blanket guarantees, mainly being confidence boosters, are not called upon (...) that the mere announcement of such guarantees suffices to stop bank runs and restore confidence in the banking system'.[23] In short, the fiscal costs of a guarantee *could* be low. In any case, against the (very visible) cost of such a mitigating device must be juxtaposed the much larger economic and social costs of a systemic collapse. This was one of the 'lessons learned' of the Asian financial crisis in 1997, during which Indonesia, Malaysia, South Korea and Thailand all guaranteed ordinary bank deposits (Delhaise 1998).[24]

The most egregious and damaging aspect of the failure of the monetary authorities in Burma to provide adequate short-term liquidity (much less a deposit guarantee) was that the costs of the crisis were transferred directly onto depositors and borrowers – the very cohort whose faith in monetary institutions was a necessary prerequisite in Burma's economic development. The stakes could hardly have been higher. Rebutting criticism of the Indonesian government's deposits guarantee declared in 1997, Enoch *et al.* (2003: 86) noted that:

> To have tried to force depositors to bear the costs of the banking failures could have led rapidly to the collapse of most, or all, banks in the country, turning Indonesia into a wasteland of financial intermediation and returning it to a cash or barter economy.

As noted earlier, it was into 'cash and barter' that Burma's economy descended in the wake of the banking crisis. The economic costs of this regression have been, and will be well into the future, severe. The role of banks in creating media of exchange is one of the crucial functions they play in an economy. Banks, through their creation of non-currency media of exchange, form the basis of the payments system in most countries. In so doing they contribute what Frydl and Quintyn (2000: 52) perceptively categorised as a valuable 'input' into a country's production potential by allowing the division of labour. This input scarcely came to function in Burma in 2003.

The recall of loans is usually a last desperate step by banks to repair their balance sheets. According to the seminal work on 'bank runs', Diamond and Dybvig (1983: 404), 'the real damage from bank runs is primarily from the direct damage occurring when recalling loans disrupts production'. Such disruption has short-run effects in the temporary loss of employment by workers displaced from the sale of enterprises and productive assets, as well as the capital loss from the 'fire-sale' of assets. But there are also longer-run effects. These include the opportunity costs to future national wealth from the projects that *no longer* go ahead. They also include what Frydl and Quintyn (2000: 51) label the 'permanent loss of wealth' that comes from the 'disruption of the combination of specific capital, knowledge and skills in the liquidated investments'. Such costs have been well documented from previous crises, including the experiences in Indonesia through 1997/98, when loan recalls were similarly (initially) entertained (Lindgren *et al.* 1999: 25). Of course, what separates these experiences from Burma's in 2003 was that, in Burma, the very authorities that should have been preventing this outcome were enforcing it.

In the final analysis, much of the blame for Burma's banking crisis in 2003 must be laid at the door of the CBM and, to the extent that it did not enjoy operational autonomy, Burma's governing institutions more broadly. The CBM did more than simply neglect its responsibilities. Throughout the crisis it not only failed to respond to the growing crisis in the way that we have come to expect central banks can and should, but it actively encouraged reactions most likely to bring about systemic instability. It gave the impression (nothing in its actions was ever entirely clear) that the banks and their customers were on their own. Early (and quickly contradicted) announcements notwithstanding, the monetary authorities in Burma did not stand behind the country's banking system.

MONEY-LAUNDERING AGAIN: PERPETRATORS AND VICTIMS

As detailed above, the concerns over money-laundering were a contributing trigger to the sudden collapse in confidence in Burma's private banks. In the wake of the crisis, however, the issue and the pressure from offshore agencies over money-laundering increased dramatically, precipitating a series of events that would bring about the downfall of the biggest names in Burmese banking.

The first of these events came in the form of a decision by FATF on 3 November 2003 to impose 'additional countermeasures' on Burma. As noted, Burma had been designated a 'non-cooperating' jurisdiction by FATF since 2001, but this latest announcement came in the wake of what FATF called the country's continuing failure to address 'major deficiencies in its anti-money-laundering regime'.[25] The already existing measures against Burma required financial institutions in FATF member countries to 'give special attention to' relationships and transactions with Burmese enterprises. The additional measures announced on 3 November were much tougher and included: (1) Stricter 'know thy customer' requirements of financial institutions to Burmese entities, to better identify the 'beneficial owners' of funds. (2) Greater scrutiny of individual transactions on the basis that, involving Burma, they were 'more likely to be suspicious'. (3) The taking into account of Burma's 'non-cooperative' designation if and when deciding upon the authorisation of local subsidiaries, branches, representative offices and the like of Burmese financial institutions. (4) Warning *non-financial* institutions that transactions with any entities in Burma 'might run the risk of money-laundering'. It was this last point that was perhaps the strongest of all of these FATF countermeasures in that its effects necessarily extended beyond simply the financial sector.

Two weeks after the latest FATF announcement came another from the United States Treasury. It declared that Burma as a jurisdiction, and the AWB and the Myanmar Mayflower Bank specifically, were of 'primary money-laundering concern'. This declaration authorised the US Treasury Secretary (under Section 311 of the USA Patriot Act[26]), in collaboration with other US government departments and agencies, to direct financial institutions in the United States to 'take certain "special measures"' against the banks in question.[27] Such measures ranged 'from enhanced recordkeeping or reporting requirements to a requirement to terminate correspondent banking relationships with the designated entit[ies]'. In the case of this ruling specifically:

> The designation of Burma is intended to deny Burmese financial institutions access to the U.S. financial system through correspondent accounts. Thus, the proposed rule would prohibit U.S. financial institutions from establishing or maintaining any correspondent account for, or on behalf of, a Burmese financial institution. This prohibition would extend to any correspondent account maintained by a U.S. financial institution for any foreign bank if the account is used by the foreign bank to provide a Burmese financial institution indirect access to the U.S. financial system. In such a case, the U.S. financial system would be required to ensure that the account no longer is used to provide such access, including, if necessary, terminating the correspondent relationship.[28]

Both the AWB and the Myanmar Mayflower Bank were covered by the measures above, but the US Treasury also took additional 'independent action' against these two in order, it said, 'to reinforce the importance of termination of relationships with these two institutions, and to ensure that no exemptions are available for them'. The action against the AWB and Mayflower was 'the first time that the Treasury Department has used its authority under Section 311 against a foreign financial institution'. The reason for singling out the pair according to the Treasury was that they had information that the two were

> ...controlled by and used to facilitate money lending for such groups as the United Wa State Army – among the most notorious drug trafficking organizations in Southeast Asia. The Burmese government has failed to take any regulatory or enforcement action against these financial institutions, despite their well-known criminal links.[29]

The ban on AWB and Mayflower would remain in place until it was 'demonstrated that they have severed their links with narcotics trafficking organizations'.[30]

The Burmese government was not inactive in response to the declarations of FATF and the US authorities, and on 5 December 2003 it (finally) issued the regulations required to bring into force its *Law to Control Money and Property Obtained by Illegal Means* (which, as we have seen, was promulgated as far back as June 2002). On paper these rules (titled 'The Control of Money Laundering Rules') met many of the requirements of FATF and the US State Department.[31] The government also established an

'Investigation Body' under the Ministry of Home Affairs to enquire into the specific money-laundering allegations against AWB and Mayflower.[32] The Investigation Body was authorised to examine all accounts (and account holders) whose deposits exceed 30 million kyat. Its membership comprised representatives of the CBM, the Auditor General's office, the Ministry of Commerce, the Myanmar Chamber of Commerce and Industry and the Bureau of Special Investigation. The Investigation Body was asked to report within three months, but was instructed that it 'should be careful not to affect the regular functions of the banks'.[33]

From this point the end for both the AWB and Mayflower came relatively quickly. Both had essentially ceased functioning in the wake of the banking crisis, but on 9 December 2003 the banking operations of both were formally suspended. This created more pain for depositors in the banks, who were prohibited from accessing their funds except during limited, specified, intervals. Of course, neither bank was allowed to take in new deposits, advance new loans or provide remittance or other services. Finally, on 31 March 2005, the banking licences of the AWB and Mayflower were revoked. Remaining deposits were refunded, but there was a sting in the tail for borrowers who may have thought they were off the hook. In an announcement published in the *New Light of Myanmar* on 2 April the CBM ordered that:

> Persons who are liable to Myanmar May Flower Bank and Asia Wealth Bank concerning loans and overdraft, credit card and other outstanding liabilities are required to contact the respective banks and their branches and to settle their liabilities *immediately*. Failure to do so, they will be taken action [sic] under the existing laws.

The end of the AWB and Mayflower banks was not the only act in Burma's money laundering play, however. On 5 August 2005 the branches of the Myanmar Universal Bank, one of Burma's 'big five' private banks before the 2002/03 crisis, were suddenly sealed off by Burmese troops.[34] The chairman and the managing director of the Bank were arrested the same day, and various government statements hinted at money-laundering and other activities 'inconsistent with CBM laws'. Rumours linking the MUB with money-laundering had been around for some time (most talking up the Shan ancestry of the Bank's founder, Tin Sein, and his purported connections with Wei Hseuh-kang, a Chinese-born business figure who had been indicted for narcotics trafficking in the United States and Thailand),

and the move was taken to signify the desire of the Burmese government to be seen to be 'getting serious' on the money-laundering question. Other accounts placed less stress on money-laundering suspicions, and more on the close connections between the MUB and the then just-deposed Burmese Prime Minister, Khin Nyunt. In the end the MUB was not closed down in the manner of the AWB and Mayflower banks, but absorbed within the state-owned Myanma Economic Bank.

Throughout all of the above Burma had remained on FATF's 'non-cooperative' list with respect to money-laundering – appearing year after year in the organisation's annual report until, by 2005, it was the *only* country so designated. In October 2006, however, Burma too was removed from the list, FATF determining that the country had 'made good progress in implementing its anti-money laundering system'. This development was not quite a complete bill of health, with FATF cautioning that it would 'continue to monitor' Burma, and called upon its regulators to give particular attention now to 'dealers in precious metals and precious stones'.[35] Finally, and although not specifically confined to money-laundering *per se*, in the wake of the SPDC's crackdown on demonstrators in September–October 2007, the long-standing financial sanctions levied by the US were joined by similar measures imposed by countries such as Australia and Canada, and an extended and stiffened response from the EU.[36] As a financial jurisdiction Burma remains, in short, something of an international pariah.

LIMPING ON: BURMA'S FINANCIAL SYSTEM AFTER THE CRISIS

The 2002/03 banking crisis brought Burma's financial system to the point of collapse. In its wake, and as a consequence of the money-laundering problems noted above, a number of the country's most prominent financial institutions disappeared entirely. Many more were rendered moribund, a situation from which few have revived. Table 10.1 (overleaf) illustrates the big picture:

As can be seen from the data below, the damage wrought by the 2002/03 crisis was both sharp and prolonged – and even by 2006 most data categories had yet to return to pre-crisis levels. As might be expected, the 'run' of anxious depositors in Burma's private banks was reflected first and most obviously in the severe decline in demand deposits, which fell by over 70 per cent between 2002 and 2003 (April to end-March). Time and fixed deposits, given their maturity structure, fell by a more modest

Table 10.1 Private Bank Loans, Deposits and CBM Assistance, 2001–2006 (kyat millions)

Year	Demand Deposits	Time and Fixed Deposits	Claims on Private Sector	Credit from CBM
2001	206,349	450,560	416,176	15,601
2002	290,520	541,307	608,401	44,251
2003	82,948	386,298	341,547	96,692
2004	139,880	594,169	428,931	48,210
2005	209,324	697,736	570,924	7,739
2006*	243,719	818,039	590,127	4,500

* As at July. Source: IMF (2007), and author's calculations.

29 per cent. Of course, this deposit flight took place during a period in which withdrawal restrictions were supposedly in place – suggesting simultaneously perhaps both the scale of the panic and the ineffectiveness of the withdrawal controls. Recovery in both categories of deposits began in 2004, particularly for time and fixed deposits which reclaimed much of their pre-crisis momentum. As at July 2006, demand deposits remained depressed.

As noted above, perhaps the most damaging aspect of the 2002/03 banking crisis had been the cessation of lending and the recall of loans. Total loans outstanding to the private sector declined by 44 per cent across 2002 to 2003. An anaemic recovery took place in 2004, but by 2006 bank lending to the private sector in Burma – the main source of any prospective growth – had not reclaimed the levels of 2002. The final column in Table 10.1 displays the level of lending to the private banks undertaken by the CBM. The data here demonstrates the dramatic increase in CBM support in the crisis period, but it will be noted that the magnitudes involved fell well short of the amounts necessary.

Despite the overall destruction wrought by the 2002/03 financial crisis, there were winners as well as losers from the drama and its aftermath and, following the disappearance of the AWB and Mayflower banks (and subsequently the MUB), some considerable 'shuffling of the pack' took place amongst the private banks. The changes were most apparent at the top of the banking tree, with the 'big five' now replaced by a 'big four' with only Kanbawza Bank common to both sets. The other three members of the four were (in rough order of size), the Myawaddy Bank, Cooperative Bank and First Private Bank.

The Kanbawza Bank, which had been the fourth-largest private bank in Burma before the 2003 crisis, had emerged by 2006 as the largest private bank in Burma. Placed under CBM administration at the height of the financial crisis, Kanbawza was permitted to resume 'normal' operations in February 2004, and by July claimed that deposits 'had increased six-fold'.[37] In 2006 these deposits stood at K50 billion, and the Bank had 45 branches across Burma. By way of comparison, and illustrative of the weakened state of Burma's private banking sector, the largest private bank *before* the crisis, the AWB, had deposits in excess of K80 billion.

The new second-placed Myawaddy Bank was officially a private bank but, as noted in the previous chapter, as an associate enterprise of Burmese military-owned companies it could be better considered 'semi-official'. Prior to the 2003 crisis, Myawaddy Bank was not particularly prominent and appeared to function as much as a corporate treasury as a bank. The difficulties experienced by other banks since 2003, however, gave Myawaddy new-found opportunities, and it numbered amongst the banks that reported a strong recovery across a range of banking activities. According to Tun Kyi, the Bank's Deputy Managing Director, deposits increased by about 40 per cent in the quarter following the crisis, with the Bank an apparent beneficiary of the flight of depositors from 'less well-connected' banks. Tun Kyi also claimed that customers of Myawaddy had been able to offer its products and services throughout the crisis period and beyond, 'which other private banks haven't been able to do'.[38]

The third-placed Cooperative Bank was a post-crisis product of a merger (in June 2004) between the already-existing Cooperative Bank and the two smaller 'cooperative' banks, the Cooperative Farmers Bank and the Cooperative Promoters Bank. The merger gave the Cooperative Bank 13 branches in Burma, of which the original Cooperative Bank contributed eight. By 2005, the Cooperative Bank claimed to have K24 billion in deposits and paid-up capital of K1.5 billion.[39] Like Kanbawza, the Cooperative Bank asserted that deposits had enjoyed rapid growth in the immediate aftermath of the financial crisis, tripling in the period from February 2003 to end May 2004. On the liabilities side, loans had 'increased more than three-fold' from when the Cooperative Bank recommenced lending in November 2003 to mid-2004.[40]

The fourth of Burma's 'big four' private banks was the First Private Bank (FPB). The FPB's chairman, Dr Sein Maung, emerged as the most prominent spokesperson of Burma's private banks following the demise of the AWB (and that of its outspoken figurehead, Aik Htun), and the Bank as one of Burma's most profitable. In 2006 the FPB reported that it had K16 billion in deposits, 15 branches, 460 employees and profits for the year of K1.49 billion (up from K865 million in 2005).[41] During 2005 and 2006 it also undertook a capital raising which increased the Bank's paid-up capital to K5 billion (from K1 billion).[42] The capital injection was a consequence of the CBM's '1:7' capital/deposits ratio (more on which below), of which Sein Maung had been critical. In an interview in October 2005, he even claimed that the FPB had returned deposits because of the need to meet the new ratio – the primary reason for the fall in bank deposits from their high in 2004 of K27 billion.[43] The FPB reported that its lending book had expanded by nearly 60 per cent in 2005, with new loans being divided between the 'service sector' (41 per cent), manufacturing (27 per cent), with the remainder to unspecified 'trading' enterprises.[44]

Beyond the new 'big four', mystery and ambiguity surrounded the operations of most of the other private banks. Nowhere was this more the case than for Yoma Bank, Burma's second-largest private bank before the 2002/03 financial crisis. Yoma Bank survived these events but, as we have seen, it was forced to both seek assistance from the CBM and 'liquidate' certain fixed and other assets. The CBM was unhappy with a number of practices (never publicly specified) of Yoma Bank prior to the crisis, and alleged that it had acted in ways inconsistent with the FIML. Though Yoma did not have the political 'connections' of banks such as Kanbawza, in contrast to the (even more entrepreneurial) Asia Wealth Bank, it continued to receive approval to conduct banking functions on a 'limited basis' after the crisis. These functions did not include, however, taking in new deposits, granting new loans, or continuing its credit card facility. At the Annual General Meeting of First Myanmar Investment (FMI) in September 2004, the ultimate parent company of Yoma Bank, FMI's Chairman, Serge Pun, announced selected financial results for Yoma Bank for the year ended 31 March.[45] According to the announced results, Yoma made profits of K231 million for the year, down from the K1.3 billion of the previous year but an astonishing (and scarcely believable) performance in the circumstances. Making the earnings result all the more remarkable was that the other figures released attested to the damage the 2003 crisis had wrought on Yoma. Deposits declined by 80 per cent from K135 billion in January 2003 to K27.6 billion as at end March 2004. Loans likewise suffered a 72 per cent fall to K31.1 billion (from K110 billion in February 2003). The *Myanmar Times* quoted Serge Pun as being 'cautiously optimistic' about Yoma Bank's future whilst acknowledging that it 'will continue to face acute challenges with the restrictions on income flows'.[46] At the equivalent meeting in 2006 similar cautious optimism was expressed – but the bank remained largely moribund nonetheless.[47]

Reports of a general revival of Burma's banks became relatively commonplace in the Burmese press after 2003, but elsewhere there were signs that cast doubt on the recovery narrative. Illustrative in this context were the reports of what was occurring in Burma's (especially Rangoon's) property market. A market normally dependent on credit, Burma's property market was in dire straights following the banking crisis. Of course, the property sector's decline was not wholly attributable to credit difficulties (the Rangoon market was almost certainly the subject of a price 'bubble'), but there can be little doubt that these were central. In the years since 2003, credit to the property market in Rangoon and elsewhere almost completely dried up – prompting complaints from property developers that they had 'to finance projects 100 per cent'. As a consequence of this, what residential construction did take place was piecemeal – each section needing to 'be completed and sold before there were funds to finance construction of a subsequent section'.[48] Most eloquent of all, however, was this complaint from a property developer from Hlaing Tharyar township, of the *practical* difficulties of business without bank credit: 'Buyers have to pay in cash, so they have to carry the money in bags, which is not very convenient (...)'.[49]

THE CBM CONTINUES ITS MONEY-PRINTING WAYS

In the wake of the 2002/03 financial crisis a number of changes were made to the regulations the CBM imposed upon the banks. By far the most important of these was a new 'gearing' requirement (noted briefly above, and captured under the broad provisions of Article 57 of the *Central Bank of Myanmar Law*), that specified that banks had to hold paid-up capital to deposits in a ratio of no less than '1:7'. This requirement was similar to the 'gearing' or 'leverage' ratios applied to banks internationally prior to the Basel capital Accords (though such ratios were invariably expressed in terms of *assets* rather than deposits). As such, and on their own, such gearing requirements had been neither unusual nor inappropriate. In the case of Burma, however, with the Basel capital accords already (formally) in place, the new measure was potentially highly restrictive. Precision in this assessment is not possible, since (depending on the nature of a particular bank and its balance sheet) the new ratio could make certain other regulations redundant (the deposit and profits reserve requirements notably) – or, in turn, it could be made redundant by *them*. Alternatively, however, it could 'piggy back' upon the other regulations and thereby create a most restrictive set of capital requirements for Burma's banks indeed. The latter view was held by Myat Thein (2004: 12), who suggested that the measure may well help prevent 'bank runs', but only at the cost of making 'legal [sic] banking unprofitable, and hence, unsustainable'. Myat Thein's conclusion came from his assessment that, since Burma's banks lent only about 70 per cent of their deposits (the remaining 30 per cent being sanctioned off into required liquid assets and reserves), the CBM's 1:7 capital/deposits ratio was equivalent to an capital/assets gearing ratio of around 1:5, or 20 per cent. Such gearing ratios globally and historically have usually been significantly below 10 per cent (in Chapter 9 we noted the 'consensus' capital/assets ratio of 1/18, or around 5.5 per cent). The overall effect then was one that potentially greatly restricted the lending abilities of Burma's banks. Unfortunately the available data on Burma's banks disallows a definitive answer to the question but, anecdotally, there was much in favour of Myat Thein's assessment. We have, for instance, already seen that one of Burma's most successful banks, First Private Bank, had complained that the 1:7 capital/deposits requirement had forced it into a position of having to ration loans, and even 'hand back' some deposits.[50] In August 2006, and in the wake of what seemed to have been active lobbying of the CBM by the private banks, the new gearing ratio was relaxed to one of 1:10. Immediate problems were thus perhaps resolved, but the issue remained problematic for the future.[51]

Meanwhile on the 'macroeconomic' side of its responsibilities, the CBM continued to function after the financial crisis more or less as it had before it – as a financing arm of the state. As Table 10.2 opposite reveals, the CBM's lending to the government, and the concomitant swelling of currency circulating outside the banks, overwhelmed the funds made available by Burma's financial system to the private sector. The principal problem of macroeconomic policy-making in Burma, in short, sailed on.

With respect to its management of Burma's exchange rate system, likewise the CBM continued to function more or less as before. Burma's currency remained officially fixed at a rate of about K6:$US1, from which the 'market rate' diverged ever more. In late 2007 Burma's market exchange rate stood at around K1,300:$US1. Meanwhile, hopes that the CBM might be granted a degree of at least 'formal' independence under Burma's 'new'

Table 10.2 CBM Lending to Government, 2001–2006 (kyat millions)

Year	Central Bank Lending to Government	Currency Outside the Banks	Bank Claims on Private Sector
2001	675,040	494,521	416,176
2002	892,581	718,633	608,401
2003	1,262,588	1,102,937	341,547
2004	1,686,341	1,347,598	428,931
2005	2,165,154	1,743,654	570,924
2006*	2,509,735	2,000,843	590,127

* As at July. Source: IMF (2007).

constitution being drafted (from late 2007) by a hand-picked committee of the SPDC have, perhaps not surprisingly, proved fruitless.[52]

One change to the CBM that did take place, in June 2006, was in its *physical* location. In November 2005 Burma's government mysteriously founded the new capital city of Napyidaw, near Pyinmana (roughly in the centre of Burma). Most government ministries relocated almost immediately, but for a while it seemed that the CBM would remain in Rangoon (which remained very much the centre of Burma's commercial and financial activity). On 3 June 2006, however, the CBM and its 200 or so staff were likewise uprooted to Napyidaw.

NOTES

1   Most of the investors in the schemes interviewed by the author were in no doubt that they were ponzi (or 'pyramid') arrangements. This is not to say, however, that they appreciated the dangers therein.

2   For more on Burma's 'private services companies', and the types of schemes that they offered, see 'Bank Crisis Reeks of a Ponzi Scheme', Kyi May Kaung, *The Irrawaddy*, 26 February 2003, online edition, <www.irrawaddy.org>.

3   For the FATF report thus naming Burma *before* the financial crisis, see 'Review to Identify Non-Cooperative Countries or Territories: Increasing the World-Wide Effectiveness of Anti-Money Laundering Measures', 21 June 2002, <http://www.fatf-gafi.org/>.

4   The relevant 'International Narcotics Control Strategy Report' was released in March 2003 and is available at the website of the US State Department, <www.state.gov>.

5   United States Department of the Treasury, Financial Crimes Enforcement Network, FinCEN Advisory, 'Transactions Involving Burma (Burma)', April 2002, <www.ustreas.gov>.

6   Ko Cho, 'Junta introduces money laundering law'.

7   The Chairman's statement was published in the same day's edition of Burma's principal state-controlled newspaper, *The New Light of Myanmar*. As the crisis wore on, Burma's press ceased to report on the crisis.

8   William Barnes, 'A run on Myanmar banks affects crony capitalists', *South China Morning Post*, 28 February 2003. See also Naw Seng, 'On shaky ground', 17 April 2003, *The Irrawaddy*, online edition, *op. cit.*

9   In some of the banks this included the issue of 'tokens' that had to be redeemed upon the withdrawal of deposits. Other banks also discriminated amongst their customers – allowing, for example, those with larger deposits to withdraw larger amounts.

10   Notwithstanding these limits, an appreciation of the extent of deposit depletion can be gleaned from reports which estimated that the AWB lost almost a third of its deposits in the first two weeks of the panic (Turnell 2003).

11   Burma's 'Foreign Exchange Certificates' (FECs) likewise appreciated during the crisis.

12   Agence France-Presse (AFP) reported on 17 February that the AWB and Yoma Banks had instructed their customers not to use or honour *their own* credit cards. A similar instruction quickly followed from the Kanbawza Bank. See Turnell (2003).

13   For more on the problems Burma's banks face in communicating with each other, see Turnell (2002).

14   For a sample, see Kyaw Zaw Moe, 'Crisis Forces Businesses to Close, Crime to Rise', *The Irrawaddy*, 17 March 2003, online edition, *op.cit.*

15   Tony Broadmoor, 'Burma's Busted Banks', *The Irrawaddy*, 8 April 2003, online edition, *op. cit.*

16   Kin Nyunt's comments were quoted by the BBC on 16 February 2003, and are here cited from Zaw Oo (2003).

17   Reports of the Minister's comments can be found in the *Business Times*, 24 February 2003, online edition <www.business-times.asiaone.com>. He did not elaborate further as to what these breaches entailed.

18   For more on the issuing of the order, see Shawn Crispin and Bertil Lintner, 'As confidence in the banks collapses', *Far Eastern Economic Review*, 17 April 2003, p. 19. Some reports suggest that the CBM *ordered* banks to recall between 20 and 50 per cent of their loans. This could not subsequently be confirmed, but who made the order is less important than the fact that it was made with (at the very least) the CBM's blessing.

19   SPDC Secretary-1, Khin Nyunt, urged businesses at the annual meeting of the Burma Federation of Chambers of Commerce and Industry to 'repay their debts quickly'. These and other urgings fell 'on deaf ears' and, notwithstanding reported threats by some of the banks, there was little evidence that much in the way of repayments were forthcoming. In April, CBM officials allegedly threatened to 'take action' against borrowers who did not repay 'at least 20 per cent of their loans'. This threat seems not to have intimidated borrowers, however – one of whom was cited as saying that the authorities could hardly 'arrest anyone because nobody has broken any bank *regulations*' (emphasis added). Naw Seng, 'Bank Crisis Rolls On', *The Irrawaddy*, 7 May 2003, online edition, *op. cit.*

20   Michael Backman, 'Burma's Banking Meltdown Goes Unnoticed Beyond its Borders', *The Age*, 20 March 2003, online edition, <www.age.com.au>.

21   Naw Seng, 'Yoma Selling Capital Assets', *The Irrawaddy*, 14 May 2003, online edition, *op. cit.*

22   For an overview of the debate regarding appropriate policy in a bank run, and the consensus emerging from it, see Latter (1997) and Goodhart (2002).

23   Such an outcome is even possible in practice, as was the case in Sweden during that country's banking crisis in 1991. See Frydl and Quintyn (2000: 56).

24   Of course such guarantees must be credible. In all four of these countries scepticism was only allayed once the guarantees had been established firmly within the law, and once they had been 'tested' in the difficult circumstances that persisted into 1998. Such credibility would have been more difficult to establish in Burma in 2003 but, given the *revealed* costs of the alternative, it should have been tried.

25   FATF's declaration on Burma, from which the following is heavily drawn, can be found at: <www.fat-gafi.org>.

26   'Providing Appropriate Tools Required to Intercept and Obstruct Terrorism' (PATRIOT) Act, 2003.

27   The following draws on the official enunciation of these measures, as set out in the *Federal Register*, vol. 68, no. 227, Tuesday, 25 November, 2003: 66305–66311.

28   *Ibid.*

29   *Ibid.*

30   *Ibid.*

31   Details of the Law, as well as Rules supposedly designed to enforce and implement it, can be found at the online research pages of *The Irrawaddy*: <http://www.irrawaddy.org/res/money.html>

32   For more, see the website of the 'Democratic Voice of Burma' at <www.dvb.no>.

33   Details of the 'Investigative Body' were published on the website of *The Irrawaddy* on 5 December 2003, *op .cit.*

34   The actions against the MUB were widely reported around the world, representative of which were: Amy Kazmin, 'Burma's junta seizes privately owned bank', *Financial Times*, 8 August 2005; 'Myanmar Universal Bank taken over', *The Irrawaddy*, 9 August 2005, online edition; 'Myanmar Universal Bank scam latest', *Democratic Voice of Burma*, 9 August 2005, <www.english.dvb.no>.

35   Burma's removal from FATF's non-cooperative list was announced at the Plenary meeting of the organisation, held in Vancouver, Canada, from 9–13 October 2006. Brief details of the decision can be found at FATF's website, <www.fatf-gafi.org>.

36   Canada's Minister for Foreign Affairs declared on 14 November 2007 that his country aimed at imposing 'the toughest sanctions in the world' on Burma, including a ban on all financial transactions. Australia produced a list of 418 individuals and businesses it identified as being members of the SPDC or connected to it, blocking their access to the Australian financial system and freezing any assets they might hold in Australia. Brodie Fenlon and Tavia Grant, 'Canada imposes new sanctions on Myanmar', *Globe and Mail*, 14 November 2007; Reserve Bank of Australia, *Banking*

(Foreign Exchange) Regulations, Sanctions Against Burma, media release, 24 October 2007, <www.rba.gov.au>.

37   May Thandar Win, 'Billions of kyat flow back to banks', *The Myanmar Times,* 19–25 July 2004, vol. 12, no. 225.

38   Moe Zaw Myint, 'Banking sector shows signs of recovery after troubled year', *The Myanmar Times,* 22–28 December 2003, Vol. 10, No. 197.

39   Moe Zaw Myint, 'Banking sector shows signs of recovery after troubled year'.

40   May Thander Win, 'Billions of kyat flow back to banks'.

41   Ye Lwin, 'FPB profits rise as loans pay off', *The Myanmar Times,* 20–26 November 2005, vol. 18, no. 343.

42   May Thander Win, 'FPB report provides new hope for banking sector', *The Myanmar Times,* 31 October–5 November 2005, vol. 15, no. 290.

43   *Ibid.*

44   'The nation's top 20 banks'

45   May Thandar Win, 'FMI posts robust financial results', *The Myanmar Times,* 20–26 September 2004, vol. 12, no. 234.

46   *Ibid.*

47   Zaw Htet, 'FMI profits beat the business blues', *The Myanmar Times,* 13–19 November 2006, vol. 18, no. 342.

48   May Thander Win, 'Economy tipped for brighter year ahead', *The Myanmar Times,* 16–22 January 2006, vol. 15, no. 300.

49   The property developer in question was Soe Myint, who was also a Director of Serge Pun and Associates (Myanmar) Ltd, a company associated with the Yoma Bank. The interview with Soe Myint appeared in Maw Maw San, 'Long awaited river-front project begins despite material prices rise', *The Myanmar Times,* 12–18 July 2004, vol. 12, no. 224.

50   May Thandar Win, 'FPB report provides new hope for banking sector'.

51   May Thandar Win, 'Banks claim a solid recovery', *The Myanmar Times,* 31 July–6 August 2006, vol. 17, no. 327. The strongest lobbyists seem to have been Dr Sein Maung of First Private Bank, and Thein Tun of Tun Foundation Bank.

52   Wai Moe, 'Junta presses on with "exclusive" constitution drafting', *The Irrawaddy,* 19 October 2007, online edition, *op. cit.*

CHAPTER 11

$\mathcal{M}icrofinance$ in $\mathcal{B}urma$

It is arguable that improvements in the availability and transparency of rural finance would do more than any other single measure to help the rural poor.

UNDP Assistance Mission to Burma,
December 2005

In recent years much excitement has accompanied the emergence of microfinance as a device for poverty alleviation and economic development. This excitement reached its apogee in 2006 when the world's most prominent microfinance institution, Grameen Bank, and its charismatic founder, Muhammad Yunus, were jointly awarded the Nobel Peace Prize. This award, coming fresh after the UN-designated 'year of microfinance' in 2005, was just the latest in a veritable cavalcade of honours bestowed upon what is now a distinctive microfinance 'movement'. Of course, if the advocates of microfinance are right, the excitement and the acclaim are richly warranted. According to these advocates, microfinance creates the means for greater employment and income-generation, allows the poor to smooth consumption and meet social, religious and other obligations, offers financial protection from crises and disasters, encourages schooling and empowers the marginalised – especially women. Inspired by the example of Grameen and other prominent microfinance entrepreneurs, microfinance *institutions* (MFIs) of all types and sizes have appeared all over the world. A myriad of models and methodologies have been employed by these MFIs, but certain key principles stand out. These include a presumption that access to credit is more important to the poor than the price of that credit, the widespread use of group and progressive lending as a substitute for collateral, the maintenance of low administration costs through simplified procedures, the mobilisation of savings through deposit products, and the use of intensive motivational techniques (McGuire and Conroy 2000: 2–3). International donors spend around $US1 billion per year on microfinance, and by 2005 almost 100 million people had access to microfinance in over 70 countries (ADB 2005: 17).

As will be apparent from the narrative outlined thus far in this book, one country greatly in need of the benefits promised by microfinance is Burma. State-supplied rural credit is both inadequate and difficult to come by, and Burma's private banks are greatly impaired institutions that face all manner of restrictions, both as a consequence of the country's poor institutional and macroeconomic environments, and those more explicitly manufactured by the state. Yet, as the quote from the UNDP at the top of this chapter attests, the provision of adequate and appropriate credit could do more than any other single initiative to alleviate the circumstances of Burma's (majority) rural poor.

Against this obvious need, various nascent microfinance schemes *have* emerged in Burma in recent years. Some of these are quite large, even by global standards, but their operations are scarcely known outside the country and the handful of workers directly involved with them. Our purpose in this final chapter, accordingly, is to attempt to shine a light on microfinance in Burma. Are such institutions Burma's last, best, hope? The chapter begins by investigating the three large microfinance schemes in Burma that operate under the auspices of the United Nations Development Programme (UNDP). This is followed by an analysis of some lesser schemes, most of which have been established by Western non-governmental organisations (NGOs). The chapter then takes up the significant challenges to microfinance in Burma, and the barriers to and opportunities for it in forming the basis of a sustainable financial system. Finally, we briefly speculate on the prospects for microfinance in Burma, and offer some concluding thoughts on financial development.

THE MAJOR UNDP MICROFINANCE SCHEMES

The most important microfinance schemes in Burma are those operating under the auspices of the UNDP, and in collaboration with the United Nations Office for Project Services (UNOPS). These schemes, which commenced operations in 1997, are organised under the UNDP's 'Human Development Initiative' (HDI) in Burma. The HDI was established in 1993 to implement basic development programs at the 'grass roots' level, and to avoid working through government authorities in Burma to the extent possible (UNDP 2001: 2).[1] The HDI has been initiated in four phases thus far, HDI-I (1994–1996), HDI-II (1996–1999), HDI-III (1999–2002) and HDI-IV (2003–2005). Delays in getting the Burmese government's approval caused a six-month hiatus in the operations of the HDI across 2002–2003, which delayed the start of HDI-IV and set its original completion date back to 2005.[2] In January 2006, following prolonged negotiations between UNDP and the Burmese government, HDI-IV was further extended to December 2007.

The UNDP's primary microfinance operations in Burma are limited to three distinct geographic regions – in the (Irrawaddy) Delta, the 'Dry Zone' ('upper Burma') and Shan State. Collectively 11 Townships and 2,400 villages are included in this 'footprint', in theory reaching around five per cent of Burma's population. The extension of the UNDP's microfinance operations to another 11 townships (in the Delta and Dry Zone regions) is currently under way. The selection of villages was initially undertaken by UNDP teams in Burma who mapped out the fields of operations for the HDI more broadly. Their criteria for including a village *in the HDI* took into account various socio-economic indicators including income estimates, measures of health, food and water security, education, remoteness and the ability of people to access formal credit of some kind. However, recognising that farmers, artisans and traders (poor, but not the poorest of the poor) were the most effective beneficiaries of microfinance, the UNDP's formal microfinance schemes were established in only 1,700 of the 2,400 villages of the HDI as a whole. Less formal schemes, which are labelled by the UNDP as 'self-reliance groups' were established in the remaining villages, and in parallel to the MFIs in others. It is, however, to what we might call the 'big three' MFIs of the UNDP that we focus our attention. By far the most important of the MFIs in Burma, they were designed for 'national replicability' and as pillars upon which a new rural finance system might be built (UNDP 2003: 6).[3]

The UNDP oversees the three MFIs it sponsors in Burma but, importantly, their creation and on-going management were originally 'subcontracted' to three international NGOs with a track record of operating microfinance schemes. Though there were marginal differences between the three MFIs, each was founded on a common methodology that was based upon that established by the Grameen Bank, and replicated in many countries since. In March 2006 the three UNDP MFIs came under the control of a single implementing agency, but each will continue to operate independently. It is to the details of each of these three MFIs that we now turn.

DELTA REGION MICROFINANCE ORGANISATION: FOUNDED BY GRAMEEN TRUST

Due to its proximity to Rangoon, and the fame of its founding agency, the most prominent of the three UNDP MFIs in Burma is the 'Delta Region Microfinance Organisation' (DRMO) which, up until 2002, was managed by the Grameen Trust. The DRMO is a Grameen Bank replication project which, for the first six years of its operations, was directly operated by Grameen Trust according to its 'Build, Operate and Transfer' (BOT) model, under which Grameen initially implements the project, trains and 'empowers' local staff and ultimately hands over the project to local operators. The BOT model is used by Grameen in circumstances where there are no viable local microfinance partners, but with the expectation that local capacities can be built up in two to four years. As it turned out, it took six years for Grameen to 'transfer' the DRMO, and even then not to a local partner, but (as detailed below) to another foreign NGO.

The DRMO was initially established in three townships, Bogolay, Mawlamyinegyun and Labuta, which are currently being joined by four more in the north of the Delta. The area is traditionally the location of Burma's famed 'rice bowl', but is now both economically and ecologically degraded. Over 70 per cent of the population in the Delta are engaged in agriculture (still primarily rice cultivation), fishing and forestry. Over half of these are landless, and have limited access to employment and income-generating opportunities beyond subsistence. Access to health and education services are greatly restricted, and the region's susceptibility to flooding, cyclones and other natural disasters means that food security is persistently precarious (UNOPS 2005: 9).

The DRMO was founded by six staff of the Grameen Bank, together with local field staff that finally numbered 116. Around 70 per cent of all the local staff were women. Provided with an initial budget of close to $US1 million by the UNDP, by 2001 the DRMO had almost 18,000 (*exclusively* female) borrowers and had disbursed nearly $US1.7 million/K1.6 billion in loans.[4] A repayment rate of 100 per cent was claimed, but the Grameen Trust reported some problems with high 'drop out' rates of both borrowers and staff. Most of the former left the scheme because the poverty of the

Delta forced them to relocate. The staff losses resulted from a mix of causes: the usual attrition that came from better opportunities elsewhere, as well as those staff who found themselves unable to cope with the demanding Grameen system, and the challenges of the Delta's physical environment. The Grameen Trust reported that some staff regarded their journeys by boat to isolated borrowers as 'highly risky', particularly during the monsoon season (Grameen Trust 2000).

Microfinance is founded upon certain methodologies that have allowed it to 'boldly go' where more conventional financial institutions have feared to tread. Such methodologies, as adopted by the DRMO (and, in essentials, by both of the other two UNDP MFIs), have allowed MFIs to transcend the limitations presented to them by the type of environment in which they usually operate. These methodologies include:

Group and Progressive Lending

The DRMO employs what Armendáriz de Aghion and Morduch (2005) call the 'non-traditional contracts' employed by Grameen (and other MFIs) to meet the special risk and information problems faced by lending to the poor. By far the most celebrated of these – and the vehicle most associated with Grameen itself – is the concept of 'peer' or 'group lending'.[5] Familiar to us in these pages via its use in Burma's cooperative credit system and later the SAB, in recent times group lending has emerged as a dominant device within the broad microfinance movement to replace collateral as the basis for secure lending.[6] Almost by definition, the poor do not have much in the way of collateral to pledge as security against their loans, and this fact is often touted as an explanation for the very high interest rates they have historically been charged by moneylenders and the like. How then to provide some sort of security against default by poor borrowers, and thereby allow lower interest rates? Group lending – which in essence involves some sort of mutual guarantee by each member of a group on the loans given to each other – is one possible answer. In place of 'physical' collateral, group lending provides 'social collateral' and a system of incentives for borrowers to monitor and supervise each other, and ultimately to enforce repayment. These incentives are not just in the form of a mutual guarantee, but also usually in devices such as 'progressive' lending, under which the ability of members of the group to access credit is predicated on the repayment performance of others in the group. Social collateral can be a powerful device, placing upon borrowers themselves tasks (monitoring and enforcing) that normally are borne by the lender. As Besley and Coate (1995: 2) point out, group lending can impose rather more exacting penalties on wayward borrowers than those available to a traditional bank, and adding 'the wrath of other group members' to the armoury of potential remedies.

Group and progressive lending is foundational to the Grameen system as employed by the DRMO in Burma. Under the traditional Grameen Bank model, borrowers are arranged into lending groups of five members each which in turn are 'federated' into 'centres' (ADB 2005: 24).[7] Groups are self-selecting, but DRMO staff will organise groups that do not spontaneously form. In addition, progressive lending according to so-called '2:2:1' staggering is applied. According to this, initially only two members of a group are eligible to borrow (from funds dispersed from the DRMO via a Centre). If, after six weeks in which these two borrowers meet their principal and interest payments, another two members of the group become eligible to borrow.

In addition to its 'collateral substituting' role, it is often claimed that group lending brings other benefits, both in improving the outreach of financial services, and in allowing for social development more broadly. Regarding the first, it is sometimes stressed that group lending is a device for simply reaching more people (Berenbach and Guzman 1994: 121). Even if not borrowers initially, for instance, members of a group are brought into the 'orbit' of financial services and practices, and could be thought of perhaps as being 'groomed' to participate eventually. Regarding social development, the idea of 'mutual trust' – clearly central to the group lending experience – is said to promote trust and other social virtues generally. Reciprocal relations between group members 'helps free borrowers from historically dependent relationships', whilst the group itself 'often becomes the building block to a broader social network' (Berenbach and Guzman 1994: 121). Today such arguments are familiar to us in the form of the emphasis upon 'social capital' as a necessary component for economic development, but is also an argument heard in Burma before – not least in the social virtues promised by the boosters of the cooperative credit system of the colonial era (as seen in Chapter 3). As with that experience, much *can* go wrong with methodologies such as group lending that are so dependent on trust, especially when the life and experiences of group members leaves little room for such trust in collective decision-making.

Interest Rates, Loan Types and Savings

The interest rates charged on loans from the DRMO average 38 per cent on an effective per annum basis, whilst 15 per cent per annum is paid on deposits (UNDP 2005: 20). Of course, neither of these rates matches Burma's inflation rate which, for the purposes of its own calculations, is assumed by the UNDP to be 40 per cent.[8] Notwithstanding that, in real terms the DRMO's interest rates are unsustainably low (more of which later), while in nominal terms they are, like the rates levied by most MFIs around the world, rather high. The cause of some angst to populist politicians and well-intentioned NGOs, the interest rates charged by MFIs are usually far in excess of those traditionally charged by formal financial institutions (but not moneylenders) in developing countries. This is certainly the case in Burma where, as we have seen, the CBM currently caps allowable interest rates on bank loans at a maximum of 18 per cent per annum (IMF 2006).

The DRMO offers four types of loan products:

(1) *General loans* are available for any approved purpose and are granted to a value of between K25,000 and K75,000. These are repaid in 50 weekly instalments of both principal and interest.

(2) *Special loans* are available only to borrowers who have already completed one successful loan cycle. They are repaid over 50 weeks, but instalments may vary according to the borrowers needs. Special loans are made for a minimum of K20,000 and a maximum of K60,000.

(3) *Micro-enterprise loans* are granted only to borrowers who have successfully completed at least two successful loan cycles. The term of these loans is up to 100 weeks, and to a maximum value of K300,000.

(4) *Health care loans* are a relatively new product offered by the DRMO. Granted up to a value of K30,000, they are meant to be repaid across 50 weekly instalments (FAO 2004b: 23).

A (somewhat controversial) requirement imposed on borrowers from Grameen replication MFIs is that of compulsory saving. The DRMO is no exception in this regard, and requires that its members save K100 per week. A member can withdraw up to half of their savings at any time and for any reason, and up to 90 per cent in an emergency. All savings withdrawals, however, have to be 'repaid' within 25 weeks. The DRMO also allows members to deposit voluntary savings (Grameen Trust 2000, FAO 2004b: 23)

Lending to Women

The DRMO lends only to landless women. Of course, a disposition to lending to women, largely if not exclusively, is a feature of many MFIs around the world. One reason for this is that lending to women delivers greater 'impact' in poverty alleviation. In contrast to men, women seem to share the benefits that derive from their participation in microfinance with their family and community (Robinson 2001). Another reason for the focus upon women amongst MFIs, however, is more narrowly focused upon institutional sustainability. Lending to women is simply good business practice for most MFIs.

The reason for this is that women borrowers are generally a better risk. It is often argued that certain 'culturally patterned behaviours' (existing in most societies) elevate the sensitivity of women to the 'shaming' that may follow from the failure to repay a loan. Intensified by the pressures of the lending-group (should this methodology also be in operation), women are much more likely to avoid loan default than men, for whom social opprobrium is perhaps more easily 'shaken off' (Rahman 1998). Less obviously, Morduch (1999: 1583) links the idea that women may be a better credit risk than men to the idea of mobility. In many parts of the world women are less physically mobile than men, and thus they have fewer alternative sources of finance, and fewer opportunities of avoiding their creditors and commitments.

Success Anecdotes

A habit applied by MFIs all over the world is to include in their promotional material inspiring 'success stories' of engagement with microfinance. They typically adopt a familiar template: a narrative that tells of an initial loan providing the breakthrough needed to establish a small enterprise, which then sets the scene for a further (expansion) loan, which begets more business success, and then usually an array of social and quality of life improvements. In this the DRMO is no exception, of which the following chronicle of 'Daw Khin Pyone' is representative:

> Having heard about the [DRMO] project and its activities, Daw Khin Pyone, who was struggling for survival with two children and her husband, decided to join a Grameen Group. She is 51. They had three acres of cultivatable land which was not enough to make ends meet. The situation became extremely difficult for them as Khin Pyone's husband became seriously ill. She did not know how to meet the medical expenses of medical treatment for her husband and manage two square meals for the family. They sold

the cultivable land and the family was in deep financial distress. In such a desperate situation, she became a member of Grameen Bogolay Township Branch. Daw Khin Pyone got her 1st loan of K6,000 in November, 1997 and bought 16 ducks. After repaying the first loan in 50 instalments with interest, she received K10,000 as a second cycle loan in November 1998. She bought a pig and pig food with this loan. The pig delivered six piglets. This gave her a boost. She was able to pay back her loan to the project by selling 4 piglets after a few months. Her asset base expanded with 16 ducks, one pig and two piglets. She applied for the third loan and received K20,000 with which she bought 160 ducks and scaled up the farm. Her micro loans not only enabled her to meet basic needs of her family, but also enabled her to go for implementation of the 15 decisions of the project members to improve the quality of their life (...) Like all the others who have joined Grameen in the Delta Zone, she now hopes to cross the poverty line very soon (Grameen Trust 2000).

Sharp-eyed readers will note that there is no mention of Daw Khin Pyone being able to buy her land back. The DRMO does not lend quite enough for this, and nor can it address the problematic nexus of credit and land in Burma.

Hand-over to EDA

In May 2003, management of the DRMO passed to EDA Rural Systems of India.[9] Established in 1983 and based in Gurgaon, India, EDA's principal activity was to manage microfinance programs, conduct microfinance personnel training and, via a subsidiary, Micro-Credit Ratings International Limited (M-CRIL), to provide credit 'ratings' for other MFIs (ADB 2005: 27). In comparison to the Grameen organisation, EDA is a very small outfit, and when it took control of the DRMO it replaced all expatriate with local staff (FAO 2004b: 25). Its subsequent management of the DRMO was not a complete success, with various cost-cutting measures undermining staff morale and inhibiting the scheme's outreach. As shall be examined in more detail below, in 2006 management of the DRMO passed to the US NGO 'PACT' which, on 28 January of that year, became the single 'implementing agency' for all three UNDP schemes.

Table 11.1 (overleaf) provides a snapshot of the DRMO as at March 2005:

Table 11.1 Selected Indicators (DRMO)

No. of Clients	57,025
No. of Active Clients	41,058
Loans Outstanding	K1,660m
Total Value of Loans Dispersed	K7,290m
No. of Loans Dispersed	208,768
No. of Credit and Savings Groups	9,514
Ave. Loan Size	K26,200
Total Savings Deposits	K700m
Repayment Rates	98–100%
Proportion Women	100%
Interest Rate (nominal)	38% p.a.

Source: UNOPS (2005: 10)

DRY ZONE MICROFINANCE ORGANISATION: OPERATED BY PACT MYANMAR

The largest and perhaps most impressive of the UNDP microfinance schemes currently operating in Burma is the 'Dry Zone Microfinance Organisation' (DZMO) which is managed by 'PACT Myanmar'.[10] Based in the United States, 'PACT' (originally 'Private Agencies Collaborating Together') was founded in 1971 as an umbrella group to assist member NGOs to access US Government aid funding. In 1992, however, PACT itself became an NGO with a vocation of poverty alleviation around the world through 'local capacity building'. PACT first entered Burma in 1997 after it was selected to manage the DZMO.

The DZMO is currently located in 624 villages centred on three townships (Chaung-U, Kyaukpadaung and Magway), but from 2005 an additional seven more townships will gradually join the scheme. The Dry Zone is one of the poorest but most densely populated regions of Burma. Water is scarce, agricultural productivity is low and much of the natural environment is severely degraded. Most of the population of the area is landless, and depends upon seasonal farm labour to survive. Beyond this, employment and income opportunities are limited. According to UNOPS (2005: 8), average incomes are not sufficient to cover basic needs for food, clothing and shelter. Access to education and health services are likewise greatly restricted. The DZMO charges an (effective) interest rate of approximately 43 per cent per annum on its loans, and claims a repayment rate of 99.6 per cent. Women comprise 98.5 per cent of borrowers, and the DZMO specifies that potential borrowers must meet one or more of the following criteria: (1) They must be a female-headed household. (2) They must be landless. (3) They must be subsistence farmers.

The DZMO organises its borrowers and savers into the familiar five-member credit and savings groups popularised by Grameen. According to PACT, creating the groups is usually a three-day process in Burma. On the first day of their arrival, local PACT employees go into a village and call a meeting at which the principles and benefits of microfinance are introduced. On day two, a number of pilot groups are formed, savings are collected and the first loans dispersed according to the 2:2:1 staggering. With this demonstration fresh in the minds of the village, on day three all of the remaining eligible and suitable MFI members are formed into their credit and savings groups. Most of these will be self-selecting, but when five-member groups do not spontaneously form, local PACT staff will act as 'facilitators'. Though group-lending is the methodology employed by the DZMO to ensure loan repayment and other requisite disciplines, PACT reports that cultural factors are just as important in achieving the DZMO's 99 per cent 'on time' repayment rate. Central to such factors is the notion of saving 'face' by ensuring repayment, not just individually or even in terms of a household, but for an entire village. According to PACT, the only time in any village that such high repayment rates were threatened occurred in 2004, when a rumour swept multiple villages that PACT had decided to convert loans into 'grants'. The rumour was quickly quashed.[11]

Once the credit and savings groups have been formed, PACT creates 'Village Credit Organisations' ('ViCOs') to serve as apex organisations to dispense the loan funds, collect the savings and monitor and supervise the groups generally. The ViCOs are managed by a village executive committee which is elected from the savings and credit groups. By centralising the savings of the village with the ViCO, credit and savings groups that are net borrowers can access a pool of funds beyond that which they could raise on their own, whilst groups that are net savers have a ready mechanism through which their savings can be placed to earn a return. To each ViCO is devolved decision-making regarding loan approvals, but decisions on interest rates and the like remain with the DZMO head-office. No PACT or UNDP staff serve on ViCOs, and there are meant to be no links to other NGOs, or Burmese government authorities of any kind. ViCOs meet weekly to make loans and collect payments of principal and interest. PACT claims, with some justification, that these weekly meetings are often the only public meetings permitted in the villages in which it operates.[12]

The DZMO offers similar 'general', 'special' and 'micro-enterprise' loans to those of the DRMO, and on similar terms. In contrast to the DRMO, however, it also offers 'agriculture loans' up to K5,000 per acre, and to a maximum of K25,000. These loans are repayable in more farmer-friendly instalments of ten bi-weekly repayments of interest, and with the principal repayable only at the end of the twenty-week term (FAO 2004b: 26).

Consistent with the Grameen philosophy, the DZMO collects compulsory savings from members, but at differential rates according to whether a member was in receipt of their first loan (in which case they had to save K40 per week), second loan (K80 per week) or third and subsequent loans (K120 per week). The DZMO pays a relatively high 25 per cent on savings balances. Cognisant of Burma's high inflation rates, the DZMO actively discourages voluntary saving, urging members instead 'to save in kind' (FAO 2004b: 26). A more telling indictment of the macroeconomic context in which 'financial institutions' must operate in Burma would be difficult to imagine.

PACT had initial high hopes that it would be able to convert the DZMO from a dependent 'project' into Burma's first formal and legalised MFI. To this end, in July 2001 a 'management board' was created to which ultimately all decision-making with regard to the DZMO would devolve. The board was supposed to function for one year as an 'advisory committee', before becoming a formal board of directors and after which PACT and the UNDP could fade from the scene.[13] Alas, this was not to be. The lack of progress in Burma with regard to the legal status of MFIs (more on which below), and other institutional constraints, meant that the board became moribund.

For most of its existence, the DZMO only lent for so-called 'productive purposes', but in 2005 this restriction was lifted to include loans for children's education and even loans for consumption. The reason for the new liberal lending strategy was twofold. Firstly, a number of borrowers were already 'avoiding' the DZMO's borrowing criteria, and in at least one instance PACT reported that groups of enterprising women had used DZMO loans to set up their own 'village banks'. Secondly, the DZMO had reached 'saturation' point in its ability to identify and fund viable business opportunities in many of its townships and villages.[14] Table 11.2 summarises the DZMO's position as at March 2005:

Table 11.2 Selected Indicators (DZMO)

No. of clients	67,770
No. of active clients	56,411
Loans Outstanding	K1,688m
Total value of loans dispersed	K9,187m
No. of loans dispersed	333,995
No. of credit and savings groups	12,928
Ave. loan size	K23,400
Total savings	K267m
Repayment rates	99.6%
Proportion women	*98.5%*
Interest Rate (nominal)	*43% p.a.*

Source: UNOPS (2005: 10)

As detailed in Chapter 9, for a brief period the DZMO was in collaboration with two of Burma's private banks, the Yoma and Kanbawza, in an innovative effort to 'connect' the MFI to the broader financial system. As we know, this collaboration was forcibly ended in 2003 under the orders of the CBM.

CREDIT FOR RURAL DEVELOPMENT INSTITUTION: OPERATED BY GRET

The third of the major UNDP microfinance schemes is the 'Credit for Rural Development Institution' (CRDI) which operates in five townships of Southern Shan State under the management of the French NGO, 'Groupe de Recherche et d'Echanges Technologiques' (GRET). GRET had been involved in a number of development projects in Burma since 1995, and was selected (like Grameen and PACT) to be a UNDP microfinance partner in 1997. Outside Burma, GRET was involved in the creation of new MFIs in Francophone Africa and, of particular relevance to Burma, in South-East Asian transition states such as Vietnam and Cambodia.[15] As with the DRMO, overall management of the CRDI passed to PACT in March 2006 upon the latter's selection as the UNDP's sole microfinance implementing agency.

The CRDI operates in the Southern Shan townships of Kalaw, Pinlaung, Pindaya, Ywangan and Nuangshwe.[16] In contrast to the other UNDP microfinance schemes, there are no plans to extend the CRDI to other townships. The Shan State is poor even relative to the rest of Burma, and the opportunities for employment and income generation are extremely limited. Greatly restricted too is access to anything in the way of health or education services, the provision of which for Shan State has not been a priority for Burma's central government. The CRDI townships are located in mountainous terrain, transportation to the area is difficult and agricultural productivity is extremely low. Indeed, the inhabitants of this area barely subsist. The proportion of the population that is landless is less than that of the other areas covered by the UNDP schemes (at about 15 per cent), but land holdings are small and title is based on customary rights (UNOPS 2005: 8).[17]

CRDI borrowers are organised into 'solidarity groups' of five people as per the Grameen model but, contrary to Grameen, CRDI loans are made to *all* group members simultaneously. Interest charged on loans is levied at the equivalent of 45 per cent per annum.[18] In another divergence from its UNDP peers, but consistent with local circumstances, the CRDI does not exclusively lend to women. In each village the solidarity groups are managed by an 'elected village credit committee', analogous to the ViCOs of the DZMO and the 'centres' of the DRMO. These committees in turn are supervised by local GRET staff from one of the five township centres.[19]

The CRDI offers four types of loans but, in contrast to the DRMO and DZMO, all are geared to agriculturalists and require the repayment of principal only at the conclusion of the loan term. The loan types are:

(1) *General loans* of a minimum of K16,000 in the first loan cycle, increasing by K6,000 in each subsequent cycle. General loans are for terms of up to twelve months, with interest (only) payable in monthly instalments.

(2) *Extra loans* for agriculture that add K6,000 on to general loans. The extra loan must be repaid in three months.

(3) *Extra loans* for health or education expenses, likewise as a margin (K4,000) on top of general loans, and also repayable in three months. These loans were recently created, reflecting the fact that the CRDI has reached near saturation point for 'productive' lending in the straightened economic circumstances of Shan State.

(4) *Micro-enterprise* loans of between K50,000 and K200,000. These are only available to borrowers who have successfully completed at least two

loan cycles. Micro-enterprise loans have a maximum term of eighteen months.[20]

The CRDI collects compulsory savings, but it has made a conscious decision to make the saving requirement as small as possible. Its 'savings to loans outstanding ratio' of 9 per cent is by far the lowest of the UNDP MFIs. The reason for this low emphasis upon savings aggregation is because of Burma's high and chronic inflation. Not unreasonably, the CRDI reckons that 'collecting savings when the inflation rate is estimated to be around 40 per cent, and when you are limited with the interest rate on credit, is not in the interests of either the clients or the MFI'.[21]

The CRDI's problems in mobilising savings draws attention to broader concerns it faces in being so reliant on the UNDP's capital contributions for its funding. As shall be examined below, these are rapidly drying up. All the UNDP MFIs face this problem to varying degrees, but the situation of the CRDI is the most acute. The UNDP itself first warned in 2003 that the CRDI was running out of capacity, and the situation has not improved since. Table 11.3 provides a snapshot of the CRDI as at March 2005:

Table 11.3 Selected Indicators (CRDI)

No. of clients	42,530
No. of active clients	39,933
Loans outstanding	K955m
Total value of loans dispersed	K4,127m
No. of loans dispersed	160,557
S&L groups	6,704
Average loan size	K23,100
Total savings	K86m
Repayment rates	99%
Proportion women	90%+
Interest rate (nominal)	45% p.a.

Source: UNOPS (2005: 10)

PACT BECOMES THE SOLE IMPLEMENTING AGENCY

On 31 March 2006, PACT became the sole implementing agency for the three UNDP microfinance schemes in Burma. Each of the existing three implementing agencies had been asked to bid for the role, but only PACT and EDA ultimately submitted tenders. By this time GRET's expatriate staff were reportedly 'exhausted' from their work in Shan State, and uninterested in bidding for the whole.[22]

PACT's success in being selected as the sole implementing agency was a surprise. EDA had been the strong favourite to win the contract, primarily on account of its low cost-base. PACT had been encouraged to put in a bid, but rumours at the time suggested that this was merely to provide some competition for EDA. As the most highly regarded of the three existing implementing agencies, PACT's ultimate success was greeted with some delight and relief by many outside observers (this author included), and spoke well of the integrity of the UNDP's tendering process.

But whilst PACT's selection was unexpected, the idea that the three implementing agencies would be replaced by a solitary one was not. Such a plan had been about for some time, especially in the wake of a recommendation to this end by a report on the projects by a UNDP-employed consultant in 2004. The consultant report identified a number of efficiencies that could be yielded by a single implementing agency, including the harmonisation and computerisation of accounting and reporting systems. The report also flagged the potential long-term and dynamic benefits of a single operator – critically, that it 'would simplify the process of building a strong governing board and funding base' (UNDP 2005: 20). The selection of PACT was confirmed in January 2006. Significantly, each of the three UNDP schemes will remain formally separate operations for the foreseeable future (under PACT as the supervising agency), and will continue to function more or less as before. As yet the (slightly) varying methodologies and philosophies of the DRMO and the CRDI are not expected to conform to those established by PACT for the DZMO.

THE FUTURE FOR THE UNDP THREE?

In 2003, the UNDP declared itself to be cautiously happy with its three major microfinance schemes in Burma. The schemes, it said, were 'making a significant contribution in promoting the income and savings of the poor', were 'well conceived and managed', and all three had achieved 'impressive financial sustainability in a difficult environment' (UNDP 2003: 2). In 2005 an independent assessment mission of the schemes essentially agreed with this judgement, but added (in what would have been music to the ears of microfinance advocates) that they had proved, in Burma, that the 'poor are bankable' (UNDP 2005: 4).

Yet, neither these verdicts, nor the broadly positive narrative suggested by the survey of their operations above, are sufficient to suggest that the future is entirely positive for the UNDP's MFIs in Burma. The general problems of attempting to operate microfinance schemes in Burma will be examined in more detail below, but there are a number of specific difficulties the UNDP MFI's face that cloud their horizon.

The first of these is that the UNDP MFIs are undercapitalised. As noted, the UNDP itself acknowledges that the CRDI has reached its capital limit, but the others are not far behind. According to surveys undertaken by the FAO across all three of the UNDP MFIs, fully 100 per cent of existing borrowers would borrow more if they could – proof, it reported, 'of high demand [for credit] that is still not met by institutional sources' (FAO 2004b: 27). The under-capitalisation of the UNDP MFI's is a particular problem since none are yet fully financially sustainable. This means that they remain dependent for their continued existence on the funds made available by the UNDP. Table 11.4 below presents the data for various sustainability indicators, as calculated by the UNDP's Assessment Mission at June 2005. It is reproduced here as it appears in their report:

Table 11.4 UNDP Microfinance Institutions Reported Operational and Financial Sustainability (as at 30 June 2005)

Sustainability Indicators	DRMO (Grameen and EDA) %	DZMO (PACT) %	CRDI (GRET) %
Operational Self-Sufficiency (= Operational Income*/Operational Expense**)	275	459	266
(Short-Term) Financial Sustainability (= Operational Income/Operational Expense + Cost of Capital + Loan Loss Provision)	192	295	265
(Long-Term) Financial Sustainability (= Operational Income/Operational Expense + Cost of Capital + Loan Loss Provision + Inflation***)	89	87	75

Source: UNDP 2005: 45

* Income includes interest and other, but excludes UNDP operational and technical assistance grants.

** UNDP reported operational expenses exclude salaries of foreign staff.

*** Inflation as per (then) UNDP estimate of 40 per cent.

As can be seen from Table 11.4, none of the MFIs has yet reached what the UNDP labels 'Long-Term Financial Sustainability'. In fact, the situation is rather worse than that presented by the UNDP, since missing from the data is the size of the subsidies (from the UNDP itself) in terms of the MFI's operational expenses *and* their cost of capital. Regarding the former, the notes to the table indicate that operational expenses *exclude* the salary expenses of foreign staff, a critical omission given that each are operated by foreign NGOs. Likewise, the cost of capital is not fully included, since the table item refers to the *actual* cost of the capital supplied to the MFIs, rather than its cost from a non-subsidised source. Thus this still begs the question – since the capital is supplied to the MFIs by the UNDP itself at a substantial subsidy. A rough calculation from the data above would suggest that the UNDP 'prices' its capital subscription at around 25 per cent per annum (a more precise figure cannot be calculated without knowing the size of loan loss provisions, which are not available).[23] This is clearly below the UNDP's own estimate of Burma's inflation rate of 40 per cent, and thus implies a substantial capital subsidy. 'True' financial stability requires that MFIs earn sufficient revenue to meet all of their operational expenses without subsidy, and at the very least to avoid their capital position from being eroded through inflation. Neither of these requirements are being met by the UNDP MFIs in Burma.

In 2005, the UNDP (through UNOPS in Bangkok) announced the objective of bringing each of its MFIs in Burma to '100 per cent' long-term financial sustainability. No details as to how this objective would be achieved were outlined, which was accompanied by the simultaneous aim of expanding the client base of each (but especially that of the DZMO) (UNOPS 2005: 11). The extension of HDI-IV beyond December 2007 will provide the UNDP with a budget of around $30 million across the additional two years, but the proportion of this that will flow on to the MFI projects likewise is unclear (UNDP 2005: 25).

Another problem that greatly constrains both the present and future of the UNDP MFIs in Burma is the lack of legal status accorded to them by the Burmese authorities. This legal ambiguity creates a number of problems, including considerable 'greyness' over the legality (or otherwise) of the interest rates they can charge. As noted above, the interest rates charged by the UNDP MFIs average around 40 per cent per annum, marginally negative in real terms, but considerably above the interest rate ceilings that are specified under Article 61 of the *Central Bank of Myanmar Law* (CBML,

1990). The CBML, under which conventional banks and other financial institutions are supervised in Burma (as we have seen), currently specifies that loan interest rates cannot exceed 18 per cent. Making matters even more uncertain, however, is the fact that the *Money Lenders Act 1945* also remains in place in Burma. This Act (outlined in Chapter 6), has its own interest rate restrictions, but also effectively disallows compound interest and determines that the total interest paid on a loan should never exceed the principal. The *Money Lenders Act* is honoured more in the breach than in the application (and in parts it contradicts the CBML), but its continued existence does little for confidence. As things stand presently, the UNDP MFIs and, indeed, all the other microfinance schemes in Burma, charge interest rates with the 'informal' sanction of the relevant authorities. Such an indulgence can be withdrawn at any time, and under any pretext.

The legal ambiguity surrounding the interest rates charged by the UNDP MFIs is matched by a more general uncertainty as to their status as legal entities. They are not 'financial institutions' as incorporated under the *Financial Institutions of Myanmar Law* (1990), even though this Law has provision for 'credit societies', as well as standard classifications for 'banks'. In short, the UNDP MFIs are in the equivalent of an institutional 'no man's land', seemingly condemned to remain as 'projects' rather than stand-alone and self-sufficient MFIs, and dependent for their on-going existence on the support of their management NGOs and UNDP funding. The 2003 UNDP Assessment Mission acknowledged the general problem of MFI legal status in Burma and linked it to their undercapitalisation:

> [The] problem of under-capitalisation in the face of excess demand brings squarely into focus the vital nature of institutionalisation of micro-finance in Myanmar. For growth and sustainability of impact, the micro-finance project needs to be able to borrow from the formal banking system and to on-lend at rates that permit a continuous expansion of activities. This requires a legal framework that provides an institutional basis for micro-finance operations in Myanmar. At the present time, neither the commercial banking law nor the cooperative legal framework offers adequate policy and regulatory instruments for the institutionalised operation of micro-finance in the country. In view of the levels of rural indebtedness to informal sources of credit and the demands for cheaper, accessible credit, the Assessment Mission considers that the *single policy change with the most impact on rural poverty* would be the creation of a legal and regulatory framework to support actively the institutionalisation of micro-finance services (emphasis added, UNDP 2003: 18–19).

In the light of assessments such as those above, the UNDP sought to remedy the legal ambiguity of its MFIs in numerous negotiations with the Burmese government. These came to naught until, unexpectedly, Burma's 'Ministry of Cooperatives' suddenly announced in 2005 that it was 'drafting legislation to frame the microfinance sector' (UNDP 2005: 21). In a fitting illustration of the care needed in Burma in getting what one wishes for, this announcement alarmed the UNDP and other interested parties. The legislation produced by the Ministry (which was not made public) fell well short of international norms and standards and, much worse, included machinery that could be used to transfer control of all MFIs to the government and/or local NGOs.[24] To all of this the UNDP had few ready answers. Its 2005 assessment mission plaintively called upon the 'international community' to provide 'as a matter of urgency' technical assistance to the Ministry of Cooperatives to come up with a better law, otherwise, it noted, it was 'not clear what options are available to UNDP/UNOPS' (UNDP 2005: 27). In early 2008 the matter remained unresolved, with the legislation seemingly set aside (temporarily?) while the Burmese government grappled with more immediate concerns. Its potential return, however, presents a cloud on the horizon for the UNDP MFIs in Burma.

OTHER MICROFINANCE PROGRAMMES IN BURMA

In addition to the UNDP microfinance schemes there are a number of others, relatively small in outreach and mostly extensions of poverty-alleviation operations of international NGOs. None are 'formal' MFIs in the accepted terminology, but are probably best described as microfinance 'providers' (ILO 2002: 4). The most prominent of the NGO-based microfinance schemes operating in Burma are:

Save the Children (USA)

This large US-based NGO with substantial global operations (45 countries) operates the 'DAWN' microfinance scheme in Shwe Pyi Thar Township on the outskirts of Rangoon.[25] Established in January 2002, by June 2005 it had over 7,600 active clients and total loans outstanding of $US84,144 (around K78 million). The DAWN scheme employs what it calls 'microfinance best practices' with a view to becoming self-sustainable. Compulsory savings are levied (roughly 4 per cent of the value of loans granted), and the scheme also collects voluntary savings. Thus far, however, the total value of savings mobilised ($US3,027/~K2.8 million in compulsory savings, $US5,322/~K4.9 million in voluntary savings) remains small.

DAWN claims a loan repayment rate of 100 per cent, and as at June 2005 reported it had never written off a loan nor had any loans either in arrears (repayments at least a day late) or at risk (repayments more than 30 days late). Financial self-sufficiency currently stands at 76 per cent. DAWN lends exclusively to women.

Save the Children has high hopes for the DAWN scheme, and it regards Burma as one of its 'focus countries' for the application of microfinance. As with so many MFI operators, however, *Save the Children* regards the lack of a legal and regulatory framework for microfinance as the principal obstacle to its microfinance ambitions in Burma. Of course, the DAWN scheme is as yet well short of financial self-sufficiency and the project remains a very small operation

World Vision

Founded in the United States in the 1950s but now operating in over 100 countries, *World Vision* is one of the largest NGOs in the world. A Christian relief and development agency, *World Vision* has in recent times emphasised programmes that aim at poverty alleviation and community development. Microfinance is central to these programmes, and in various guises *World Vision* MFIs are ubiquitous in much of the developing world.

In Burma, *World Vision* established microfinance operations as a component of its 'Micro-Enterprise Development Program' (MEDP). The MEDP commenced in 1997, and currently functions in four townships, three on the outskirts of Rangoon, and one in Chan Mya Tha Zi Township on the outskirts of Mandalay.[26] The MEDP lends money to individuals organised in groups of five to seven borrowers and requires set weekly repayments of principal and interest. There is no joint-liability within the loan groups, but members are said to be 'accountable to one another in how they use and repay their loan'. Before getting a loan 'a poor entrepreneur must demonstrate trust worthiness, a good work ethic and a sound business plan', and the MEDP combines its lending with 'basic training in handling credit and basic business'. Loans vary from small (around K15,000) to the comparatively large (up to K75,000). The maximum loan term is relatively short at six months, and an interest rate of 48 per cent per annum is charged on loans. The MEDP does not lend exclusively to women, but no data is available on the precise gender divide in lending (64 per cent of World

Vision's global MFI clients are women). The MEDP claims a repayment rate on its loans of 99 per cent.

CARE

The 'Cooperative for Assistance and Relief Everywhere', better known by its acronym CARE, is one of the world's largest private, and secular, NGOs.[27] Created in the United States just after the Second World War, the organisation is now a federation of 11 country-based organisations working in over 70 countries. Microfinance schemes, of various types, are regarded by CARE as a key ingredient in their avowed objective of increasing 'self-help' capacities in the communities in which they operate. CARE's operations in Burma are 'sub-contracted' out to CARE Australia. The Australian government's principal aid agency, 'Ausaid', is also a major financial backer.[28]

CARE's microfinance operation in Burma is based in Rakhine State. Known as the 'Saving Mobilisation and Income Generation Program' (SMIG), it is based on a similar project developed by CARE Cambodia. By 2006, the SMIG had around 1,200 members in nine credit and savings groups of an average size of over 130 members each. CARE says that the SMIG is based on a group lending methodology. However, the large size of the groups raises questions as to how effective this might be. The SMIG lends to women exclusively. The SMIG has issued a cumulative total of around 2,500 loans (2006) of an average size of around K16,000. It charges relatively high interest rates that have ranged from between 4 and 6.25 per cent per month (60 to 107 per cent per annum). As will be examined in more detail below, however, the SMIG's interest rates are determined by its members. Notwithstanding its relatively high interest rates, however, the SMIG is not yet fully financially sustainable.[29]

Savings are an important component of the SMIG. Members must place on deposit an initial K200, and thereafter are required to make compulsory monthly deposits of K100 each. Voluntary savings are also encouraged. By 2006 the SMIG had accumulated around K3.5 million in compulsory savings, and (a tiny) K40,000 in voluntary savings. The SMIG's deposit liabilities are not sufficient to fund its lending, which continues to made primarily out of CARE's initial and subsequent capital contributions of just over $US5 million.

Since its creation, the SMIG has dispensed around K40 million in loans. The SMIG loans are officially for 'productive' purposes only, but there are provisions for loans to be made for 'emergency' purposes too. Amongst the purposes to which the SMIG's 'productive' loans have been applied include crop cultivation, small trading, the establishment of small shops, basic food processing, and even buying a ferry. The 'emergency loan' component is surprisingly liberal – an allowable emergency comprising anything from the usual accident and illness events, to necessary expenditures for marriage, education and 'court appearances'.

The SMIG sets great store on developing the savings and lending groups. An initial village meeting is first organised with the relevant 'Village Peace and Development Council' (more on which below), at which the details of the SMIG and its procedures are discussed. At this first meeting, and reflecting the gender divide in Rakhine State, men and women are briefed separately. A second meeting (of women only) quickly follows, at which groups are formed and group leaders are elected. For the first six months thereafter various training takes place, including workshops on 'Saving Mobilisation and Action Planning' and saving and loan group 'Bye-laws and Policies'. Savings begin in this period, at the end of which the first loans are dispersed. Loans will only be made, however, when a borrower meets certain 'preliminary performance criteria' such as: (1) meeting the compulsory savings requirements over the last six months; (2) attending at least 85 per cent of the weekly meetings of their savings and lending group; (3) achieving a score of at least 85 per cent in an examination of saving and loan group bye-laws and policies.

A notable feature of CARE's SMIG is that, based as it is in Rakhine State, most of its members are Muslim. The levying of interest (*riba*) is illegal under Islamic *Sharia* law, based on the philosophy that profit should accrue only to the provision of goods and services and not money, and that the 'risk' of any particular project should be borne by all parties to it, not just the debtor (El Hawary and Grais 2005). A number of devices have developed over the centuries in Islamic banking to both avoid and make lending consistent with the injunction on interest. The one chosen by the SMIG is the concept of *hibah* (gift), under which borrowers voluntarily give the lender a 'donation' along with the repayment of principal. The most common form of *Sharia*-consistent lending, *mudharabah* (profit sharing), is also implicitly employed by SMIG, in that the *hibah* payments are dependent upon the profits collectively made by the lending groups from their loans.

THE CHALLENGES AHEAD

Burma's Macroeconomic Instability and Inflation

A stable macroeconomic environment is a critical condition for financial intermediaries of any stripe. The needs of MFIs are not exceptional to this requirement even if, almost by definition, they are designed for application in the most challenging of circumstances. Burma has a deeply unstable macroeconomic environment. The country lacks the fundamental institutions of a market economy, policy-making is arbitrary and uninformed, inflation is rampant, the currency is distrusted and trades via a multiple of exchange rates, unemployment is endemic, taxation is chaotic and the Government finances its spending by printing money. To this list can be added all-pervasive corruption, a growing trade deficit, foreign debt arrears, the imposition of economic sanctions and negligible foreign investment (Turnell 2006a, 2006b). Burma, in short, is in possession of almost every conceivable macroeconomic malady.

In such an environment, the MFIs in Burma face a near-insurmountable array of macroeconomic obstacles. That some continue to function in positive ways regardless is testimony no doubt to the doggedness of staff on the ground. Of course, the diversion of their energies into simply surviving in Burma's chaotic economy can do little towards delivering the outcomes promised by microfinance.

As we have seen, inflation is a particular problem for the MFIs operating in Burma. Conservatively estimated to average around 40 per cent per annum over the last decade (by the UNDP), Burma's high inflation rates have the effect of persistently eroding the capital base of all the MFIs operating there. With savings likewise inhibited by the diluting effects of inflation, without constant injections of donors' funds the ability of Burma's MFIs to lend diminishes precipitously with each passing year. More broadly, high inflation in Burma distorts any incentive to use the country's financial resources to invest long term and for productive purposes, and increases uncertainties generally. In its commentary on MFIs throughout the Asia-Pacific, the Asian Development Bank (ADB 2005) remarked that 'nothing is more harmful for microfinance than high inflation'.

Is There Sufficient Effective Demand?

Inflation is one of the two pathologies that stand out in the modern global macroeconomy. The second, that there may be insufficient effective demand to match a country's output potential, is just as pervasive and, in many ways, rather more intractable. The word 'effective' in this context is, of course, crucial. There is no question that in Burma there is great *demand* for all the goods and services the country is capable of producing. Burma is not short of 'wants'. The real question, however, is whether people have the wherewithal to match their needs and desires with their purchasing power – in other words, to make their demand 'effective'. In the rich industrial world a lack of effective demand is manifested in unemployment, and a certain degree of relative poverty. In the poorer countries of the world such as Burma deficient effective demand is more obvious: it is economic stagnation, and grinding poverty.

In an environment of insufficient demand the promoters of microfinance must take great care since, for all the best of intentions, they could just be saddling their clients with debt. As the ILO (2002: 92) puts it:

> One problem that exists in almost all microfinance development projects for poor people is that the product (service or goods) is developed first (…) A lesson learned by many people to date is that there is simply no market for their products and that no matter how hard they work, without an assured market they will remain in debt.

Of course, this is not to say that microfinance itself is not a *part* of the solution to the problem of insufficient effective demand. By providing finance to entrepreneurs and the self-employed whose principle constraint *is* a lack of access to capital, microfinance helps generate the economic activity – and with it the effective demand – sorely needed. But most people in Burma and elsewhere are not budding entrepreneurs constrained simply by a lack of finance. What most people in Burma crave is 'wage employment' of some kind. Microfinance aids employment creation, but the great driver of employment broadly is economic growth. The processes determining economic growth contain ingredients that range from the importance of secure private property rights to openness to trade, ingredients in short supply in Burma and likely to remain so in the absence of profound reform in the country's political economy. As Morduch (1999: 1610) notes, '[m]icrofinance may be able to help some households take advantage of those processes [of economic growth], but nothing so far suggests that it will ever drive them'.

The question of whether the supply of credit is a 'first-order' need for the poor is a critical one for the microfinance movement everywhere. A suspicion routinely aired, for instance, is that many NGOs 'provide credit to the poor when it is the NGO that wants to supply it, not because the demand is there' (ILO 2002: 23). This is a particularly sensitive issue in Burma, where NGOs often find themselves in a position of needing to justify their entry into the country. The political situation in Burma precludes the involvement of many NGOs (and even UN agencies), and the NGOs that do decide to go in are often at pains to demonstrate that their money does not end up in the hands of the military regime or its allies. In this context microfinance might provide a convenient screen for NGOs: money goes into the country, but it is only used for loans that must be paid back. Of course the problem that arises here is whether this a diversion of funds that could be better employed in other ways.

Poor Savings Mobilisation

In recent years, great attention has been paid to the role of MFIs in promoting savings amongst their clients. In the early era of microfinance, when the movement was mostly (and revealingly) referred to as micro*credit*, savings were (in the redolent phrase of Robert Vogel, 1984) the 'forgotten half' of financial intermediation for the poor. Such myopia has now all but disappeared, and since what Robinson (2001) refers to as the 'paradigm shift' in microfinance, the importance of savings in poverty alleviation has become widely acknowledged.

The role that savings can play in poverty alleviation is much the same as that which can be played by access to credit. Indeed, as Robinson (2001) points out, in talking about savings and access to credit we are effectively talking about two sides of the same coin. A household can save now and over time build up a stock of 'wealth' for use later; or, it can borrow to get access to such a 'stock' and use it for spending now. Given certain assumptions regarding interest rates and the discount factor we might employ over the benefits of accessing money now or later, the differences between savings and borrowing can come down simply to a matter of time preference. In just the same ways as access to affordable credit, savings allow the poor to accumulate capital resources for productive investment, cushions them against financial catastrophe and income instability, and provides them with the means to smooth consumption. Of course, there is an additional benefit of savings to the MFI client: interest payments now work to their advantage, rather than to that of the lender.

The importance of savings for MFIs themselves is also a widely acknowledged component of Robinson's 'paradigm shift' in the microfinance literature. Mobilising savings provides MFIs with a cheap and reliable source of capital. On the other side of the balance sheet, it is also the case that savers tend to become good borrowers. A savings record is a good way for an MFI to accumulate information on the financial character of potential future borrowers. According to the International Labour Organisation's study of microfinance 'best practice' (2002: 31), '[p]utting into place viable savings products rather than providing credit is the best first step for any financial services project'.

Savings mobilisation is not, however, the widespread practice of Burma's MFIs. Two reasons stand out as to why this is so. Firstly, most of Burma's MFIs are operated by NGOs as a 'sidelight' to their other activities and they have neither the experience nor the expertise for collecting savings. Even the 'big three' MFIs of the UNDP show a marginal interest in collecting savings. Consistent with their origins as Grameen replications, the UNDP MFIs collect a small flow of 'compulsory savings' from their members, but this is more for the purposes of creating quasi-loan collateral and instilling regular payment disciplines than an effort to consciously mobilise deposits. Of the remaining MFIs in Burma, some make references to savings, but few collect savings of any magnitude.

A second reason why savings mobilisation has not been a key feature of microfinance in Burma relates to how such efforts are undermined by the country's macroeconomic and political instability. Savings are highly vulnerable, in the absence of compensating interest rates, to erosion through inflation. As noted earlier in this chapter, this was the reason why two of the three UNDP MFIs actively discouraged their clients from making voluntary savings – and why one even urged people to save in 'non-monetary' forms. But there is also a broader uncertainty of savings preservation that evokes Burma's troubled monetary history. Stated baldy, there is a profound mistrust in the currency in Burma and, especially since the wholesale collapse of banks in the country in 2002–2003, even less trust in financial institutions. Privately a number of MFIs in Burma have confided to the author that one reason that they hold off from a 'final push' towards financial sustainability is that they fear their assets will be seized by the state.[30] Long experience tells the Burmese people that whatever 'savings' they hold are likely to be better off in other places, and in other forms.

Legal Status and Financial System Linkage

There is, at present, no legal or regulatory framework governing the operations of MFIs in Burma (the inadequate 2005 draft legislation of the Ministry of Cooperatives notwithstanding). As noted above in the context of the UNDP MFIs, this creates great uncertainty with respect to interest rates, and more fundamentally in terms of the sustainability of MFIs as stand-alone institutions. The importance of legal recognition for MFI development is universally recognised amongst microfinance practitioners around the world, but it is perhaps most sincerely manifested in the efforts of those 'dozens of countries' that are designing legislation and regulations specifically for MFIs (ILO 2002: 13).

The question of legal status has a direct impact upon the ability of MFIs to enter into contractual relationships with the economy more broadly, but particularly with other 'formal' financial institutions. As Littlefield and Rosenberg (2004: 40) note, the original challenge of microfinance was a 'methodological' one that set out to demonstrate that the poor were 'bankable'. With this arguably achieved (certainly it is claimed by the 'UNDP three' in Burma), the challenge now is a 'systematic' one in integrating MFIs with conventional financial institutions and drawing from them the 'vast amounts of human, physical, and financial resources and management know-how' that they command (ADB 2005: 18). Though 'unthinkable just a decade ago', linkages between MFIs and conventional financial institutions are fast becoming commonplace. This is particularly the case in Latin America, where the microfinance sector is well down the road to integration and commercialisation (Christen 2001: 17). But such linkages and transformations are increasingly common throughout Asia too. Moreover, the ADB reports (2005: 21) that, contrary to some fears, increased linkages and commercialisation has not reduced the outreach of MFIs to the poor. Indeed, to the contrary, 'in most cases it has had a positive effect on both the breadth and depth of their outreach (...) all transformed institutions in Asia are now serving a larger number of poor households than they did previously'.

As has been noted, MFIs in Burma do not have legal status and whatever standing they have is dependent upon the whim of the country's military regime and the esteem of their founding NGOs. Of course, given the current state of Burma's formal financial system, the benefits yielded from MFI integration may be less apparent than it has been elsewhere, though longer term the potential benefits surely remain to be yielded. As also discussed earlier, something of an experiment in bank/MFI linkages was briefly attempted in Burma in 2001 when the Yoma and Kanbawza banks supplied funds for on-lending under the UNDP's Integrated Community Development Project in the Dry Zone. The subsequent 'cease and desist' order from the CBM is, alas, suggestive that such an experiment is unlikely to be repeated anytime soon. In an account otherwise very 'bullish' on microfinance in Burma, Rahman (2003:10) commented that MFI 'graduation' into the country's formal economy, and into self-sustaining institutions is 'not realisable at the present time due to the weak legal framework and supportive policies and government administrative machinery'. Fukui and Llanto (2003: 5) are just as blunt on Burma: 'The country lacks the policy framework, legal structure for registering microfinance NGOs, and administrative structure that are needed for dealing with microfinance undertakings'.

Problems of Group-Lending in Burma

As has been noted throughout these pages, group lending is central to most MFI methodologies – narrowly as a collateral substituting device, more broadly as a way of building 'social capital'. But if group lending can build trust, it also requires it: trust amongst group members, trust between members and group leaders, trust in the management of an MFI, trust in the NGO sponsoring or operating it, and trust that external forces will not interfere in harmful ways. Group lending is about information sharing but it is also about sanction and (hopefully benign) social pressure. Joining an MFI creates vulnerabilities as well as opportunities. Trust is the true currency of an MFI, just as it is for financial institutions generally.

Does such multi-faceted trust exist in contemporary Burma? Burma is under a military dictatorship whose political control in many parts of the country is almost complete, and whose intrusion into everyday life is often shocking to those unfamiliar with the country. At the highest level Burma is ruled via a military committee that styles itself the 'State Peace and Development Council' (SPDC). But, as we have seen, this is replicated down through the levels of government in Burma, even to the village level where Village Peace and Development Councils (VPDCs) have pushed aside the 'head man' (*thugyi*) and other traditional forms of local authority. Such organs, working in (willing or unwilling) collaboration with Military Intelligence, the Ministry of Information and other arms of the central state, have created in Burma an atmosphere of profound *mis*trust. The existence of a vast army of informers for the State (real and perceived) has, moreover, created throughout Burma 'extraordinary levels of fear, covertness, suspicion and self-censorship' (Skidmore 2004: 77). Such perceptions are widely shared amongst Burma watchers and confirmed by the testimonies of those in the country who suffer from them.[31] People in Burma 'do not trust each other and cannot talk freely, even in their own neighbourhoods' (Fink 2001: 127).

The overt extension of the state into the lives of Burmese villagers is supplemented by various 'parastatal' organisations that ostensibly exist to promote various social and health objectives (Skidmore 2004: 105). Such organisations are equivalent to NGOs elsewhere but with the obvious caveat that, in Burma, 'non-government' is a label that has little meaning – the regime fearing 'all dynamic organizations to have the potential to rally people in opposition to the government' (Fink 2001: 135). Accordingly, most genuine domestic NGOs in Burma 'have been crushed or absorbed' (Fink 2001: 135). What remains are the 'Government Organised Non-Governmental Organisations' ('GONGOs') such as the Myanmar Maternal Child Welfare Association (MMCWA), the Myanmar Red Cross, and numerous village-level education, health, sanitation and other 'improvement' vehicles that have proliferated throughout the country in recent years (Skidmore 2004: 102). By far the largest (and most notorious) GONGO in Burma, however, is the Union Solidarity and Development Association (USDA). An organisation established in 1993 seemingly for various social welfare purposes, in reality the USDA is a mass political organisation – even, according to one of the leading figures of the SPDC, an 'auxiliary national defence force' (International Crisis Group 2001: 10).[32] The USDA has over eleven million members and its authority extends deep into villages throughout Burma (Steinberg 2001: 110). USDA members routinely infiltrate township and village meetings, whatever the topic or circumstances.

The nature and extent of state/GONGO control of civil and social space in Burma has important implications for microfinance in the country. Above all, it creates another avenue via which interpersonal trust (outside of the immediate family) is greatly compromised. What member of a village lending group, for instance, would voluntarily divulge business and other difficulties to groups that were (at the very least) perceived to be shaped and infiltrated by other organs whose existence was to deny or repress free exchange? The Burmese military regime's mouthpiece, the *New Light of Myanmar,* has on numerous occasions declared that GONGOs should not consider themselves as independent of the government, and that it was the 'national duty of all (...) social organizations as well as the public to cooperate with the Government's nation-building endeavours' (Skidmore 2004: 104). Such instructions, imbibed by the leaders of these 'social organisations' for varying motives (including career advancement, other perks and simply 'protection'), have an especially insidious effect upon free expression when it is combined with traditional Burmese notions of *ah nah day* (which roughly translates as a desire not to impose on others) and a deference for elders (Fink 2001: 120). The International Crisis Group (2001: 12) describes the phenomenon thus:

> In organisations and community meetings, those perceived to have higher status dominate discussions, while others who are perceived as having lower status (and so perceive themselves) will either not attend or stay silent.

The presence of GONGOs and other actors compromise group activity in other, more basic, ways. In particular, the credit and savings groups of MFIs are especially vulnerable to capture by 'connected' elites. The 2005 UNDP Assessment Mission reported, for example, 'numerous instances in which project benefits accrued mainly to the village elite and/or to committee members' (UNDP 2005: 11). Confidential anecdotes received by the author suggest that even though the major UNDP MFIs have managed to stay clear of *explicit* GONGO partnerships, it is still the case that leadership of lending groups (and higher committees within the MFIs) accrue mostly to village MMCWA office bearers, the wives of headmen and ward officers, and other 'connected' individuals. More generally, the UNDP MFIs are in a more or less persistent struggle to keep various government and semi-government organisations at bay.

The narrowing of the 'humanitarian' space in Burma since the ousting of Prime Minister Khin Nyunt in October 2004 has had serious implications for all international NGOs in the country, including MFIs. The UNDP's 2005 Assessment Mission, an account that otherwise tended (diplomatically) to downplay Burmese government obstructionism, contained this testimony;

> ...the Mission was told of numerous incidences of increased scrutiny of humanitarian programmes; problems of access by foreign staff of humanitarian agencies to certain areas of the country; insistence that Government personnel accompany both local and foreign staff on field trips,

combined with the need for three weeks' notice of field travel; and requests for information on the background of local staff (UNDP 2005: 11).[33]

FINAL WORDS

Microfinance in Burma has reached a critical juncture. In the opaque world of Burma's political economy few things are ever entirely clear-cut, but it does seem that certain of the MFIs currently operating there are at a tipping point. From this place they *could* transform into sustainable financial institutions. Alternatively, microfinance could fail to make this leap, and continue in the dismal tradition of Burma's financial sector – of just another idea, well-intentioned and sound in theory, gone wrong in application.

But whatever the fate of the current MFIs in Burma, such institutions are ameliorative rather than transformative. The amelioration of the symptoms of Burma's economic crisis is both necessary and important, but even more important is that the country's political economy is transformed into one in which modernisation and economic development can take place. A first order condition for the economic development and modernisation of Burma is the creation of a viable financial system more broadly. Burma remains primarily an agricultural country whose financial needs are highly skewed to those of its cultivators. But the financial needs of agriculturalists in Burma, highly co-variant in both volume and risk, will not be met by microfinance. Strong and diversified commercial financial institutions are what Burma needs. The creation of these, however, will require a yet more profound transformation in the country.

NOTES

1   The HDI in Burma is meant to be governed by strict criteria with respect to interactions with the Burmese authorities, and as originally set out in a decision (No. 93/21) of the UNDP's Governing Council in 1993 (UNDP 2001: 2).

2   Broad details of the UNDP's HDI programmes can be found at the website of the UNDP's Burma Office, <www.mm.undp.org>, accessed 19 February, 2008.

3   And interviews with UNDP staff.

4   The UN currently employs a reference exchange rate of the US dollar to the kyat of $US1:K930 (UNOPS 2005: 1). For the purposes of comparative consistency, this rate will also be applied throughout this chapter.

5   In fact, whilst still *de rigueur* for the Grameen replications around the world, group lending is no longer central to the methodology in use at the Grameen Bank itself. Under what Grameen refers to as 'Grameen Bank II', a borrower's 'word' as well as

a form of 'staggered' individual lending have emerged as the dominant repayment–security devices. Flexibility in loan terms, and allowing for seasonal variability in agriculture, have also been introduced. These changes were motivated by the problems that became apparent in what some have regarded as the excessive 'rigidity' of the older Grameen model, some of which are discussed in these pages. For more details of Grameen Bank II, see Armendáriz de Aghion and Morduch (2005).

6   There is a solid literature on the virtues and otherwise on group lending methodologies – in which Stiglitz (1990), Besley and Coate (1995) and Prescott (1997) could be regarded as seminal.

7   This description of Grameen's credit delivery system is taken from the Bank's website, <www.grameen-info.org>, accessed 14 December, 2007.

8   In 2004 the IMF's estimate of inflation in Burma stood at 57 per cent (IMF 2005).

9   The following details regarding EDA are based largely on the company's website, <www.edarural.com>. Additional information has been supplied to the author by confidential sources.

10   The following information on PACT's operations in Burma have been obtained, except where indicated, from the NGO's website: <www.pactworld.org>, and via interviews and correspondence with PACT staff.

11   Interview with PACT staff undertaken by the author.

12   *Ibid.*

13   Details of the proposed 'Board' can be found at the PACT website, *op. cit.*

14   Interview with PACT staff undertaken by the author.

15   GRET website, <www.GRET.org>, accessed 2 June, 2007.

16   Much of the information here was supplied to the author by Christian Baron of GRET, as well as other staff of the CRDI and their clients.

17   And *ibid.*

18   *Ibid.*

19   *Ibid.*

20   *Ibid.*

21   *Ibid.*

22   Information here and below supplied through correspondence by the author with staff of the three UNDP implementing partners.

23   In arriving at the '25 per cent' estimate, the author has assumed loan loss provisions of around 3 per cent of the outstanding loan portfolios of the MFIs. Such a provision ratio is suggested by CGAP's Consensus Guidelines for MFIs (see CGAP website, www.cgap.org), but it is probably larger than those applied by the UNDP MFIs. If this is indeed the case, then the degree of subsidy implicit in the UNDP's funding of the MFIs is even higher.

24   A copy of the proposed Law was viewed by the author.

25   The information here on the DAWN programme was provided via interviews by the author with Save the Children staff, and from the NGO's website: <www.savethechildren.org>, accessed 15 June, 2007.

26 Information in this section was provided to the author in correspondence with World Vision staff. See also the World Vision website at <www.worldvision.org.uk>.

27 Information provided to the author by CARE Australia.

28 Details of Ausaid's financial contributions to CARE's operations in Burma can be found at: <www.ausaid.gov.au>.

29 Information provided to the author by CARE Australia.

30 One MFI official told the author that 'in such a country, it is dangerous to create an institution if you don't have some security that the state will not try to get back'.

31 For confirmation of this the reader can consult what is becoming a veritable avalanche of reports as to both the repressive nature of the Burmese state, and its incursions into almost every aspect of life in the country. For a representative, and authoritative sample, however, see the annual and other reports of such groups as Amnesty International, <http://web.amnesty.org>, Human Rights Watch <http://hrw.org>, and the International Crisis Group <www.crisisgroup.org>.

32 The 'leading figure' quoted was General Maung Aye, Deputy Chairman of the SPDC and the second most senior figure in Burma's military regime. USDA's patron is the Chairman of the SPDC, Senior-General Than Shwe.

33 The shrunken 'humanitarian space' within which NGOs can function is the subject of two recent (December 2006 and January 2008) reports of the International Crisis Group (2006, 2008).

Afterword

Banks and financial institutions are proprietary networks of information and trust that are microcosms of the societies they inhabit. As such, it is not surprising that in countries where information flows are inhibited, and in which trust has been compromised, financial institutions struggle.

Sixty years after it achieved independence Burma remains without a properly functioning financial system. The most significant reason for this – the traces of which are plain in every chapter of this book – is the almost universally destructive role of government. Together with famine, fire, flood and plague, 'government' is one of the five traditional pestilences confronting the people in Burmese folklore. In the context of creating viable financial institutions the validity of the belief is hard to deny.

The state in Burma has played a harmful role in a number of ways, but not least has been its own insatiable financial demands that have left little room for non-state enterprises. For decades Burma's governments have run substantial budget deficits which, more often than not, have been 'financed' by simply borrowing from the CBM and its predecessors. The predictable result of this practice has been inflation and a depreciating value of the kyat. If to this we add well-reasoned fears of arbitrary property seizure, doubts about contract enforcement, demonetisation anxieties, an inability to pledge collateral and (proven) doubts about the solvency of Burma's financial institutions – then it is safe to say that 'property rights' over financial assets do not exist in Burma.

THE IMPORTANCE OF PROPERTY RIGHTS

In recent decades, the importance of creating clearly defined and enforceable property rights as a central pillar of an economic development strategy has come to be recognised by economists, development specialists and policy-makers. Property 'rights' have two critical elements. Firstly, they grant the individual exclusive entitlement to use their property as they see fit (subject to the proviso that this does not infringe on the rights of others), and to enjoy the fruits of this use. Secondly, the right to sell or otherwise transfer those rights according to their desire. The first element provides the basis of the incentives to work, to produce, to save, to invest and to conduct all those other activities that collectively provide the motor of the capitalist economy. The second element is just as important since it provides the *means* through which capital itself can be created. Clearly defined property rights – and their expression in formal legal documentation – have been the basis of collateralised lending for investment in the industrial world for two centuries. Hernando de Soto, the Peruvian economist who has perhaps done more than anyone else to underline the importance of this 'second element' of property rights, described its capital-creating mechanism in his seminal book, *The Mystery of Capital*, thus:

> In the West (...) every parcel of land, every building, every piece of equipment or store of inventories is represented in a property document that is the visible sign of a vast hidden process that connects all these assets to the rest of the economy. Thanks to this representational process, assets can lead an invisible, parallel life alongside their material existence. They can be used as collateral for credit. The single most important source of funds for new businesses in the United States is a mortgage on the entrepreneur's house. These assets can also provide a link to the owner's credit history, an accountable address for the collection of debts and taxes, the basis for the creation of reliable and universal public utilities, and a foundation for the creation of securities ... By this process the West injects life into assets and makes them generate capital (de Soto 2000: 6–7).

The 'representational process' articulated by de Soto above scarcely functions in Burma. As a consequence, physical property in Burma is left purely in its 'material existence' and is assuredly not a device, in conjunction with a properly functioning financial system, for the introduction of 'life' into assets, and 'self-replication' into capital.[1]

FAILURE OF THE FUNDAMENTAL FINANCIAL
ASSET: 'MONEY' IN BURMA

The importance of a credible regime of property rights for banking and financial systems hardly needs explanation. Financial assets such as bank deposits are, after all, little more than claims on the issuer, an abstract representation of the real assets and resources into which they are meant to be redeemable. They are symbolic, backed up by nothing other than the trust their holders are willing to invest in the corporate (or government) entity issuing them. In the developed financial markets of the world this trust has been hard won. In Burma, such trust is notable only by its absence.

The most fundamental financial asset is what we think of as 'money', the basic function of which is as a medium of exchange. A more efficient substitute for barter, in this role money allows for the division of labour – famously the driver that Adam Smith posited that explained the 'wealth of nations'. But money, especially in its modern form, is much more than simply a means of exchange. As a store of value, money allows for 'inter-temporal' decision-making by economic agents. Participants in an economic transaction do not need to instantly consume the products of their exchange. Rather, money allows consumption to be postponed, brought forward and more generally 'liberated' from its initiating transaction. In a practical sense, this allows for saving, investment and the longer-term consumption decisions that people make. Finally, money is a unit of account. Often overlooked, it is this virtue that makes possible the calculation of relative prices, debts, wages, profits – the signals that allow for the 'progressive rationalisation of social life' (Ingham 2004: 4).

It is when we pause to consider the nature of money that the importance of property rights becomes apparent. Once valued since it was a commodity of intrinsic worth (gold and silver for instance), modern money is merely a socially-constructed 'promise to pay'. In its most recognisable form (that is, as embodied in a nation's currency) this promise is made by the state.

Currency is at the peak of the money hierarchy in terms of its widespread acceptability but it is, of course, only a component – and in modern economies with a proper functioning financial system, an increasingly small component – of what we regard as 'money'. The major component of money in modern financial systems is those financial assets created by financial institutions (in the recognisable forms of deposits, credit cards and so on) that are transferable and, as such, widely accepted for payment.

Burma has failed to establish credible money at every level of this hierarchy. The currency, weakened by chronic inflation, a collapsing exchange rate and ever-present demonetisation fears, functions as a low-value medium of exchange, but scarcely as a store of value and unreliably so as a unit of account.[2] In purchasing power, one kyat today is unlikely to be worth one kyat tomorrow. Money in its other forms, as the liabilities of Burma's financial institutions, has all the problems of its currency of denomination but – as the 2002–2003 crisis revealed – with that extra uncertainty that these institutions may be of dubious standing themselves.

The failure to create reliable money in Burma means the country is greatly inhibited in its ability to generate internal sources of financial capital. Much angst is exercised amongst Burma watchers that the country is without much in the way of foreign investment or external aid. Yet such avenues are *not* the most important sources of national capital accumulation. From the United Kingdom as 'first mover' in the industrial revolution to the Asian 'tigers', internal capital accumulation through the creation of claims against a country's own financial institutions has been the dominant pool from which capital is financed.[3] The mechanism by which this pool is formed is the simple deposit/lending 'money creation' process described in Chapter 2 of this book.

As Collignon (2004: 91) notes, the recognition that domestic financial systems create money in this way discredits the idea that the principal problem facing countries such as Burma is that of a 'financing gap' which must be filled by external borrowing or aid. Instead, such a gap can be 'filled' by a country's own financial system – so long as it is able to function in the ways indicated. In terms of a role for government then, a principal objective should be ensuring that the right institutions are in place to allow this to happen. Of course, this is not to say that a country such as Burma is not in need of foreign investment, nor that foreign investment could not play a positive role in the country's economic development. There are certain goods and services, certain types of expertise, that can only be sourced offshore and secured through financial resources beyond the ability of the domestic financial system to create. Nevertheless, it is the case that the means through which Burma can realise its potential, as implied by its (oft cited) substantial physical factor endowments, are largely in its own hands.

THE ESSENTIAL PROBLEM

Solving the essential problem of creating a viable financial system in Burma will require fundamental institutional reform of the country's political economy. Such reform will require, at a minimum, the creation of effective property rights, freedom to contract, a government of laws rather than of men [sic], and a modicum of macroeconomic stability. These attributes elsewhere and in history have emerged from domestic constituencies possessing the incentives and freedoms to bring about change. Burma has such constituencies, and the incentives are apparent. Freedom awaits.

NOTES

1   Amongst studies examining ways to improve agricultural productivity in Burma, there is near unanimity about the important role that can be played by establishing private land title (see, for example, ADB (2003), Copland (2004), James (2003), and the World Bank (1995)). An instructive example for Burma in this respect might be Vietnam. Vietnam introduced private land title in 1995, leading to an almost instantaneous increase in investment on the land, increased yields and various other efficiencies. For details, see Do and Iyer (2003).

2   Burma's government seems to have learnt the lessons of past demonetisations, and have been at pains at various times (such as when a new note is introduced) to reassure that such measures will not be repeated. Nevertheless, in monetary matters, fear is a difficult emotion to dispel.

3   The importance of this point, in the specific context of Burma, is made with great verve and authority by Collignon (2001: 90–94).

Bibliography

OFFICIAL SOURCES

Burmese Official Documents

Burma Currency Board (1947) *Report of the Burma Currency Board, for the Six Months Ended 30 September 1947.* London: Burma Currency Board.

—— (1948) *Report of the Burma Currency Board, for the Period 1st April 1947 to 30 September 1948.* London: Burma Currency Board.

—— (1949) *Report of the Burma Currency Board, for the Period 1st April 1948 to 30 September 1949.* London: Burma Currency Board.

—— (1950) *Report of the Burma Currency Board, for the Period 1st April 1949 to 30 September 1950.* London: Burma Currency Board.

—— (1951) *Report of the Burma Currency Board, for the Period 1st April 1950 to 30 September 1951.* London: Burma Currency Board.

—— (1952) *Report of the Burma Currency Board, for the Period 1st April 1951 to 30 September 1952.* London: Burma Currency Board.

Burma Intelligence Bureau (1943) *Burma During the Japanese Occupation,* vol. 1. Simla: Government of India Press.

—— (1944) *Burma During the Japanese Occupation,* vol. 2. Simla: Government of India Press.

Burma Provincial Banking Enquiry (BPBE) (1930a) *Report of the Burma Provincial Banking Enquiry Committee, 1929–1930, Volume I: Banking and Credit in Burma.* Rangoon: Superintendent of Government Printing.

—— (1930b) *Report of the Burma Provincial Banking Enquiry Committee, 1929–1930, Volume II: Surveys, Appendices and Questionnaire.* Rangoon: Superintendent of Government Printing.

Government of Burma (1900) *The Upper Burma Land Revenue Manual.* Rangoon: Superintendent of Government Printing.

—— (1915) *Report on the First Regular Settlement in the Myingyan District, 1909–1913.* Rangoon: Superintendent of Government Printing.

—— (1916) *Report on the Third Settlement of the Tharrawaddy District, 1913–1915.* Rangoon: Superintendent of Government Printing.

—— (1920) *A Handbook of Co-operation for Burma.* Rangoon: Superintendent of Government Printing.

—— (1929) *Report of the Committee on Co-operation in Burma, 1928–1929.* Rangoon: Superintendent of Government Printing.

—— (1930) *Report on Settlement Operations in Upper Chindwin District, 1926–1928.* Rangoon: Superintendent of Government Printing.

—— (1932) *Commissioner of Settlement and Land Records, Crop Report for 1930–1931.* Rangoon: Superintendent of Government Printing.

—— (1938) *Report of the Land and Agriculture Committee, Part III: Agricultural Finance; Colonisation; Land Purchase.* Rangoon: Superintendent of Government Printing.

—— (1939) *Report of the Riot Enquiry Committee.* Rangoon: Superintendent of Government Printing.

Government of the Union of Burma (1948a) *The Constitution of the Union of Burma.* Rangoon: Superintendent of Government Printing.

—— (1948b) *Two-Year Plan of Economic Development for Burma.* Rangoon: Superintendent of Government Printing.

—— (1949) *Report of the Committee on State Agricultural Bank 1948.* Rangoon: Superintendent of Government Printing.

—— (1950), *The Law and Principles of Co-operation in Burma.* Rangoon: Superintendent of Government Printing.

—— (1951) *Economic Survey of Burma 1951.* Rangoon: Superintendent of Government Printing.

—— (1952) *Economic Survey of Burma 1952.* Rangoon: Superintendent of Government Printing.

—— (1953) *Economic Survey of Burma 1953.* Rangoon: Superintendent of Government Printing.

—— (1954) *Economic Survey of Burma 1954.* Rangoon: Superintendent of Government Printing.

—— (1955a) *Economic Survey of Burma 1955.* Rangoon: Superintendent of Government Printing.

—— (1955b) *The Burma Code,* Volume X. Rangoon: Superintendent of Government Printing.

—— (1956) *Economic Survey of Burma 1956.* Rangoon: Superintendent of Government Printing.

—— (1957) *Economic Survey of Burma 1957.* Rangoon: Superintendent of Government Printing.

–– (1958a) *Economic Survey of Burma 1958*. Rangoon: Superintendent of Government Printing.

–– (1958b) *Tenth Anniversary Yearbook*. Rangoon: Superintendent of Government Printing.

–– (1959) *Economic Survey of Burma 1959*. Rangoon: Superintendent of Government Printing.

–– (1960a) *Economic Survey of Burma 1960*. Rangoon: Superintendent of Government Printing.

–– (1960b) *Is Trust Vindicated?* Rangoon: Director of Information, Government of the Union of Burma.

–– (1961a) *Economic Survey of the Union of Burma 1961*. Rangoon: Superintendent of Government Printing.

–– (1961b) *Second Four-Year Plan for The Union of Burma 1961–1962 to 1964–1965*, Rangoon: Government Printing Office.

–– (1975) *The Constitution (Fundamental Law) of the Socialist Republic of the Union of Burma*. Translation by Maya Swa Shin. Washington D.C.: Library of Congress.

Government of the Union of Myanmar (1990a) *Central Bank of Myanmar Law*. Rangoon: State Law and Order Restoration Council.

–– (1990b) *Financial Institutions of Myanmar Law*. Rangoon: State Law and Order Restoration Council.

–– (1996) *Review of the Financial, Economic and Social Conditions of the Union of Myanmar, 1995/96*. Yangon: Ministry of National Planning and Economic Development.

–– (2002) *Myanmar, Facts and Figures 2002*. Yangon: Ministry of Information.

Revolutionary Government of the Union of Burma (1962) *Economic Survey of the Union of Burma 1962*. Rangoon: Superintendent of Government Printing.

–– (1963) *Economic Survey of the Union of Burma 1963*. Rangoon: Superintendent of Government Printing.

–– (1967) *People's Bank of the Union of Burma Act, 1967*. Rangoon: Superintendent of Government Printing.

State Commercial Bank of the Union of Burma (1963) *Annual Report and Accounts, 1962*. Rangoon: State Commercial Bank.

Union Bank of Burma (1948) *Annual Report 1948*. Rangoon: Union Bank of Burma.

–– (1950) *Annual Report 1950*. Rangoon: Union Bank of Burma.

–– (1952) *The Union Bank of Burma Act, 1952*. Rangoon: Superintendent of Government Printing.

–– (1962) *Annual Report 1962*. Rangoon: Revolutionary Government of the Union of Burma.

–– (1963) *Annual Report 1963*. Rangoon: Revolutionary Government of the Union of Burma.

–– (1964) *Annual Report 1964*. Rangoon: Revolutionary Government of the Union of Burma.

Foreign Government and Multilateral Agencies

Asian Development Bank (ADB) (2003) *Asian Development Outlook 2003*. Manila: ADB.

–– (2004a) *Asian Development Outlook 2004*. Manila: ADB.

–– (2004b) *Asian Economic Monitor 2004*. Manila: ADB.

–– (2005) *Asian Development Bank Annual Report 2004*. Manila: ADB.

European Union (2005) 'Council common position of 21 February 2005, reviewing restrictive measures against Burma/Myanmar'. *Official Journal of the European Union*, L49, pp. 37–39.

Food and Agriculture Organisation of the United Nations (FAO) (2004a) *Myanmar: Agricultural Sector Review and Investment Strategy, Volume 1 – Sector Review*. Rome: FAO.

–– (2004b) *Myanmar: Agricultural Sector Review and Investment Strategy, Working Paper No. 9, Rural Finance*. Rome: FAO.

Government of Australia (1997) *The New ASEANS: Vietnam, Burma, Cambodia and Laos*. Canberra: East Asia Analytical Unit, Department of Foreign Affairs and Trade.

Government of India (1915) *Report of the Committee on Co-operation in Burma*. Simla: Government of India.

–– (1928) *Report of the Royal Commission of Agriculture in India*. London: His Majesty's Stationary Office.

–– (1930) *Madras Provincial Banking Enquiry Committee Report*, vol. III, *Written Evidence*. Madras: Government of India.

Government of the United Kingdom (1930) *Report of the Indian Statutory Commission*. London: His Majesty's Stationary Office (HMSO).

–– (1937) *The India and Burma (Burma Monetary Arrangements) Order, 1937*. London: HMSO.

International Labour Organisation (ILO) (2002) *Micro-Finance Interventions: Tools to Combat the Worst Forms of Child Labour Including Trafficking*. Bangkok: ILO.

International Monetary Fund (IMF) (1966) *International Financial Statistics, Yearbook 1966*. Washington D.C.: IMF.

–– (1968) *International Financial Statistics, Yearbook 1966*. Washington D.C.: IMF.

–– (1979) *International Financial Statistics, Yearbook 1979*. Washington D.C.: IMF.

-- (1989) *International Financial Statistics, Yearbook 1989.* Washington D.C.: IMF.

-- (1991) *International Financial Statistics, Yearbook 1991.* Washington D.C.: IMF.

-- (1995) *International Financial Statistics, Yearbook 1995.* Washington D.C.: IMF.

-- (1998) *International Financial Statistics, Yearbook 1998.* Washington D.C.: IMF.

-- (1999) *Myanmar: Statistical Appendix.* Washington D.C.: IMF.

-- (2003) *International Financial Statistics.* Various issues. Washington D.C.: IMF.

-- (2004) *International Financial Statistics.* Various issues. Washington D.C.: IMF.

-- (2006) *International Financial Statistics.* Various issues. Washington D.C., IMF.

-- (2007) *International Financial Statistics.* Various issues. Washington D.C., IMF.

United Nations Development Programme (UNDP) (2001) *Future Assistance to Myanmar.* Note by the Administrator of the UNDP's assistance programme in Myanmar and prepared for the Second Regular Session of the Executive Board of t h e UNDP, 10–14 September 2001. New York: UNDP.

-- (2003) *Human Development Initiative, Myanmar: Report of Independent Assessment Mission.* New York: UNDP.

-- (2005) *Human Development Initiative, Myanmar: Report of Independent Assessment Mission.* New York: UNDP.

United Nations Office for Project Services (UNOPS) (1998) *Micro-Credit Project: Myanmar.* Yangon: UNOPS.

-- (2005) *Sustainable Microfinance to Improve the Livelihoods of the Poor Project: Myanmar.* Bangkok: UNOPS.

United States Embassy (1998) *Burma, Country Commercial Guide 1998.* Rangoon: US Embassy.

World Bank (1972) *The Economy of the Union of Burma.* Washington D.C.: World Bank.

-- (1974) *Agricultural Development and Credit in the Union of Burma.* Washington D.C.: World Bank.

-- (1989) *World Development Report 1989.* New York: Oxford University Press for the World Bank.

-- (1995) *Myanmar: Policies for Sustaining Economic Reform.* Report no. 14063. Washington D.C.: World Bank.

-- (1999) *Myanmar: An Economic and Social Assessment.* Washington D.C.: World Bank.

-- (2002) *World Development Report 2002: Building Institutions for Markets.* New York: Oxford University Press for the World Bank.

MANUSCRIPT SOURCES

Archives of the Bank of England
Overseas Department, Burma, 1935–1970, OV/79.

The National Archives (Public Record Office), United Kingdom, Kew
Foreign Office: Political Departments, General Correspondence, Burma, FO371

Treasury: Finance, Overseas Development Division and Successors, T317

Treasury: Imperial and Foreign Division, T220

Treasury: Overseas Finance Division, Burma, T236

National Archives of Australia, Canberra
File of the High Commissioner, New Delhi, 1949, SN.1838/2

Oriental and India Office Collection, British Library

India Office Papers
Burma Miscellaneous, L/P, O/4

Burma Office Papers, M/3

Burma Office Private and Intelligence Files, M/5

Governor of Burma's Office, R/8

India Office Select Materials, Private Papers
Frank Siegfried Donnison, MSS Eur B357.

Arthur Kingscote Potter, MSS Eur C414

Echols Collection on Southeast Asia, Cornell University
Louis Walinsky Papers, Rare Manuscript Collection, no. 4874

South Asian Archive, Centre of South Asian Studies, University of Cambridge
C.W. Dunn Papers

British Empire and Commonwealth Museum, Bristol
Steel Brothers Records

NEWSPAPERS AND PERIODICALS

Business Times

Far Eastern Economic Review

The Financial Times

The Irrawaddy

The Myanmar Times and Weekly Review

The New Light of Myanmar

New Times of Burma

Rangoon Times

Times of Burma

JOURNAL ARTICLES AND MONOGRAPHS

Adas, M. (1974a) *The Burma Delta: Economic Development and Social Change on an Asian Rice Frontier, 1852–1941.* Madison: University of Wisconsin Press.

–– (1974b) 'Immigrant Asians and the economic impact of European imperialism: The role of the South Indian Chettiars in British Burma'. *The Journal of Asian Studies.* vol. 33, no. 3, pp. 385–401.

Alba, P. (1999) 'Financial liberalisation and the capital account: Thailand, 1988–1997'. *World Bank Policy Research Working Paper* 2188.

Allen, L. (1984) *Burma, The Longest War 1941–45.* London: J.M. Dent and Sons.

Allen, R.L. (1958) 'Burma's clearing accounts arrangements'. *Pacific Affairs,* vol. 31, no. 2, pp. 147–162.

Andrus, J.R. (1936) 'Three economic systems clash in Burma'. *The Review of Economic Studies,* vol. 3, no. 2, February, pp. 140–146.

–– (1948) *Burmese Economic Life.* Stanford: Stanford University Press.

Ardeth Maung Thawnghmung (2004) *Behind the Teak Curtain.* London: Kegan Paul.

Arianto, S.A. (2004) 'Commercialization of microfinance and linkages between microfinance and commercial banking', paper presented to the International Microfinance Workshop, 8–9 December 2004, Phnom Penh, Cambodia.

Armendáriz de Aghion, B and J. Morduch, (2005) 'Microfinance: Where do we stand?'. In C.A.E. Goodhart (ed), *Financial Development and Economic Growth.* London: Palgrave Macmillan.

Asian Economic Research Institute (AERI) (1961) *Economic Development in Burma.* Asian Economic Research Institute: Tokyo.

Aung Din Taylor, D. (2002) 'Signs of distress: Observations on agriculture, poverty, and the environment in Myanmar', paper delivered to the Conference on Burma: Reconciliation in Myanmar and the Crises of Change, School of Advanced International Affairs, Johns Hopkins University, Washington D.C., 22 November 2002.

Aung San Suu Kyi (1995) *Freedom from Fear,* revised edn. London: Penguin Books.

Aye Hlaing (1958) 'Some aspects of seasonal agricultural loans in Burma'. *Department of Economics, Statistics and Commerce Working Paper No. 14.* University of Rangoon: Rangoon.

Bagchi, A.K. (1989) *The Presidency Banks and the Indian Economy, 1876–1914.* Calcutta: Oxford University Press.

—— (2000) 'The past and the future of the development state'. *Journal of World Systems Research,* vol. 6, no. 2, pp. 398–442.

Bagehot, W. (1873 [1999]) *Lombard Street.* London: John Wiley and Sons.

Banerji, S.C. (1963) 'Burma: nationalisation and aftermath'. *Far Eastern Economic Review,* 12 April 1963: 106–107.

Bannerjee, A., T. Besley, and T. Guinnane (1994) 'Thy neighbor's keeper: The design of a credit cooperative, with theory and a test'. *The Quarterly Journal of Economics,* vol. 109, no. 2, pp. 491–515.

Basch, A. (1964) *Financing Economic Development.* New York: Macmillan.

Bauer, P. and G.M. Meier (1994) 'Traders and development'. In G.M. Meier (ed), *From Classical Economics to Development Economics: Essays in Honour of Hla Myint.* London: Macmillan, pp. 135–143.

Bayly, C. and T. Harper (2004) *Forgotten Armies: The Fall of British Asia, 1941–1945.* London: Allen Lane.

Berenbach, S. and D. Guzman (1994) 'The solidarity group experience worldwide'. In M. Otero and E. Rhyne (eds), *The New World of Microenterprise Finance: Building Healthy Financial Institutions for the Poor.* West Hartford: Kumarian Press, pp. 119–139.

Besley, T. and S. Coate (1995) 'Group lending, repayment incentives and social collateral'. *Journal of Development Economics,* vol.46, February, pp.1–18.

Binns, B.O. (1946) *Agricultural Economy in Burma.* Rangoon: Government of Burma Printing and Stationery.

Bodenhorn, H. (2000) *A History of Banking in Antebellum America.* Cambridge: Cambridge University Press.

Bonus, H. (1986) 'The cooperative association as a business enterprise: A study in the economics of transactions'. *Journal of Theoretical and Institutional Economics,* vol. 142, pp. 180–207.

Boquérat, G. (2001) 'India's confrontation with Chinese interests in Myanmar'. In F. Grare and A. Mattoo (eds), *India and ASEAN: The Politics of India's Look East Policy.* New Delhi: Manohar CCH.

Boyle, A. (1967) *Montagu Norman.* London: Cassell.

Bradford, W. (2004a) 'Purchasing power estimates for Burma'. *Burma Economic Watch,* no. 1 2004, pp. 4–18.

–– (2004b) *'Fiant fruges?* Burma's *sui generis* growth experience'. *Burma Economic Watch,* no. 2 2004, pp. 6–14.

Brown, I. (2005a) *A Colonial Economy in Crisis: Burma's Rice Cultivators and the World Depression of the 1930s.* London: Routledge Curzon.

–– (2005b) 'Blindness which we mistake for sight: British officials and the economic world of the cultivator in colonial Burma'. *The Journal of Imperial and Commonwealth History,* vol. 33, no. 2, May, pp. 181–193.

Brown, R. (1990) 'Chinese business and banking in South-East Asia since 1870'. In G. Jones (ed), *Banks as Multinationals.* London: Routledge.

–– (1993) 'Chettiar capital and Southeast Asian credit networks in the inter-war period'. In G. Austin and K. Sugihara (eds), *Local Suppliers of Credit in the Third World, 1750– 1960.* New York: St. Martin's Press.

Butwell, R. (1963) *U Nu of Burma.* Stanford: Stanford University Press.

Cady, J.F. (1958) *A History of Modern Burma.* Ithaca: Cornell University Press.

Cain, P.J and A.G. Hopkins (2001) *British Imperialism, 1688–2000.* 2nd edn. Harlow: Longman.

Callahan, M.P. (2000) 'Cracks in the edifice: Military-society relations in Burma since 1988'. In M. Pedersen, E. Rudland and R.J. May, *Burma Myanmar: Strong Regime Weak State.* Adelaide: Crawford House, pp. 22–51.

–– (2003) *Making Enemies: War and State Building in Burma.* Ithaca: Cornell University Press.

Calvert, H. (1959) *The Law and Principles of Cooperation.* Calcutta: Thacker Spink.

Chakravarti, N.R. (1971) *The Indian Minority in Burma.* London: Oxford University Press.

Chan, Won-Loy (1986) *Burma: The Untold Story.* Novato, California: Presidio Press.

Chapman, S. (1985) *The Rise of Merchant Banking.* London: Unwin Hyman.

Cheng, L. (2003) *Banking in Modern China: Entrepreneurs, Professional Managers, and the Development of Chinese Banks, 1897–1937.* Cambridge: Cambridge University Press.

Cheng Siok-Hwa (1968) *The Rice Industry of Burma, 1852–1940.* Kuala Lumpur: University of Malaya Press.

Chew, E. (1979) 'The fall of the Burmese kingdom in 1885: Review and reconsideration'. *Journal of Southeast Asian Studies,* vol. 10, pp. 372–380.

Chidambaram Trust (2004) *The Unfinished Journey: The Story of M.Ct.M Chidambaram Chettyar.* Chennai: Chidambaram Trust.

Christen, R.P. (2001) 'Commercialization and mission drift: The transformation of microfinance in Latin America'. *CGAP Occasional Paper,* no. 5, Washington D.C.: World Bank.

Christian, J.L. (1942) *Modern Burma.* Berkeley: University of California Press.

—— (1945) *Burma*. London: Collins.

—— (1945) *Burma and the Japanese Invader.* Bombay: Thacker and Company.

Collignon, S. (2001) 'Human rights and the economy in Burma'. In R.H. Taylor (ed), *Burma: Political Economy under Military Rule.* London: C. Hurst.

Collis, M. (1956) *Last and First in Burma.* London: Faber & Faber.

—— (1965) *Wayfoong: The Hongkong and Shanghai Banking Corporation.* London: Faber & Faber.

Consultative Group to Assist the Poorest (CGAP) (2004) 'Key principles of microfinance'. Document released by CGAP and endorsed by the Group of Eight leaders at the G8 Summit, 10 June 2004.

Cook, P. and M. Minogue (1993) 'Economic reform and political change in Myanmar (Burma)'. *World Development,* vol. 21, no. 7, pp. 1151–1161.

Cooper, C.L. (1959) *Moneylenders and the Economic Development of Lower Burma – An Exploratory Historical Study of the Role of the Indian Chettyars.* Unpublished doctoral dissertation, The American University, Washington, D.C.

Copland, J. (2004) 'The agricultural sector and the role of international assistance in promoting agricultural reform in Myanmar', paper presented to the *Burma Update Conference,* Australian National University, Canberra, 18–19 November 2004.

Dapice, D. (2003) 'Current economic conditions in Myanmar and options for sustainable growth'. Global Development and Environment Institute Working Paper no. 03–04, Tufts University, May.

Darling, M. (1932) *The Punjab Peasant in Prosperity and Debt,* 3rd edn. Bombay: Oxford University Press.

—— (1947) *The Punjab Peasant in Prosperity and Debt,* 4th Edn. Bombay: Oxford University Press.

Davies, G. (1994) *A History of Money: From Ancient Times to the Present Day.* Cardiff: University of Wales Press.

Dayer, R.A. (1988) *Finance and Empire: Sir Charles Addis, 1861–1945.* New York: St Martin's Press.

De Juan, A. (1996) 'The roots of banking crises: Microeconomic issues and regulation and supervision'. In R. Hausammn and L. Rojas-Suarez (eds), *Banking Crises in Latin America.* Washington D.C.: John Hopkins University Press: pp. 83–102.

De Soto, H. (2000) *The Mystery of Capital: Why Capitalism Triumphs in the West and Fails Everywhere Else.* London: Bantam Press.

Delhaise, P. (1998) *Asia in Crisis: The Implosion of the Banking and Financial Systems.* Singapore: John Wiley and Sons.

Diamond, D.W. and P.H. Dybvig. (1983) 'Bank runs, deposit insurance, and liquidity'. *Journal of Political Economy,* vol. 91, pp. 401–419.

Do, Q.T. and L. Iyer (2003) 'Land rights and economic development; Evidence from Vietnam'. *World Bank Policy Research Working Paper Series*, no. 3120.

Donnison, F.S.V. (1956) *British Military Administration in the Far East, 1943–46*. London: Her Majesty's Stationery Office.

Drake, P.J. (1980) *Money, Finance and Development*. Oxford: Martin Robertson.

—— (2004) *Currency, Credit and Commerce: Early Growth in Southeast Asia*. Aldershot: Ashgate.

Economist Intelligence Unit (EIU) (2002) *Myanmar (Burma), Country Profile 2002*. London: Economist Intelligence Unit.

—— (2003a) *Myanmar (Burma), Country Report May 2003*. London: Economist Intelligence Unit.

—— (2003b) *Myanmar (Burma), Country Report August 2003*. London: Economist Intelligence Unit.

—— (2004) *Myanmar (Burma), Country Report* August. London: Economist Intelligence Unit.

—— (2006) *Myanmar (Burma), Country Profile 2006*. London: Economist Intelligence Unit.

Eichengreen, B. and C. Arteta (2000) 'Banking crises in emerging markets: Presumptions and evidence'. *Center for International and Development Economics Research Paper*. University of California, Berkeley, no. 115.

El Hawary, D. and W. Grais (2005) 'The compatibility of Islamic financial services and microfinance'. *Microfinance Matters*, no. 14, July.

Emery, R.F. (1970) *The Financial Institutions of Southeast Asia*. New York: Praeger.

Enoch, C., O. Frecaut, and A. Kovanen (2003) 'Indonesia's banking crisis: What happened and what did we learn'. *Bulletin of Indonesian Economic Studies*, vol. 39, pp. 75–92.

Fase, M.M.G. and R.C.N. Abma (2003) 'Financial environment and economic growth in selected Asian countries'. *Journal of Asian Economics*, vol. 14, pp. 11–21.

Ferrars, M and B. Ferras. (1901) *Burma*. London: Sampson Low and Marston.

Fink, C. (2001) *Living Silence: Burma under Military Rule*. Bangkok: White Lotus.

Foucar, E.C.V. (1956) *I Lived in Burma*. London: Dobson.

Fraser, J.F. (1998[1899]) 'Pawnshops and pagodas'. In N. Greenwood (ed) *Shades of Gold and Green: Anecdotes of Colonial Burmah, 1886–1948*. New Delhi: Asian Educational Services.

Frydl, E.J. and M. Quintyn (2000) 'The benefits and costs of intervening in banking crises'. *IMF Working Paper* 00/147. Washington D.C.: International Monetary Fund.

Fujita, K. and I. Okamoto (2006) 'Agricultural policies and the development of Myanmar's agricultural sector'. *Institute of Developing Economies, Working Paper No.63*. Chiba, Japan: Institute of Developing Economies.

Fukui, R. and G.M. Llanto (2003) 'Rural finance and microfinance development in transition countries in Southeast and East Asia'. *Philippine Institute for Development Studies Discussion Paper Series*, no. 2003–12, August.

Furnivall, J.S. (1909) 'Land as a free gift of nature'. *The Economic Journal*, vol. 19, no. 76, December, pp. 552–562.

–– (1956) *Colonial Policy and Practice*. New York: New York University Press.

–– (1958) *The Governance of Burma*. New York: Institute of Pacific Relations.

Galbraith, J.K. (1987) 'Robert R. Nathan'. In J. Eatwell, M. Milgate and P. Newman (eds), *The New Palgrave: A Dictionary of Economics*. London: Macmillan.

Gershenkron, A. (1962) *Economic Backwardness in Historical Perspective*. Cambridge, Mass.: Harvard University Press.

Ghate, P. (1992) *Informal Finance: Some Findings from Asia*. Oxford: Oxford University Press for the Asian Development Bank.

Golay, F.H., R. Anspach, M. Pfanner, and E.B. Ayal (1969) *Underdevelopment and Economic Nationalism in Southeast Asia*. Ithaca: Cornell University Press.

Goldsmith, R.W. (1969) *Financial Structure and Development*. New Haven: Yale University Press.

–– (1983) *The Financial Development of India, 1860–1977*. New Haven: Yale University Press.

Goldstein, M. and P. Turner (1996) 'Banking crises in emerging economies: Origins and policy options'. *BIS Economic Papers* 46. Geneva: Bank for International Settlements.

Gonzalez-Vega, C. (1998) 'Microfinance: Broader achievements and challenges'. *Economics and Sociology Occasional Paper* no. 2518, Rural Finance Program, Ohio State University.

Goodheart, C.A.E. (1995) *The Central Bank and the Financial System*. Cambridge, Mass.: MIT Press.

–– (ed) (2002) *Financial Crises, Contagion, and the Lender of Last Resort; A Reader*. Oxford: Oxford University Press.

Gotts, H.C. (1973) 'Operation Shylock'. *The Dark Horse* (Lloyds Bank staff magazine). September, pp. 508–510.

Grameen Trust (2000) 'Myanmar: Hope for Women'. *Grameen Dialogue*, no. 42, April, <http://asp.grameen.com/dialogue>.

Guinnane, T. (1997) 'Cooperatives as information machines: German Rural Credit Cooperatives, 1883–1914. *University of Copenhagen, Department of Economics, Discussion Paper no. 97–20*.

Gurley, J.G. and E.S. Shaw (1955) 'Financial aspects of economic development'. *American Economic Review*, vol. 45, no. 3, pp. 515–538.

Harvey, G.E. (1946) *British Rule in Burma: 1824–1942*. London: Faber & Faber.

Helms, B. and X. Reilla (2004) 'Interest rate ceilings and microfinance: The story so far'. *Consultative Group to Assist the Poorest, Occasional Paper*, no. 9, September.

Hempel, G.H. and D.G. Simonson (1999) *Bank Management*. New York: John Wiley and Sons.

Hla Maung (1971) 'Beginning of American aid to Burma'. In S.P. Hayes (ed), *The Beginning of American Aid to Southeast Asia: The Griffin Mission of 1950*. Lexington, Mass: Heath Lexington Books, pp. 201–222.

Hla Myint (1958) 'The classical theory of international trade and the undeveloped countries'. *Economic Journal*, vol. 68, June, pp. 317–337.

— (1963) *The Economics of Developing Countries*. London: Hutchinson.

— (1971) *Economic Theory and the Underdeveloped Countries*. Oxford: Oxford University Press.

Hla Pe (1961) *U Hla Pe's Narrative of the Japanese Occupation of Burma*. Recording by U Khin. Ithaca: Department of Far Eastern Studies, Cornell University.

Hoggarth, G., P. Jackson and E. Nier (2005) 'Banking crises and the design of safety nets'. *Journal of Banking and Finance*, vol. 29, pp. 143–159.

Honda, Y. (2002) 'Microfinance in Myanmar'. *DBJ Dispatch*, vol. 10, March, p. 7.

Honohan, P. (1997) 'Banking system failures in developing and transition economies: Diagnosis and prediction'. *BIS Working Paper* 39. Geneva: Bank for International Settlements.

Indian Institute of Bankers (1963) 'Editorial comment: Nationalisation of banks in Burma'. *The Journal of the Indian Institute of Bankers*, vol. XXXIV, no. 2, February: 78–79.

International Crisis Group (2001) *Myanmar: The Role of Civil Society*. Asia Report No. 27. Bangkok/Brussels: International Crisis Group.

International Crisis Group (2006) *Myanmar: New Threats to Humanitarian Aid*. Asia Briefing no. 58. Yangon/Brussels: International Crisis Group.

International Crisis Group (2008) *Burma/Myanmar: After the Crackdown*. Asia Report no. 144. Yangon/Jakarta/Brussels: International Crisis Group.

Jain, L.C. (1929) *Indigenous Banking in India*. London: Macmillan.

Johnston, D. (1999) *Roman Law in Context*. Cambridge: Cambridge University Press.

Jones, G. (1993) *British Multinational Banking 1830–1990*. Oxford: Clarendon Press.

Jost, P.M. and H.S. Sandhu (2000) *The Hawala Alternative Remittance System and its Role in Money Laundering*. Lyon: Interpol General Secretariat.

Keeton, C.L. (1974) *King Thebaw and the Ecological Rape of Burma*. Delhi: Manohar Book Service.

Keynes, J.M. (1913) *Indian Currency and Finance*. London: Macmillan.

Khin Mar Cho and R. Boland (2002) *Participatory Learning for Agricultural Extension and Future Development in Myanmar*. Paper presented to Deutscher Tropentag 2002, University of Kassel, Witzenhausen, Germany, 9–11 October 2002.

— (2004) 'Agricultural training in Myanmar: Extension agents' perceptions of training needs'. *Journal of International Agricultural and Extension Education,* vol. 11, no.1, Spring, pp. 5–15.

Khin Maung Kyi, R. Findlay, R.M. Sundrum, Mya Maung, Myo Nyunt and Zaw Oo (2000) *Economic Development of Burma: A Vision and a Strategy.* Stockholm: Olaf Palme International Centre.

Khin Maung Nyunt (1990) *Foreign Loans and Aid in the Economic Development of Burma, 1974/75 to 1985/86.* Bangkok: Institute of Asian Studies, Chulalongkorn University.

Khin San Yee (1997) *Cooperatives in Myanmar: Performance and Perspective.* Kiel: Wissenschaftsverlag Vauk Kiel KG.

Khin Than Kywe (1960) 'Financing the small manufacturing establishments of Burma'. *Burma Research Society Fiftieth Anniversary Publications,* no. 1, January, pp. 107–147.

King, F.H.H. (1987) *The History of the Hongkong and Shanghai Banking Corporation, Volume I: The Hongkong Bank in Late Imperial China, 1864–1902.* Cambridge: Cambridge University Press.

— (1988a) *The History of the Hongkong and Shanghai Banking Corporation, Volume II: The Hongkong Bank in the Period of Imperialism and War, 1895–1918.* Cambridge: Cambridge University Press.

— (1988b) *The History of the Hongkong and Shanghai Banking Corporation, Volume III: The Hongkong Bank Between the Wars and the Bank Interned, 1919–1945.* Cambridge: Cambridge University Press.

— (1990) 'Structural alternatives and constraints in the evolution of exchange banking'. In G. Jones (ed), *Banks as Multinationals.* London: Routledge.

— (1991) *The History of the Hongkong and Shanghai Banking Corporation, Volume IV: The Hongkong Bank in the Period of Development and Nationalism, 1941–1984.* Cambridge: Cambridge University Press.

King, R.G. and R. Levine (1993a) 'Finance and growth: Schumpeter might be right'. *Quarterly Journal of Economics,* vol. 108, August, pp. 717–737.

— (1993b) 'Finance, entrepreneurship, and growth: Theory and evidence'. *Journal of Monetary Economics,* vol. 32, December, pp. 513–542.

Kisch, C.H. (1928) *Central Banks.* London: Macmillan.

Knappen, Tippetts and Abbott Engineering Company (KTA) (1953) *K.T.A. Comprehensive Report, Economic and Engineering Development of Burma.* Rangoon: Knappen Tippetts Abbett McCarthy, Engineers, in association with Pierce Management, Inc., and Robert R. Nathan Associates.

KPMG (1995) *Investment in Myanmar.* Singapore: KPMG Peat Marwick.

Kumar, D. (1983) *The Cambridge Economic History of India, Volume 2: 1757–1970.* Cambridge: Cambridge University Press.

Kyaw Min (1945) *The Burma We Love.* Calcutta: Bharati Bhavan.

La Porta, R., F. Lopez-de-Silanes, A. Shliefer and R.W. Vishny (1998) 'Law and Finance'. *Journal of Political Economy,* vol. 106, no. 6, pp. 1113–1155.

Latter, T. (1997) 'Causes and Management of Banking Crises'. *Handbooks in Central Banking* 12. London: Centre for Central Banking Studies, Bank of England.

Ledgerwood, J. (1999) *Micro-finance Handbook: An Institutional and Financial Perspective.* Washington D.C.: World Bank.

Levine, R., L. Norman, and B. Thurston (2000) 'Financial intermediation and growth: Causality and causes'. *Journal of Monetary Economics,* vol. 46, pp. 31–77.

Lieberman, V. (1991) 'Secular trends in Burmese economic history, c.1350–1830, and their implications for state formation'. *Modern Asian Studies,* vol. 25, no. 1, pp. 1–31.

Lindgren, C, G. Garcia and M. Sal (1996) *Bank Soundness and Macroeconomic Policy.* Washington D.C.: International Monetary Fund.

Linter, B. (1990) *Outrage: Burma's Struggle for Democracy.* London: White Lotus.

—— (1999) *Burma in Revolt: Opium and Insurgency since 1948.* Bangkok: Silkworm Press.

Littlefield, E. and R. Rosenberg (2004) 'Microfinance and the poor'. *Finance and Development,* vol. 41, no. 2, June, pp. 38–40.

Longmuir, M. (2002) *The Money Trail: Burmese Currencies in Crisis, 1937–1947.* DeCalb, Illinois: Southeast Asian Publications.

McGuire, P.B. and J.D. Conroy (2000) 'The microfinance phenomenon'. *Asia–Pacific Review,* vol. 7, Is. 1, May, pp. 109–130.

McKinnon, R.I. (1973) *Money and Capital in Economic Development.* Washington D.C.: Brookings Institution.

Mackenzie, C. (1954) *Realms of Silver: One Hundred Years of Banking in the East.* London: Routledge.

Marshall, A. (2002) *The Trouser People.* London: Viking.

Maung Hla Thing (2004) *The Establishment of Myanmar Securities Market and the Role of the MSEC.* Rangoon: Central Bank of Myanmar.

Maung Thin Aung (1965) *The Stricken Peacock: Anglo-Burmese Relations, 1752–1948.* The Hague: Inhofe.

Maung Maung (1969) *Burma and General Ne Win.* New York: Asia Publishing House.

—— (1980) *From Sangha to Laity: Nationalist Movements of Burma, 1920–1940.* Delhi: Menorah.

—— (1989) *Burmese Nationalist Movements 1940–1948.* Honolulu: University of Hawaii Press.

Maung Hla (1960) 'Some aspects of central banking in Burma'. *Burma Research Society Fiftieth Anniversary Publications,* no. 1, January, pp. 147–155.

Maw Than and Nun Sew (2000) 'Overview of demand for capital for Myanmar's development'. In Mya Than and Myat Thein (eds), *Financial Resources for Development in Myanmar: Lessons from Asia.* Singapore: Institute of Southeast Asian Studies, pp. 25–52.

Meier, G.M. (ed) (1994) *From Classical Economics to Development Economics: Essays in Honor of Hla Myint.* London: Macmillan Press.

Mi Chafing (1956) *Burmese Family.* Bangkok: Aver House.

Mieno, F. (2006) 'Determinants of debt, bank loan and trade credit of private firms in the transitional period: The case of Myanmar'. In Mariko Watanabe (ed), *Recovering Financial Systems: China and Asian Transition Economies.* Hampshire: Palgrave Macmillan.

Morduch, J. (1999) 'The microfinance promise'. *Journal of Economic Literature,* vol. 37, no. 4, December, pp. 1569–1614.

Mya Maung (1965) 'Agricultural co-operation in Burma: A study on the value orientation and effects of socio-economic action'. *Social and Economic Studies,* vol. 14, pp. 321–338.

–– (1966) 'The elephant catching co-operative society of Burma: A case study on the effect of planned socio-economic change'. *Asian Survey,* vol. 6, June, pp. 327–337.

–– (1971) *Burma and Pakistan: A Comparative Study of Development.* New York: Praeger.

–– (1991) *The Burma Road to Poverty.* New York: Praeger.

–– (1998) *The Burma Road to Capitalism.* New York: Praeger.

Myint Tin (2000) 'Creating domestic investment via the banking system in Myanmar'. In Mya Than and Myat Thein (eds), *Financial Resources for Development in Myanmar: Lessons from Asia.* Singapore: Institute of Southeast Asian Studies, pp. 72–107.

Mya Than (1988) *Growth Pattern of Burmese Agriculture: A Productivity Approach.* Occasional Paper no. 81. Singapore: Institute of Southeast Asian Studies.

–– (1997) 'Economic transformation in mainland Southeast Asia: The case of Myanmar'. In J.H. Brandon (ed), *Burma/Myanmar: Towards the Twenty-First Century.* Bangkok: Open Society Institute.

–– (2000) 'Changing faces of the Myawaddy (Irrawaddy) Delta (1850–2000)'. *The Chaos Praia Delta: Historical Development, Dynamics and Challenges of Thailand's Rice Bowl.* Conference, Kasetsart University, 12–14 December.

Mya Than and N. Nishizawa (1990) 'Agricultural policy reforms and agricultural development in Myanmar'. In Mya Than and J.L. Tan (eds), *Myanmar Dilemmas and Options: The Challenge of Economic Transition in the 1990s.* Singapore: Institute of Southeast Asian Studies, pp. 89–116.

Mya Than and J.L. Tan (eds) (1990) *Myanmar Dilemmas and Options: The Challenge of Economic Transition in the 1990s.* Singapore: Institute of Southeast Asian Studies.

Mya Than and Myat Thein (eds) 2000, *Financial Resources for Development in Myanmar: Lessons from Asia.* Singapore: Institute of Southeast Asian Studies.

Myat Thein (1990) 'Monetary and fiscal policies for development'. In Mya Than and J.L. Tan (eds), *Myanmar Dilemmas and Options: The Challenge of Economic Transition in the 1990s.* Singapore: Institute of Southeast Asian Studies, pp. 53–88.

–– (2004) *Economic Development of Myanmar.* Singapore: Institute of Southeast Asian Studies.

Myat Thein and Mya Than (1995) 'Transitional economy of Myanmar: Performance, issues and problems'. In S.F Naya and J.L.H. Tan (eds) *Asian Transitional Economies: Challenges and Prospects for Reform and Transformation.* Singapore: Institute of Southeast Asian Studies.

Nagarajan, G. and R.L. Meyer (2005) 'Rural finance: Recent advances and emerging lessons, debates and opportunities'. *Department of Agricultural, Environmental, and Development Economics Working Paper,* no. AEDE-WP-0041-05. Ohio State University.

Nash, M. (1965) *The Golden Road to Modernity.* Chicago: University of Chicago Press.

Oak, M.P. and A.V. Swamy (2005) 'Only twice as much: A rule for regulating lenders'. Paper presented to the Northeastern Universities' Development Consortium Conference, Brown University, Providence, Rhode Island, 23–25 September 2005.

Okamoto, I., K. Kurita, T. Kurosaki and K. Fujita (2003) *Rich Periphery, Poor Center: Myanmar's Rural Economy under Partial Transition to a Market Economy.* Institute of Economic Research, Hitotsubashi University, Discussion Paper Series, no. 03–23.

Peam, B.R. (1946) *The Indian in Burma.* Ledbury: LePlay House Press.

Pfanner, D.E. (1962) *Rice and Religion in a Burmese Village,* unpublished doctoral dissertation, Faculty of the Graduate School, Cornell University.

Pham, J. (2005) 'J.S. Furnivall and Fabianism: Reinterpreting the "plural society" in Burma'. *Modern Asian Studies,* vol. 39, no. 2, pp. 321–348.

Pierce, J.L. (1997) 'Developments in Myanmar: New frontiers for banking'. *Journal of International Banking Law,* vol. 11, pp. 441–445.

Pointon, A.C. (1974) *Wallace Brothers.* Oxford: Oxford University Press.

Pollack, O.B. (1980) *Empires in Collision: Anglo-Burmese Relations in the Mid-Nineteenth Century.* London: Greenwood Press.

Prescott, E.S. (1997) 'Group lending and financial intermediation: An example'. *Federal Reserve Bank of Richmond, Economic Quarterly,* vol. 83, no. 4, Fall, pp. 23–48.

Rahman, A (1998) 'Microcredit initiatives for equitable and sustainable development: Who pays?'. *World Development,* vol. 27, no. 1, January, pp. 67–82.

Rahman, M.S. (2003) *Direct Aid Delivery – Reaching the Hardcore Poor: UNDP/CBO Case Study in Myanmar.* New York: United Nations Department of Economic and Social Affairs.

Ray, R.K. (1995) 'Asian capital in the age of European domination: The rise of the bazaar, 1800–1914'. *Modern Asian Studies,* vol. 29, no. 3, pp. 449–554.

Richter, H.V. (1968) 'State agricultural credit in postwar Burma'. *The Malayan Economic Review,* vol. XIII, no. 1, April.

Robert, B.L. (1983) 'Agricultural credit cooperatives, rural development, and agrarian politics in Madras, 1893–1937'. In J.D. Von Pishke, D.W Adams and G. Donald (eds) 1983, *Rural Financial Markets in Developing Countries: Their Use and Abuse.* Baltimore: Johns Hopkins Press for the Economic Development Institute of the World Bank, pp. 354–362.

Roberts, T.D. (ed) (1968) *Area Handbook for Burma*. Washington D.C.: Foreign Area Studies, American University and U.S. Government Printing Office.

Robinson, J. (1933) *The Economics of Imperfect Competition*. London: Macmillan.

–– (1952) 'The generalization of the General Theory'. In *The Rate of Interest and Other Essays*. London: Macmillan.

Robinson, M.S. (2001) *The Microfinance Revolution: Sustainable Finance for the Poor*. Washington D.C.: World Bank.

Robinson, M. and L.A. Shaw (1980) *The Coins and Banknotes of Burma*. Manchester: Lancashire and Cheshire Numismatic Society.

Rudner, D.W. (1989) 'Bankers' trust and the culture of banking amongst the Nattukottai Chettiars of colonial South India'. *Modern Asian Studies*, vol. 23, no. 3, pp. 417–458.

–– (1994) *Caste and Capitalism in Colonial India: The Nattukottai Chettiars*. Berkeley: University of California Press.

Saito, T. (1997) 'Rural monetization and land-mortgage *Thet-Kayits* in Kon-baung Burma'. In A. Reid (ed), *The Last Stand of Asian Autonomies*. London: Macmillan.

Sayers, R.S. (1952) *Banking in the British Commonwealth*. Oxford: Clarendon Press.

–– (1957) *Central Banking after Bagehot*. Oxford: Clarendon Press.

Schumpeter, J. (1911) *The Theory of Economic Development*. Cambridge Mass: Harvard University Press.

Sharma, A. (2002) 'Developing sustainable microfinance systems'. In *Rejuvenating Bank Finance for Development in Asia and the Pacific*. New York: Economic and Social Commission for Asia and the Pacific, United Nations, and Asian Development Bank.

Shaw, E.S. (1973) *Financial Deepening in Economic Development*. New York: Oxford University Press.

Sheng, A. (1996) *Bank Restructuring Lessons from the 1980s*. Washington D.C.: World Bank.

Seshadri, R.K. (1982) *A Swadeshi Bank from South India*. Bombay: Orient Longmans.

Siegleman, P. (1962) *Colonial Development and the Chettyar: A Study in the Ecology of Modern Burma, 1850–1941*, unpublished doctoral dissertation, University of Minnesota.

Silverstein, J. (1977) *Burma: Military Rule and the Politics of Stagnation*. Ithaca: Cornell University Press.

Singh, B. (2001) *Burma's Democratic Decade 1952–1962: Prelude to Dictatorship*. Tempe, Arizona: Arizona State University.

Skidmore, M. (2004) *Karaoke Fascism: Burma and the Politics of Fear*. Philadelphia: University of Pennsylvania Press.

Smith, A. (1910 [1776]) *An Inquiry into the Nature and Causes of the Wealth of Nations*. London: Dent and Son.

Starr, P. (2002) *Citibank: A Century in Asia*. Singapore: Editions Didier Millet.

Steinberg, D.I. (1981a) 'Burmese economics: The conflict of ideology and pragmatism'. In F.K. Lehman (ed), *Military rule in Burma Since 1962*. Singapore: Maruzen Asia in association with the Institute of Southeast Asian Studies.

— (1981b) *Burma's Road Toward Development: Growth and Ideology Under Military Rule*. Boulder: Westview Press.

— (2001) *Burma: The State of Myanmar*. Washington D.C.: Georgetown University Press.

— (2005) 'Burma/Myanmar: The role of the military in the economy'. *Burma Economic Watch*, no. 1/2005, pp. 51–78.

Stiglitz, J.E. (1990) *'Peer* monitoring in credit markets'. *World Bank Economic Review*, vol. IV, pp. 315–366.

Sundrum, R.M. (1994) 'Exports and economic growth'. In G.M. Meier (ed), *From Classical Economics to Development Economics: Essays in Honour of Hla Myint*. London: Macmillan, pp.104–120.

Swinnen, J.F.M. and H.R. Gow (1999) 'Agricultural credit problems and policies during the transition to a market economy in central and eastern Europe'. *Food Policy*, vol. 24, pp. 21–47.

Tamaki, N. (1990) 'The Yokohama Specie Bank: A multinational in the Japanese interest 1879–1931'. In G. Jones (ed) *Banks as Multinationals*. London: Routledge.

Tandon, P. (1988) *Banking Century: A Short History*. New Delhi: Penguin.

Taylor, R.H. (ed) (2001) *Burma: Political Economy under Military Rule*. London: C. Hurst.

Thant Myint-U (2001) *The Making of Modern Burma*. Cambridge: Cambridge University Press.

— (2006) *The River of Lost Footsteps: Histories of Burma*. New York: Farrar, Strauss and Giroux.

Theroux, P. (1971) 'Burma'. *The Atlantic Monthly*, vol. 228, no. 5, November, pp. 37–45.

Thet Tun (2001) *The Contemporary Myanmar: Selected Writings of U Thet Tun*. Yangon: Myanmar Business Magazine.

Thurston, E. (1909) *Castes and Tribes of Southern India*. Madras: Government of India.

Timberg, T.A. and C.V. Aiyer (1984) 'Informal credit markets in India'. *Economic Development and Cultural Change*, vol. 33, no. 1, pp. 43–59.

Tin Maung Thet (2000) 'Creating domestic investments via the financial system in Myanmar'. In Mya Than and Myat Thein (eds), *Financial Resources for Development in Myanmar: Lessons from Asia*. Singapore: Institute of Southeast Asian Studies, pp. 93–107.

Tin Soe and B.S. Fisher (1990) 'An economic analysis of Burmese rice-price policies'. In Mya Than and J.L. Tan (eds), *Myanmar Dilemmas and Options: The Challenge of Economic Transition in the 1990s*. Singapore: Institute of Southeast Asian Studies, pp. 117–166.

Tin Yee (2004) *The Socio-Economic Life of the Wah National.* Yangon: National Centre for Human Resource Development, Ministry of Education, Government of the Union of Myanmar.

Tinker, H. (1957) *The Union of Burma: A Study of the First Years of Independence.* London: Oxford University Press.

— (1959) *The Union of Burma: A Study of the First Years of Independence,* 2nd edition. London: Royal Institute of International Affairs and Oxford University Press.

— (1961) *The Union of Burma: A Study of the First Years of Independence,* 3rd edition. London: Royal Institute of International Affairs and Oxford University Press.

— (1963) 'Economic development in Burma, 1951–1960, by Louis Walinksy', book review, *Pacific Affairs,* September, pp. 325–327.

— (ed) (1983) *Burma: The Struggle for Independence 1944–1948. Volume 1: From Military Occupation to Civil Government, 1 January 1944 to 31 August 1946.* London: Her Majesty's Stationery Office.

Toe Hla (1987) *Money-Lending and Contractual Thet-Káyits: A Socio-Economic Pattern of the Later Kon-Baung Period, 1819–1885,* unpublished doctoral dissertation, Northern Illinois University.

Trager, F.N. (1958) *Building a Welfare State in Burma, 1948–56.* New York: Institute of Pacific Relations.

— (1966) *Burma, From Kingdom to Republic.* London: Pall Mall Press.

Tucker, S. (2001) *Burma: The Curse of Independence.* London: Pluto Press.

Tun Wai (1953) *Burma's Currency and Credit.* Bombay: Orient Longmans.

— (1961) *Economic Development of Burma from 1800 till 1940.* Rangoon: University of Rangoon.

— (1962) *Burma's Currency and Credit,* 2nd revised edition. Bombay: Orient Longmans.

— (1977) 'A revisit to interest rates outside the organized money markets of underdeveloped countries'. *Banca Nazionale del Lavoro Quarterly Review,* vol. XXX, no. 122, pp. 291–312.

— (1990) 'The Myanmar economy at the crossroads'. In Mya Than and J.L. Tan (eds), *Myanmar Dilemmas and Options: The Challenge of Economic Transition in the 1990s.* Singapore: Institute of Southeast Asian Studies, pp. 18–52.

Turnell, S.R. (2001) 'Burma's FECs'. *Burma Economic Watch,* no. 1, 2001, pp. 5–6.

— (2002) 'Reforming the banking system in Burma: A survey of the problems and possibilities'. *Technical Advisory Network of Burma, Working Papers* 7. Washington D.C.: The Burma Fund.

— (2003) 'Myanmar's banking crisis', *ASEAN Economic Bulletin,* vol. 20, no. 3, December, pp. 272–282.

— (2004) 'Burma bank update'. *Burma Economic Watch,* no. 1, 2004, pp. 19–29.

— (2006a) 'Burma's economic prospects'. Testimony, United States–Burma Relations. Hearing before the Committee on Foreign Relations, United States Senate, Wednesday, 29 March, 2006.

–– (2006b) 'Burma's economy: Crisis masking stagnation'. In T. Wilson (ed), *Myanmar's Long March to National Reconciliation.* Singapore: Institute of Southeast Asian Studies.

U Nu (1953) 'Towards a welfare state', *Burma Looks Ahead.* Rangoon: Ministry of Information, Government of the Union of Burma.

–– (1954) *Burma Under the Japanese.* London: Macmillan.

–– (1955) *Forward with the People.* Rangoon: Ministry of Information, Government of the Union of Burma.

–– (1957) *Premier U Nu on the 4-Year Plan.* Rangoon: Director of Information, Government of the Union of Burma.

–– (1975) *U Nu, Saturday's Son.* New Haven: Yale University Press.

U Po Sa (1955) *A Brief Outline of Buddhism.* Rangoon (privately published).

Van Schendel, W. (1991) *Three Deltas: Accumulation and Poverty in Rural Burma, Bengal and South India.* New Delhi: Sage Publications.

Vicary, A.M. (2004) 'The state's incentive structure in Burma's sugar sector and inflated official data: A case study of the sugar industry in Pegu Division'. *Burma Economic Watch,* no. 2, 2004, pp.15–28.

Vogel, R.C. (1984) 'Savings mobilization: The forgotten half of rural finance'. In D.W. Adams, D.H. Graham and J.D. Von Pishke (eds), *Undermining Rural Development with Cheap Credit.* Boulder: Westview Press.

Von Pishke, J.D, D.W. Adams and G. Donald (eds) (1983) *Rural Financial Markets in Developing Countries: Their Use and Abuse.* Baltimore: Johns Hopkins Press for the Economic Development Institute of the World Bank.

Wajima, T. (1999) 'Recent banking sector developments and current monetary status in Myanmar'. In M. Kiryu (ed), *Industrial Development and Reforms in Myanmar.* Bangkok: White Lotus Press.

Walinsky, L.J. (1962) *Economic Development in Burma, 1951–1960.* New York: The Twentieth Century Fund.

Webster, A. (1998) *Gentlemen Capitalists: British Imperialism in South East Asia.* London: I. B. Tauris.

–– (2000) 'Business and Empire: A reassessment of the British conquest of Burma in 1885'. *The Historical Journal,* vol. 43, no. 4, pp. 1003–1025.

Weerasooria, W.S. (1973) *The Nattukottai Chettiar Merchant Bankers in Ceylon.* Delhiwala, Sri Lanka: Tisara Prakasakayo.

Weller, C.E. (2001) 'Financial crises after financial liberalisation: Exceptional circumstances or structural weaknesses'. *The Journal of Development Studies,* vol. 38, no. 1, pp. 98–127.

Wickizer, V.D. and M.K. Bennett (1941) *The Rice Economy of Monsoon Asia.* Stanford: Stanford University Press.

Williamson, J. (1995) *What Role for Currency Boards?* Washington D.C.: Institute forindex International Economics.

Wolff, H.W. (1893) *People's Banks: A Record of Social and Economic Success.* London: Longmans Green.

Won Zoon Yoon (1973) *Japan's Scheme for the Liberation of Burma: The Role of the Minami Kikan and the 'Thirty Comrades'.* Athens, Ohio: Ohio University Centre for International Studies.

Wrench, G.T. (1939) *The Restoration of the Peasantries.* London: C.W. Daniel Company.

Wydick, B.W. (1999) 'Can social cohesion be harnessed to repair market failures? Evidence from group lending in Guatemala'. *The Economic Journal,* vol. 109, no. 457, July, pp. 463–475.

Yin Yin Mya (2000) 'Establishment of a capital market in Myanmar: Perspectives and problems'. In Mya Than and Myat Thein (eds), *Financial Resources for Development in Myanmar: Lessons from Asia.* Singapore: Institute of Southeast Asian Studies, pp. 53–71.

Young, K.B., G.L. Cramer and E.J. Wailes (1998) *An Economic Assessment of the Myanmar Rice Sector: Current Developments and Prospects.* Arkansas Agricultural Experiment Station, University of Arkansas, Research Bulletin 958, February.

Youngjohns, B.J. (1983) 'Cooperatives and credit: A re-examination'. In J.D. Von Pishke, D.W. Adams and G. Donald (eds), *Rural Financial Markets in Developing Countries: Their Use and Abuse.* Baltimore: Johns Hopkins Press for the Economic Development Institute of the World Bank, pp. 346–353.

Yunus, M. (1998) *Banker to the Poor: The Story of the Grameen Bank.* London: Aurum Press.

–– (2005) *Grameen Bank at a Glance.* Dhaka: Grameen Bank, <www.grameen-info.org>.

Zaw Oo (2003) 'Throwing good money after bad: Banking crisis in Burma'. *Burma Fund Policy Brief* 3. Washington D.C.: The Burma Fund.

Index

A

A. Scott and Co., stockbrokers, 106, 117
advance purchase, 7, 224, 282
  as replacement for other forms of
    agricultural credit, 244–247, 252
AFPFL, *see* Anti-Fascist People's Freedom
  League
Agricultural and Rural Development
  Corporation (ARDC), 191
agricultural finance,
  continuing poor performance of,
    283–289
  performance in parliamentary
    democracy era, 192–202
  and reforms of 1990, 281–282
  under the Revolutionary Council
    government, 240–248
Agriculturalists Loans Act 1883, 188, 199–
  201
Aik Htun, 261–262, 277, 311
All-Burma Peasants Organisation (ABPO),
  200
Anti-Fascist People's Freedom League
  (AFPFL), xxii, 142, 144–145, 169–
  170, 176, 200, 203, 216
Ardeth Maung Thawnghmung, 221, 252,
  254–255
Asia Wealth Bank (AWB),
  and accusations of moneylaundering,
    261–262
  and banking crisis 2002, 300, 302,
    308–309, 312, 316
  banking licence revoked, 308, 310, 311
  established, 260-263, 275, 278
  named by US Treasury, 277–278,
    306–309
Aung San, xxi, xxii, 137, 142, 144, 169–170
  and economic plans, 175, 219
Aung San Suu Kyi, xxiii, 49, 256
Australian Agency for International
  Development (Ausaid), 340, 352
Ava Bank, 210, 212–213, 226
Aye Hlaing, U, 192–194
Azad Hind Bank, 133

B

Ba Maw, xxi, xxii, 70, 87, 101, 131, 176, 220
Balwant Singh, 238-239
Bank Law 1975, 278–279, 289
Bank of Burma (BoB), 82, 84–85, 87, 89
Bank of Chettinad, 32, 51, 132
Bank of China, 106, 116, 210, 226, 228
Bank of Chosen, 133
Bank of Communications, 106, 116, 210,
  226
Bank of England (BoE), xiv, 78, 82–83,
  94, 114, 134–136, 169–171, 190,
  204–205, 220–222
  role in creation of Burma Currency
    Board, 141–144, 147

role in creation of Union Bank of
Burma, 157–164
Bank of France,
as model for the Bank of Burma, 83-85
Bank of Upper Burma, 212, 222
Basel Capital Accord, 51, 267–269, 313
Binns, Sir Bernard Ottwell, 38, 71, 73, 135,
192–195
'black market' banking, 135, 236–237, 244,
254, 295
Bogyoke interlude
and expansion of GA Loans, 216–219
Bradford, Wylie, xv, 12, 284
Brown, Ian, xiii, 22, 41, 107, 116, 122,
124–126
budget deficits,
and financing via the central bank,
166–167, 353
Burma Agriculturalists' Debt Relief Act
1947, 156, 189
Burma Currency Board (BCB),
establishment of, 145–147
objections to, 151–154
performance of, 147–150
planning for, 138–145
wound up, 154
Burma Economic Development
Corporation (BEDC), 212–213
Burma Provincial Banking Enquiry
(BPBE), 123, 188, 192–193
and central banking in Burma, 76,
78–90, 101
and the Chettiars, 17–35, 39–48,
50–52, 119, 123, 126
commissioning of, 70, 81
and cooperative credit, 63, 70, 73
membership, 81
Burma Road, 116
Burma Socialist Programme Party (BSPP),
xxii, 244, 248–250, 254–255
Burma State Bank (BSB),
as central bank during Japanese
occupation, 132, 220
Burmah Oil Company, 114, 225
Burmese National Army (BNA), 137
Burmese National Bank, 210–213, 222, 226
Burmese Way to Socialism, xxii, 223, 238,
249

C

Callahan, Mary, 212, 216
Calvert Committee, 54, 65–71
CARE Australia,
and Saving Mobilisation and Income
Generation Program (SMIG), 340–
341, 352
Central Bank of India, 106–107, 116, 132,
210, 226
Central Bank of Myanmar (CBM),
establishment 1990, 258, 267, 290
performance in the banking crisis
2002, 301–305
printing money to finance the state,
313–315
Central Bank of Myanmar Law 1990, 258,
267, 289, 313, 336
Chartered Bank of India, Australia and
China, 1, 32, 106–107, 111–116,
125, 129, 131–132, 134, 210, 226
Chettiars,
capital sources, 21–25
deposit types offered, 27–29, 51
education of, 35
extent of operations, 17–20, 50
as financiers of the 'rice bowl', 14–17
and Hundis, 29–32, 51–52
interest rates charged, 40–49, 52
and land alienation in Burma, 35–40,
52
and modern economic theory, 44–48,
52
origins in India, 20–21, 50–51
in the parliamentary democracy era,
188–189, 193–194, 220
reasons for success in Burma, 32–35,
51–52
relationship with exchange banks,
24–25, 51
their banking business, 25–32, 51
and their internal organisation,
33–35, 51–52
China Development Finance Corporation,
113
Constitutions, Burma
of 1937, xxi, 141, 144
of 1947, 141, 174, 186, 189, 223
'Dyarchy' constitution 1923, xix, 86
Cooperative Bank, 260, 264, 266, 310–311

cooperative credit,
    Calvert Committee and, 65–69
    growth and collapse in colonial
        Burma, 63–65, 73
    historical foundations, 53–58, 72–73
    in the parliamentary democracy era,
        176, 182, 186, 195, 197–199
    structure in colonial Burma, 58–63
Cooperative Farmers' Bank, 260, 266, 311
Cooperative Promoters' Bank, 260, 266, 311
Cox and Co., 114
Credit for Rural Development Institution
    (CRDI), 331–335, 351
    established by GRET, 331–333
    taken over by PACT, 333–335
Currency and Coinage Act 1946, 145, 154, 162

D

Dapice, David, xiii, 10, 273, 285
Dawson, Lawrence, 39, 81, 117–118, 120, 127, 130, 135–136
Dawson's Bank, 1, 39, 81, 105–106, 117–
    120, 127–130, 136, 190, 220, 254
    interest rates charged, 46–47, 119–120
    and the *Land Nationalisation Act*,
        190, 222, 256
    liquidation and restructure during
        great depression, 120, 127–128
    outreach philosophy and, 118
    relationship to Chettiars, 39, 46–47
    relationship to exchange banks, 105,
        119–120
de Soto, Hernando, 354
Defence Services Institute (DSI), 212–213
Delta Region Microfinance Organization
    (DRMO), 322–328
    absorbed by PACT, 333–335
    group lending and, 323–324
    interest rates charged, 325
    and lending to women, 326
    loan types, 325
    takeover by EDA Rural Systems, 327
demonetisation, 2, 135, 143, 354, 357–358
    of 1987, xxii, 7, 252–254
    and *Currency Notes Demonetisation
        Bill* 1985, xxii, 252–253

and *Demonetisation Act* 1964, 6, 224,
    237–240, 254
Drake, Peter, 109–110, 150, 153, 169
Dry Zone Microfinance Organization
    (DZMO), 328–335
Dunn, C.W., 102–103

E

economic planning,
    and the Nagi Ni (Red Dragon) book
        club, 175
    in the post-independence era, 6, 172–
        176, 182–185
    Pyidawtha (Eight-Year) Plan, xx, 154,
        165–166, 173, 182–185, 214, 220
    Two-Year (Sorrento Villa) Plan, 148,
        154, 175–176
enforceable property rights, lack of,
    354–355
exchange banks,
    entry into Burma, 105–107, 135
    and the great depression, 124–126
    and the Japanese invasion, 129–133,
        135–136
    lending to Chettiars, 107–109, 135
    in the parliamentary democracy era,
        203–210, 213
    provision of bills of exchange, 109–
        110, 135
    return after Second World War, 133,
        135–136
exchange controls, 124, 171, 292
exchange rate policy, 138–140, 145–146,
    163, 251, 291–293, 314, 342
Export Import Bank, 210, 212, 216, 226

F

Farmers' Rights Protection Law 1963, 234
Federal Fund of the Federated Shan States,
    99
Financial Action Task Force (FATF),
    and banking crisis trigger, 299, 306
    sanctions against Burma, 276, 295,
        306–309, 315, 317
Financial Institutions of Myanmar Law
    1990, 257–258, 267, 278, 281, 337
financial sector reform 1990,
    and agriculture, 281–289, 295

and the CBM, 267–271, 289–293, 296
and the return of private banks, 258–267, 293–295
and the state-owned banks, 278–281, 293–294
Findlay, Ronald, 11
First Private Bank, 260, 265, 275
   growth following banking crisis, 311–312, 314, 318
Fitchen, Paul, 158–159, 163
foreign exchange certificates (FECs), 281, 292–293, 316
Foreign Investment Law, 257
Furnivall, John S., 14, 16, 18, 38, 50–52, 122, 176–180, 187, 220

G

General Administrative (GA) Loans, 188, 191, 193, 199–200, 217–218, 233–234
Gillander Arbuthnot (stockbrokers), 106, 117
government organised non-government organisations (GONGOs), and microfinance, 348–349
Grameen Bank, 57, 319, 321, 329–333, 345, 350–351
   and Delta Region Microfinance Organization (DRMO), 322–327, 335
   leaves Burma, 327
Great Depression, xxi, 54, 64, 66, 74
   and the Chettiars, 3, 13–14
   and the commercial banks, 5, 119, 124

H

Hla Myint, 11, 177, 220, 256
Hong Kong and Shanghai Banking Corporation (HSBC),
   nationalisation 1963, 213, 226
   operations in colonial Burma, 111–113, 124–125, 130, 133–134

I

Imperial Bank of India, 24–25, 30–32, 41, 65–66, 104, 107–108, 110–111, 120–121, 125, 130, 209
   as central bank for Burma, 75, 78–103

establishment, 74–75
Indian Bank, 81, 106, 117, 209
Indian Overseas Bank, 210, 226
Indian Paper Currency Act 1882, 75
Industrial Development Bank (IDB), 217, 230–231, 260, 266, 275
Industrial Development Corporation, 191, 215
Innwa Bank, 260, 265–266

J

Japan
   banking institutions established during occupation of Burma, 131–133
   invasion of Burma 1942, 129–131
   occupation of Burma 1942–1945, 131–133
Japanese Military Administration rupees ('JM' rupees), 132–134

K

Kanbawza Bank,
   establishment, 260–261, 264
   growth following banking crisis, 300, 302, 310, 316
   and UNDP's microfinance schemes, 272, 347
Kershaw, Raymond, 136, 142–147, 157, 162–163, 169–171
Keynes, John Maynard, 10, 75–79, 82, 88, 94, 101, 160, 175, 184
Khin Maung Kyi, 11
Khin Nyunt, Major General, 302, 309, 316, 349
Knappen Tippetts Abbett Engineering (KTA), 167, 182–187, 191, 196, 203–204, 221
Konbaung Dynasty, 16–17
Korean war, 148, 152, 172, 184
Kyaw Nyein, 170, 203–204, 219–221

L

Land and Agriculture Committee Report 1938, 70–72, 154–155, 192
Land Improvement Loans Act 1883, 188
Land Nationalisation Act 1948, 174, 189–190

Law of Establishment of the Socialist Economic System 1965, 257
Law to Control Property Obtained by Illegal Means 2002, 277, 299, 307
least developed status for Burma, xxi, 256
Lister, Thomas, 87–103
Lloyds Bank, 24, 32, 106–107, 114, 119–120, 124–126, 133–134, 158, 190, 209, 220–222
Longmuir, Marilyn, 12, 136

M

Marshall, Andrew, 276
Mercantile Bank of India, 106, 114, 226
microfinance,
    and Burma's macroeconomic instability, 334–336, 342
    and a lack of effective demand in Burma, 342–343, 351–352
    and legal status in Burma, 336–338, 346–347, 351–352
    and poor savings mobilisation, 344–347, 351–352
    and problems of group-lending in Burma, 347–350, 351–352
military intelligence, 347
Ministry of Cooperatives, 266, 338, 346
Ministry of Finance and Revenue, 290, 293, 295–296
money laundering,
    and FATF, xxiii, 7, 276–278, 295, 299, 306–307, 309, 315, 317
    and US sanctions, 276–278, 306–307
Money Lenders Act 1945, 154–155, 337
Mya Maung, 11, 122, 145, 182, 194, 198–199, 220, 223, 229, 237–239, 246, 248–249, 252–253, 255, 273, 275, 293
Myanma Agricultural Development Bank (MADB),
    establishment, 258, 281–282
    performance, 282–288, 296
Myanma Economic Bank (MEB), 250, 278–281, 285–289, 293, 295, 309
Myanma Foreign Trade Bank (MFTB), 250–251, 279–281, 292–293
Myanma Small Loans Enterprise (MSLE), 279, 288–289, 296
Myanmar Agricultural and Rural

Development Bank Law 1990, 257, 281
Myanmar Citizens Bank, 260, 275, 278
Myanmar Economic Corporation (MEC), 266
Myanmar Investment and Commercial Bank (MICB), 280–281, 293, 296
Myanmar Livestock and Fisheries Development Bank, 266, 278
Myanmar Maternal Child Welfare Association (MMCWA), 348–349
Myanmar Mayflower Bank,
    and accusations of moneylaundering, 263–265, 308
    and banking crisis 2002, 275
    dissolution of, 308–310
    establishment, 260, 262
    and joint-venture partner, 278
    named by US Treasury, 277, 306–307
Myanmar Universal Bank, 260, 264–265, 275, 308, 317
Myawaddy Bank
    established, 260, 264
    growth following banking crisis, 310–311
    and links to the military, 265–266

N

Nash, Manning, 191, 199, 201–202, 218–219
National Bank of India, 106–108, 114
National Bank of Scotland, 114
National City Bank of New York (Citibank), 24, 32, 106–107, 115, 125, 129, 209
National League for Democracy (NLD), xxi
Ne Win, General, xxii, xxiii, 242, 247–248, 253
    caretaker government in 1958, 216
    takeover of power in 1962, 223–225
Niemeyer, Sir Otto, 141, 169
Norman, Montagu, 114, 142

O

official exchange rate, 236, 251, 291–292
Overseas Chinese Banking Corporation, 106, 116, 210

P

PACT Myanmar,
  becomes single implementing agency
    for all UNDP microfinance schemes,
    327, 334–335, 351
  establishes DZMO, 328–331
Panglong Agreement, xxii
Pegu Central Cooperative Bank, 52, 81,
  132
People's Bank of the Union of Burma, xxii,
  6, 224, 242, 244, 249
  creation of, 223, 231–232
  dissolution, 249–251
Pfanner, David, 196–199
'ponzi' schemes, 297–298, 315
Presidency banks, 74–80, 85, 104, 111
private banks,
  collapse in 2002–2003, 297–318
  growth 1992–2002, 270–278
  return of, 1992, 258–267
Private Industrial Enterprise Law 1990,
  257
property rights, 121, 174, 343, 353–357
Pyidawtha (eight-Year) Plan, xxii, 154,
  165–166, 173, 182–183, 185, 214,
  220
Pyithu Hluttaw, 248–249

R

Reid, J.C., 157–159, 171, 204
Reserve Bank of India (RBI), 74, 91, 94, 97,
  100, 103, 106, 108, 141, 147, 157,
  162, 170
Revolutionary Government of the Union
  of Burma (RGUB),
  and agricultural finance, 233–235,
    240–248
  and bank nationalisation, 224–232,
    254–255
  and the demonetisation of 1964,
    237–239, 255
  and monetary policy, 235–237
Robert R. Nathan Associates, 183
Royal Bank at Mandalay, 135

S

San Lin, U, 147, 157, 160, 162–163, 170–
  171, 225, 238

sanctions, xxiii, 280–281, 295, 309, 317–
  318, 342
Save the Children (USA), 338–339, 351
Saw Pah Dwai, 52, 104
Saya San,
  rebellion of 1931, xxi, 101, 127
Serge Pun, 262, 312, 318
Skidmore, Monique, xiii, 49, 348–349
SLORC, *see* State Law and Order
  Restoration Council
social capital, 57–58, 68
  importance for microfinance, 324, 347
  and the MADB, 282
SPDC, *see* State Peace and Development
  Council
State Agricultural Bank (SAB),
  absorption into PBUB, 231, 233–235,
    241–243
  establishment, 182, 185
  Furnivall's proposals, 176–182
  performance in parliamentary
    democracy era, 195–197, 218–219,
    221
  and village bank network, 178–180,
    185
State Agricultural Marketing Board
  (SAMB), 164, 166, 191, 194, 208,
    216, 244
State Commercial Bank (SCB), 204–213,
    216–217, 227, 230–232
State Law and Order Restoration Council
  (SLORC),
  and economic reforms, 7, 257–296
  takeover 1988, xxiii, 256
State-owned enterprises (SOEs), 230, 270
State Pawnshop Management Board
  (SPMB), 187, 248
State Peace and Development Council
  (SPDC), 257–296, 302, 309, 315–
    317, 347
Steel Brothers, 114
Steinberg, David, xiii, 212, 225, 241, 253–
    254, 348

T

Tatmadaw (armed forces), 212, 216, 223
Tavoy Bank, 210, 212, 222, 226
Thakin movement, xxi, 175, 219–220

Thant Myint-U, 9, 16–17, 50, 101, 141, 144, 156, 219, 254
Thomas Cook and Sons, 106, 115
Tin Tut, U, 71, 144–145, 169
Transfer of Immoveable Property Act 1948, 159, 210
Tun Foundation Bank, 260, 264–265, 275, 318
Tun Wai, U, 1, 11, 22–23, 41–43, 46, 51, 63, 74, 95, 99–106, 109–112, 114, 116–118, 120–124, 127, 147, 151–154, 165, 185, 188, 197, 201, 208–209, 211–212, 221
Turner, Sir Sidney, 147, 149, 170

U

U Nu, xviii, xxi, xxii, 145, 172, 175, 182–184, 189, 200, 216–217, 219–221
U Po Sa, 211
U Rai Gyaw Thoo and Company, 106, 117, 120–121
UNDP, *see* United Nations Development Programme
Union Bank of Burma (UBB),
  drafting issues and, 156–158, 162–164, 170–171
  establishment as full central bank, 1952, 159–162, 171
  performance in parliamentary democracy era, 164–171
Union Bank of Burma Act 1947, 151, 156
Union Bank of Burma Act 1952, 159, 231, 250, 291
Union of Burma Bank (UBB*),
  as purely central bank 1975, 250
  as re-named PBUB, 224, 232, 248
Union of Burma Cooperative Bank, 211–212, 226
Union of Myanmar Economic Holdings (UMEH), 265–266
United Commercial Bank (UCB), 209–211, 226
United Nations Development Programme (UNDP), xix, 264, 272, 320–338, 342, 345–347, 349–351
  and the Human Development Initiative (HDI) in Burma, 320–321, 350
  and lack of legal status for microfinance schemes, 336–338
United Nations Office for Project Services (UNOPs), 320, 322, 328, 331–333, 336, 338, 350
Union Solidarity and Development Association (USDA), 348, 352
United Wa State Party,
  and Myanmar Mayflower Bank, 263, 294
USDA, *see* Union Solidarity and Development Association

V

Vicary, Alison, xv

W

Walinsky, Louis, 171, 183–184, 195–196, 200, 220–221
Wallace Brothers, 104–105, 114, 134–135
World Bank, 44, 232, 234, 238, 241, 243–248, 260, 267, 274, 295, 357
World Vision (Myanmar), 339–340, 352

Y

Yokohama Specie Bank (YSB), 24, 106, 115–116, 119–120, 124, 209
  as competitor to the exchange banks, 115–116
  role in Japanese occupation of Burma, 131–132
Yoma Bank, 260, 262–263, 275, 278, 294
  during banking crisis 2002, 300, 302–303, 316–317
  establishment, 262
  survival, 312–313, 318
  and UNDP microfinance schemes, 264, 272, 331, 347

Z

Zaw Oo, xi, 300, 302, 316

NIAS Press is the autonomous publishing arm of
NIAS – Nordic Institute of Asian Studies, a research institute
located at the University of Copenhagen. NIAS is partially funded by the
governments of Denmark, Finland, Iceland, Norway and Sweden
via the Nordic Council of Ministers, and works to encourage and
support Asian studies in the Nordic countries. In so doing, NIAS
has been publishing books since 1969, with more than two
hundred titles produced in the past few years.

COPENHAGEN UNIVERSITY

Nordic Council of Ministers